What did it mean to be Irish in the seventeenth century? This fundamental question is addressed in this important and innovative volume, the latest in a sequence published in association with the Folger Shakespeare Library in Washington, DC. Distinguished international scholars conduct the first in-depth analysis of seventeenth-century Irish political thought and culture, shed new light on the leading political theorists of the day, and draw attention to previously neglected writers (Irish Catholics in particular) and overlooked political treatises. The contributors address major topics including the constitutional relationship between England and Ireland and the extent to which Ireland was a kingdom or colony; Ireland's intellectual links with Catholic Europe and the influence of Counter-Reformation ideology; and the place of Irish political thought in its wider 'Three Kingdoms', imperial and Atlantic contexts. The dramatic impact on political thought of the civil wars of the 1640s and 1688–91 is also examined. The volume as a whole adds an essential new dimension to our understanding of the formation of early modern Irish identity.

The editor, JANE OHLMEYER, is a Senior Lecturer in history at the University of Aberdeen. She is author of *Civil War and Restoration in the Three Stuart Kingdoms: The Career of Randal MacDonnell, Marquis of Antrim, 1609–1683* (1993) and editor of *Ireland from Independence to Occupation, 1641–1660* (1995). She also edited, with the late John Kenyon, *The Civil Wars: A Military History of England, Scotland and Ireland, 1638–1660* (1998).

T0381565

Political Thought in Seventeenth-Century Ireland

Political Thought in
Seventeenth-Century Ireland

Kingdom or Colony

Edited by

Jane H. Ohlmeyer

Published in association with the Folger Institute,
Washington, DC

CAMBRIDGE
UNIVERSITY PRESS

CAMBRIDGE UNIVERSITY PRESS
Cambridge, New York, Melbourne, Madrid, Cape Town, Singapore,
São Paulo, Delhi, Dubai, Tokyo, Mexico City

Cambridge University Press
The Edinburgh Building, Cambridge CB2 8RU, UK

Published in the United States of America by Cambridge University Press, New York

www.cambridge.org
Information on this title: www.cambridge.org/9780521157728

First published 2000
First paperback edition 2010

A catalogue record for this publication is available from the British Library

Library of Congress Cataloguing in Publication Data

Political thought in seventeenth-century Ireland: kingdom or colony / edited by Jane H.
Ohlmeyer.
        p.   cm.
Includes bibliographical references and index.
ISBN 0 521 65083 6
1. Political science – Ireland – History – 17th century. I. Ohlmeyer, Jane H.
JA84.I76P66   2000
320'.09415'09032–dc21   99–048704

ISBN 978-0-521-65083-0 Hardback
ISBN 978-0-521-15772-8 Paperback

Contents

List of plates   *page* ix
List of contributors   x
Acknowledgements   xiii
Conventions   xv
List of abbreviations   xvi

1   Introduction: for God, king or country? Political thought
    and culture in seventeenth-century Ireland   1
    JANE OHLMEYER

Part I Ireland and England

2   Patrick Darcy and the constitutional relationship between
    Ireland and Britain   35
    AIDAN CLARKE

3   Counter-currents in colonial discourse: the political
    thought of Vincent and Daniel Gookin   56
    PATRICIA COUGHLAN

4   Recasting a tradition: William Molyneux and the sources
    of *The Case of Ireland . . . Stated* (1698)   83
    PATRICK KELLY

5   Political ideas and their social contexts in
    seventeenth-century Ireland   107
    RAYMOND GILLESPIE

Part II Ireland and the continent

6   Representations of king, parliament and the Irish people in
    Geoffrey Keating's *Foras Feasa ar Éirinn* and John Lynch's
    Cambrensis Eversus (1662)   131
    BERNADETTE CUNNINGHAM

viii   Contents

7   'Though Hereticks and Politicians should misinterpret their
    good zeale': political ideology and Catholicism in early
    modern Ireland   155
    TADHG Ó HANNRACHÁIN

8   Gaelic Maccabeanism: the politics of reconciliation   176
    JERROLD CASWAY

**Part III Irish political thought and the new British and
Irish histories**

9   Covenanting ideology in seventeenth-century Scotland   191
    ALLAN I. MACINNES

10 The political economy of Britain and Ireland after the
    Glorious Revolution   221
    DAVID ARMITAGE

11 From ancient constitution to British empire: William
    Atwood and the imperial crown of England   244
    CHARLES C. LUDINGTON

12 The Third Kingdom in its history: an afterword   271
    J. G. A. POCOCK

Index   281

Plates

Plate 1 John Speed, *Theatre of the Empire of Great Britain* (1612)
(by permission of Aberdeen University Library)   *page* 11

Plate 2 William Petty, 'The Down Survey' (by permission of
Aberdeen University Library)   12–13

Plate 3 John Speed's portrayal of the 'wild Irish' (by permission
of Aberdeen University Library)   14

Contributors

DAVID ARMITAGE is Associate Professor of History at Columbia University. He is the author of *The Ideological Origins of the British Empire* (2000), the editor *of Bolingbroke: Political Writings* (1997) and *Theories of Empire, 1450–1800* (1998), and the co-editor of *Milton and Republicanism* (1995). He is now working on a study of political thought and international relations from Locke to Bentham.

JERROLD CASWAY is a Professor of History and Chairman of the Social Sciences Division at Howard Community College in Columbia, Maryland. He has written more than thirty articles on early modern Irish topics and is the author of *Owen Roe O'Neill and the Struggle for Catholic Ireland* (1984). More recently his research has focused on Irish influences on American baseball and his biography of Ed Delahanty will be published in 2000.

AIDAN CLARKE is Erasmus Smith's Professor of Modern History at Trinity College, Dublin, and a past president of the Royal Irish Academy. He is the author of numerous articles on early modern Irish history and his books include *The Old English in Ireland 1625–1642* (1966; reprinted 2000), *The Graces* (1968) and *Prelude to Restoration in Ireland: The End of the Commonwealth* (1999).

PATRICIA COUGHLAN teaches in the English Department at the National University of Ireland, Cork. She has edited the collection *Spenser and Ireland: An Interdisciplinary Perspective* (1989) and has published several essays and articles on seventeenth-century writings about Ireland, including those of Henry Burkhead, the Hartlib circle and the Irish natural history project in the 1650s, and William Petty. She has also written extensively on later Anglo-Irish literature.

BERNADETTE CUNNINGHAM is Deputy Librarian at the Royal Irish Academy, Dublin. She has written numerous articles on early modern Irish history and literature and is currently completing a book on *The World of Geoffrey Keating*.

RAYMOND GILLESPIE teaches in the Department of Modern History at the National University of Ireland, Maynooth. He is the author of a numerous works on early modern Ireland. His books include *Colonial Ulster: The Settlement of East Ulster 1600–1641* (1985) and *Devoted People: Religion and Belief in Early Modern Ireland* (1997). He is currently working on the experience of reading and writing in early modern Ireland.

PATRICK KELLY is a Senior Lecturer in Modern History at Trinity College, Dublin. He has edited *Locke on Money* (2 vols., 1991) in *The Clarendon Edition of the Works of John Locke*, and has published articles on Locke and on various topics in Irish political and intellectual history of the seventeenth and eighteenth centuries. He is currently completing a critical edition of William Molyneux's *The Case of Ireland ... Stated* for the Irish Legal History Society.

CHARLES C. LUDINGTON is completing his doctoral thesis on the politics, consumption and culture of wine in early modern Britain and Ireland, at Columbia University. He has published articles on Anglo-Irish relations in the late seventeenth century and on the Huguenot community in Ireland.

ALLAN I. MACINNES holds the Burnett-Fletcher Chair of History at the University of Aberdeen. He has written extensively on covenants, clans and clearances and his main publications include *Charles I and the Making of the Covenanting Movement, 1625–41* (1991), *Clanship, Commerce and the House of Stuart, 1603–1788* (1996) and *The British Confederate: A Political Biography of Archibald Campbell, Marquess of Argyll 1607–61* (2000).

TADHG Ó HANNRACHÁIN is a College Lecturer in the Department of Modern Irish History, University College, Dublin. He is the author of several articles on the confederate era and his monograph on the papal nuncio Rinuccini in Ireland has just been submitted for publication.

JANE OHLMEYER is a Senior Lecturer in History and an associate member of the Research Institute of Irish and Scottish Studies at Aberdeen University. Her books include *Civil War and Restoration in the Three Stuart Kingdoms: The Career of Randal MacDonnell, Marquis of Antrim, 1609–1683* (1993) and *Ireland from Independence to Occupation, 1641–1660* (editor, 1995). She has also co-edited *The Civil Wars: A Military History of England, Scotland and Ireland, 1638–1660* (with John Kenyon, 1998) and *The Irish Statute Staple Books, 1596–1687* (with Eamonn ó Ciardha, 1998). She is currently working on the crisis of the Irish elite in the seventeenth century.

J. G. A. POCOCK is Professor Emeritus of History at the Johns Hopkins University. His principal publications include *The Ancient Constitution and the Feudal Law: A Study of English Historical Thought in the 17th Century* (1957; re-issued with a retrospect in 1987), *Politics, Language and Time: Essays in Political Thought and History* (1971), *The Machiavellian Moment: Florentine Political Thought and the Atlantic Republican Tradition* (1975), *The Political Works of James Harrington* (edited, 1977), *Virtue, Commerce and History: Essays on Political Thought and History* (1985), and (with Gordon Schochet and Lois Schwoerer), *The Varieties of British Political Thought 1500–1800* (1993). His two-volume study of Edward Gibbon and his world was published under the title *Barbarism and Religion* in 1999.

Acknowledgements

This collection of essays stems from a seminar series organised under the auspices of the Centre for the History of British Political Thought at the Folger Shakespeare Library, Washington, DC. It was the second of three events (the first co-ordinated by Hiram Morgan and the third by Sean Connolly) designed to draw scholarly attention to Irish political discourse and culture in the early modern period. Originally entitled 'From Darcy to Molyneux: Political Thought in Seventeenth-Century Ireland', this seminar series aimed to examine the development of Irish political thought and culture between 1641 and 1700. During the late spring of 1997 nine distinguished speakers from both sides of the Atlantic presented papers that situated Irish political discourse in its wider 'Three Kingdoms', European and even Atlantic contexts; drew attention to less well-known writers and theorists (especially Catholic ones) and overlooked political treatises, usually composed in Irish or Latin; and examined the dissemination of political culture throughout seventeenth-century Ireland. These papers were interspersed with congenial and constructive discussions together with informal presentations by scholars attending the seminar series. The success of the seminar series stems in large part from the enthusiasm of the contributors, David Armitage, Aidan Clarke, Bernadette Cunningham, Raymond Gillespie, Patrick Kelly, Allan Macinnes, Tadhg ó hAnnracháin, and Breándan ó Buachalla, and of the participants, Jerrold Casway, Clare Carroll, Edward Furgol, Catriona Logan, Chad Ludington, Bob Mahony, Sean Moore, George O'Brien, John Pocock, Lahney Preston, Eileen Reilly and Paul Romney. I am very grateful to them all for the intellectual stimulation and inspiration that they collectively provided.

The seminar series was made possible by the vision of the members of the Steering Committee of the Folger Institute's Centre for the History of British Political Thought (John Pocock, Gordon Schochet, Lois Schwoerer and Linda Levy-Peck). I was greatly honoured by their invitation to co-ordinate the seminar series and greatly appreciated the financial support provided by the Folger Institute. The Department of

Foreign Affairs, Dublin, generously contributed towards the travel costs of a number of speakers. The British Embassy kindly hosted a welcome reception in the Great Hall of the Folger Library while the proceedings ended with an equally convivial evening at the Irish Embassy. These events and the ebullience of the representatives of the two embassies – Janet McIvor, Don Alexander, Adrian O'Neill and Michael Moloney – were greatly appreciated by everyone.

I owe a special debt of gratitude to John Pocock. He played a seminal role in organising the series and enlivened each seminar with his wit and erudition. Without his enthusiasm and support neither the seminar nor the book would have been possible. The staff of the Folger Institute, especially Barbara Mowat, the Chair, and Kathleen Lynch, executive director, played a key role in facilitating the seminar, as did Martha Fay and Mariann Payne. They were a delight to work with and I should like to thank them for making my stay in Washington so pleasurable and memorable. The smooth transition from an informal seminar series to a published volume has been made possible by the tact and patience of Richard Fisher of Cambridge University Press who has served as a model editor.

On a more personal note I am grateful to the University of Aberdeen and particularly my head of department, Allan Macinnes, for granting me leave of absence in the spring term of 1997, my colleagues in the History Department, especially David Ditchburn and William Naphy, for their support, and the members of my 1998 Special Subject on 'The Irish Mind'. Last but not least I should like to thank my family, Richard and Jamie Parker-Green, Alex Green, and Shirley Ohlmeyer, and my au pairs, Dagmar Heyer and Vera Votrubova, who shared the delights of Washington with me and have indulged and humoured me as I edited this volume.

Jane Ohlmeyer

Conventions

Dates throughout are given according to the Old (Julian) Calendar, which was used in Ireland and Britain but not in most of continental Europe. The beginning of the year is taken, however, as 1 January rather than 25 March.

Spellings from contemporary sources have not been modernised but with proper names the modern spellings have been preferred.

List of abbreviations

BL	British Library, London
Add. MSS	Additional Manuscripts
Bodl.	Bodleian Library, Oxford
Cal SP Ire	*Calendar of State Papers relating to Ireland*
Commons Jnl, Eng	*Journals of the House of Commons 1547–1714* (17 vols., London, 1742–)
Commons Jnl, Ire	*Journals of the House of Commons of the kingdom of Ireland* ... (20 vols., Dublin, 1796–1800)
DNB	*Dictionary of National Biography*, ed. Sir Leslie Stephen and Sir Sidney Lee (66 vols., London, 1885–1901; reprinted with corrections, 22 vols., London, 1908–9)
EHR	*English Historical Review*
FFÉ	Geoffrey Keating, *Foras Feasa ar Éirinn: The History of Ireland* [*c.* 1634], ed. and trans. David Comyn and P. S. Dinneen (4 vols., Irish Texts Society, London, 1902–14)
Gilbert (ed.), *Contemporary History*	J. T. Gilbert (ed.), *A Contemporary History of Affairs in Ireland from 1641 to 1652* (3 vols., Irish Archaeological Society, Dublin, 1879–80)
Gilbert (ed.), *Irish Confederation*	J. T. Gilbert (ed.), *History of the Irish Confederation and War in Ireland, 1641–1649* (7 vols., Dublin, 1882–91)

HMC	Historical Manuscripts Commission
IHS	*Irish Historical Studies*
IMC	Irish Manuscripts Commission
JCHAS	*Journal of the Cork Historical and Archaeological Society*
Lords Jnl, Eng	*Journals of the House of Lords 1578–1714* (17 vols., London, 1767–)
Lords Jnl, Ire	*Journals of the House of Lords of the kingdom of Ireland* (8 vols., Dublin, 1779–1800)
MS/MSS	Manuscript(s)
NHI, III	T. W. Moody, F. X. Martin and F. J. Byrne (eds.), *A New History of Ireland*, III, *Early Modern Ireland 1534–1691* (Oxford, 1976, reprinted 1978)
SHR	*Scottish Historical Review*
NA	National Archives, Dublin
NLI	National Library of Ireland
NS	New series; or, in dating, New Style
OS	Old series; or, in dating, Old Style
PRO	Public Records Office, London
SP	State Papers
RIA	Royal Irish Academy
TCD	Trinity College, Dublin

I   Introduction: for God, king or country?
     Political thought and culture in seventeenth-
     century Ireland

Jane Ohlmeyer

The real attraction of this volume – and the seminar series from which it
derives – is that it offers an opportunity to open up a fresh field of
study: that of seventeenth-century Irish political thought and culture.[1]
Throughout, the term 'political thought' has been loosely defined to
include anything generated about politics in Ireland by thinkers of all
ethnic and religious backgrounds irrespective of whether they resided in
Ireland or not. Many of the writers who feature in this volume could be
more accurately labelled propagandists rather than political theorists; yet
their works critically shaped ideas about politics and political culture in
early modern Ireland. These essays discuss the traditional canon of
works, together with 'alternative' texts and the political prose of lesser-
known scholarly and literary figures, and the historical contexts in which
they were written and/or published.[2] The four chapters in Part I focus on

[1] This is an area of study that has been hopelessly neglected; there are, of course, a number
of important exceptions. See for example C. E. J. Caldicott on Patrick Darcy in *The
Camden Miscellany*, 31 (Royal Historical Society, London, 1992); Aidan Clarke on Anglo-
Irish relations and the constitutional relationship between the two kingdoms and their
parliaments (see particularly 'Colonial Constitutional Attitudes in Ireland, 1640–1660',
Proceedings of the Royal Irish Academy, 90 Section C no. 11 (1990) and 'Alternative
Allegiances in Early Modern Ireland', *Journal of Historical Sociology*, 5:3 (1992), pp.
253–66); Jacqueline Hill, 'Ireland without Union: Molyneux and His Legacy' in John
Robertson (ed.), *A Union for Empire: Political Thought and the British Union of 1707*
(Cambridge, 1995); Patrick Kelly on 'William Molyneux and the Spirit of Liberty in
Eighteenth Century Ireland', *Eighteenth-Century Ireland: Idris an da chultur*, 3 (1988), pp.
133–48; Breándan Ó Buachalla on loyalty to the Stuarts and Jacobitism (especially 'James
Our True King: The Ideology of Irish Royalism in the Seventeenth Century' in G. Boyce,
Robert Eccleshall and Vincent Geoghegan (eds.), *Political Thought in Ireland since the
Seventeenth Century* (London, 1993), pp. 1–35).
[2] All of the important political works relating to seventeenth-century Ireland have been listed
in Tony Sweeney, *Ireland and the Printed Word: A Short Descriptive Catalogue of Early Books,
Pamphlets, Newsletters and Broadsides Relating to Ireland. Printed: 1475–1700* (Dublin, 1997).
Also see M. Walsh, 'Irish Books Printed Abroad, 1475–1700', *The Irish Book*, 2:1 (1962–3),
pp. 1–36 and William Sessions, *The First Printers in Waterford: Cork and Kilkenny pre-1700*
(York, 1990). All of the leading writers of the period are discussed in the remarkable, though
poorly organized, compilation by Sir James Ware and Walter Harris, *The Writers of Ireland in
two books written in Latin by Sir James Ware . . . now newly translated into English, revised
improved with many material additions . . .* (2 vols. in one, Dublin, 1746). For a summary of
this see Thomas Darcy McGee, *The Irish Writers of the Seventeenth Century* (Dublin, 1846).

the constitutional relationship between England and Ireland and the extent to which seventeenth-century Ireland was a kingdom, a colony, or a combination of both. The essays in Part II examine Ireland's intellectual links with Catholic Europe and the ways in which Counter-Reformation ideology in particular shaped Irish political discourse. Finally, the contributions to Part III situate Irish political thought and culture in its wider 'three kingdoms', imperial and Atlantic contexts.

Throughout, the threads of continuity have been emphasised.[3] The political discourse of 1690 enjoyed much in common with that of 1641, which in turn drew on sixteenth-century and medieval precedents. However, this thematic approach should not detract from the dramatic impact which the political, social and economic turmoil of the 1640s and the years between 1688 and 1691 had on shaping political thought and culture. From the Catholic perspective the civil war offered the Irish confederates an almost unique opportunity to become 'constitutional nationalists' and to secure religious freedom and political autonomy within the context of the Stuart monarchies.[4] That they failed to achieve their goals stemmed from domestic political divisions, which the perfidiousness of Charles I in turn exacerbated. Ironically defeat after 1649, accompanied by the revolution in Irish landholding, merely served to increase their dependence on the Stuarts, especially James II, as the best means of securing the future position of the Catholic Church and the Catholic political nation. Yet the dogged determination of Catholic Ireland to support the Stuarts during the Wars of the Three Kings (1688–91) ultimately proved its undoing. The events of these years undermined the personal character of Irish kingship and transformed the nature of English parliamentary sovereignty, setting it on a collision course with its Dublin counterpart which, in the wake of the Revolution, met more regularly and became increasingly belligerent. Thus the civil wars of the 1640s and 1688–91 left a permanent scar on political discourse and intensified a brand of sectarianism and religious bigotry that permeated many forms of political thought well into the eighteenth century and beyond.[5] Closely linked to the growing power of the Westminster parliament was the importance of London as a financial centre and the fact that trade and commerce had, by the late seventeenth century, become a determining

[3] The essays in this volume focus on the years after 1641. For the earlier period see Hiram Morgan (ed.), *Political Ideology in Ireland, 1541–1641* (Dublin, 1999) and for the later period Sean Connolly (ed.), *Patriots and Radicals: Political Ideas in Eighteenth-Century Ireland* (Dublin, forthcoming).

[4] For an excellent recent assessment see Micheál Ó Siochrú, *Confederate Ireland 1642–1649* (Dublin, 1999), especially the conclusion.

[5] Chapter 4 below and Hill, 'Ireland without Union', p. 282. Also see T. C. Barnard, '1641: A Bibliographical Essay' in Brian MacCuarta (ed.), *Ulster 1641* (Belfast, 1993), pp. 173–86.

reason of state. Ireland's economic position and England's need to regulate its burgeoning economy with restrictive legislation (such as the Navigation and Cattle Acts or legislation controlling the woollen industry) influenced the nature of political ideas and catapulted discussions about Ireland's constitutional status to the forefront of the British and imperial political agenda.[6]

I

To date, English-language political texts, written by Protestants, usually of English extraction, have attracted the greatest scholarly attention.[7] Equally interesting – though much less well known – is the political prose written in English by Irish Catholics: Patrick Darcy's *An Argument*; the various blueprints for government generated by the confederates during the 1640s; or political treatises by exiled clerics. If the political prose written by Irish Catholics has been overlooked, works in languages other than English have been virtually ignored.[8] Michael Cronin recently attributed this to the fact that Ireland suffered from 'linguistic schizophrenia': 'English-language histories ignore Irish-language material and Irish-language histories focus on exclusively Irish-language material.'[9] Yet during the early decades of the seventeenth century works in vernacular Irish became increasingly popular and a concentration of scholars skilled in Irish and other languages at St Anthony's, the Franciscan College at Louvain (which in 1611 acquired a printing press with Irish characters), generated a wealth of Counter-Reformation literature. Though their primary mission was to train priests for the Irish and Scottish missions, the academic community there, which included

---

[6] See chapters 10 and 11 below.
[7] Though the bulk of ordinary people continued to speak Irish (that said, bilingualism was very common), the language of government, of the law and of commerce was English. The publication of Seamus Deane's masterly edited volume, *The Field Day Anthology of Irish Writing* (3 vols., Derry, 1991) and Andrew Hadfield and John McVeagh (eds.), *Strangers to that Land: British Perceptions of Ireland from the Reformation to the Famine* (Gerrards Cross, Buckinghamshire, 1994) has provided easy access to some of the more important English-language political works. Recently a number of key texts have also appeared. See, for example, Graham Kew (ed.), *The Irish Sections of Fynes Moryson's Unpublished Itinerary* (IMC, Dublin, 1998) and John Toland, *Christianity not Mysterious*, ed. Philip McGunniess, Alan Harrison and Richard Kearney (Dublin, 1997).
[8] For an excellent introduction see Brian O Cuiv, 'The Irish Language in the Early Modern Period' in *NHI*, Ill and also 'Irish Language and Literature 1691–1845' in T. W. Moody and W. E. Vaughan (eds.), *A New History of Ireland*, IV, *Eighteenth-Century Ireland, 1691–1800* (Oxford, 1986), pp. 374–423.
[9] Michael Cronin, *Translating Ireland: Translation, Languages, Culture* (Cork, 1996), p. 2. The linguistic barrier remains a very real one; however, given the wealth of material that has been translated into English by bodies like the Irish Texts Society, it should not be an insurmountable one.

hereditary historians (the Conrys and the Ó Cléirighs) together with hereditary poets (such as the Ó hEodhasas of Fermanagh) generated texts, such as the *Annals of the Four Masters,* aimed at an Irish audience.

The Latin-language material is equally inaccessible to the modern reader, largely because so much remains untranslated. This is ironic since these Latin tracts, composed in the *lingua franca* of early modern Europe, were specifically written for an international, scholarly audience. As Bernadette Cunningham and Tadhg ó hAnnracháin demonstrate in chapters 6 and 7, their purpose was threefold: to placate the Vatican and their host nation (and occasionally the Stuarts as well); to defend the reputation of the Irish; and to shape continental attitudes about the prevailing political culture in Ireland.[10] For instance, the publication in 1602 of a German edition of Giraldus Cambrensis' *Expugnatio Hibernica* provoked the Old English cleric, John Lynch, to pen a response (*Cambrensis Eversus*) on the grounds that Cambrensis' 'very vilest relations of Ireland were taken for confessedly true'.[11] In turn the English authorities regarded these publications by Catholic writers as politically subversive and maintained that their objective was to stir up 'open rebellion to disturb the quiet of that kingdom'.[12] The eighteenth-century antiquarian Walter Harris noted that the Franciscan Paul King allegedly published *Epistola Nobilis Hiberni* (1649) – circulating copies 'over all the popish countries of Europe' – 'with design to instigate those powers against the English and Protestant interest of Ireland'.[13] Whatever their intent, these writings quickly secured 'credit and reputation', especially throughout Catholic Europe, and provoked a counter-attack from Protestant polemicists during the later decades of the seventeenth century.[14]

Protestant writers sought to secure national and international support for the continued 'civilization' of Ireland. In an attempt to promote their political agenda, they addressed their works to individuals, especially in London, who formulated Irish policies. For instance, the publication in 1633 of Sir James Ware's edition of Edmund Spenser's *View* offered those in power, at home and in England, a blueprint for the continued

[10] For an excellent introduction see Benignus Millet, 'Irish Literature in Latin, 1550–1700' in *NHI*, III, pp. 561–86.
[11] [Peter Walsh], *A prospect of the state of Ireland from the year of the World 1756 [sic] to the year of Christ 1652* (London, 1682), p. [34]. Lynch also translated Geoffrey Keating's history from Irish into Latin, making a work originally aimed at an Irish audience available to continental clerics and scholars.
[12] Cathaldus Giblin, 'The Contribution of Irish Franciscans on the Continent in the Seventeenth Century' in Michael Maher (ed.), *Irish Spirituality* (Dublin, 1981), p. 93.
[13] Ware and Harris, *Writers*, II, p. 141.
[14] See for example, Edmund Borlase, *The History of the Irish Rebellion . . .* (Dublin, 1743), p. iii.

colonisation of Ireland.[15] Ware dedicated the book to Lord Deputy
Thomas Wentworth, later earl of Strafford, and encouraged him to accept
Spenser's suggestions 'for the reformation of abuses and ill customes'
since 'none come so neere to the best grounds for reformation, a few passages excepted, as Spenser hath done in this'.[16] Of equal significance in
shaping English attitudes about the Irish (and about themselves)[17] was
the publication in 1646 of *The Irish Rebellion* by Sir John Temple, a New
English planter and the master of the rolls.[18] John Adamson has demonstrated the impact that Temple's hyperbole exerted on Westminster politics and how the book served as a manifesto for a faction, centred on
Viscount Lisle (an intimate of Temple), that advocated a scorched earth
policy in Ireland.[19] Almost at once government propagandists, including
John Milton, imbibed Temple's prejudices and maintained that their barbarism and incivility denied the Irish individual rights and liberties.[20]
However, the publication of Vincent Gookin's pamphlets in 1655 sought,
as Patricia Coughlan argues convincingly in chapter 3, to temper these
hard-line views and to convince the government to moderate its policies,
especially with regard to transplantation, and thereby to preserve the economic interests of the Old Protestant community.

Just as the readership for Irish political writings varied, so too the nature
of the discourse itself was heterogeneous and ranged from political treatises, that bristled with legal precedents and convoluted argument, to
poetry and plays. Of particular interest was the way in which writers used
history as a 'political weapon'.[21] The purpose of histories, according to a
later Protestant commentator, was 'to inform their own people, as well as

[15] Ware omitted criticisms of Irish families and offensive depictions of the Irish, Edmund
Spenser, *A View of the State of Ireland: From the First Printed Edition*, ed. Andrew Hadfield
and Willy Maley (Oxford, 1997), p. xxiv and appendices I and II. Walter Harris proved
more critical of Spenser, Ware and Harris, *Writers*, II, p. 327.
[16] Edmund Spenser, *A View of the State of Ireland* (Dublin, 1633), dedication.
[17] B. Bradshaw, A. Hadfield and W. Maley (eds.), *Representing Ireland: Literature and the
Origin of Conflict, 1534–1660* (Cambridge, 1993); Keith Lindley, 'The Impact of the 1641
Rebellion upon England and Wales, 1641–1645', *IHS*, 18 (1972), pp. 143–76; Ethan
Howard Shagan, 'Constructing Discord: Ideology, Propaganda, and English Responses to
the Irish Rebellion of 1641', *Journal of British Studies*, 36:1 (1997), pp. 4–34; and Kathleen
Noonan, '"The Cruell Pressure of an enraged, barbarous people": Irish and English
Identity in Seventeenth-Century Propaganda', *Historical Journal*, 41 (1998), pp. 151–77.
[18] Sir John Temple, *The Irish Rebellion . . . Together With the Barbarous Cruelties and Bloody
Massacres which ensued thereupon* (London, 1646).
[19] John Adamson, 'Strafford's Ghost: The British Context of Viscount Lisle's Lieutenancy
of Ireland' in Jane Ohlmeyer (ed.), *Ireland from Independence to Occupation, 1641–1660*
(Cambridge, 1995), pp. 131, 137n, 138–41.
[20] Willy Maley, 'How Milton and Some Contemporaries read Spenser's *View*' in Bradshaw,
Hadfield and Maley (eds.), *Representing Ireland*, pp. 191–208.
[21] Bernadette Cunningham, 'Seventeenth-Century Interpretations of the Past: The Case of
Geoffrey Keating', *IHS*, 25 (1986), p. 116.

foreigners, what they were and what they are'.[22] Thus criticism of the past served as an oblique commentary on the present and as a manual for future action. Many of the Catholic histories specifically aimed to glorify Ireland's past and to refute work by hostile Protestant commentators. For example the synthesis of Irish history from earliest times to the Anglo-Norman invasion – *Foras Feasa ar Éirinn* (translated as *A Basis of Knowledge about Ireland*) – by Geoffrey Keating, an Old English priest from County Tipperary, defended the native and Old Irish against their many critics:[23]

> Whereof the testimony given by Cambrensis, Spenser, and Stanihurst . . . Moryson, Davies, Campion, and every other new foreigner who has written on Ireland from that time, may bear witness; inasmuch as it is almost according to the fashion of the beetle they act, when writing concerning the Irish. For it is the fashion of the beetle, when it lifts its head in the summertime, to go about fluttering, and not to stoop towards any delicate flower that may be in the field, or any blossom in the garden, though they be all roses or lilies, but it keeps bustling about until it meets with dung of horse or cow, and proceeds to roll itself therein. Thus it is with the set above named; they have displayed no inclination to treat of the virtues or good qualities of the nobles among the old foreigners and the native Irish who then dwelt in Ireland.[24]

Keating, together with the Counter-Reformation historians based at Louvain, set out both to preserve and at the same time to remould the Gaelic past 'in accordance with their own values' and, as a result, created 'the basic source-book of the emerging Irish Catholic nation'.[25] Bernadette Cunningham demonstrates (chapter 6) how Keating's work profoundly influenced later writers who also used history to defend and justify Catholic behaviour, particularly during the 1640s. For instance, John Lynch argued that the Old English only joined forces with the insurgents when 'my countrymen discovered that the parliamentarians were in open and infamous war against the king'. He added: 'The confederate Irish . . . flew to arms, not, like the English, to depose, but to support him

---

[22] In 'An Essay on the Defects in the Histories of Ireland', Harris hoped to 'excite others to consider a subject, which hitherto has been little attended to, and which stands in need of such Reformation'. In particular he lambasted depictions of the Irish as a barbarous, uncivilised and promiscuous people as 'groundless' fables and urged future commentators to rely on written and other factual records. In this historiographical survey Harris criticised histories generated by Catholics and Protestants alike. He dismissed Keating's *Foras Fasa* on the grounds that it relied too heavily on 'the unfaithfulness of oral tradition'; while the enormous gaps in his sources marred Sir Richard Cox's history: Walter Harris, *Hibernica* (2 vols., Dublin, 1747, 1750), I, pp. 273–4, 258, 284–5, 262 and 274; Ware and Harris, *Writers*, II, p. 209.
[23] Cunningham, 'Geoffrey Keating', pp. 116–28 and chapter 6 below. Brendan Bradshaw, 'Geoffrey Keating: Apologist of Irish Ireland' in Bradshaw, Hadfield and Maley (eds.), *Representing Ireland*, pp. 166–90.   [24] *FFÉ*, I, pp. 3–5.
[25] Bernadette Cunningham, 'The Culture and Ideology of Irish Franciscan Historians at Louvain 1607–1650' in C. Brady (ed.), *Ideology and the Historians* (Belfast, 1991), p. 20.

[Charles I].'[26] Lynch also tried to shift the stigma of massacre on to Protestant shoulders: Sir Charles Coote, 'a most bloodthirsty monster . . . a bad crow from a bad egg, perpetrated horrible massacres in several parts of Meath and Leinster, before either had been involved in the flame of war'.[27] Similarly Nicholas French, bishop of Ferns, in *The Bleeding Iphigenia* (1674) condemned the atrocities committed by Protestant soldiers and argued that 'We are not accountable for what murthers, some of the common people . . . committed against poore Protestants . . . which we pittied with all our h[e]arts'.[28] These histories also reflected contemporary fears about the future of the Catholic political nation and repeatedly emphasised the loyalty of the Irish in the volatile world of Restoration Irish politics.[29] These Catholic narratives immediately attracted the scorn of increasingly beleaguered Protestant writers. In the preface to *Hibernia Anglicana* (1689) Sir Richard Cox, later lord chancellor, condemned Keating's history as 'no more than an ill-digested heap of very silly fictions'.[30] With the exceptions of the works by Richard Bellings ('one of the greatest and wisest of them') and the Franciscan Peter Walsh, he dismissed all of the other Catholic histories of the 1640s as lies.[31] Taking their lead from Temple, Cox and his compatriots sought to use the events of the 1640s to whip up anti-Catholic hysteria at times of political crisis, particularly during the 1670s and 1680s, and by vilifying the Irish to justify hard-line Protestant policies, especially expropriation.[32]

[26] John Lynch, *Cambrensis Eversus*, trans. Matthew Kelly (3 vols., Dublin, 1848–52), I, pp. 15, 19. Patrick Corish, 'Two Contemporary Historians of the Confederation of Kilkenny: John Lynch and Richard O'Ferrall', *IHS*, 8 (1953), p. 230.
[27] Lynch, *Cambrensis*, III, p. 93
[28] Nicholas French, *The bleeding Iphigenia . . .* (Louvain, 1674; published Dublin, 1848), p. 28.
[29] For a fascinating account of Richard Belling's history, written in the 1670s at the height of anti-Catholic paranoia, see Raymond Gillespie's essay in Micheál Ó Siochrú (ed.), *Catholics and Confederates* (Dublin, forthcoming).
[30] Published shortly after William and Mary's accession, Sir Richard Cox, *Hibernia Anglicana: or, The History of Ireland from the conquest thereof by the English to this present time* (London, 1689), covered the years 1603 to 1689.
[31] He particularly vented his spleen against Conor O'Mahony's *Disputatio* – 'a most treasonable and scandalous book': Cox, *Hibernia Anglicana*, preface to vol. II and p. 198. Also see Ware and Harris, *Writers*, II, pp. 164–5.
[32] Walter Harris acknowledged the particular problems of writing any account of the 1640s – 'rendered amazingly intricate by the writings of historians of different parties and interests, some making it a most hideous rebellion, and [others] palliating it into a necessary civil resistance': *Hibernica*, I, p. 278. Edmund Borlase's history (first published in 1670) focused primarily on the 1640s and relied heavily on Temple's *History*, together with 'records, publick evidences, credible relations, or my own knowledge': Borlase, *History*, p. iii. For a critique of it see Ware and Harris, *Writers*, II, p. 351. Roderic O'Flaherty believed Temple's work to be 'so falsified in most particulars': Roderic O'Flaherty, *A Chorographical Description of West or H-Iar Connaught, written AD 1684*, ed. James Hardiman (Irish Archaeological Society, Dublin, 1846; republished, Galway, 1978), p. 432.

Whether penned by Protestants or Catholics, a sense of providentialism permeated all of these histories.[33] The Protestants, influenced by Archbishop Ussher and Temple, interpreted the 1641 rebellion as God's punishment on an irreligious settler population and their willingness to tolerate Catholicism. It was due to God's providence that the plot for the rising had been discovered in the first place and during the 1640s (and again during the war of 1688–90/1) Protestants remained convinced that God was on *their* side.[34] An apocalyptic vision also infused these Protestant histories, as it had during earlier periods of crisis; the Catholic writers responded by emphasising their role as martyrs for the true cause. They believed that God supported their struggle to preserve and promote Catholicism and attributed military successes to divine intervention.[35] In a fascinating discussion of Gaelic Maccabeanism (chapter 8), Jerrold Casway argues that during the course of the early seventeenth century 'the biblically conscious native Irish . . . frequently identified their misfortunes with the plight of the ancient Israelites'.[36] Certainly Nicholas French later noted that without the Catholic religion 'there is no salvation'. He added that: 'This was the judgement the pious and valiant Maccabees made of the war they undertook, and nobly pursued for their religion and laws, which they preferred before their wives and children, and all temporal things most dear unto them.'[37]

To a large extent the written word has understandably been the focus of whatever work on Irish political thought that has been done. Yet other sources – especially visual ones – are also worthy of interrogation. According to one scholar of early modern English cartography, 'In many contexts maps would have articulated symbolic values as part of a visual language by which specific interests, doctrines and even world views were communicated.'[38] From the later sixteenth century maps became an

[33] Marc Caball, 'Providence and Exile in Early Seventeenth Century Ireland', *IHS*, 29 (1994), pp. 174–88; Raymond Gillespie, *Devoted People: Belief and Religion in Early Modern Ireland* (Manchester, 1997), p. 57; and John McCafferty, 'St. Patrick for the Church of Ireland: James Ussher's *Discourse*', *Bullán*, 3:2 (1997/8), pp. 87–101. Similar themes permeated the 'political' poetry; for further details see Michelle O Riordan, '"Political" Poems in the Mid-Seventeenth-Century Crisis' in Ohlmeyer (ed.), *Ireland*, pp. 112–27.
[34] Gillespie, *Devoted People*, pp. 50–5; T. C. Barnard, 'The Uses of 23 October 1641 and the Irish Protestant Celebrations', *EHR*, 106 (1991), pp. 891–2, 894, 918.
[35] See for example O'Mellan's account of the war, in Robert Young (ed.), *Historical Notices of Old Belfast* (Belfast, 1896), pp. 206, 242.   [36] See p. 177 below.
[37] French, *The bleeding Iphigenia*, p. 38. The Scottish covenanters also believed that they were the chosen people, see chapter 9 below.
[38] J. B. Harley, 'Meaning and Ambiguity in Tudor Cartography' in Sarah Tyacke (ed.), *English Map-Making 1500–1650* (London, 1983), p. 22. For a good introduction see Peter Barber, 'England II: Monarchs, Ministers and Maps, 1550–1625' in D. Buisseret (ed.), *Monarchs, Ministers and Maps: The Emergence of Cartography as a Tool of Empire* (Chicago, 1992).

increasingly important 'tool of government' in the English colonial experience, especially in Ireland. In an effort to facilitate military conquest, administrative assimilation and legal imperialism, late Tudor bureaucrats (such as Lord Burghley or Sir George Carew) constantly commissioned new maps of the 'moving frontier' in Ireland and, prior to settling lands, the government ordered extensive surveys of Munster (1584), Ulster (1608), North Wexford (1609), Wicklow and the Midlands (1637–38) and Connacht (1636–40). With the publication, in 1612, of John Speed's *Theatre of the Empire of Great Britaine* cartography took on an even greater symbolic importance. First, Speed's maps, which promoted James VI and I as the imperial sovereign of all three kingdoms, were 'designed to proclaim an ideological belief about his country, about the course of its history, and about its political system and destiny'.[39] Second, as J. H. Andrews has noted, the provincial (rather than the English county) format of his Irish maps 'deliberately relegated Ireland to second-class geographical status and no doubt reflected his assessment of contemporary interest in the country'.[40] Finally, Speed's map (see Plate 1) – peppered with forts and other symbols of imperial power – highlighted English control over Ireland and helped to pave the way for plantation and other 'civilising' policies. Speed's image of Ireland as a conquered nation, ripe for civilisation, was distributed throughout the known world (the *Theatre* became an international atlas in 1627).[41] Yet it was not until the 1650s that Ireland was systematically measured and accurately mapped by Sir William Petty in what is now known as the 'Down Survey' (see Plate 2).[42] This marked the first attempt to carry out a large-scale survey in a scientific manner and facilitated a revolution in landholding during the 1650s. Petty's maps also testify to the emergence of a new type of discourse in Ireland – that of the political economy – which in the words of Petty himself used only 'arguments of sense' which rested on 'visible foundations in nature'.[43]

---

[39] Harley, 'Meaning and Ambiguity in Tudor Cartography', p. 37.

[40] J. H. Andrews, *Shapes of Ireland: Maps and Their Makers 1564–1839* (Dublin, 1997), pp. 91 and 93, 107, 114. Also see Linda Levy Peck (ed.), *The Mental World of the Jacobean Court* (Cambridge, 1991), pp. 9–10.

[41] In addition to 'Speed's Lesser Maps', Ormond's library contained atlases by Blaeu, Seller, Janssen, Ortelius and Ptolemy, together with atlases of Japan and Africa: HMC, *Calendar of the Manuscripts of the Marquis of Ormonde*, NS (8 vols., London, 1902–20), VII, pp. 519, 513–14. Wadding's library included an 'atlas in longo folio': Patrick Corish (ed.), 'Bishop Wadding's Notebook', *Archivium Hibernicum*, 29 (1970), p. 57.

[42] T. Larcom (ed.), *History of the Down Survey* (Dublin, 1851). Andrews, *Shapes*, pp. 127, 137, 148–9, 153. Petty's maps circulated widely in manuscript from the 1660s but his *Hiberniae delineatio* was only published in 1685.

[43] Preface to Petty's *Political Arithmetic, or a Discourse*... reprinted in *Tracts chiefly relating to Ireland* (Dublin, 1769), p. 207. Also see chapter 10 below.

Just as maps highlighted the extent of English control over Ireland, contemporary images of the Irish reinforced popular perceptions and geo-political doctrines.[44] For example, Speed's illustrations, particularly his portrayal of the native Irish as 'wild' barbarians (see Plate 3), reinforced ethnocentric attitudes, confirming the racial superiority of the English over the Irish.[45] In chapter 5 Raymond Gillespie draws attention to the importance of state rituals and pageantry, glorifying the position of the chief governors, in conveying a powerful political message during the later decades of the seventeenth century.[46] In a similar vein domestic architecture illustrates the extent to which the physical landscape was being 'briticised' while, at the same time, serving to disseminate further the 'civilising' message.[47] As extant surveys and buildings illustrate, planters in Ireland built English-style, stone and timber dwelling-houses and improved their holdings, either by fencing, draining or planting a garden. This served as a symbolic barrier between the 'wild' world – where, as one anonymous critic noted, the Irish farmer 'never buildeth, repaire, or enclosethe the grownde'[48] – and the 'civilised' one they were creating. Regional powerbrokers increasingly adopted these architectural styles. In 1618 the fourth earl of Clanricard spent £10,000 he could ill afford building a grand fortified house, with mullioned bay windows and an ornate interior, at Portumna, near Galway.[49] Though the outer buildings of the earl of Antrim's principal seat at Dunluce remained defensive in

[44] Hiram Morgan, 'Festive Irishmen – an "Irish" Procession in Stuttgart, 1617', *History Ireland*, 5:3 (1997), pp. 14–20. Many contemporary images are reproduced in H. F. McClintock, *Old Irish and Highland Dress* (Dundalk, 1950); John Telfer Dunbar, *The Costume of Scotland* (London, 1981); Lucas de Heere, *Beschrijving der Britsche Eilanden* ed. T. M. Chotzen and A. M. E. Draak (Antwerp, 1937); and Francis A. Yates, *The Valois Tapestries* (London, 1959). Also see Arthur Williamson, 'Scots, Indians and Empire: The Scottish Politics of Civilization 1519–1609', *Past and Present*, 150 (1996), pp. 46–83. The political significance of Irish art during this period has been largely neglected. For the later years see Jane Fenlon, 'French Influence in Late Seventeenth-Century Portraits', *Irish Arts Review* (1989–90), pp. 158–65 and Anne Crookshank, 'The Visual Arts, 1603–1740' in Moody and Vaughan (eds.), *NHI*, IV, pp. 471–97.

[45] To some extent these were early forms of political cartoons and served a similar function, see Perry Curtis, *Apes and Angels: The Irishman in Victorian Caricature* (revised edition, Washington DC, 1997), p. x.

[46] For a vivid account of the pageantry laid on for Rinuccini upon his arrival in Kilkenny in November 1645 see C. P. Meehan, *The Confederation of Kilkenny* (Dublin, 1882), pp. 138–40.

[47] Also see Raymond Gillespie, 'Irish Funeral Monuments and Social Change 1500–1700: Perceptions of Death' in Raymond Gillespie and Brian Kennedy (eds.), *Art into History* (Dublin, 1994), pp. 155–68 and 'The Image of Death, 1500–1700', *Archaeology Ireland*, 6 (1992), pp. 8–10 where the political importance of funeral monuments is discussed.

[48] Hadfield and McVeagh (eds.), *Strangers to That Land*, p. 64.

[49] Jane Fenlon (ed.), *Clanricard's Castle, Portumna* (Dublin, 1999).

Plate 1 John Speed's map of Ulster, with Enniskillen fort in the lower left-hand corner, highlighted English control over this troublesome province. The numerous editions of Speed's *Theatre of Empire* circulated throughout the known world and included a pocket-sized edition published in 1627.

Plate 2   During the 1650s, under the direction of Sir William Petty,
Ireland was for the first time systematically mapped in what is now
known as the 'Down Survey'. The country and barony maps were first
published in *Hiberniae delineatio* (1685).

The *Wilde Irish* man   The *Wilde Irish* Woman

Plate 3   John Speed's *Theatre of Empire* was heavily illustrated and included unflattering depictions of the 'wilde Irish man' and the 'wilde Irish woman' alongside their 'civill' counterparts. These images reinforced geopolitical doctrines and popular perceptions of the native Irish.

character, the inner great house resembled an English manor house with two-storied bay windows and leaded diamond-shaped panes of glass. Likewise Antrim's 'pleasant house' at Glenarm was built to impress both his followers and his peers and to demonstrate his 'Englishness'.[50]

II

Whatever the nature, language or readership, it is critical to situate political discourse in its relevant contexts, which tend to be multi-faceted, mellifluous and overlapping. Certainly they transcended national boundaries and so any discussion cannot simply be limited to the realm of early

[50] Jane Ohlmeyer, '"Civilizinge of those rude partes": Colonization within Britain and Ireland, 1580s-1640s' in Nicholas Canny (ed.), *The Oxford History of the British Empire*, I, *The Origins of Empire: British Overseas Enterprise to the Close of the Seventeenth Century* (Oxford, 1998), p. 142.

modern Irish history; the British, imperial and continental contexts are also vital.[51] To begin with, Irish political thought and ideas cannot be examined without reference to England which – like it or not – effectively ruled Ireland as a colony for much of the seventeenth century. The English legal and parliamentary systems, together with the work of English political theorists, shaped Irish political prose. Patrick Darcy, as Aidan Clarke argues in chapter 2, drew on contemporary English as much as Irish precedents when drafting his treatise, while his *Argument* was a reaction to specific political developments both in Ireland and England during the later 1630s. The political philosophy of William Molyneux, as Patrick Kelly shows in chapter 4, can only be understood with reference to the influence of John Locke, particularly his views on natural right and contract theory of government, and to the constitutional and economic climates prevailing in England during the 1680s and 1690s.[52]

So much for England. What of the other Stuart kingdom, Scotland? During the early modern period, Irish and Scottish Gaeldom formed a distinct cultural entity, with bards composing works aimed at audiences in Ireland and Scotland and with restless Jacobites seeking succour and refuge on both sides of the North Channel. After 1603 this 'North Channel World' expanded to include Protestant preachers, planters and profiteers who shuttled back and forth between Antrim and Ayrshire, forming a homogeneous unit which, like Catholic Gaeldom, was united by the sea rather than the land. These migrants brought with them distinctive political ideas and religious beliefs.[53] In chapter 9 Allan Macinnes explains how covenanting ideology was transformed during the seventeenth century from a doctrine of power to one of protest and how interaction across the North Channel facilitated this shift. During the 1620s and 1630s the re-export of evangelical fervour from Ulster fuelled the growth of nonconforming Presbyterianism in south-west Scotland and strengthened the conventicling movement. After 1642 the presence of a large Scottish army of occupation not only transferred to Ulster covenanting 'constitutional fundamentalism' but also consolidated Presbyterianism there. Cross-fertilisation between the two kingdoms occurred in other ways. For instance after 1638 the covenanting movement 'served as a model for terminating the personal rule of Charles I';[54] while during the

---

[51] David Armitage and John Pocock make convincing calls for such an approach in chapters 10 and 12. For a more general discussion of the 'New British and Atlantic Histories' see *American Historical Review*, 104 (1999).   [52] Also see chapters 10 and 11.
[53] Ian Michael Smart, 'The Political Ideas of the Scottish Covenanters, 1638–88', *History of Political Thought*, 1:2 (1980), pp. 167–93; John Coffey, 'Samuel Rutherford and the Political Thought of the Scottish Covenanters' in John R. Young (ed.), *Celtic Dimensions of the British Civil Wars* (Edinburgh, 1997), pp. 75–95; the chapters by Edward Cowan and John Ford in Roger Mason (ed.), *Scots and Britons: Scottish Political Thought and the Union of 1603* (Cambridge, 1994).   [54] See p. 203 below.

later seventeenth and early eighteenth centuries Scottish theorists drew on the writings of Irish theorists, like William Molyneux, in their own constitutional struggle with the expansionist English parliament.[55]

Closely linked to the 'British' context is the imperial one and the recognition that, during the seventeenth century, Ireland served as a 'laboratory' of empire. In chapter 3 Patricia Coughlan examines the nature of the English colonial impulse during the 1650s, especially the debate between the assimilationist, reforming views of Vincent Gookin and the segregationist, hard-line attitudes of his opponents. Of particular interest is the discourse of barbarity and savagism which, in an Irish context, dated from the twelfth century, and the accompanying emergence of the ethnocentric mentalities, which later characterised English rule in the Americas, Africa and the Indian sub-continent.[56] Dr Coughlan highlights these personal linkages between County Cork and Massachusetts and shows how Daniel Gookin imbibed his cousin's ideas and transmitted them to North America. Thus, 'The Gookins' treatises afford a striking example of the kinship of ideas about colonial ideology and ethnicity and even about the moral status of colonists on one Atlantic seaboard with those on the other.'[57] With the emergence of political economy as a distinctive discourse and with trade increasingly determining the reason of state, Ireland's colonial status became more apparent still. In chapter 11 Charles Ludington notes how the Whig theorist William Atwood developed an imperial ideology – with the king in his English parliament at its centre – and then applied it not simply to Ireland, but to the American colonies and Scotland as well.

Yet seen from the perspective of mid-seventeenth-century Ireland the continental context was more important than the imperial one. As one might expect, Irish Catholic writers, often trained on the continent, were acquainted with the terminology of canon and civil law and drew on this when writing their political treatises.[58] More significant still was the impact that humanist thought had on Irish writers of all denominations

[55] See chapters 10 and 11.
[56] Ohlmeyer, '"Civilizinge of those rude partes"', pp. 130–4, 146.   [57] See p. 57 below.
[58] For instance see the 'Queries' produced by Peter Walsh in 1648: Patrick Corish, 'The Crisis in Ireland in 1648: The Nuncio and the Supreme Council: Conclusions', *Irish Theological Quarterly*, 22 (1955), p. 250. Also see Peck, 'Beyond the Pale', pp. 124, 137, 143. Cross-fertilisation occurred at other levels. English theorists resorted to continental traditions to strengthen their common law discourse. For example, Davies made selective use of Roman law conquest doctrine and even canon law to justify his civilising agenda: Hans Pawlich, 'Sir John Davies, the Ancient Constitution, and Civil Law', *Historical Journal*, 23 (1980), pp. 695–700 and Glenn Burgess, *The Politics of the Ancient Constitution: An Introduction to English Political Thought, 1603–1642* (University Park, PA, 1992), p. 127. Also see Donal Cregan, 'The Confederate Catholics of Ireland: The Personnel of the Confederation, 1642–9', *IHS*, 29:116 (1995), pp. 490–512 and 'The Social and Cultural Background of a Counter-Reformation Episcopate, 1618–60' in A. Cosgrove and D. MacCartney (eds.), *Studies in Irish History Presented to R. Dudley Edwards* (Dublin, 1979), pp. 85–117.

throughout the course of the century.[59] Counter-Reformation ideology also tempered the political prose of Catholic thinkers, as did the theological storms stirred up by Jansenism.[60] In other instances international politics influenced the nature of a discourse. For instance Conor O'Mahony, a Jesuit priest from County Cork who had spent his adult life in Portugal, wrote his *Disputatio apologetica de Iure Regni Hiberniae* (1645) in Lisbon at the height of the (ultimately successful) struggle for independence from Spain. O'Mahony was undoubtedly familiar with Portuguese arguments, often penned by his Jesuit colleagues, denying Habsburg rights and he simply adapted these to suit an Irish model of resistance. Thus exceptional circumstances facilitated the writing of an unusual work.[61]

Any attempt to contextualise political texts must also take account of the intellectual, cultural and social circles in which individual writers moved. Temple's *History* emerged from the embittered Protestant exiles who gathered at the home of Katherine, Lady Ranelagh (an intimate of Samuel Hartlib and John Milton), as did Boate's *Ireland's Naturall History*.[62] The 'learned triumvirate' of Roderic O'Flaherty, John Lynch and Dubhaltach Mac Fhirbhisigh 'had long resided together in Galway'. Yet O'Flaherty also corresponded with leading Protestant scholars, such as Edmund Borlase and William Molynuex;[63] while Mac Fhirbhisigh translated and transcribed ancient Irish texts for the Protestant antiquarian, Sir James Ware.[64] In short, considerable cross-fertilisation occurred

[59] Helga Robinson-Hammerstein, *European Universities in the Age of Reformation and Counter-Reformation* (Dublin, 1998), pp. vii–x; Clare Carroll and Vincent Carey (eds.), *Solon His Follie or A Politique Discourse Touching the Reformation of Common-Weales Conquered, Declined or Corrupted* (Medieval and Renaissance Texts and Studies, Binghamton, NY, 1996); Kew (ed.), *The Irish Sections of Fynes Moryson's*.

[60] Corish, 'Two Contemporary Historians', p. 227; Joseph O'Leary, 'The Irish and Jansenism in the Seventeenth Century' in Liam Swords (ed.), *The Irish–French Connection 1578–1978* (Paris, 1978), pp. 31–7.

[61] See chapters 7 and 8. Its hostile reception in Ireland can, in part, be attributed to fears that Owen Roe O'Neill aspired to the crown of Ireland. For his part, O'Neill distanced himself from the tract.

[62] T. C. Barnard, 'The Hartlib Circle and the Cult and Culture of Improvement in Ireland' in Mark Greengrass, Michael Leslie and Timothy Raylor (eds.), *Samuel Hartlib and the Universal Reformation* (Cambridge, 1994), p. 282 and his seminal article, 'The Hartlib Circle and the Origins of the Dublin Philosophical Society', *IHS*, 19 (1974), pp. 56–71.

[63] O'Flaherty, *A Chorographical Description*, p. 421; Ware and Harris, *Writers*, II, 163. Archbishop Ussher's intellectual environment has been effectively reconstructed, particularly his cordial relations with Franciscan scholars and other members of the Catholic hierarchy (such as David Rothe, bishop of Ossory). He allowed them access to his personal library and loaned them precious manuscripts and copies of his own writings and they reciprocated in kind: Aubrey Gwynn, 'Archbishop Ussher and Father Brendan O Conor' in Franciscan Fathers (eds.), *Father Luke Wadding Commemorative Volume* (Dublin, 1957), pp. 265, 272–3. Also see Joep Leerssen, 'Archbishop Ussher and Gaelic Culture', *Studia Hibernica*, 22 (1982), pp. 50–8.

[64] Nollaig Ó Muraíle, *The Celebrated Antiquary* (Maynooth, 1996), pp. 20, 93, 99–101, 108, 110, 116, 190, 192, 194–5, 230, 242, 248–50, 264; Dudley Loftus was also in touch with him: Ware and Harris, *Irish Writers*, II, pp. 156, 217.

between different religious and ethnic groups at all levels: the native Irish
borrowed ideas about kingship from English planters, while Old English
ideas about the constitutional relationship between Ireland and England
influenced Protestant writers.[65]

III

This collection falls far short of being a comprehensive history of seventeenth-century Irish political thought and culture.[66] However these
essays indicate the parameters within which further research might fruit-
fully be conducted and highlight a number of closely interrelated themes.
First, the central role played by kingship and the way that this underpinned the constitutional relationship between England and Ireland
dominated political discourse in seventeenth-century Ireland. Yet what
defined the character of kingship in an Irish context? Right of conquest,
divine right, or a contractual relationship between the sovereign and his
subjects? How did the Catholic and Protestant peoples of Ireland perceive their allegiances to an English monarch? How did the nature of
kingship change over time? Second the role that the English parliament
played in determining Irish affairs engaged theorists of all religions. Did
the two parliaments enjoy equal status? What laws governed Ireland? Did
Ireland merit the status of a kingdom (like Scotland), a colony (like those
in North America) or an annexed province (like Wales)? Third, the tor-
turous relationship between temporal and spiritual authority confounded
Irish political discourse throughout these years. To whom did the
Catholic peoples of Ireland owe ultimate allegiance: the king or the pope?
Finally, all of these issues impinged on identity formation in early modern
Ireland. What did it mean to be Irish in the seventeenth century? How did
ethnicity and religious affiliation shape identity formation?

As elsewhere in early modern Europe, political ideas in Ireland invari-
ably focused on the changing nature of kingship, in both its personal and
institutional forms, and the relationship between the king and his sub-

---

[65] For further details see chapter 5 below.

[66] Just as a number of the key political texts (many of them discussed in this volume) are
worthy of translation and/or (re)publication, so too many important topics remain unexplored. For example, the contribution to seventeenth-century Irish political thought and
culture made by various 'interest groups' – the lawyers, the clerics, the literary classes and
the antiquarians – and by ideologies such as royalism, republicanism, constitutionalism
or Jacobitism needs to be explored much more fully. Despite some recent pioneering
studies, particularly by Toby Barnard and Raymond Gillespie, the dissemination and
reception of political ideas, especially among the lower orders, is another neglected area.
Finally it is critical to draw insights from other disciplines – especially historical geogra-
phy, anthropology, sociology, literary theory and gender studies – in an attempt to understand better the subtleties and complexities of Irish political discourse and culture.

jects.[67] As Bernadette Cunningham shows (chapter 6), Keating and Lynch used discussions of kingship in early Ireland to interpret the nature of sovereignty and parliament in the seventeenth century and to emphasise the sense of continuity between the early kings and the Stuarts. They highlighted the importance of good kingship to the wellbeing of the Irish political nation and the fact that the 'sovereignty of the king depended on the willingness of the people to be his subjects'.[68] From a constitutional perspective it was the passage of the Kingship Act in 1541 that transformed Ireland's status from a lordship into an imperial kingdom:

That his Majesty, his heirs and successors, be from henceforth named, called, accepted, reputed, and taken to be kings of this land of Ireland, to have, hold, and enjoy the said style, title, majesty, and honours of king of Ireland . . . for ever, as *united and knit* to the imperial crown of the realm of England.[69] (italics mine)

The phrase 'united and knit' implied that the two kingdoms were equal, albeit under the rule of the English sovereign (but *not* his English parliament).[70] Yet according to the English statute that gave legislative sanction to the act, it '*united and annexed* [Ireland] forever to the Imperial crown of this highness' realm of England'.[71] Thus from the outset the roles played by the English and Irish parliaments in defining the nature of kingship in its Irish context were ambiguous and understandably resulted in a variety of interpretations, particularly during the 1640s and after 1688 when the tortured working relationship between the king and his English parliament disintegrated.

Debate about the nature of the conquest fuelled the ambiguity about Ireland's constitutional status. Had the Norman invaders conquered Ireland; or did the Irish submit willingly to Henry II? Irish theorists maintained that Ireland was not a conquered nation. Keating, for instance, argued that Ireland had submitted willingly to the English king provided he maintained and protected the nation's privileges;[72] while the anonymous chronicler of *Aphorismical Discovery of Treasonable Faction* and O'Mahony contended that Ireland had never been conquered but had

---

[67] For important insights, albeit from a Scottish perspective, see J. H. Burns, *The True Law of Kingship: Concepts of Monarchy in Early Modern Scotland* (Oxford, 1996) and Roger Mason, *Kingship and Commonweal: Political Thought in Renaissance and Reformation Scotland* (Edinburgh, 1997). [68] See p. 146 below.

[69] Constantia Maxwell, *Irish History from Contemporary Sources (1509–1610)* (London, 1923), pp. 101–2.

[70] Quoted in Michael Perceval-Maxwell, 'Ireland and the Monarchy in the Early Stuart Multiple Kingdom', *Historical Journal*, 34 (1991), p. 285.

[71] C. H. Williams (ed.), *English Historical Documents, c.1485–1558* (London, 1967), p. 474. I am grateful to David Menarry for bringing this reference to my attention.

[72] See chapter 6. Lynch and Keating differed in their views on the nature of the conquest and particularly the role the papacy played in it.

been occupied as a result of the internal divisions among the Irish. Though Giraldus Cambrensis had suggested that Ireland legitimately belonged to the English kings, he stressed that it was not a conquered nation. Writing in 1612, the English legal imperialist Sir John Davies concurred, arguing that only the suppression of Ireland at the end of the Nine Years War (1594–1603) constituted a legitimate conquest which in turn paved the way for the assimilation and civilisation of the Irish.[73] English victories during the 1640s and after 1688 simply reinforced Ireland's position as a vanquished nation. With the passage of the Adventurers' Act (1642) and the Acts of Settlement (1652, 1662 and 1665) the English parliament flexed its legislative supremacy, and it continued to do so for the rest of the seventeenth century.[74] In his *The Case of Ireland's Being Bound by Acts of Parliament in England and elsewhere Stated* (1698), Molyneux vigorously challenged this encroachment, constructing his argument around the concept of conquest in the context of post-Revolutionary Ireland.[75] Drawing on a variety of earlier sources (outlined in chapter 4), he argued that neither Henry II nor the English rulers of the sixteenth and seventeenth centuries had conquered Ireland and only laws passed by the Irish parliament could bind the political nation (which by this point constituted an exclusively Protestant body):

To conclude all, I think it highly inconvenient for England to assume this authority over the kingdom of Ireland . . . The Laws and Liberties of England were granted above five hundred years ago to the People of Ireland, upon their submissions to the Crown of England, with a design to make them easy to England, and to keep them in the allegiance of the King of England. How consistent it may be with true policy, to do that which the people of Ireland may think is an invasion of their rights and liberties, I do most humbly submit to the parliament of England to consider.[76]

The English House of Commons censured Molyneux's *Case*, and numerous responses, including one from the Whig polemicist William Atwood, reiterated Ireland's subordinate status to the English parliament and the

---

[73] Anthony Carty, *Was Ireland Conqurered? International Law and the Irish Question* (London, 1996), pp. 29, 30–5. Coke's position, including an analysis of the Merchants of Waterford Case, is fully discussed in Barbara Black, 'The Constitution of Empire: The Case for the Colonists', *University of Pennsylvania Law Review* 124:5 (1976), pp. 1157–1211.

[74] As Arthur Williamson recently noted after 1603, 'The cultural assumptions of English constitutionalism could never allow for a Britain formulated as other than an expanded England': Arthur Williamson, 'Union with England Traditional, Union with England Radical: Sir James Hope and the Mid-Seventeenth-Century British State', *EHR*, 110 (1995), p. 307.   [75] Carty, *Was Ireland Conquered?*, pp. 69–72.

[76] William Molyneux, *The Case of Ireland's Being Bound by Acts of Parliament in England and elsewhere Stated* (Dublin, 1698), pp. 171–2. Also see Patrick Kelly, 'William Molyneux and the Spirit of Liberty in Eighteenth-Century Ireland', *Eighteenth-Century Ireland*, 3 (1988), pp. 133–48; 'A Pamphlet Attributed to John Toland'; and chapter 11 below.

country's dependence for survival, especially during times of crisis, on English support.[77]

Whatever the status of the Irish parliament, the position of the king remained central even for Protestants. For as Jackie Hill noted in a fascinating article on Molyneux: 'without a king there could be no kingdom, and without a kingdom there could be no Irish parliament consisting of king, lords and commons, no ancient constitution to be inherited'.[78] The problem arose when kingship broke down, as it did in the 1640s and after 1688. Toby Barnard has elegantly argued that the onset of the First English Civil War in 1642 forced Irish Protestants to choose between king and the English parliament and resulted in something of an identity crisis for many.[79] Similarly, after 1660, even though many Protestants found the Stuart proclivity for 'popery' odious, they simply wanted more political autonomy and greater control over the army, judiciary and administration within the context of the Stuart monarchies.[80] Thus many Irish Protestants reluctantly tolerated James II and only shifted their allegiances after William III had established himself as the victor on the battlefield.[81] Archbishop William King's *The State of the Protestants of Ireland* (1691) conveniently justified their actions and in chapter 1 King argued: 'That it is lawful for one Prince to interpose between another Prince and his subjects when he uses them cruelly or endeavours to enslave or destroy them'.[82]

What then of the Stuarts' Catholic subjects? Like many of their Protestant countrymen, those of Norman ancestry stressed their 'Englishness' often at the expense of their 'Irishness'.[83] Aidan Clarke's definitive work on the political connections and cultural makeup of this Old English community clearly demonstrates that throughout the seventeenth century they perceived themselves as the crown's loyal and devoted servants. In return they expected to enjoy access to the person of the monarch and looked to the crown 'to protect their interests through

[77] Discussed at length in chapter 11.
[78] Hill, 'Ireland without Union' in Robertson (ed.), *Union for Empire*, p. 281.
[79] T. C. Barnard, 'The Protestant Interest, 1641–1660' in Ohlmeyer (ed.), *Ireland*, pp. 218–40.
[80] T. C. Barnard, 'Settling and Unsettling Ireland: The Cromwellian and Williamite Revolutions' in Ohlmeyer (ed.), *Ireland* and J. Hill, 'Ireland without Union' in Robertson (ed.), *Union for Empire*.
[81] J. I. McGuire, 'The Church of Ireland and the "Glorious Revolution" of 1688' in Cosgrove and McCartney (eds.), *Studies in Irish History*, pp. 137–49.
[82] William King, *The State of the Protestants of Ireland under the Late King James's Government* (London, 1691), p. 6.
[83] Joep Leerssen, *Mere Irish and Fíor-Ghael: Studies in the Idea of Irish Nationality, Its Development and Literary Expression prior to the Nineteenth Century* (Cork, 1996) offers the best overview of identity formation among the Catholic population in early modern Ireland.

the benevolent exercise of the royal prerogative'.[84] Above all, the Old
English writers asserted that their Catholicism in no way jeopardised
their fealty to a Protestant prince and drew on Bellarmine's theory of
indirect power to support their position.[85] John Lynch, for instance,
maintained that the king enjoyed supreme power over the temporal
matters of his kingdom; since the English kings also ruled Ireland, they
held supreme political power there as well.[86] Recent studies, largely by
Gaelic literary scholars, suggest that after their defeat in the Nine Years
War and the 'flight of the earls' in 1607 the native Irish, while acknowledging the centrality of Catholicism to their national identity, increasingly
adopted the same conciliatory, politique attitude towards the crown
which had traditionally characterised the Old English.[87]

The relationship between temporal and spiritual authority proved less
clear-cut for Irish Catholics living on the continent. The body of literature emanating from Louvain – histories, genealogies, devotional works
catechisms and the lives of saints – 'featured a sense of unquestioning
loyalty to the pope, and was defined by a sense of grievance against persecution on the grounds of religion'.[88] But these works saw the 'heretics'
and not the English as their enemy and many continued to regard the
Stuarts as the legitimate monarchs.[89] More overtly political were the treatises by the exiles who fled to the continent in the wake of rebellion at

---

[84] See p. 36 below.

[85] Aidan Clarke, 'The Policies of the "Old English" in Parliament, 1640–1' in J. L.
McCracken (ed.), *Historical Studies, V* (London, 1965); 'Colonial Identity in Early
Seventeenth Century Ireland' in T. W. Moody (ed.), *Historical Studies. XI. Nationality and
the Pursuit of National Independence* (Belfast, 1978); and 'Alternative Allegiances', p. 253.
Bellarmine, together with Suarez, argued that 'by divine institution the Popes have no
direct power over the secular or political sphere: the Pope's authority is formally a spiritual not a temporal one. But in virtue of his spiritual authority he has the right and power
to intervene in the field of politics, if and when the political ruler is acting contrary to the
spiritual interests of his subjects': James Brennan, 'A Gallican Interlude in Ireland', *Irish
Theological Quarterly*, 24 (1957), p. 226. This article provides an excellent insight into the
theological background, as does Cregan, 'Counter-Reformation Episcopate', pp. 114–17.

[86] Corish, 'Two Contemporary Historians', p. 229 and chapter 6, IV below.

[87] Mícheál Mac Craith, 'The Gaelic Reaction to the Reformation' in S. G. Ellis and S.
Barber (eds.), *Conquest and Union: Fashioning a British State 1485–1725* (London, 1995),
pp. 139–61; Bernadette Cunningham, 'Irish Language Sources for Early Modern
Ireland', *History Ireland*, 4:1 (1996), pp. 41–8; Marc Caball, 'Bardic Poetry and the
Analysis of Gaelic Mentalities', *History Ireland*, 2:2 (1994), pp. 46–50 and *Poets and
Politics: Reaction and Continuity in Irish Poetry, 1558–1625* (Cork, 1998); O Riordan,
'"Political" poems' and *The Gaelic Mind and the Collapse of the Gaelic World* (Cork, 1990);
Ó Buachalla, 'James our true king', pp. 7–35.

[88] Cunningham, 'The Culture and Ideology of Irish Franciscan Historians', p. 30.

[89] Many, influenced by Franciscan ideas about the nature of kingship, maintained that
loyalty was not necessarily unconditional. Franciscan ideology derived from the writings
of the thirteenth-century theorist Duns Scotus, who asserted that sovereignty originated
not with God but with the consent of the people; see chapter 8 for details. O'Mahony also
emphasised the contractual nature of kingship and linked this to the need for the king to
be a good Catholic; see chapter 7.

home, and who, according to Hiram Morgan, 'fused the patriotic ideals associated with Commonwealth reform with Counter-Reformation militancy'.[90] A number of contemporary histories – including those by Peter Lombard and Philip O Sullivan Beare, and Ludhaid Ó Cléirigh's account of Red Hugh O'Donnell – imbibed this rhetoric of 'faith and fatherland' and transmitted it back to Ireland.[91] This reached its apogee, as Jerrold Casway argues in chapter 8, with Owen Roe O'Neill and his exiled followers who modelled themselves after the Maccabean freedom fighters of ancient Judea and promoted 'an embryonic nationalism' first on the continent and after 1642 in Ireland itself.

Yet the accession of James VI and I undoubtedly changed the tone of the rhetoric for many. For instance, the exiled Archbishop Peter Lombard of Armagh dedicated his *Episcopion Doron* to James and in the preface congratulated him on his accession as Ireland's legitimate ruler. He went on to beg the king to end the persecution of Irish Catholics and to grant liberty of conscience since the Irish were, Lombard maintained, his faithful and loyal subjects. Secular writers followed suit. For example, 'The Appeal of the Catholics of Ireland' (*c.*1623), which was probably drafted by Jenico Preston, Viscount Gormanston, on behalf of the 'Catholics of Ireland', articulated a peaceful compromise based on a consensus settlement between the two religious communities.[92] However, the hope that James would grant toleration proved misplaced.[93]

The apparent mutual exclusiveness between loyalty to the crown and to Catholicism, which flew in the face of the contemporary doctrine of *cuius regio, euius religio*, confounded the Irish political nation for much of the seventeenth century and particularly during the 1640s.[94] Despite the fact that the confederates blatantly violated the king's royal prerogatives and consistently refused to obey his instructions, they still referred to themselves as 'loyal subjects' and the majority operated 'within the context of loyalty to the Crown'.[95] John Lynch clearly delighted in pointing out that:

---

[90] Hiram Morgan, 'Faith and Fatherland in Sixteenth Century Ireland', *History Ireland*, 3:2 (1995), p. 15.
[91] Hiram Morgan, 'Faith and Fatherland or Queen and Country? An Unpublished Exchange between O'Neill and the State', *Dúiche Néill*, 9 (1994), pp. 9–65.
[92] Glyn Redworth, 'Beyond Faith and Fatherland. The Appeal of the Catholics of Ireland, c.1623', *Archivium Hibernicum*, 52 (1998). I am grateful to Dr Redworth for letting me see his interesting article in advance of publication.
[93] John Silke, 'Primate Lombard and James I', *Irish Theological Quarterly*, 22 (1955), p. 131.
[94] In chapter 9 Allan Macinnes offers an interesting parallel. In Scotland loyalty to the crown and Presbyterianism became inextricably intertwined. However a person's obedience to God was unconditional whereas allegiance to a king depended on good government and the sovereign's willingness to accept religious imperatives. This contractual and limited notion of monarchy became a constitutional imperative again after 1685.
[95] Cited in Aidan Clarke, *The Old English in Ireland 1625–42* (New York, 1966), pp. 179–80 and Gilbert (ed.), *Irish Confederation*, I, p. lxv, II, p. 85. Also see chapter 2.

> The Scotch had sold; the English slew their king
> The Irish faithful to his banners cling.[96]

Throughout the war Gaelic poets lauded Charles I as 'their rightful king', and saw themselves as 'Charles's people'.[97] Moreover, royalism was not confined to members of the elite, and insurgents throughout the country interpreted the tumultuous events surrounding the rebellion in the language of kingship.[98] Oaths of association and 'union', usually administered by the clergy, reinforced this loyalism and ordinary Catholics took them very seriously.[99] For example, an entry dated 21 August 1646, in the corporation book for the confederate town of Clonmel, noted that: 'We have taken an oath [the second Oath of Association] to be true to our soveraigne lord the king . . . and to maintaine and defend the holie catholiq romaine religion'; significantly the entry ended 'the oath is the tye between God and man'.[100]

Even though 'embryonic republicanism' and the model of Maccabean resistance developed by the exiled native Irish combined with constitutional royalism after 1642, the confederates rejected any attempt to redefine the nature of kingship in Ireland or to question the legitimacy of Stuart sovereignty. For example, as Tadhg ó hAnnraháin shows (chapter 7), the publication of O'Mahony's *Disputatio*, which urged the Irish to complete the massacre of any Protestants remaining in Ireland, to abandon Charles I, and to choose in his stead a king from amongst the native nobility, infuriated many. The confederate supreme council burned the book in Kilkenny, as did the mayor and corporation of Galway, deeming it 'full of venemous and virulent doctrines, and damnable treasons against our King and country'.[101] An anonymous poet praised this censure:

> A book, so worth of light, may it shine in the burning flames,
> Likewise, may the writer himself be a companion for his book
> For both author and work have been treason's spark,
> As they deserve, I ask that both be brought forth to perish.[102]

---

[96] Lynch, *Cambrensis*, III, p. 135 and chapter 7, III.

[97] Ó Buachalla, 'James our true king', p. 23.   [98] See chapters 2 and 5 for further details,.

[99] The importance of covenanting in Scotland is examined in chapter 9 below. A similar analysis could be usefully applied to Ireland.

[100] NLI, MS 19,171, f. 365. Others promoted oaths of 'union', see James Hardiman, *The History of the Town and County of Galway* (Dublin, 1820), p. 111. The parallels here with the Scottish covenanters are striking; see chapter 9 for details.

[101] Hardiman, *Galway*, p. 123.

[102] I am grateful to my colleague, Dr William Naphy, for providing a translation of this Latin verse: *Dignus luce liber, modo flammis luceat ustus,/Et scriptor sit comes ipse suo/ Seditionis erat nam fax authorque liberque,/ Ambo perire pari sic meruere rogo*: O'Flaherty, *A Chorographical Description*, p. 432.

Even the Catholic clergy dissociated themselves from the *Disputatio* because, as Dr ó hAnnraháin astutely observes, the Oaths of Association provided them with the moral and political leverage that they needed.[103] Yet the book was allegedly castigated against the wishes of the papal nuncio, Rinuccini, 'who saved John Bane, a parish priest of Athlone, upon whom the book was found, from punishment'.[104] Equally serious, 'divers copies' were allegedly 'dispersed into severall partes of this kingdome'.[105]

Ultimately it was the debate surrounding Rinuccini's censure in 1648 of those who adhered to a truce with the royalists that provoked the greatest crisis within the confederate movement.[106] John Callaghan, a priest from Cork, in *Vindiciarum Catholicorum Hiberniae* (1650) defended the action of the supreme council. He argued that Rinuccini's decision to interfere in civil government was arbitrary and maintained that he 'sowed discord among the Catholics of Ireland, whom he found united and left disunited'.[107] Callaghan's history generated much controversy, particularly among clerics on the continent. John Lynch, though he thought Callaghan prone to exaggeration, shared many of his views and his *Alithinologia* (St Malo, 1664) devoted over 300 pages to a discussion of confederate affairs.[108] Others took umbrage at what they perceived as an unjustified attack on Rinuccini. The Capuchins Richard O'Ferrall and Robert O'Connell, who enjoyed exclusive access to the nuncio's personal papers, responded to it by compiling the *Commentarius Rinuccinianus* (not actually published until this century) where they blamed confederate failure on the 'half-hearted Catholicism and political and worldly interests of the Anglo-Irish'.[109]

With the restoration of Charles II as 'the prince of the three kingdoms',

---

[103] See chapter 7, I below.
[104] Ware and Harris, *Writers*, II, p. 122. See chapter 7 for a detailed discussion of Rinuccini's position.　　[105] Hardiman, *Galway*, p. 123.
[106] As Allan Macinnes shows in chapter 9, the covenanting movement disintegrated over the summer of 1648 over very similar issues.
[107] Cited in Patrick Corish, 'John Callaghan and the Controversies among the Irish in Paris 1648–54', *Irish Theological Quarterly*, 21 (1954), p. 48. Also see Brennan, 'A Gallican Interlude', p. 229.
[108] Corish, 'Two Contemporary Historians', pp. 217–36 and 'Bishop Nicholas French and the Second Ormond Peace, 1648–9', *IHS*, 6 (1948), p. 100. Unfortunately there is no recent edition of Lynch's *Supplementum Alithinologiae* (St Malo, 1667).
[109] Cited in Corish, 'Two Contemporary Historians', p. 221. Richard O'Ferrall and Robert O'Connell, *Commentarius Rinuccinianus, de sedis apostolicae legatione ad foederatos Hiberniae Catholicos per annon . . . .* ed. Rev. Stanislaus Kavanagh (6 vols., IMC, Dublin, 1932–49). A modern translation of this invaluable work might encourage scholars to use it more extensively. For a recent reassessment of Rinuccini's policies see Tadhg ó hAnnraháin, '"Far from *Terra Firma*". The Mission of GianBattista Rinuccini to Ireland, 1645–49' (unpublished PhD thesis, European University Institute, 1995).

this acrimony became embroiled in the Remonstrance controversy.[110] In an attempt to clarify the nature of allegiance between the Protestant king and his Catholic subjects, Richard Bellings, former secretary to the Confederation, drafted a Remonstrance that paraphrased the 1606 Oath of Allegiance. By promising to 'disclaim and renounce all foreign power be it wither papal or princely' which in any way threatened 'your majesty's person, royal authority . . . the state or government', it aimed to neutralise Protestant hostility by minimising papal claims.[111] Peter Walsh, a Franciscan and an intimate of Lord Deputy Ormond, offered clerical support for this compromise.[112] Ultimately the Remonstrance controversy 'only served to reopen the old cleavage among the clergy between Ormondists and Nuncioists on a new basis' and, in the face of hostility from Rome, only a small minority accepted it.[113] However Walsh continued to parade the loyalty of the Catholic community to the crown. In *The History and Vindication of the Loyal Formulary* – addressed to the 'British and Irish Catholics' inhabitants of 'this famous Empire of Great Brittaine' – he reassured the king and parliament 'of our steadfast and inflexible loyalty'. He beseeched them never to perceive the Irish 'as men whose faith is faction, and whose religion is rebellion'.[114] His pleas fell on deaf ears and only the accession of a Catholic king briefly resolved the dilemma. However by supporting James II with such enthusiasm Irish Catholics merely alienated their Protestant compatriots, the English parliament and the new sovereigns. The Catholic strategy for survival which had centred on kingship and the ability of the monarch to protect them was no longer a viable option.[115]

IV

Between the idea
And the reality
Between the motion
And the act
Falls the Shadow   (T. S. Eliot, *For Thine is the Kingdom*)

[110] Ó Buachalla, 'James our true king', p. 28 and chapter 2, III. Also see Anselm Faulkner, 'Anthony Gearnon, OFM (c.1610–1680) and the Irish Remonstrance', *Louth Archaeological and Historical Journal*, 17:3 (1971), pp. 141–9.
[111] Quoted in Brennan, 'A Gallican Interlude', p. 232.
[112] Peter Walsh, *The Controversial Letters, or the grand controversie concerning the pretended temporal authority of popes over the whole earth and the true sovereign of kings within their own respective kingdoms* (2nd edn, London, 1674) and *The History and Vindication of the Loyal Formulary, or Irish Remonstrance . . .* (London?, 1674), pp. xxiii–xxiv.
[113] T. Ó Fiaich, 'Edmund O'Reilly, Archbishop of Armagh, 1657–1669' in Franciscan Fathers (eds.), *Father Luke Wadding*, p. 202.   [114] Walsh, *History*, p. xxxv.
[115] Clarke, 'Alternative Allegiances', p. 263.

No discussion of Irish political thought and culture would be complete without examining what 'the Shadow' signifies. In chapter 5 Raymond Gillespie illuminates how Irish people interpreted political ideas and untangles the conceptual maps they constructed in order to help them better understand their political worlds, particularly during periods of national and personal crisis. How then did political ideas circulate within Ireland? How did the 'idea' influence the 'reality' of Irish politics?

One of the most effective ways of disseminating political ideas was through the pulpit and 'Theology was in many ways as important and fundamental a language for political discussion as the common law.'[116] Through sermons and homilies the clergy called for submission to the ruler, promoted images of a godly prince, and fuelled anti-Catholic rhetoric. Toby Barnard, in a fascinating study of sermons preached on the anniversary of the Irish rebellion (23 October), has shown how these perpetuated Temple's interpretation of the rebellion and his hostility towards Irish Catholics.[117] Catholics also used the pulpit to disseminate a political message. For example, Peter Walsh 'preached nine sermons against the evil tendency of O'Mahony's opinions in St Kenny's church, at Kilkenny'.[118] Whatever the religion, schools and colleges served as mediums for indoctrinating the young with religious and political ideologies.[119] Despite government censure, Catholic schools operated and even prospered, particularly in urban areas. The Jesuits were particularly active and came to the fore during the 1640s when, under the leadership of the respected scholar Stephen White, they established schools and colleges throughout the country.[120] The political message of one Jesuit play, *Titus; or the Palme of Christian Courage*, performed by the scholars at Kilkenny in the midst of negotiations between the Confederation of Kilkenny and the king, is clear: 'the religious principles of Catholicism could not be

---

[116] Burgess, *The Politics of the Ancient Constitution*, p. 131.

[117] Barnard, 'The Uses of 23 October 1641', pp. 890–2, 894, 918. Also see McCafferty, 'St. Patrick for the Church of Ireland', p. 97.   [118] Ware and Harris, *Writers*, II, p. 122.

[119] For example while at Eaton Conn O'Neill read books – such as *Deus et Rex being King James Intermediate under God* – designed to inculcate obedience to the ruler: Robert E. Ward, *An Encyclopedia of Irish Schools, 1500–1800* (Lewiston, NY, 1995), p. 206. Interestingly Catholic and Protestant schools both used the same texts except that in the former the page which referred to the monarch as 'Defender of the Faith' was removed: Raymond Gillespie, 'Church, State and Education in Early Modern Ireland' in Maurice O'Connell (ed.), *Education. Church and State* (Dublin, 1992), p. 42. Monasteries or Catholic schools often acquired substantial libraries. For instance the Jesuit College in Kilkenny allegedly possessed 'a large library containing an excellent selection of books': John Leonard, *A University for Kilkenny* (Kilkenny, 1996), p. 52. Also see Ward, *An Encyclopedia*, pp. 160–1, 212–13.

[120] White and Ussher enjoyed a close relationship (Corcoran (ed.), *State Policy*, pp. 23–4) and the archbishop thought him 'a man of exquisite knowledge in the antiquities not only of Ireland, but also of other nations' (Ware and Harris, *Writers*, II, p. 103).

compromised and there was divine sanction for maintaining a religious position'.[121] In chapter 5 Dr Gillespie also discusses the broader significance of theatre in diffusing political ideas to a wider audience. For instance, the post-Restoration plays by Roger Boyle, earl of Orrery, redefined the nature of kingship; while George Farquhar's *Love and a Bottle* embodied many of Molyneux's ideas.[122]

The texts of many plays were also printed; but how many people could actually read? Dr Gillespie has argued that while an absence of evidence makes determining precise levels of literacy problematic, there was 'a significant reading public in Ireland' by the end of the seventeenth century, particularly in urban areas and among the elite, professional, merchant and (increasingly) trading classes.[123] In addition to the printed word, people read manuscript works. In the preface to *A Prospect of the State of Ireland* Peter Walsh noted that 'When I was a young man I had read Geoffrey Ke[a]ting's Irish Manuscript History of Ireland.'[124] A rather battered and heavily annotated copy of Keating's manuscript is extant in the National Library of Scotland and clearly passed through many hands. One of its early owners was Maurice King from County Antrim, who described himself as a 'miner'; it eventually ended up in Argyllshire where a number of people read it, including Patrick McFarland. McFarland clearly prized the volume and noted in the margin that if anyone stole it he 'shall be hanged till a tree till the corbies [crows] pi[c]k out the eyes'.[125]

Important though the manuscript tradition was, print remained a more effective medium for spreading political ideas. During the 1640s the confederates quickly realised the power of print in shaping popular opinion and rallying support for the Catholic cause. 'And as soldiers with swords,

---

121 See p. 119 below. Also see Patricia Coughlan, '"Enter Revenge": Henry Birkhead and *Cola's Furie*', *Theatre Research International*, 15:1 (1990), pp. 1–17.
122 Also see Nancy Klein Maguire, *Regicide and Restoration: English Tragicomedy, 1660–1671* (Cambridge, 1992), pp. 11, 182–3.
123 Gillespie, *Devoted People*, p. 75; 'Church, State and Education', pp. 50–1, 54; and 'The Circulation of Print', pp. 32–3. Also see chapter 5, II. Lists of devotional works circulated by Luke Wadding to 'Relations, friends, benefactors, poore gentry and widdowes, children etc' in County Wexford during the later seventeenth century suggest that there was a literate Catholic population: Corish, 'Bishop Wadding's Notebook', pp. 55–87.
124 Walsh, *A Prospect*, pp. [10], 16. By the early seventeenth century, even people who spoke and read vernacular Gaelic had problems comprehending literary Gaelic: Samantha Meigs, *The Reformations in Ireland: Traditionalism and Confessionalism, 1490–1690* (London, 1997), p. 109.
125 King noted in the margin that the book belonged to him and requested in both English and Irish that it be returned to him if he lost it, NLS, Advocates MSS 33.4.11, f. vi. By the end of the seventeenth century the Advocates Library had acquired two further copies of Keating's history, NLS, Advocates MSS 72.2.1 and 72.2.8 and in 1850 another copy NLS, Advocates MSS 72.1.43.

pikes, and guns doe fight for the restitution of the only true religion', wrote the Waterford printer Thomas Bourke, 'so it is meet, and expedient that the pen and the print bestirre themselves also for so worthy a cause.'[126] For much of the seventeenth century, the inadequacy of national presses meant that the bulk of books were imported from England and even then the book trade centred on Dublin.[127] Other publications, despite government prohibitions, were brought in – often clandestinely – from the continent. For instance, the earl of Clanricard used merchants in Lisbon to buy books.[128] Bishop Wadding managed to acquire many of the more controversial works published on the continent (including Peter Lombard's *De Regno Hiberniae*, John Lynch's *Cambrensis Eversus*, and Nicholas French's *Bleeding Iphigenia*), probably from a supplier in Rotterdam.[129] Wadding was not an exception. The Protestant historian Edmund Borlase noted with horror how French's *Bleeding Iphigenia* ('a virulent and scurrilous piece') and other seditious Catholic pamphlets were readily available 'at home and abroad'.[130]

In an attempt to control the flow of books into and within Ireland, the state regulated the trade and closely monitored the activities of predominantly Dublin-based booksellers and printers.[131] During the 1640s the confederates proved equally vigilant. Between 1642 and 1650 the confederate presses published ninety-two books, pamphlets and broadsheets. As the figures in Table 1.1 show, the bulk (83 per cent) of these publications can be classified as either propaganda or political works. They included copies of important pieces of legislation (such as the 1643 cessation);

---

[126] Quoted in William Sessions, *The First Printers in Waterford, Cork and Kilkenny pre 1700* (York, 1990), p. 8.

[127] Robert Munter, *A Dictionary of the Print Trade in Ireland, 1550–1775* (New York, 1988), Mary Pollard, *Dublin's Trade in Books, 1550–1800* (Oxford, 1989), James W. Philips, *Printing and Bookselling in Dublin 1670–1800* (Dublin, 1998) and R. J. Hunter, 'Chester and the Irish Book Trade, 1681', *Irish Economic and Social History*, 15 (1988), pp. 89–93. Between 1603 and 1641 only ninety-six titles were produced in Dublin: Raymond Gillespie, 'Irish Printing in the Early Seventeenth Century', *Irish Economic and Social History*, 15 (1988), p. 81.

[128] Raymond Gillespie, 'The Book Trade in Southern Ireland 1590–1640' in Gerard Long (ed.), *Books beyond the Pale: Aspects of the Provincial Book Trade in Ireland before 1850* (Dublin, 1996), p. 7.

[129] Lombard's *De Regno* was suppressed by Wentworth in November 1633: Corish (ed.), 'Bishop Wadding's Notebook', pp. 55–87.   [130] Borlase, *History*, pp. iii, iv, viii, xii.

[131] Between 1603 and 1660 roughly twenty-five individuals (stationers, booksellers, binders and printers) were involved in the Irish book trade; only eight (or 32 per cent) were not based in Dublin; between 1660 and 1700 this figure had nearly quadrupled to ninety-five; however only six originated from outside Dublin. These figures derive from Munter, *Dictionary*. In Dublin books were sold and traded by individual booksellers and stationers and in local shops or markets, in taverns (one of the most popular was the 'Rose and Crown' on Dame Street) or, increasingly, in the coffee houses; chapmen and peddlers serviced the 'country trade'.

Table 1.1 *The nature of publications produced by the confederate presses, 1642–50.* *

Nature of the publication	Waterford, 1643–6	Cork, 1648–50	Kilkenny, 1642–9	Total
Political/propaganda	18 (20%)	17 (18%)	41 (45%)	76 (83%)
Military	1		1	2 (2%)
Play/literature	2	1	1	4 (4%)
Sermon	1			1 (1%)
Almanac/news/other	2	6	1	9 (10%)
Total	24 (26%)	24 (26%)	44 (48%)	92 (100%)

Note:
* Data extracted from Sessions, *First Printers* and E. R. Dix, 'Printing in the City of Kilkenny in the seventeenth century', *Proceedings of the Royal Irish Academy*, 32, section C, 7 (1914).

discussions and editorials on major political events (particularly negotiations with Charles I); political treaties (such as Patrick Darcy's *Argument*); and works of popular propaganda, which were usually pro-royalist and always anti-parliamentarian.

Apart from one pamphlet, clearly written for a clerical audience, these were all printed in English and were sold in well-known locations, such as 'the printhouse ar Roche's building' in Cork or 'the White Swanne' in Kilkenny. Others, especially proclamations, could be purchased 'upon market dayes, betweene the houres of ten and two . . . in the market place of each corporation, and market towne in this kingdome'.[132] The only real battle for men's minds in Catholic Ireland occurred in 1648 when civil war between the confederates erupted in the wake of Rinuccini's censure (discussed above), and the nuncio's subsequent failure to gain control of the Kilkenny press (which, ironically, he had procured in France in 1645) did his cause untold damage. The output, particularly of broadsheets, increased very significantly during these months as the anti-clerical faction tried to whip up popular support against the nuncio and his chief military supporter, Owen Roe O'Neill. One broadsheet of 28 July accused Rinuccini of having 'introduced a civill war among the Confederates, and thereby exposed the Catholick Religion and this Kingdome to apparent hazard of destruction'.[133] Another, published a few weeks later, threatened to punish severely any

[132] Quoted in Sessions, *First Printers*, p. 246.   [133] *Ibid.*, p. 248.

person 'who shall join with, or adhere unto, supply, relieve or assist the said Owen O'Neyll'.[134]

The impact that the controversies surrounding the 1648 censure had on the Catholic political nation both at home and abroad was profound and dragged on into the later decades of the seventeenth century. What influence did other works have? Primate Boyle noted with horror in 1685 that Nicholas French's *The Settlement and Sale of Ireland* had been reprinted 'to serve a turn and to make the people mad' about the land settlement. He had questioned the 'papist bookseller' William Weston, who had sold about a hundred copies in Dublin, and discovered that 'There were many of them bought up here and gave great disturbance to the people.'[135] William King's *State of the Protestants* became an immediate bestseller and by the early eighteenth century virtually every country house library in Ireland held a copy.[136] According to the Scottish cleric and historian Bishop Gilbert Burnet, it was 'the best book that hath been written for the service of the government . . .[and] it is worth all the rest put together, and will do more than all our scribblings for settling the minds of the nation'.[137] Jack Greene has noted the popularity of the ideas of a number of Irish writers – Sir John Davies, William Petty, and more especially William Molyneux – among the American colonists, especially in the 1770s.[138]

The popularity of Molyneux and a few other prominent – largely Protestant – theorists should not, however, detract from the great variety of political discourses generated within and about Ireland during the seventeenth century. Though primarily the domain of the elite, these discourses embraced all ethnic, religious and political traditions and captured the imaginations of both contemporary and later writers at home and abroad. Many of the riches of the Irish political tradition remain to be tapped; this volume – hopefully – marks a beginning.

---

[134] *Ibid.*, p. 251.   [135] HMC, *Ormonde*, NS, VII, pp. 398–9.
[136] By 1768 it had been reprinted twelve times.   [137] Cited in *DNB*, 'William King'.
[138] Jack P. Greene, *The Intellectual Heritage of the Constitutional Ear* (Philadelphia, 1986), pp. 16, 19, 23.

Part I

Ireland and England

2   Patrick Darcy and the constitutional relationship between Ireland and Britain

Aidan Clarke

Two contexts are appropriate to the consideration of the celebrated speech made by Patrick Darcy at a conference committee of the Lords and Commons of the Irish parliament in the great dining hall of Dublin Castle on 9 June 1641 and published two years later. One is the context in which it was delivered and has to do with particular issues arising from recent governmental practice and political developments. The other is the context in which it was published and has to do with the relationship between two propositions about the nature of the dependency of Ireland upon England. The more famous of these was Darcy's assertion of Ireland's legislative independence of the English parliament. That constitutional position has come to stand, so to speak, as the diagnostic feature of the emerging colonial identity of the eighteenth-century Protestant ascendancy and historians have found both an interesting continuity and a pleasing irony in tracing its lineage back to a Catholic, rebel source. The result has been a tendency both to overstate the originality of Darcy's view of the public law relationship between the two parliaments and to overlook its secondary place in his carefully structured argument. In reality, the claim to legislative independence did not stand alone. It was a logically sequential complement to an older and larger proposition, sanctioned by the act of the Irish parliament that had converted Ireland from a lordship to a kingship in 1541: that Ireland was a separate kingdom, subject to the same crown as England, but distinct from it. The union of the crowns of England and Scotland in 1603 retrospectively provided a useful parallel for this relationship, but it was not until the breakdown of authority in the multiple Stuart kingship in the early 1640s that the underlying assumptions of Irish politics were found to be in need of definition and justification and it became necessary to defend the position that Ireland was a dependency, not of England, but of the English crown.

    In Ireland, the immediate context of Darcy's 'Argument' was provided by the manner of government introduced by Lord Deputy Wentworth and the entourage of lay and clerical administrators who came with him to Ireland in the 1630s. Local conventions and established procedures were overturned and both the formal and the informal distribution of power was subverted as the new administration routinely governed through accentuated prerogative powers which were enforced not only by direct conciliar jurisdiction, but through the Courts of Castle Chamber and High Commission and the Commission for the Remedy of Defective Titles. The power of the legislature was circumscribed as the executive applied to parliament the statutory controls that had been designed to restrict its own discretion when they were set in place in Poynings' Act in 1494. Access to the king, both in person and by petition, was systematically suppressed. The formerly influential were displaced and in some prominent cases called to account, often it seemed vindictively.

This altered configuration of governmental authority was associated with the pursuit of unpopular policies. For the Catholic colonial community – the Old English, as they called themselves – the crux was the frustration of the successful conclusion to which a series of royal Graces granted in 1628 had brought their sustained effort to preserve their property by securing a waiver of royal title to the lands they occupied. The withdrawal of those concessions in the 1634 parliament, the consequent resumption to the crown of land in Connacht for plantation purposes and the sinister transformation of the Defective Titles Commission into an agency concerned to establish the title of the crown rather than to confer rights against it were all confirmations of official unwillingness to honour the promise that the existing property rights of the Catholic colonists would be confirmed. The inference that systematic expropriation and religious proscription would follow was plain. Heightening both of these linked threats was the loss of the means to withstand them: a steady decline of political influence had begun with the augmentation of Protestant parliamentary membership to a majority in 1613, had been made manifest in the restrictions imposed upon parliament's independence in 1634, and continued thereafter with a systematic attack on Catholic constituencies which resulted in sharply reduced Catholic representation in the parliament which met in March 1640. The natural reaction was to try to recover the ground that had been lost and to seek to set the political clock back to the 1620s. But the regression that had taken place in the 1630s had one vital corollary. In the 1620s, the power of final decision had lain outside Ireland: in the 1630s, that was no longer so. As parliament ceased to be a useful means of defence and the Old English could no longer realistically rely upon traditional constitutional protections, the alternative was to return to the approach that had succeeded in 1628 and to protect their interests through the benevolent exercise of the royal prerogative.

The need to switch the emphasis from politicing in the legislature to

supplicating at court was disguised for some time by the apparent convergence of Old English aims with those of their Protestant fellow colonists –
the New English. Deprived as they were of places of honour, profit and
power; required as they were to subscribe to a new set of religious norms
which they thought suspiciously close to popery; subjected as they were to
rent increases and the surrender of church property; governed as they
were in a style which they saw as a denial of their rights as Englishmen;
and inclined, as some of them certainly were, to sympathise with the
opponents of royal policies in England and Scotland, the New English,
like the Old English, had every reason to wish the new style of government at an end. It is clear from Professor Perceval-Maxwell's recent dis-
section of the parliamentary record that members of that group played a
leading part in the opposition movement which developed in the Irish
parliament in 1640.[1] It is circumstantially clear that they were part of a
multiple opposition which was brought into being to counter a multiple
monarchy. Just as the English parliamentary leaders conspired with the
Scots rebels before the convention of the English parliament in
November 1640, so they also plotted with their counterparts in Ireland
whose initial part in the plan was to arrange for the delivery of a petition
of remonstrance from the Irish parliament which would serve as a spring-
board for the impeachment of Wentworth, who was now the king's first
minister in England. It was to be presented to the English Commons at
the first opportunity by the politically well-connected Antrim planter Sir
John Clotworthy. The success of the Irish government in delaying the execution of this scheme for a critical two weeks or so has obscured its central
place in the tactics of the English parliamentary opposition. The initiation
of the proceedings against Wentworth was improvised, with Clotworthy
playing a prominent part, until the belated arrival of the remonstrance
from Ireland made it possible to proceed to the formulation of charges.
Soon after, parliamentary committees from Ireland arrived in London to
support the petition and to provide informed assistance in the preparation of detailed articles of impeachment, the majority of which related to
Wentworth's Irish administration.

Intercolonial cooperation in Ireland and London did not preclude the
pursuit of sectional interests by traditional non-parliamentary means.
Both groups sought the redress of their particular grievances in direct
negotiation with the king, and the Old English members of the parliamentary committee were spectacularly successful in March 1641 when
they prevailed upon the beleaguered king to order the preparation of bills
to enact the principal Graces and to revoke the plantation proceedings in

---

[1] M. Perceval-Maxwell, *The Outbreak of the Irish Rebellion of 1641* (Dublin, 1994).

Connacht. The agreed area of common action that did develop between Catholic and Protestant colonists included a determination to make use of the opportunity to mount a campaign for governmental reform as well as their willingness to cooperate in the impeachment of Wentworth. The coalition, identifying those for whom they spoke as the 'loyal and dutiful people of this land of Ireland, being now for the most part derived from British ancestors', claimed the 'birthright and best inheritance' that their ancestry entitled them to, which was to be governed according to law and due process, and set out to achieve three objectives.[2]

The most fundamental of these was to establish the illegality of the recent administrative practices that were alleged to have 'altered the Face of the Government' in Ireland.[3] To that end, in February 1641, a checklist of complaints was compiled which became known as the 'Queries' because it took the form of a series of questions addressed to the Irish judges for their collective, itemised confirmation that the rule of law had been abrogated. The first of these inquired 'Whether the subjects of this kingdom be a free people, and to be governed, only, by the common laws of England, and statutes of force in this kingdom?' The remainder questioned the legality of the jurisdiction of the council, the chief governor and the Court of Castle Chamber; the subservience of the judges to the government rather than the law; the execution of martial law in times of peace; the use of acts of state to alter the law; the disfranchisement of parliamentary boroughs; and the granting of monopolies. There was no suggestion that the answers to these questions were in doubt. They were framed to elicit the 'manifestation and declaration of a clear truth' and the aim was said to be 'the good of posterity',[4] though the fact that a number of them touched directly on incidents specified in the articles of impeachment against Wentworth suggests a more immediate purpose. The second objective was to restore the Irish parliament to its traditional status through the passage of an act which would reinstate the historic understanding of the statutory controls that had regulated meetings of the Irish parliament since it had passed Poynings' Act in 1494 and amended it in 1557.[5] They demanded that it be made clear that the requirements that the Act imposed for the transmission of proposed legislation to England for certification in advance of their formal considera-

---

[2] *Commons Jnl, Ire*, I, pp. 164–6.   [3] *Ibid.*, pp. 176–7.   [4] *Lords Jnl, Ire*, I, p. 161.
[5] 10 Henry 7, c. 9. 3 & 4 Philip & Mary, c. 4. The original act required all proposed legislation to be transmitted to England for certification by the king and Privy Council before the summoning of a parliament in Ireland. The amendment removed the English Privy Council from the process and allowed for the transmission of bills while Parliament was in session. The first change followed from the Act of Kingly Title of 1541; the second was dictated by the need to make procedural provision for the recertification of bills amended in passage.

tion by parliament were intended to limit the discretion of the Irish government, not to restrict the right of parliament to initiate legislative proposals.[6] The third aim was to establish the right of the Irish parliament to exercise the judicial power of impeachment. There were proximate reasons for doing this because the Irish parliament wished to discredit four potential defence witnesses in Wentworth's trial, but the issue quickly assumed an importance beyond the specific cases. Since there was no precedent for impeachment in Ireland, the king refused to allow the proceedings to continue. This reasoning challenged the undifferentiated claim of the colonists to enjoy both the rights specific to Ireland and the rights 'held by the subjects of England' which had been conferred on them by King John and to which the Irish parliament was 'co-heir with the parliament in England'.[7] They responded by protesting that the powers and functions of parliaments were inherent, irrespective of usage, and claimed the validity of English parliamentary precedents for Irish purposes.

The presumption of the equivalence of the two parliaments which was implicit in this declaration, adopted on 24 May, twelve days after Wentworth's execution, had been stated explicitly two months earlier. In March, when the judges had tried to avoid answering the 'Queries' on the grounds that some of the matters dealt with were under consideration in the English parliament, the Irish House of Lords had reproved them for speaking 'as if this parliament were subordinate to the parliament of England'.[8] The Commons had proposed to deal with this judicial obstruction by requesting the English parliament to give its opinion on the points of law involved. In doing so they were expressing a sense not of inferiority, but of partnership; more particularly, partnership in securing the conviction of Wentworth, whose reputation the 'Queries' were designed to damage. The Lords, more attuned to the constitutional nuances, did not concur. Their rebuke to the judges had been fully in accordance with received opinion. The only available edition of the Irish statutes, which had been published in 1621 by Richard Bolton, now lord chancellor and one of those whom the Commons was attempting to impeach, had cited two fifteenth-century declaratory acts of the Irish parliament to show that the relationship between the two parliaments was one of equality.[9] Coincidentally, in the same year the nature of that relationship had been adverted to in the English House of Commons when a

---

[6] Aidan Clarke, 'Historical Revision: XVIII The history of Poynings' Law, 1615–41', *IHS*, 18:70 (1972), pp. 207–22.
[7] *Captaine Audley Mervin's Speech, Delivered in the Upper House to the Lords in Parliament, May 24 1641* (London, 1641).   [8] *Lords Jnl, Ire*, I, p. 161.
[9] Richard Bolton, *Statutes of Ireland* (Dublin, 1621), p. 67.

number of members moved to regulate the rising imports of Irish cattle on the hoof to England. King James insisted that the matter was not within the parliament's competence and Sir John Davies, the most celebrated of Irish attorney generals and a former speaker of the Irish Commons, matter-of-factly informed the House that 'Ireland is a member of the crown of England' and that 'this kingdom here cannot make laws to bind that kingdom, for they have there a parliament of their own'.[10] This position received the authoritative support of Sir Edward Coke, who defended the right of the Commons to discuss the matter as a grievance, but not to determine it: the proper procedure, he explained, was to refer the grievance to the king to deal with, either by order or by referring it to the Irish parliament for consideration. In so far as this episode was perceived to have constitutional implications, it was the propriety of the king's action in determining the bounds of his own prerogative by removing matters from parliament's purview that was contentious, not the relationship between the two parliaments.[11]

What was unproblematic in 1621 and continued to be taken for granted in Ireland was, however, coming into question in England twenty years later. In the negotiations towards an Anglo-Scottish treaty in the winter and spring of 1641, the Scots representatives, who were anxious to ensure that the king did not retain control of independent force in Ireland, persistently assumed that Ireland was subject to the English parliament. Conrad Russell has speculated that this may have been not a misunderstanding but 'a concealed item in a programme for the security of Protestantism'.[12] Whatever the truth of that, there is no doubt that the concurrent management of the trial of Wentworth was greatly extending the English parliament's informal involvement in Irish affairs, while the desire to secure the disbandment of the new, largely Catholic, Irish army that had been raised for service against the Scots in the previous year tempted both English Houses to discuss proposals about the Irish military establishment. The point of crystallisation came late in April, when the opposition leader, Oliver St. John, who had recently been appointed solicitor general, was called upon to justify to the House of Lords the Bill of Attainder against Wentworth which had been substituted when the impeachment collapsed. St. John needed to establish the jurisdiction of the English parliament over offences committed in Ireland and he did so

[10] Hans Pawlisch, *Sir John Davies and the Conquest of Ireland* (Cambridge, 1985), p. 32. Barbara Black, 'The Constitution of Empire: The Case for the Colonists', *University of Pennsylvania Law Review*, 124 (1976), pp. 1157–1211.

[11] This issue arose again, more clearly, in 1624, when James denied parliament's competence to deal with Virginia.

[12] Conrad Russell, *The Fall of the British Monarchies, 1637–1642* (Oxford, 1991), p. 169.

by deduction from the competence of the English parliament to legislate for Ireland. He conceded that the question of whether Ireland was bound by English acts which did not specifically refer to Ireland was unsettled, but 'if named, no doubt'.[13] The forensic effect of this admission of uncertainty about the scope of general legislation was to reinforce the competence that was claimed, and that was presumably St. John's intention. In reality, there was no doubt whatever as to whether Ireland was bound when it was not named. Almost 150 years earlier, the parliament that had passed Poynings' Act had provided for 'all statutes, late made within the said Realm of England, concerning or belonging to the common and public weal' to be given the force of law in Ireland[14] and successive governments ever since had proceeded on the principle that English legislation needed to be re-enacted in Ireland. Once the critical moment had passed, moreover, the claim was not renewed.

The Irish judges, having failed to hide behind the English parliament, resorted to hiding behind the royal prerogative. The answers presented by them in May systematically evaded the points at issue by appealing to the discretionary authority of the crown, leaving it to be understood that it was for the king to decide upon the proper extent of executive authority. The Commons 'did hold it not fit it should be called an answer' and deputed to Patrick Darcy and a consultative committee the task of refuting it and of determining precisely what constituted lawful authority within the state.[15] Darcy had taken his seat in the Irish Commons only three weeks previously. A leading opposition spokesman in the 1634 parliament, he had, as he reminded his audience in his prefatory remarks, suffered from Wentworth's 'high hand', having been both imprisoned and disbarred for his part in bringing local resistance to the finding of the king's title to the lands of County Galway to the royal court. His incongruous return in a by-election as knight of the shire for Tyrone was part of a collaborative pattern, for by-elections from boroughs in the same plantation county had already returned his brother-in-law and fellow Galway agent, Richard Martin, and, even more improbably, Sir Phelim O'Neill who was soon to become notorious as 'the arch rebel of all Ireland'.[16] Darcy's electoral provenance underlines the fact that it was not as an Old English spokesman that he replied to the judges in his address on 9 June but as the representative of a colonial opposition in which Catholics and

---

[13] John Rushworth, *The Trial of Strafford* (2nd edn, London, 1700), p. 698. For a recent account of the trial see Maija Jansson (ed.), *Proceedings in the Opening Session of the Long Parliament (Including the Trial of Strafford)* (Rochester, NY, and London, forthcoming).
[14] 10 Henry 7, c. 22.   [15] *Commons Jnl, Ire*, I, pp. 219–20, 223.
[16] Bríd McGrath, 'The Membership of the Irish House of Commons, 1640–1' (University of Dublin, PhD thesis, 1997), sub Darcy, Patrick and chapter 5 below.

Protestants had come together to contest what Darcy characterised as 'the late introduction of an arbitrary government'.[17]

This language was borrowed from the charge against Wentworth and it reflected Darcy's decision to confront the equivocation of the judges by drawing on contemporary English developments rather than Irish precedents. It was not that Irish precedents were wanting. The principles that Darcy upheld were those of the Tudor conquest itself, which had proclaimed its determination to replace the tyranny of the Irish polity with the rule of law, and also those of a commission of inquiry in 1622 which had disclosed the failure to introduce due process and had urgently recommended forty-seven reforms of administrative and judicial procedure.[18] The truth was that executive discretion in Ireland had always been large, and controls ineffective, and Wentworth had not so much extended the bounds of authority as used it to the full, while closing off the customary safety valve of final resort to the monarch. In short, the Irish precedents would have diluted the case that was being made – that the reign of Charles and the rule of Wentworth had seen a major transformation in the nature of government – and Darcy took as his starting point the king's acceptance of the Petition of Right presented to him by the English parliament in 1628, by which he had conceded, in Darcy's rendering, 'that his prerogative is to defend the people's liberty and the people's liberty strengthens the king's prerogative'. These were not the king's words: rather, they closely echo the words used by John Pym in the characterisation of the prerogative powers that he had presented in his closing speech at Wentworth's trial on 13 April.[19] Moreover, Darcy followed Pym to the same conclusion: that there was no uncertainty about the place of the prerogative in government. The prerogative was defined by law and subordinate to it and the power of the king was 'never in greater spendour or majesty than in parliament' which alone was responsible for 'the making, altering or regulating of laws and the correction of all courts and ministers'.[20] Darcy's complementary task, of establishing by what laws Ireland was governed, was performed indirectly and cumulatively through the methodical examination of each of the 'Queries' in turn. The effect was a

---

[17] Patrick Darcy, *An Argument Delivered by the express order of the House of Commons in the parliament of Ireland, 9 Junii, 1641* (2nd edn, Dublin, 1764), p. 46.

[18] G. J. Hand and V. W. Treadwell, 'His Majesty's Directions for Ordering and Settling the Courts within his Kingdom of Ireland, 1622', *Analecta Hibernica*, 26 (IMC, Dublin, 1970), pp. 177–212.

[19] Pym argued that the king's prerogative and the people's liberty 'are a support and a security to one another, the prerogative a cover and defence to the liberty of the people, and the people by their liberty are entitled to be a foundation to the prerogative'. J. P. Kenyon, *The Stuart Constitution* (2nd edn, Cambridge, 1986), p. 196.

[20] Darcy, *An Argument*, pp. 98, 113–14, 117.

demonstration that Ireland, like England, was governed according to a combination of custom and common and statute law. Of these, it was the common law that presented Darcy with difficulties in making his case, for the plain truth was that the juridical systems of England and Ireland were not independent of one another. With considerable dexterity, Darcy argued that entitlement to the full benefit of the common law included the right of access to all the remedies available, so that the king's subjects in Ireland had the right to have recourse to the court of king's bench in England and to the English House of Lords. By contrast, the legislative position was clear-cut: the statutes which had force in Ireland were those of the Irish parliament, which alone had the authority to receive and enact English statutes. This was stated as a matter of fact, not of opinion, and like Sir John Davies twenty years before Darcy coupled it with the proposition that Ireland was 'annexed to the crown of England'.[21] Both propositions were asserted as axioms in support of particular points: the first to deny the authority of the Irish council to introduce English statutes without reference to the Irish parliament; the second to rebut the validity of a proclamation forbidding movement between Ireland and England without official licence.

There are five salient features of this episode. First, the parliamentary opposition for which Darcy spoke combined members of both colonies under a leadership in which Protestants were more prominent than the Catholics. Second, this faction co-operated with the parliamentary opposition in England, shared some of its priorities and borrowed some of its ideas. Third, the central purpose of the opposition was to restrict executive discretion by asserting the rule of law and defining what that meant. Fourth, the matter of Ireland's legislative independence was becoming problematic as the English parliament found it expedient to match the scope of the king's authority by following it out of England into England's dependent kingdom. Fifth, when Darcy spoke he was not addressing this challenge but assumed that both Ireland's status as a dependency of the crown and its legislative independence were uncontroversial and incontrovertible.

It seems unlikely that was still the case when the Irish Commons set about concluding the business of the 'Queries' on 26 July. In defiance of an explicit government prohibition and without dissent in a house in which Protestants outnumbered Catholics by two to one, the Commons adopted a series of declarations on each of the questions along the lines mapped out by Darcy, answering the first with a concise formula which excluded both executive discretion and English statutes altogether: 'the

[21] *Ibid.*, p. 108.

subjects of this His Majesty's kingdom of Ireland are a free people, and to be governed only according to the common law of England, and statutes made and established by parliament in this kingdom of Ireland, and according to the lawful customs used in the same'.[22] There is a suggestive change of emphasis in this wording. The question had referred only in general terms to the 'statutes of force in this kingdom': the declaration took care to specify what statutes these were. The clarification is unlikely to have been fortuitous, for by this time an aggressive attempt to extend the English parliament's competence to Ireland had been initiated, involving precisely the area of judicial competence that Darcy had obfuscated by emphasising the rights of the king's subjects in Ireland rather than the jurisdiction of the legislature in England.

In May the English House of Lords had entertained a number of petitions relating to Irish matters. One was from Daniel O'Neill, a Protestant nephew of Owen Roe O'Neill and an officer in the royal army, who sought repossession of his family estates in County Down from Viscounts Montgomery and Clandeboye; four others were presented by a group of Scottish settlers in Ulster who complained of their imprisonment by the Court of Castle Chamber in 1639 for refusing to take an oath – the infamous 'Black Oath' – renouncing the Scottish National Covenant. In July, the Lords' committee of petitions summoned the two viscounts to appear before the house to answer O'Neill's petition and the entire Irish council, including six peers and the lord chancellor, to attend likewise to answer the complaints of the Scots. On 27 July, the speaker of the Irish Lords reported to his English counterpart that 'the House thinks not fit to licence them so to do, conceiving those proceedings being in time of parliament here sitting and properly here determinable to be prejudicial to the rights and privileges of the House'. He concluded by expressing his confidence that the English house would 'remit the same to the parliament of Ireland'.[23] In fact, the English Lords 'took it in great indignation', according to the Irish master of the rolls, and 'made protestation to be entered for the declaring the subjection of the parliament in Ireland to this of this kingdom'.[24] A search was instituted for evidence of Ireland's dependency and the king was requested to uphold the position of the Lords by declaring that the Irish parliament was subject to the English parliament and to exert pressure to enforce compliance by intermitting the passage of the 'Acts of Grace and Favour' which he had conceded in March until the business had been concluded. The king agreed to the

[22] *Ibid.*, pp. 133–4.
[23] HMC, *Fourth Report: Appendix, House of Lords MSS* (London, 1874), pp. 61, 64, 83, 85, 91.
[24] HMC, *De L'Isle and Dudley MSS*, VI, pp. 407–8.

latter request on 5 August.[25] The response of the earl of Leicester, who had been appointed lord lieutenant of Ireland in mid-June and whose adviser on Irish matters was the New English master of the rolls, Sir John Temple, was to note that Ireland was 'annexed to the crown in propriety' and that parliament had no role in its government.[26]

The matter fizzled out within days. The Lords referred the 'Irish letter' to its Committee of Privileges, which never reported, and the certified bills had been returned to Ireland by 25 August. By then the Irish parliament had been in recess for three weeks and the king was in Scotland. The reality seems to have been that the king's concurrence with the Lords had been entirely tactical: the bills were already being deliberately held back until the adjournment of the Irish parliament in order to allow time to pair them with measures that would compensate for the revenue losses that would result from their enactment. The constitutional issue, however, remained. In the second week of October the English Privy Council, noting that the complementary revenue bills were still not ready, advised the king that it would be wise to prorogue the Irish parliament for a further four months and that he should avail of the delay to invite the English parliament to consider both Poynings' Law and the 'Queries'. In Ireland, the return of the members of the Irish parliamentary committees from London brought a heightened awareness of the danger presented by the English parliament's accelerating encroachment on the royal prerogative and led to a reassessment of priorities and a parting of the colonial ways. For the Old English, the need to curtail the power of the executive in Ireland was superseded by the greater need to uphold the royal authority that they believed to be fundamental to their preservation. Ultimately, it was to the crown that they looked for protection against the avarice of Protestants, for tolerant connivance at their failure to comply with the statutory requirements of religious conformity and for forbearance from pressing inherited claims against their property. In the face of the developing threat to their position from the English parliament, the desire to change governmental arrangements in Ireland gave way to the need to defend the anterior principle that the place of the king in the Irish political system was independent of his role in the government of England and therefore could not be affected by any change in the distribution of power there. They depended precariously on royal goodwill, and they could not survive without it. The same conclusion had already been reached by a number of native Irish gentry, among them some members of parliament,

[25] *Lords Jnl, Eng*, IV, pp. 339, 342, 345, 348.
[26] Conrad Russell, 'The British Background to the Irish Rebellion of 1641', *Historical Research*, 145 (1988), p. 168, citing Kent Archives Office, U 1475/Z 47.

who were planning a pre-emptive defence against the threat posed by both the English parliament and Scots to their religion and property. The Scottish threat receded when the king travelled north to seek assistance against parliament, but the extent of the English threat was confirmed by his doing so. Two months later, they rose in arms.

I

The nature of their rising provides the second context within which what Darcy said needs to be considered, for it reflected altered perspectives. In the past, rebellion in Ireland had been associated with the transfer of allegiance. In the 1530s, the earl of Desmond had dabbled in treason with the Spanish; in the 1570s, James Fitzmaurice had invited the king of Spain to nominate a king of Ireland; and in the 1590s, Hugh O'Neill had followed him in placing the crown of Ireland at the disposal of the Spanish king. In the seventeenth century, that tradition was continued by exiles who worked for the establishment of a separate Irish state on the principle that the authority presently exercised in Ireland was usurped. In 1618, they offered the throne to the king of Spain's brother; in the 1620s, they proposed an Irish republic under Spanish protection. Whether they were continuing an authentic sixteenth-century tradition or creating a new one from continental borrowings is open to debate, for the notion of an Irish state was itself untraditional.

What is certain is that a very different tradition was invoked at home in Ireland by those who conspired with the exile community in 1641. The rightful authority that was called upon then was that of Charles I, king of Ireland by virtue of the Kingship Act. From the outset, the rebels claimed to have risen in defence of the royal prerogative against the pretensions of the English parliament and announced their determination to continue in arms until 'we be at better leisure to make our great grievances known unto his Majesty, and he have more power to relieve us'.[27] The point was driven home by the publication of a forged commission in which Charles was represented as commanding them to take arms in his defence. Although the background to this stratagem is obscure, two implications are plain. First, that the leaders of the rising, whatever the truth of their own loyalties, believed that in seeking support it was to their advantage to claim to be fighting for the king rather than against him and, second, that those who followed them were affirming rather than renouncing their allegiance. Thus the rebellion assumed a character that was entirely consistent with both the political principles and the anxieties of the Old

---

[27] Gilbert (ed.), *Irish Confederation*, I, 360–1.

English. When the Catholic colonists in north Leinster joined the Irish shortly after the outbreak, they did so because they shared the perception of imminent danger and because they received an absolute assurance that the cause that was being pursued was the king's cause. 'It was a blessing of God', they reported, 'that the Irish had proposed to themselves fair ends' and they invited their fellow colonists to assist them in their fight 'to vindicate the honour of our sovereign, assure the liberty of our consciences, and preserve the freedom of this kingdom under the sole obedience of his sacred Majesty'.[28] Within months, the passage in England of the Adventurers' Act, which not only raised money for the suppression of the rebellion on the security of Irish land that would be forfeited as a result of it, but overrode the prerogative by reserving to the English parliament the sole right to determine when the rebellion was at an end, starkly affirmed the right of the English parliament to legislate for Ireland.[29] From that point it became imperative that any settlement must confirm that the king's authority in Ireland was independent of his authority in England and was not transferable to the English parliament – that Ireland was, in Darcy's words, 'annexed to the crown of England'.

Amidst the almost impenetrable complexities of the wars of the 1640s, with returned exiles, papal emissaries and diplomatic missions introducing extra dimensions in Ireland and the onset of civil war in August 1642 complicating relations with England, one thing at least is clear: the separatist tendencies of earlier contestations were not revived. Although the confederation of native and colonial Catholics sought external assistance, they did not offer allegiance to secure it, and they fell a good way short of subservience to their papal paymaster. What was consistently sought in negotiations with the earl of Ormond and other representatives of King Charles was a settlement that would combine continued allegiance to the crown of Ireland, which was inseparably linked to the crown of England by the Act of 1541, with guarantees of the preservation of existing religious and constitutional interests. These were terms that depended on the king winning his war with parliament and on English parliamentary competence being confined to England. Although the loyalists who negotiated on behalf of the confederate Catholics did not always enjoy the trust of those for whom they acted, the points of difference were tactical and concerned the questions of how far, in the short term, the king's present weakness could or should be turned to advantage and of how far, in the longer term, demands upon him should be tempered by a realistic

---

[28] Thomas Carte, *Life of Ormond* (6 vols., London, 1851), V, pp. 280–1, 285–6. Ulick, Marquis of Clanricard, *Letters and Memoirs* (London, 1757), p. 70.

[29] Formally entitled 'An Act for the speedy and effectual reducing of the rebels in His Majesty's Kingdom of Ireland', 16 Car. I, c. 33.

consideration of the constraints imposed upon him by his other roles as Protestant king of two Protestant countries.

The evolution to this point is simply stated. The constitutional tradition, embodying the colonists' view of the relationship between Ireland and England, had superseded an episodic and poorly formulated instinct towards separatism which had been the initial reaction of some alienated colonists and, at a later stage, of many influential Irish to the process of sixteenth-century conquest. The notion of severing the connection with England and entering into an alternative allegiance to an appropriate European power was replaced by the notion of containing English influence through the protection afforded by a crown that was common to both England and Ireland, but separate in each, according to the principle 'that the subjects of Ireland are immediately subject to your Majesty as in right of your crown'.[30] Thus when Darcy's 'Argument' was published in 1643, the year in which negotiations between the royal government and the rebels commenced and a cessation was agreed, its significance had altered. Its compelling feature was no longer its delineation of executive authority but its characterisation of the public law relationship between England and Ireland and, in particular, the support it gave to the case against the Adventurers' Act. Legislative independence was not, however, an issue that Darcy had addressed directly and the need for a more elaborate treatment of the subject was met in the following year by the preparation of a 'Declaration how, and by what means, the laws and statutes of England, from time to time, came to be of force in Ireland'.[31]

The position adopted by the author of this unpublished tract differed from that of Darcy in the greater elaboration of his approach to the difficulty of reconciling the inclusive claim to be governed by the English common law with the exclusive claim that only statutes confirmed by the Irish parliament had force in Ireland. He did this by distinguishing between the power of the English parliament to make law, which was confined to England, and its power to determine and declare what the law was, which was not territorially bound because it was not jurisdictional in character, but interpretative. It followed that acts of the English parliament that were declaratory of the common law were part of the body of law by which Ireland was governed. Otherwise, though the anonymous author conceded the 'precedency and seniority' of the English parliament, he maintained that Ireland had been governed since the reign of King John 'according to the model of England' and that the English

---

[30] Gilbert (ed.), *Irish Confederation*, III, pp. 128–33.
[31] Walter Harris (ed.), *Hibernica* (2 vols., Dublin, 1747, 1750), II, pp. 1–21.

parliament had no more jurisdiction in Ireland than it had in Scotland. A review of the historical precedents showed that the authority of the English parliament to bind Ireland had been never claimed, never acknowledged, and more than once explicitly denied. It is revealing that the authorship of this unpublished but widely circulated tract has been attributed to both the Old English rebel, Patrick Darcy, and the New English lord chancellor, Richard Bolton.[32] There is some slender evidence for the latter ascription, none for the former.[33] Neither is probable, but neither is incredible. The position taken by the author was not alone one on which both colonial communities had been agreed when they had been united in peacetime, but one which remained fundamental in wartime to everyone in Ireland who remained loyal to the crown.

The negotiating stance of the confederate Catholics on the constitutional issue was at first complicated by the fact that the relationship of the Irish parliament to the king was of more urgent concern to them than its relationship with the English parliament. Their fear was that because the treaty terms that they sought included legislative measures, the king might be tempted to use the cumbrous procedures required by Poynings' Act to escape commitments made on his behalf. After an initial muddled attempt to include provision for a review of the act in the treaty itself, they settled for the simpler requirement that the articles of the treaty should be exempted from the act. When the 1646 treaty was being negotiated, this was an issue of trust rather than constitutional principle for

---

[32] There is no evidence to support Caldicott's assumption that the Declaration was published. C. E. J. Caldicott (ed.), 'Patrick Darcy, an Argument', *Camden Miscellany*, 31 (Royal Historical Society, London, 1992), Introduction, n. 19.

[33] As Patrick Kelly notes below in chapter 4, the earliest known attribution of the Declaration to Bolton was in 1700. Neil Longley York's assertion that Samuel Mayart, 'who was in a position to know', identified Bolton as the author in the *Answer* which he published in 1644 is a misreading of Mayart's opening sentence. This referred to Bolton, who was speaker of the Lords, as having defined the issue to be debated, not as having written the work under debate. Neil Longley York, *Neither Kingdom nor Nation: The Irish Quest for Constitutional Rights, 1698–1800* (Washington, DC, 1994), p. 16n. 'Sergeant Samuel Mayart's Answer to a Book Entitled a Declaration, in Harris (ed.), *Hibernica*, II, p. 23. The likelihood that Darcy rather than Bolton had written the Declaration was first suggested by Walter Harris in his introduction to the second volume of *Hibernica* in 1750 because of its resemblance to *An Argument*. An erroneous citation perhaps renders both attributions unlikely. In a marginal gloss on 10 Henry 7, c. 22, in his edition of the Irish statutes, Bolton drew attention to acts of two Irish parliaments, of 10 Henry IV and 29 Henry VI, which declared 'That the Statutes made in England should not be of force in this kingdom, unless they were Allow'd and Publish'd in this Kingdom by Parliament'. The records of both of these parliaments were missing, but Bolton claimed to have seen exemplifications of the acts in the treasury in Waterford. Bolton, *Statutes of Ireland*, p. 67. In *An Argument*, Darcy cited these two acts, without reference to Bolton. The author of the Declaration, also without acknowledging Bolton but with a tell-tale reference to the Waterford exemplifications, wrongly cited a parliament of 19 Edward II instead of that of 10 Henry IV. Bolton and Darcy were the two men least likely to have made this mistake.

the confederates, but Charles was acutely aware that 'the whole frame of government of that Kingdom would be shaken' if the repeal of Poynings' Act were to be perceived as negotiable.[34] When the 1649 treaty was concluded, the king was a defeated captive and the future was uncertain. It was by no means clear how the act could be complied with and the marquis of Ormond conceded that the Irish Houses of parliament 'may consider what they shall think convenient touching the repeal or suspension of the statute commonly called Poynings' Act'.[35] In both negotiations the confederates dealt with the substantive matter of the pretensions of the English parliament by demanding that the treaty include an article requiring the passage of a declaratory act of legislative independence in the next Irish parliament. The difficulty was that because such an act could not bind the English parliament, it would derive its authority only from the royal assent. Charles was in no position to take sides on the issue and insisted that it was for the two parliaments to resolve their differences since he was 'equally interested in the rights of both parliaments'.[36] In fact, as the confederates pointed out, he had already endorsed the English parliamentary claim by assenting to the Adventurers' Act, and its invalidation was the counterpart to their demand for a Declaratory Act. The argument did not prevail: all that they succeeded in extracting in the successive treaties was a worthless agreement that the Irish parliament should 'make such declaration therein as shall be agreeable to the laws of the kingdom of Ireland'.[37]

Among the New English, there were two positions on the issue. The view of those who upheld the authority of the English parliament, covertly or otherwise, was expressed in an answer to the Declaration prepared for the House of Lords by the second justice of the common pleas, Samuel Mayart, in which he stated baldly that Ireland 'was and is a member of England united to it, and as a part or province of England governed'.[38] The appropriate analogy, in other words, was not Scotland but Wales, and his case relied on the fact that Ireland, unlike Scotland, had been acquired by conquest. Though his work was both long and densely argued, its political essence was conveyed in its initial premise, that the issue had been 'implicitly resolved of late by his Majesty, the lords and commons of England' in the Adventurers' Act.[39] The reluctance of the rump of the Irish parliament to debate the issue despite his urgings is elucidated by the stance of the government's negotiating team, which was led by Lord Chancellor Bolton. With arguments repeated from the

---

[34] Gilbert (ed.), *Irish Confederation*, II, pp. 360–1.   [35] *Ibid.*, VII, pp. 184–211.
[36] *Ibid.*, III, pp. 177, 296.   [37] *Ibid.*, V, p. 294; VII, p. 194.
[38] 'Sergeant Samuel Mayart's Answer to a Book Entitled a Declaration' in Harris (ed.), *Hibernica*, II, p. 127.   [39] *Ibid.*, p. 24.

anonymous Declaration, they bluntly dismissed the proposition that the English parliament could bind Ireland as 'absurd' and on Bolton's authority they asserted that the issue had long since been determined by two declaratory acts of the kind demanded by the confederates. Their language was plain, but their recommendation was circumspect. They endorsed the king's own view that concessions that would damage his position in England could 'be of no use or avail' in Ireland: 'It was to be wished that there were such an act,' they reported, 'but the time was not seasonable to desire it.'[40]

That judgement remained valid. For some years after the execution of Charles in 1649 Ireland was ruled by the English parliament; for some further years it was part of Oliver Cromwell's Lord Protectorate and had token representation in a union parliament of the three nations. When Oliver Cromwell died and the protectorate regime disintegrated in acrimonious disagreement, the Long parliament returned to government, if not to power, and the possibility that the monarchy could be restored became increasingly real. In Ireland, the established Protestant colonists plotted to secure control over the process. In December 1659, a *coup d'état* overthrew the government and an oddly assorted consortium of established settlers and opportunist Cromwellian newcomers assumed control of the government and command of the army. The bond that brought them together was their joint interest in ensuring that the overthrow of the commonwealth and the restoration of the king should not involve the restoration of Irish property rights and the overturning of the land settlement. But they were also concerned to re-establish the old government. Denouncing the English parliament for having usurped, 'contrary to all Laws, the Supreme Power not only of *England*, but also of *Ireland* and *Scotland*', they laid down the condition that in future these countries were not to be taxed 'without their own free consent, given by their representatives in their several and respective parliaments'.[41] Ireland's watching brief on the negotiations which brought Charles II back to the thrones of his three kingdoms in May 1660 was held by a 'general convention', a surrogate parliament of New English collaborators and recent army settlers which assembled in Dublin in March. Its first business was to endorse the objectives previously announced and the convention availed of the opportunity to assert belligerently that 'the right of having parliaments held in Ireland, is still justly and lawfully due and belonging to Ireland, and that the parliament of England never charged Ireland in any Age with any Subsidies, or other publick Taxes or Assessment, until after the violence

---

[40] Gilbert (ed.), *Irish Confederation*, III, pp. 286–7.
[41] *The declaration of Sir Charles Coote and the rest of the Council of Officers* (London, 1660).

offered to the parliament of England in December 1648, since which time, they who Invaded the Rights of the parliament of England, Invaded also the Rights of the parliament of Ireland, by imposing Taxes and Assessment upon them'.[42] The Convention drove home the point by ignoring the tax assessment ordinance passed by the English parliament and instead assumed authority to impose a poll tax for the support of both government and army.

It seems clear that both the experience of direct rule and the uncertainty of the future had narrowed the focus of New English concerns. The immediate priority was to restore the Irish parliament, and the arguments for doing so were founded on the classic grounds of the right to consent to taxation – which drew enhanced force from the fact that Ireland had indeed been disproportionately taxed in recent years. A related grievance arising from the imposition of duties on Irish trade with England and Scotland during the Commonwealth led to the addition of a related demand that the Irish parliament alone should be responsible for the regulation of Irish trade and manufactures. The New English were also concerned to secure their position by guaranteeing their own control of the Irish parliament, and the request that they presented to the king on his restoration in May was for the speedy summons of a parliament confined to Protestants. The question of the status of that parliament and its relationship to the parliament of England was still not 'seasonable' because it was not yet clear in which parliament it would be more expedient to have the land settlement confirmed.

In London in July, however, the newly appointed attorney general for Ireland, William Domville, presented Ormond with 'A disquisition touching that great question whether an act of parliament made in England shall bind the kingdome and people of Ireland without their allowance and acceptance of such act in the kingdom of Ireland' in which he concurred with the conclusion of the anonymous Declaration of 1644.[43] He departed significantly from his predecessor's treatment only in confronting Mayart's argument that Ireland was England's by conquest with the counter-claim that the country had submitted willingly to Henry II and received from him the laws of England and the right to hold parliaments. Otherwise he traversed familiar ground, invoking the Scottish parallel once again and demonstrating at length that 'our forefathers' 'were both parties and privy to the enacting of all such laws as were at any time of force among them'. The origins and purposes of the 'Disquisition' are undocumented but it is likely that Ormond was prepar-

---

[42] *A new declaration of the General Convention now assembled at Dublin in Ireland, 12 March 1659 [1660]* (London, 1660).   [43] Molyneux Papers, TCD, MS 890.

ing for the possibility of discussions on the terms of the treaties that he had negotiated with the confederates in the 1640s. In the event, Domville's advice was received in silence. Ormond himself took care to have his lands in Ireland restored to him by act of the English parliament in advance of the summoning of an Irish one and, though there is tenuous evidence to suggest that the 'Disquisition' was made available to the New English commissioners who had come from Ireland on behalf of the general convention, they refused to debate with rival Old English commissioners the question of whether English acts 'ought to bind Ireland'.[44]

On the face of it, this refusal was perverse. The sole legal foundation of the land settlement that the Protestant commissioners were concerned to preserve was the Adventurers' Act of 1642. Their most effective course of action would have been to uphold its validity against the Catholic claim that it was *ultra vires*. They did not do so. Instead, they constructed a tortuous counter-argument in three stages. The land forfeited by rebellion was legally vested in the king and at his disposal; the Adventurers' Act comprised the terms of a collaboration entered into by the king and his English parliament to validate measures to be taken in England to procure the resources needed to suppress the rebellion in Ireland; the measures taken in Ireland derived their authority not from the act but from the king's entitlement to resume and dispose of the lands concerned.[45] This nonsense wrote the civil war and the interregnum out of recent history, but it was the only way to retain the benefit of the Act without accepting that it had force in Ireland. In short, though the commissioners did not press the point of legislative independence, they went to considerable lengths not to concede it.

II

The strategy of the Protestant community in Ireland succeeded. Charles II repudiated all of the works of the usurping governments of the 1640s and 1650s except the Irish land settlement. When the readjustments required by the reinstatement of the unequivocally loyal were complete, the transfer of 40 per cent of Irish land from Catholic to Protestant ownership had been confirmed. The inequity of these new arrangements was manifest. The alleged justification for the expropriation of the former owners was their rebellion, but many of the new owners had either fought against their king or collaborated with those who had deposed him. The reality was that the line of division was religious. The experience of civil

[44] One copy of the 'Disquisition' is inscribed 'For the Irish Comrs', NLI, MS 40.
[45] TCD, MS 587, ff. 133–65.

war, regicide and the abolition of both monarchy and the established church had revealed, however, that the connections between religious belief and political obedience were less simple than they had once seemed. The antithesis between the innate disloyalty of Catholics and the loyalty of Protestants could no longer be maintained without acute Protestant embarrassment.[46]

Not unnaturally, colonial Catholics saw allegiance as the central issue. The response of a number of self-appointed leaders of their community to the loss of both land and the right of political participation was to draw attention to the unfairness of their treatment and to seek to protect what remained to them by giving assurances of their loyalty. They promoted the widespread adoption of a petition in which influential Catholics in Ireland would reaffirm the traditional stance of the Old English: that their allegiance to the pope did not affect their allegiance to the king. By doing so, they hoped to supply a justification for the toleration of Catholicism that had been promised in the hitherto ineffective peace treaties negotiated with Ormond. The effort failed signally, largely because the Remonstrance that they prepared met with widespread disapproval from the clergy, whose experience in exile in Counter-Reformation Europe in the 1650s had persuaded them that it was wrong to derogate from the plain obligation to obey the pope.

Constructive opposition proved impossible, but hope was not denied. In the early 1670s, the news of the conversion to Catholicism of the king's brother and heir, the duke of York, opened up the possibility that the land settlement and the polity based upon it might be reviewed. The remainder of the reign was a period of waiting, and the first years of James a time of probing, but events in England dictated that Irish contradictions would be resolved by force. The Glorious Revolution simplified the situation and disposed of the ambiguities by inversion. The English transferred their allegiance to William and Mary, and most Protestants in Ireland followed them. Catholics in Ireland were unwilling to do so. For a brief period in 1690, Ireland enjoyed the rare experience of a resident monarch, from whom the Catholic colonists in particular expected a sympathetic understanding appropriate to one who was, like themselves, Catholic and English. They did not appreciate that James' view of England's interest in Ireland had been formed before his religious preferences. In the parliament that he convened they did not show the same sensitivity to the demands of his English exigencies as had been shown to his brother in the 1640s and they forced the constitutional aspiration of

[46] Aidan Clarke, 'Alternative Allegiances in Early Modern Ireland', *Journal of Historical Sociology*, 5 (1992), pp. 263–5.

the confederates to a sterile conclusion. James managed to preserve the royal interest by resisting pressure for the repeal of Poynings' Act, but he could not protect the interest of the English parliament and gave his consent to a Declaratory Act which both asserted Ireland's legislative independence and enlarged upon the historic goal by repudiating the jurisdiction of the English courts, including that of the House of Lords.[47]

James' deposition in England was confirmed by his defeat in Ireland and this epilogue concluded the tradition of Catholic parliamentary constitutionalism. Catholic allegiance to the crown lived on. The principle that Ireland was annexed to the crown of England dictated the contention that the usurpation of William and Mary had violated the linkage of the crowns established by the Kingship Act: the tradition of loyalty now belonged to Ireland, not to England, and to Catholics, not Protestants, in Ireland. Thereafter, Catholics withheld their allegiance from the English monarch in favour of a retrospective, nostalgic and constitutionally proper loyalty to the house of Stuart. By contrast, the Protestant colony became the sole inheritor of the commitment to legislative independence. Muted as it had been by the perils of the 1640s and the uncertainties of 1660; breached as it had been by the English parliament's systematic regulation of Irish trade after the Restoration; and contaminated as it now was by its associations with King James' Irish parliament, the ideal of a colonial Ireland that was separate, not from England but from English political process, remained as attractive to some members of the emergent ascendancy as it had been to an earlier generation of Protestant settlers and their Catholic allies.

[47] J. G. Simms, *Jacobite Ireland, 1685–91* (London, 1969), pp. 77–81.

3   Counter-currents in colonial discourse: the political thought of Vincent and Daniel Gookin

Patricia Coughlan

Few episodes in Irish history have had more resonance than the policy of transplantation formulated in the wake of the Cromwellian conquest. To the Irish long a touchstone of nationalist indignation, the plan for the forcible removal of Catholics from their dwelling-places and their consignment to the barren wastes of the west has also struck students of the past from outside Ireland as a signal instance of inhumanity in the discharge of power. This chapter focuses primarily on one contemporary view of that policy, and considers it in the context of an investigation of the developing discourse about the English colonisation of Ireland. It also explores opposing views expressed at the time, and briefly examines a parallel discussion of questions to do with the treatment of indigenous inhabitants in another theatre of colonial activity, the Massachusetts Bay Colony.

The primary focus of the chapter is on the contributions of Vincent Gookin, a Corkman of English planter descent and friend and colleague of William Petty, to the 1655 pamphlet controversy about the policy of dealing with the Irish former rebels and their adherents by wholesale forced transplantation from their land to the uncultivated territories of Connacht. In *The great case of transplantation in Ireland discussed* (1655), and in its sequel later that year, Gookin developed a discourse of moderation and assimilation. The chapter seeks to place Gookin, who has not to date been the subject of any extensive study, in his background as the son of a New English Munster settler and office-holder and as a member of the Old Protestant interest.[1] It contrasts his assimilationist perspective on the problem of colonist–colonised relations with the irredentist position set out the same year in *The interest of England in the Irish transplantation stated* by his opponent Colonel Richard Lawrence, military governor of Waterford and an ardent Baptist. The last part of the discussion will

---

[1] Those English whose ancestors had settled in Ireland only during the fifty or so years leading up to 1641 were in the 1650s known as 'Old' (or sometimes 'antient') 'Protestants', to distinguish them from the new arrivals from the 1640s wars onwards.

consider, as an analogue to Vincent Gookin's writings, those of his first cousin Daniel Gookin, also from a County Cork settler family, who in the 1670s wrote *Historical Collections . . . of the Indians in New England* (*c.* 1674) and *An Historical Account of the Doings and Sufferings of the Christian Indians in New England in the Years 1675, 1676, 1677*. Daniel Gookin migrated from Cork to Virginia in 1631 and later joined the Massachusetts Bay Colony. A convinced Puritan, friend of John Eliot and enthusiastic champion of the 'Praying Indians', he became an important figure in New England colonial government who was, for a time, discredited because of the perception of excessive and inappropriate sympathy on his part with the position and interests of the Native Americans. The chapter will consider the parallels that may be drawn between the two men's writings, and the possible influence of Vincent's unusually liberal thought on Daniel's later work. The Gookins' treatises afford a striking example of the kinship of ideas about colonial ideology and ethnicity and even about the moral status of colonists on one Atlantic seaboard with those on the other.

These texts rehearse important issues which go to the heart of colonial attitudes; this chapter aims to explore the ideology revealed in their rhetoric, particularly Vincent Gookin's pamphlets, which are important above and beyond their narrow context in the transplantation controversy because of their eloquence, which arises not merely from the rhetorical talent of their author but also from the exceptionally clear-sighted and humane exploration they make of the moral position of the colonist. It may seem an exaggeration to call Gookin's writings an enquiry into the ideology of colonialism, but at their most intense moments they certainly tend that way, and generate a distinct sense that the pressure on the author's mind of the difficult question of the proposed wholesale transplantation has produced a coherence and clarity of thought which rises well above the norm of the many merely controversial texts of the period. So far few historians have been prepared to consider this ideological aspect of the matter at any length, having concentrated for the most part on brief reference to Gookin's texts to elucidate facts or to illustrate opinions during narratives or analyses of the period's events and of the complex and crucial subject of the transplantation itself.[2]

---

[2] The ideological significance of Gookin's arguments was, however, acknowledged by Nicholas Canny. See the brief account in 'Dominant Minorities: English Settlers in Ireland and Virginia, 1550–1650' in A. C. Hepburn (ed.), *Minorities in History* (London, 1978), p. 64, and the extended and very valuable discussion by T. C. Barnard in 'Crises of Identity among Irish Protestants 1641–1685', *Past and Present*, 127 (1990), pp. 39–83. There is now a very large bibliography on the general question of colonial discourse, see note 90 below.

I

To be able to interpret these texts, it is necessary as far as possible to keep in mind the contexts of the debate, so as to grasp the interests of its various participants which, as is always the case, underlay their arguments, and also to understand the wider situation of competing factions among the parliamentary ruling elite within which the controversy was played out.[3] The idea of dealing with the former rebels – a large proportion of the population of Ireland – by transplantation away from their localities was mooted in an Adventurers' petition of April 1652.[4] This preceded by a few months the Act of Settlement (August 1652) which concentrated on the listing under five 'qualifications' of those among former rebels exempt from pardon for their lives or estates. The confiscation and redistribution of lands was projected from the start, but it appears that the mechanism for removing the incumbents only developed piecemeal. The commissioners for settling Ulster had proposed in April 1653 that 'those popular men in these parts' who could not be trusted to remain 'dutiful and peaceable' should be transplanted into other suitably distant Irish counties (though not to Connacht). Finally, in July 1653, a document from Westminster specifically directed the transplantation of 'all persons in Ireland who have a right to any favour and mercy' under any of the Act's qualifications to 'remove and transplant themselves into the province of Connaught and the county of Clare' before 1 May 1654.[5] However, the logistics of the policy were not thought out, and its formulation was far from clear or sharp-edged. In the perennial *décalage* between London and Ireland, the lines of demarcation even between the broad categories of delinquents and those exempt became more blurred, and the overwhelming practical difficulties of enforcing the uprooting of thousands and their settlement far away in unknown country interposed

---

[3] Among specific discussions of the transplantation, the clearest extended account is that of Corish, which approaches the subject primarily from the point of view of events in Ireland and which includes some detailed regional examples which are a help in imagining the actuality: Patrick J. Corish, 'The Cromwellian Régime' in *NHI*, III, pp. 364–73. Gardiner's long discussion, though written in 1899, remains indispensable in gaining a sense of the evolution of the official policy, seen largely from the viewpoint of the state papers and associated documents: S. R. Gardiner, 'The Transplantation to Connaught', *EHR*, 14 (1899), pp. 700–34. Many of the relevant documents are printed in R. Dunlop (ed.), *Ireland under the Commonwealth* (2 vols., Manchester, 1913). R. C. Simington's 'Introduction' to his *The Transplantation to Connacht* (IMC, Shannon, 1970) supplements Gardiner and shows, on the one hand, the lack of coherence in official policy and, on the other, the very impossibility of its execution because of the sheer insufficiency of land to meet the needs of the disbanding army, in spite of the transplantation of all Catholic landowners to points west of the Shannon.

[4] Quoted in Gardiner, 'Transplantation', p. 701.

[5] Both quoted in Gardiner, 'Transplantation', pp. 706–7.

themselves in all their immediacy between plan and execution. This left a fair amount of room for argument and manoeuvre about the whole matter and it could be argued that during the summer of 1654 the whole policy of transplantation itself was still under question in London.[6] When Charles Fleetwood was sent to Ireland as lord deputy in August, his instructions allowed wide discretion in the implementation of the transplantation. In the end it very gradually emerged that only proprietors and any fighting men remaining would actually be transplanted, leaving other classes *in situ*; but during the latter half of 1654, when Gookin's first pamphlet must have been written, this eventual result could not have been easily foreseen even by those close to the authorities, and still less by the bulk of the Irish populace, who were or perceived themselves liable to transplantation.

The category of 'Irish' was, of course, a highly complex one; the interests of those making up the prospective initial transplanters could and did diverge from one another quite markedly (as indeed they had, with fatal results, during the Confederation). For instance, there were large-scale Catholic proprietors of Old English origin – specifically Nugent, Barnewall and Esmond – who in 1654 managed to pressure Cromwell directly in London for a larger grant of lands in Connacht after their prospective transplantation; and this in spite of their being specifically exempted by name in the Act for the Settling of Ireland from pardon for life or estate, i.e. automatically sentenced to death. A manuscript petition among the papers of Cromwell's secretary of state, John Thurloe, for May 1654 seems to reflect this kind of lobbying. It pointedly insists on the allegiance of the petitioners to Englishness, concluding with the contention that

the petitioners and their progenitors have since theire arrivall there affected and continued the Civilitie, breeding, language, lawes, and manners, of the English, theire extraction, interest, education and affection natura[lly] inclining thereto; whose example[s] have been forcible meanes to introduce among the people the same, who are now to be proscribed to a wilderness devoid of all accomodation [*sic*], as to diswont them from theire accustomed Civilitie, and betray the same to barbaritie, Custom being a second nature.[7]

In addition, the petitioners complained, with some bitterness, that 'farmers and those of inferior qualitie are not to be transplanted though

---

[6] Some of it in the form of a draft parliamentary proviso of September 1653 allowing for retention of some of the Irish perhaps by Gookin, as detailed by Gardiner, 'Transplantation', p. 709. Notes of a debate in council about sending an expedition to the West Indies, mentioned in Gardiner, 'Transplantation', p. 719, and quoted in C. H. Firth (ed.), *Clarke Papers* (4 vols., Camden Society, London, 1899), III, p. 207.

[7] Bodl., Rawlinson MSS A 14 and summarised in *Analecta Hibernica*, 1 (1930), pp. 20–1.

not so innocent as most of the proprietors who are compelled to goe'.[8]
They also lamented the total absence in Connacht of the 'artificers' who
would be needed to build any kind of dwelling.

Among the military faction and those whom Gookin acidly called 'the
godly', many continued to cry out stridently for what they called justice,
in the form of retributive punishment of the Irish for the 1641 atrocities.
For instance, early in 1655, officers stationed in Ireland circulated a
blood-and-thunder petition calling for universal transplantation of the
Irish. Studded with Old Testament and apocryphal quotations about not
'committing of corporal and spiritual fornication [as] at Peor' and
'root[ing] them out before you', and with references to 'the land which
ye go to possess' as 'an unclean land because of the filthiness of the
people that dwell therein', this text by its rhetoric strikingly rehearsed
fundamental colonial fears of contamination by the otherness of indigenes whom it conceived as idolatrous, alien and inveterately corrupt.[9]
In doing so, it recapitulated the tone and feeling of diatribes against the
Irish from an earlier phase of intensive colonisation, such as the writings
of Edmund Spenser and Barnabe Rich. It also highlighted the contrasting impulses of colonists either towards extirpation of the pre-existing
population, or towards an ultimately shared existence (reached, to be
sure, via the assimilation of native culture and identity into those of the
colonists, not *vice versa*). 'I like', wrote Bacon in his essay 'Of
Plantations', 'a *Plantation* in a Pure Soile', by which he meant, in plainer
language, a land empty of prior inhabitants.[10] The longing for a totally
new beginning, so much a part of all seventeenth-century Puritan and
millenarian aspiration, also haunted the American colonial adventure
(discussed below, IV).

II

Before turning to Gookin's two texts, it is worth determining what is
known about him and his family that may have influenced his motivation
and his thinking. Of Kentish gentry extraction, his father, Sir Vincent,
had settled during the early seventeenth century in County Cork, at
Castle Mahon in the barony of Ibane and Barryroe as a tenant in fee
simple to Phane Beecher, who had been one of the original undertakers in

---

[8] *Ibid.*
[9] Published in *Mercurius Politicus* during March 1655 (BL, E. 831(7)) and quoted in full in
Gardiner, 'Transplantation', pp. 723–7. See Peter Stallybrass and Allon White, *The Poetics
and Politics of Transgression* (London, 1986), for an illuminating discussion of the importance of motifs of purity and contamination in early modern bourgeois culture.
[10] Francis Bacon, *The Essayes or Counsels, Civill and Morall*, Essay 33, ed. Michael Kiernan
(Oxford, 1985), p. 106.

the Munster plantation. Sir Vincent's brother Daniel also came to County Cork, but left Ireland in 1621 with his son Daniel and fifty of his followers for Virginia, where he settled Newport News. Having earned commendations for a dogged resistance on his own plantation in the 1622 over-running and killing of settlers, the elder Daniel returned to Cork, where he acquired the castle and lands of Carrigaline, further east in the county.[11] Yet the Gookins were not grandee landowners. As T. C. Barnard has pointed out, their economic foothold in south Cork was originally acquired as a result of government service and their status in Munster Protestant society was considerably lower than that of the exalted Boyles, owners of the vast estates accumulated, often in dubious ways, by the first earl.[12] Still, the lands Sir Vincent did inhabit, dotted about the stretch of territory between the inlets of Timoleague to the east and Clonakilty to the west, were in an area of rich and fertile soil and enjoyed the mild and moist coastal climate of south Cork. As his will shows, he evidently profited from the abundant fisheries of Courtmacsherry Bay, as well as from cattle and a wool business, though on nothing like the scale of Richard Boyle.

When it comes to evaluating Gookin's arguments and the attitudes they reveal, it should be remembered that relations between New English settlers and the existing population differed markedly in Munster from those obtaining elsewhere in Ireland. Less than half of that province had been planted, which meant that in an area such as the barony of Ibane and Barryroe the position the incoming Gookins would have had to occupy was far from one of outright hegemony over previous landholders.[13] Instead they had perforce to interweave themselves to a degree into the prevailing social grouping. In this region these arrangements still left at the top of the pyramid the septs of old Gaelic gentry such as the McCarthy Riabhach, and then the powerful local baronial

---

[11] The information in this paragraph is based on the following: *DNB* entries on all the Gookins; T. C. Barnard, 'Lord Broghill, Vincent Gookin, and the Cork Elections of 1659', *EHR*, 88 (1973), pp. 352–65; James Coombes, 'The Benedictine Priory of Ross', *JCHAS*, 73 (1968), pp. 152–60; C. M. Tenison, 'Cork MPs, 1559–1899', *JCHAS*, 1 (1895), p. 421; George Bennett, *History of Bandon* (Cork, 1869); Charles Smith, *The Ancient and Present State of the County and City of Cork* (Cork, 1815); F. W. Gookin, *Daniel Gookin, 1612–1687* (Chicago: privately printed, 1912); Guy L. Lewis, 'Daniel Gookin, Superintendent and Historian of the Massachusetts Indians: A Historiographical Study' (PhD thesis, University of Illinois at Urbana-Champaign, 1973).

[12] See Barnard, 'Cork Elections', for a convincing exposition of this point, based on the dispute between Gookin and Lord Broghill about William Petty's prospective candidacy for a Cork constituency.

[13] See Michael MacCarthy Morrogh, 'The English Presence in Early Seventeenth-Century Munster' in Ciaran Brady and Raymond Gillespie (eds.), *Natives and Newcomers: The Making of Irish Colonial Society 1534–1641* (Dublin, 1986), pp. 171–90, especially pp. 188–90.

families, especially the gaelicised Norman Barrys and to a lesser extent the Hodnett-MacSherrys.[14] The Hodnetts were themselves originally English incomers from more than three hundred years before, but had long been gaelicised as 'Mac Séafraidh', from which came the name 'Courtmacsherry'. Sir Vincent became a tenant of these Hodnetts, but a humbler branch of the Barrys were in turn tenants of the Gookins.[15] It is not difficult to see why Vincent, bred in such a milieu, should have formed different notions of the most viable social arrangements for the future in Ireland from those of Lawrence.[16]

One of the main questions to be considered in relation to the genesis of Vincent's writings is the extent to which the rebellion and wars of the 1640s affected the Gookins' security, physical or mental, and the young Vincent's attitude to the local Catholic gentry on the ground. Admittedly, during the earlier phases of the 1641 rebellion, south Munster had to some extent escaped the more major upheavals, dispossessions of planters and widespread killings that marked the period elsewhere in the country. This was especially true of the area – from Youghal at the east all along the Blackwater, across to Mallow and down to Bandon in the south-west – protected by the earl of Cork's defence plan.[17] But the land between Timoleague and Clonakilty where the Gookins lived lies south of Bandon and west of Kinsale, and so outside even the Boyles' initial cordon. Thus the English population of Clonakilty fled to Bandon for protection in mid-January 1642, having been 'robbed, spoiled and their cattle carried away'.[18] Eventually the rebels possessed every County Cork town except Kinsale, Bandon, Youghal and Cork itself.[19] In these circumstances, the Gookins could very well have found themselves repeatedly exposed to danger between 1641 and 1650, whether resulting from the

---

[14] See K. W. Nicholls, 'The Development of Lordship in County Cork 1300–1600' in Patrick O'Flanagan and Cornelius G. Buttimer (eds.), *Cork: History and Society* (Dublin, 1993), pp. 157–212 and Rev. E. Barry, 'Records of the Barrys', *JCHAS*, 6 (1900), pp. 127–46.   [15] Barry, 'Records of the Barrys', p. 131.

[16] It is not clear what lands Vincent Gookin himself may have owned or leased before the 1650s; see the Books of Survey and Distribution, compiled *c.*1680, listing a Vincent Gookin as holder of the 50 acres at BallymcWilliam and Cruary (on the western side of Barryroe, nearest Clonakilty) held by Sir Vincent before 1641; this may be a son of our Vincent's. Curiously, his father did not name him as a beneficiary of his will (as he did his younger brothers and the 'servant' John Burrowes). This may have something to do with the fact that Vincent, the eldest son, would already have attained the age of majority at the time of his father's will in 1637, whereas the land and rents bequeathed to the other sons were directed to be retained by the executors until one was twenty and the other twenty-four. A settlement may have been made upon Vincent if he married early, and perhaps his inheritance took the form of money rather than land.

[17] See T. O. Ranger, 'The Career of Richard Boyle, First Earl of Cork, in Ireland, 1588–1643' (DPhil thesis, University of Oxford, 1959), conclusion.

[18] Smith, *County and City of Cork*, p. 127.   [19] *Ibid.*, p 133.

activities of the changeable but militarily formidable Lord Inchiquin in the Munster theatre of fighting, or locally.[20] Certainly both the local Barrys (William and Redmond) and the Hodnetts (Edmond and his son and brother) joined the insurrection; Hodnett allegedly 'kept Courtmcsherry with men and Armes for the Irish against the English', and 'the Said Hodnett and Barry had comand of att least 400 men who did oppose a States Ship that were coming into the Harb[ou]r of Courtmacsherry'.[21]

There is also direct evidence about the dealings of these rebel Catholic gentry with Gookin property and with individuals associated with the Gookins, most probably their servants. Several depositions, taken in Kinsale during February of 1653/4, mentioned in the usual vivid terms the seizing of livestock, goods and money – variously £2,000 and £3,000, a very large sum – from 'Esquire Gookin', and one also named 'Mr Burres' as having been similarly robbed.[22] It seems that Burrowes lost not only his 'house, goods and estate', but his life also, when he was tried and hung by one of the neighbouring McCarthys at the rebels' camp at Kilvarrig wood, in Kilmalooda parish.[23] Burrowes acted as steward to the elder Gookin, managing Sir Vincent's cattle business, his fishery at Lislee, and also his lease of Courtmacsherry from Hodnett.[24]

There was probably a close connection between these depositions and the letter of June 1654 from Oliver Cromwell to Fleetwood about Gookin. This acknowledged 'sufferings' undergone by Gookin 'by plunder, sequestration, and imprisonment' for his 'constant adhering' to the parliamentary side, and directed that he receive a grant of lands in fee farm in the barony of Barrymore (some distance away, in east Cork) in compensation.[25] The sequestration – a formal legal process – may have referred either to the Hodnetts' and the Barrys' activities in 1641, or to what took place in 1648–9 when the alliance between Protestant and Catholic royalist factions, earlier at odds, enabled formal joint action in areas which

---

[20] See Scott Wheeler, 'Four Armies in Ireland' in Jane Ohlmeyer (ed.), *Ireland from Independence to Occupation, 1641–1660* (Cambridge, 1995), pp. 43–65.
[21] TCD, MS 828, f. 45, deposition by John Arthour, 21 February 1654.
[22] TCD, MS 828, ff. 38, 39, 42, 45 and 47, depositions of Richard White, John Arthour and John Danuye[?], 21 February 1653/4. [23] Bennett, *History of Bandon*, pp. 365–6.
[24] John T. Collins, 'Some Cork Wills, Deeds and Indentures', *JCHAS*, 64 (1959), pp. 104–8. Sir Vincent's will is dated 1 February 1637. There is no deposition from any of the Gookins themselves, however. Why did Vincent Gookin not depose on his own behalf on this occasion? Simply because he was absent from the area in February 1654, or did he for some reason deliberately refrain? Perhaps he was motivated by pragmatic caution in troubled times, or even, after all that had passed, can a trace of neighbourly feeling have existed given the dense interweaving of incoming and existing, Catholic and Protestant, landholders in Ibane and Barryroe?
[25] Quoted by Gardiner, 'Transplantation', p. 734, n.76.

these factions controlled against Protestant adherents to parliament such as the Gookins.[26] Gookin presumably alluded to some such event when he noted wryly that 'I have lost as good an estate almost, as Collonel Lawrence has got by them [the Irish]'.[27]

Were Gookin's own Catholic neighbours transplanted? The surviving lists do not include the names either of the relevant Barrys, or of any Hodnetts.[28] If they ever were transplanted the Hodnetts or some of them certainly came back, as happened in many such instances. Like many others they escaped the death sentence for treason which had been pronounced on the father and son (together with eleven hundred other Catholic gentlemen of Munster) in Youghal in August 1642.[29] But, as the *Books of Survey and Distribution* clearly show, they certainly were dispossessed, like all the Catholic gentry in Barryroe. Edmund Hodnett's 810 acres at Courtmacsherry ended up, like so much else, in the hands of Roger Boyle, Lord Broghill and later earl of Orrery.[30] In the case of the Hodnetts, Robert Gookin acquired some of their land, at Abbeymahon slightly north of Courtmacsherry. Yet nearly fifty years later Hodnetts lived in the area, one still designated 'gent. of Courtmacsherry', who were outlawed in the Jacobite wars.[31] Finally, Hodnett marriages in plenty were recorded in the Church of Ireland diocese of Cork and Ross from 1689 onwards.[32]

It is possible that Vincent Gookin did not return to Barryroe: it is known that about 1652 he built a house 'near Cork' on lands in the barony of Barrymore, further east, which he then held on a short lease. In June 1654 Cromwell's letter directed that he be granted the fee farm of 'the lands now in his possession in the barony of Barrymore with the two ploughlands of Ahada, at such rent as they think fit'.[33] Yet in June 1655 he was still found petitioning the authorities to extend his lease in Barrymore 'lest any future Act of State prevent his just right of pre-emption in these

---

[26] See Patrick J. Corish, 'Ormond, Rinuccini, and the Confederates' in *NHI*, III, pp. 333–5. I am grateful to K. W. Nicholls who suggested this possibility to me and to Pádraig Lenihan for helpful further discussion of it.   [27] *Author and Case*, p. 41.

[28] 'List of Transplanted Irish, 1655–1659' in HMC, *Calendar of the Manuscripts of the Marquis of Ormonde*, OS (3 vols., London, 1895–1909), II, pp.142–76. It is not known whether this list is complete.

[29] See 'J.C.', 'The Old Castles around Cork Harbour', JCHAS, 21 (1915), pp. 109–10.

[30] See *Books of Survey and Distribution*, Barryroe half of Ibane and Barryroe barony, parishes of Templeomalice and Lislee.

[31] The Jacobite Hodnetts outlawed were 'Edward Hodnett, Esq., and David Hodnett, gent., of Courtmacsherry', see James Coombes, *A History of Timoleague and Barryroe* (Timoleague, 1969), p. 38.

[32] See Herbert W. Gillman, 'Index to the Marriage Licence Bonds of the Diocese of Cork and Ross . . . 1623–1750', JCHAS, 2 and 3 (1896 and 1897), p. 57.

[33] Printed in Gardiner, 'Transplantation', p. 734, n. 76.

lands', and to add a lease of 'certain lands near thereunto for convenience of fuel'.[34] Gookin's supplication specifically connected the building of this house with the discharging of his public duties, 'to which', he said in a curious phrase emphasising his own modesty, 'he was called without his knowledge'.[35] A surviving copy of an official Dublin document mentioned the grant of lands to him by a specific order of the lord protector in 1656, though unfortunately the barony name is illegible in the copy.[36] S. R. Gardiner's interpretation of the situation was that because of factional enmity to Gookin during 1654–5, Fleetwood dragged his feet in executing the order to secure Gookin in possession in Barrymore, and therefore Cromwell himself had to repeat it.[37]

During the 1650s, Vincent was actively involved in political life and in constant contact with and service to the authorities both in Dublin and in London. He was a personal friend of Sir William Petty and, together with Petty and others, oversaw the distribution of allotted lands to the army in the context of an extreme shortage of available property. Furthermore, as well as holding other civil offices both in England and in Dublin throughout the latter half of the 1650s, Gookin was repeatedly appointed to small three- or four-man committees who were entrusted with the execution in Ireland of government directives and the carrying out of specific tasks which arose from the redistribution of land.[38] In the closely connected area of religious reform, he served with six others on a committee of 'Triers' for the approbation of suitable candidates for the ministry in County Cork, perhaps in particular for the exclusion of Episcopalian inclined ministers.[39] On one occasion in 1657 he worked together with Richard Lawrence, his very adversary of two years before, and three others, in treating with 'persons, being Protestants' offering to be tenants of Irish lands in various counties which would become disposable by the protector (having been forfeited by various categories of previous

---

[34] As for Aghada, the *Books of Survey and Distribution* name James Magner, 'Irish Papist', as pre-1641 holder of the 255 acres (together with some glebe land) of which the parish consisted, and Redmond Magner and Thomas Mitchell as joint owners of it afterwards. Perhaps Gookin never did get his grant there.

[35] See *Cal SP Ire, 1640–1660, Addenda,* pp. 803 and 573 respectively.

[36] 'Ordered that it be and it is hereby referred to Ben Worsley Surveyor Gen for lands to preserve the letter of his Highness in behalf of Vincent Gookin Esq. touching certain lands in the barony of Barrine[nr] *or* [m]y & Co of Cork to be held in fee farm . . .', References of Petitions Vol. XII, 1656–7, NA, T.5183. The barony name may be simply a mistake for 'Barrymore'.   [37] Gardiner, 'Transplantation', p. 734, n.74.

[38] Dunlop *Commonwealth,* II, documents 762, 829, 844, 915, 956; Barnard, 'Elections', pp. 356–7. In 1657 the mayor and corporation of Gloucester also appointed Vincent as their attorney to take possession of the Irish lands they expected to be allotted 'for their adventure', HMC, *12th Report, Appendix 9* (London, 1891), p. 515.

[39] St. John D. Seymour, *The Puritans in Ireland 1647–1691* (Oxford, 1912), p. 90.

holders), and also of town houses and tenements.[40] All this shows that, at least after the displacement from dominance of Fleetwood and the military party by the more moderately inclined Henry Cromwell, Gookin belonged, so to speak, to the *nomenklatura* of the protectorate in Ireland. He was evidently considered to be both capable of effective work and steadfast in discharging the tricky role of upholding, to both the London and Dublin authorities, the interests of the Old Protestant settlers in Ireland, whose County Cork electors returned him to three parliaments in succession.[41] Within this ultimately broader allegiance Gookin was, however, so conspicuously identified with the protectorate and parliamentary side that in autumn 1659 when the Restoration seemed imminent he was putting out feelers about a possible appointment to the governorship of Barbados; in the event he died suddenly that October.[42] As for Lawrence, a military man and enthusiastic Baptist, even if his underlying ideological position remained unchanged perhaps his growing stake in Ireland was already disposing him under the aegis of an emerging common interest to co-operate even with those less godly.[43]

III

Gookin wrote two pamphlets, *The great case of transplantation in Ireland discussed* and *The author and case of transplanting the Irish into Connaught vindicated*, published in January and May 1655 respectively, the second in answer to Colonel Lawrence's *The Interest of England in the Irish transplantation stated*, which appeared in between. Gookin's two pieces were published in London and Lawrence's in Dublin, underlining the fact that Gookin's purpose was to influence policy at its source, and perhaps also reflecting the hostility of the Dublin administration, still under Fleetwood until September 1655, to the Old Protestant viewpoint being represented, or at least being elaborated in such a surprisingly liberal direction, by Gookin.

Why was Gookin's attitude to the 'Irish' (which really means the Catholics, since it refers to those of both Gaelic and Old English origin)

---

[40] Dunlop, *Commonwealth*, II, document 945.

[41] See R. Caulfield (ed.), *Council Book of the Corporation of Kinsale* (Guildford, 1879), pp. xliv, 44, 45 for glimpses of his local role. He was also early made an alderman of the restored corporation of Cork city in 1656 (Cork Court of D'Oyer Hundred Book, Caulfield papers, University College Cork library, UC/RC/B.10/8/1).

[42] BL, Add. MSS 11411, letter of Thomas Povey, a London agent for many Barbados merchants, to Daniel Searle, himself then governor, 20 October 1659; printed in *Analecta Hibernica*, 4–5 (1932–4), pp. 240–2.

[43] For Lawrence's role as prominent Baptist see Kevin Herlihy, '"A gay and flattering world": Irish Baptist Piety and Perspective, 1650–1800' in Kevin Herlihy (ed.), *The Religion of Irish Dissent 1650–1800* (Dublin, 1996), pp. 59–67.

on the whole so free of the rhetoric of bitter abuse which pervaded most of the period's writings? Robert Dunlop, writing in 1913, somewhat optimistically explained this exceptionally positive view of the Irish as 'evidence of how residence in Ireland has always tended to draw English settlers and Irish natives together in one common interest'.[44] Certainly the fact of his not being a first-generation settler was one of the most sharply differentiating factors between him and the newly arrived Lawrence. The *Great Case* referred pointedly to the poor judgement of those who are 'strangers to Ireland' and the *Argument* insisted that lack of experience in Ireland led to his opponents' wrong-headed views.[45]

A broader consideration of Gookin's mentality, however, indicates other variances. As well as sharp divergences in religious complexion, social status and its accompanying intellectual formation may play a role in these differences. Gookin's many allusions to ancient history and literature, his deployment of rhetorical effects, and some explicit references to the methods used in his time to impart logical skills suggest that he had a classical, and probably a university, education.[46] There was a sophisticated use of metaphor in both texts, usually to deepen a serious argument but sometimes also to score points, often to entertaining effect. Thus he deployed a military image to make fun of Lawrence's alleged ineptitude in argument, pointedly implying that this can be attributed to his opponent's *déclassé* status as an under-educated soldier: 'he has suffered two Objections to struggle from their company, to the Rear of his Book, Pag. 26. which I shall desire to march up into their proper place, that so I may take a view of them with the rest here, and the Reader see the whole strength he musters at one view.'[47] Lawrence's more pragmatic and less than elegant writing style entirely lacks these flavours. But as well as his rhetorical skills Gookin also showed other kinds of knowledge, most evidently in *The Author and Case . . . Vindicated*, when he referred to Plato and More and especially when he cited modern history, in particular the works of Sir John Davies, Edmund Campion and Spenser. He must presumably have read these authors in Sir James Ware's 1633 compilation, and his acquaintance with them revealed a reflective and philosophical interest in Ireland and in the history of English settlement there. *The Great Case* was on the whole less allusive; it seems that Gookin was stung by Lawrence's sneers into a fuller grounding of his arguments in the appropriate historical authorities the second time round. But both Gookin's pamphlets occasionally rose to moments of eloquence, and this effect was always associated with a group of topics which the times had

[44] Dunlop, *Commonwealth*, II, p. 609, n.2.   [45] *Great Case*, p. 32 and *Argument*, p. 25.
[46] I have not however found any record of Gookin at Trinity College, Dublin or at the universities of Oxford or Cambridge.   [47] *Author*, p. 47.

bound inextricably together: namely, giving the reader an adequate sense of how terrible the condition of the Irish really was; getting his audience to acknowledge the exercise of compassion as a moral imperative; and solving the problem, immemorially incumbent upon the victorious, of reconciling justice with mercy.

Of course, much of the argument in these writings, however enlightened and humane, can be understood as also pragmatic and connected with economic self-interest. When, for instance, Gookin pleaded for the retention *in situ* of husbandmen and labourers, it is easy to discern the consternation of a landed gentleman at the prospective removal of the labour necessary to sustain farm, household and fishery as profitable going concerns.[48] Certainly there was no sign of Gookin feeling compunction specifically at the removal from their traditional habitations of the Catholic upper and gentry classes. But it is inadvisable to adopt too reductionist attitudes to what are, by any standards, ideologically remarkable texts. After due acknowledgement of the role of self- and class-interest in these writings, there remains an excess of expressed compassion and even of self-exploration which is altogether exceptional in the period and in the context.

In *The Great Case*, Gookin divided his argument into three sections: whether transplanting was appropriate or necessary to further the 'principles' of religion, 'in order to the purity of the Gospell'; of public good, 'in order to the preservation of the English Nation and Interest entire'; and finally of 'Advantage, in order to the fixing English Estates, where the hazard may be least, and profit greatest'.[49] He added an unsignalled last section which discussed 'the impossibility of this transplanting'.[50] In the first section, on religion (pp. 1–14), he maintained that the conversion of the Irish could be achieved *if* they remained among the English. A governing image and idea throughout the whole work was that of unification. At the very outset he merged the aim of religious conversion with his anti-transplantation argument by referring to 'the unitive principles of Christianity' which teach that 'separations of persons, are then onely Lawfull when necessary'.[51] He took the opportunity to criticise sharply the bitter divisions among Protestants themselves as the reverse of edifying, to lament the scarcity of ministers, and pointedly to remark that 'it is sad [to] observe how Garrisons are placed in every quarter where the Irish inhabit, Ministers in none; as if our business in Ireland were onely to set up our own interess [sic], and not Christs [sic]'.[52] He also attacked what he saw as the 'lamentable ignorance' or 'blasphemous haeresies' of

[48] *Great Case*, pp. 15–17.   [49] *Ibid.*, p.1.   [50] *Ibid.*, p.1.   [51] *Ibid.*, pp. 1–2.   [52] *Ibid.*, p. 3.

some who had been employed as preachers and of 'gifted men'; in this he revealed his own position as firmly resistant to the religious experiments and innovations of the period, which especially characterised the recent military incomers to Ireland.[53] In a memorable metaphor he even discredited preaching itself, so central to the practice of Independents and Baptists: 'mans soul is like a narrow mouth'd bottle, the means to fill it is not to pour buckets of water over it, but to take it singly, and pour in the water gently by little and little; publick preaching may be compared to the former, but private catechizing and family duties to the lat[t]er.'[54]

One can only imagine how infuriating Lawrence and other members of the more radical factions must have found this rather traditionalist position, with its distaste for a pre-eminence of preaching in religious exercise. Gookin's privileging here of private, familial and indoor piety over those dramatic group expressions of faith and self-abasement which characterised the English public culture of the Puritan Reformation in general is particularly striking; in a passage such as this, his views may seem far from the centre of gravity among his fellow members of the 1650s parliaments. They were, however, close to those of Edward Worth, dean of Cork, who during the period of Fleetwood's deputyship and the consequent dominance of the Munster military governors was struggling to carry out his aim for the re-establishment and consolidation of centralised religious organisation with a parochial ministry and against 'itinerant preachers and voluntaryism'.[55] Worth, who was Presbyterian in his position, enjoyed the support of Henry Cromwell and Gookin seems to have been of like mind: a January 1657 letter in the Thurloe correspondence attributed to him discussed the recruitment of suitable ministers for Dublin and approvingly mentioned the 'many hopefull young men being ordained by the presbytery of London' as well as more specifically selecting one 'Newcomen, of the Presbyterian way . . . in Suffolke . . . whom I am now designing to get over'.[56] In this connection it may be worth recalling Alan Ford's recent observation that the 'disparate strands' of the Protestantism imported from England and Scotland were in fact held together in Ireland in the two decades before 1660 to a surprising degree, and that this was done 'partly through amnesia and carelessness, partly through the principled construction of a tolerant framework . . . in a

---

[53] *Ibid.*, pp. 4, 5–6.   [54] *Ibid.*, pp. 6–7.

[55] T. C. Barnard, *Cromwellian Ireland: English Government and Reform in Ireland 1649–1660* (Oxford, 1975), p. 127.

[56] John Thurloe, *A Collection of State Papers of John Thurloe*, ed. T. Birch (7 vols., London, 1742), V, pp. 19–21. See Seymour, *The Puritans in Ireland*, especially pp. 54, 65–8, 154, 157, 162, 180–1, 199 and Barnard, *Cromwellian Ireland*, pp. 117–32 for accounts of Worth and of the various religious tendencies in Ireland in the period.

peculiarly Irish compromise'.[57] Such a view helps to account for the
apparent range of religious affiliations among the Munster Protestants:
on the April 1655 committee of Triers, for example, Gookin sat together
not only with Worth, but with Claudius Gilbert, a Limerick minister with
well-known Independent views; and when later that year the Quakers
preached in Kinsale, Worth's own wife Susannah was converted.[58]

The real focus of this section of Gookin's argument, however, was
hardly upon the hope of mass conversions at all. He very soon embarked
on a topic that evidently fascinated him and worried his conscience: the
validity of the notion of a 'national bloud-guilt' of the Irish. In spite of
the well-known centrality of this belief to English official attitudes after
the dissemination of the 1641 propaganda, he worked energetically at dis-
mantling the certainty with which this guilt was collectively assigned to a
whole nation, first questioning the infallibility and human unreliability of
the English judicial system.[59] Then he disaggregated the nation into its
particular members to point out that 'it is unnecessary that punishment
should be inflicted in common, when triall of the guilt and execution of
the guilty may be single'.[60] He stoutly maintained that the involvement of
many of the Irish was produced by a degree of 'ignorance or infirmitie' as
well as by coercion, which he attributes to *both* sides in the early stages of
the rising. Then he returned to query the very nature of punishment and
the morality of continuing 'punishment against a Nation'.[61] There
follows a fine passage of deep compunction about the moral viability of
the role of the English in so far as they were bent upon revenge for 1641.
What was the purpose of punishment? 'The ends thereof are commonly
mistaken', he argued, with 'men making punishment the end of punishment, and the gratifying either the Law it self . . . or God (who delights not
in suffering, as such) or the partly injured (the scratching of whose itch, in
the way of revenge, barely, is utterly unlawful)'.[62] At the climax of this
argument he acknowledged with simple dignity that 'the truth is, an
injury done is unrepealable, and neither God, nor the law of Reason
delights in accumulation of suffering, or are pleased with pain'.[63] It followed therefore that 'justice is not Anger but Caution; to devise how one
may bite him that bites us, is the part of a beast'. To insist on punishment
even when it was not 'in connexion with the ends' (that is, not likely to
prevent the committing of a fault) was the act of 'the vulgar, who are as

[57] Alan Ford, 'The Origins of Irish Dissent' in Herlihy (ed.), *The Religion of Irish Dissent*, p.
30.
[58] See Raymond Gillespie, '"Into another intensity": Prayer in Irish Nonconformity,
1650–1700', in Herlihy (ed.), *The Religion of Irish Dissent*, p. 31; for Susannah Worth, see
Seymour, *The Puritans in Ireland*, p. 132.   [59] *Great Case*, pp. 6–7.
[60] *Ibid.*, p. 8.   [61] *Ibid.*, p. 9.   [62] *Ibid.*, p. 10.   [63] *Ibid.*, p. 10.

inexorable as Nemesis, and thinks him the justest man, that like Draco, writes all his Lawes in Blood'.[64]

Again and again in both pamphlets, Gookin staged the key moment of compassion. A passage from *The Great Case* which described the abject condition of the Irish common people is often quoted:

for the poor Commons, the Sun never shined (or rather not shined) upon a Nation so miserable . . . There are not one hundred of them in 10000, who are not . . . under the penalty of losing life and estate; the Tax sweeps away their whole Subsistence; Necessity makes them turn Theeves and Tories, and then they are prosecuted with fire and sword for being so. If they discover not Tories, the English hang them, if they do, the Irish kill them . . .[65]

The passage ended with a less frequently noted but equally passionate self-exculpation from blame for showing sympathy for their suffering: 'if any person melted with the bowels of a man, or moved by the Rules of Common Equitie, labour to bring home to them that little Mercy which the State allowes, there are some ready to asperse them as Tories, coverers of bloud-guiltiness . . .'.[66] In a remarkably direct repudiation of the governing rhetoric of the period's discourse about Ireland, the morally corrosive nature of self-righteous avenging rage was stressed: 'Must we still cry justice, justice? . . . the fair vertue of justice (overdon) degenerates into the stinking weed of Tyranny . . .'.[67] This passage is lent further resonance by the echo of the quasi-proverbial conclusion – 'Lilies that fester, smell far worse than weeds' – of Shakespeare's sonnet 'They that have powre to hurt, and will doe none'.[68] The attitude to the Irish in these passages finds an echo in what at first may seem a curious quarter, the Quaker John Perrot's letter to the pope. Describing how at this same time he pleaded with the military governor of Kilkenny that a group of Irish sentenced to be transported to Barbados might be spared, Perrot used a strikingly similar language of pity: 'I had written about three sheets of Paper, that represented the sore Grievances and heavy Oppressions of all thy Children in the Land, which none of them instigated me unto, but was only carried forth thereunto in the Mercies, Pities and Compassions that God had put in my soul, beholding them *a bleeding People*' (italics in original).[69]

It is important to be aware that Gookin's whole discourse in both pamphlets was constantly addressing the moral attitudes and condition of the English themselves in so far as they were settlers. Throughout, then,

---

[64] *Ibid.*, p. 10. [65] *Ibid.*, pp. 13–14. [66] *Ibid.*, p. 14. [67] *Ibid.*, p. 14.
[68] William Shakespeare, *Shake-speares sonnets. Never before imprinted*. London, 1609 (Menston, 1968), p. 90.
[69] John Perrot, *Battering Rams against Rome, or the Battel of John, the Follower of the Lamb* . . . (London, 1661), pp. 123–4.

he considered the specific position of the planter in Ireland as distinct from that of the English subject or Protectorate citizen in general. His writings therefore marked a formative moment in the development of the whole characteristic mentality of the Protestant interest in Ireland, an attitude which would eventually shape Protestant Ascendancy culture and, from within it in the course of time, colonial nationalism. The fundamental injustice of the fate of the Catholic proprietors should not overshadow Gookin's crucial gesture of assuming a certain degree of moral responsibility for present actions and therefore for future consequences. That concession was not the product primarily of pragmatism or self-interest, nor even of an exceptional degree of individual intelligence; true to its time, it was motivated by religious understanding and insight. The *Great Case* passage beginning 'The Sun never shined . . . upon a Nation so miserable', quoted above, rose to a climax with a protest that 'the Lord knows I spoke only from the bowels of a man towards men, and the charity of a Christian to miserable blinded Christians, and one who had read a little what has happened to others by this practice, and therefore would that we should avoid such rocks'.[70]

It is noticeable that what was really focused on here was the inner state of the English, those with the power and therefore the responsibility. When he referred to 'what has happened to others by this practice', he clearly thought of the effect upon those in power of the misuse of that power. Such moments recurred throughout both the pamphlets, and in particular they dominated the concluding parts of *The Great Case*. To be sure, arguments about moral status such as 'it being an Heroickness not to insult upon an humbled Enemy' were accompanied by practical concessions like 'and Wisdome not to make him desperate', but the intensity of tone was most marked in the former, as for instance: 'God hath complicated our good with this mercy, as if he would not let Men be too cruel to those poor blind Natives, without being so to themselves'.[71] In a ringing final passage, he represented the moral good of refraining from all action entailing destruction, urging that 'the most contemptible things carry Engins of death along with them; a Gnat, a Hair, a Rasin-stone can destroy, but great glorious universal agents (like the Sun) are the Parents of life'.[72] Furthermore, 'a storm or accident may throw down a house, but art and industry are required to build it; and this way treads a destructive path, as hath been shewn, and therefore should no longer be trodden in'.[73]

Gookin's whole conception of colonial development was predicated upon assimilation. Leaving aside the specific question of implementing

---

[70] *Argument,* pp. 41–2.   [71] *Great Case,* p. 29.   [72] *Ibid.,* p. 29.   [73] *Ibid.,* p. 31.

the transplantation, it was perhaps in this basic aspiration that he was most at odds with Lawrence. He predicted that the Irish, now 'so abated' by famine, the sword and foreign transportation, were no longer likely to 'overgrow the English as formerly', but that 'being mixed with, they are likelyer to be swallowed up by the English, and incorporated into them; so that a few Centuries will know no difference present'.[74] Those parts of Lawrence's text which were most sequential, effective and urgent were precisely those passages where he elaborated his argument that only by consolidating English settlement and keeping the Irish outside these enclaves would the English interest in Ireland ever be secured.[75] Sounding quite a bit like Spenser in fundamental outlook, though not in style, he argued that the very cause of English weakness in 1641 was their 'not being embodied or . . . not cohabiting together'.[76] He developed a scenario of concentrating English plantations, such as the Ards peninsula, whose successful resistance to the 1641 insurrection he derived from this consolidation. Earlier English settlers, according to him, did well as long as they remained within the Pale or the English baronies in Wexford, whereas by their subsequent 'promiscuous and scattered inhabiting among the Irish', in the period of their 'degeneration', they were 'even as sheep prepared for the slaughter'.[77] In the spring of 1655 the authorities evidently supported Lawrence's views about effecting separate enclaves for Irish and English. This is shown by an official document of April 1655 about transplantation in the Cork area. Acting upon the report of an enquiry by a committee of six including Lawrence himself into 'what persons fell within the rules of the Act of Transplantation [*sic*]', this directed that any five of a large group headed by Broghill and Sir William Fenton but otherwise made up entirely of army officers were to 'take care that such Irish inhabiting the County Cork, as shall be thought fit to be dispensed with from Transplantation, do not live scatteringly, but be drawne together into townships'.[78] Further, it was ordered that 'watch and ward' be kept, allegedly 'for the better defence of the said inhabitants against disturbers of the Public peace', to catch 'Tories and other Felons'.[79] It continued that there should be 'no person inhabit[ing] without the lines of protection, or planting upon lands without the ancient declared lines' unless by a special licence.[80] The emphasis was laid on protection, but even if this was not disingenuous, the shared mentality between the document and Lawrence's own arguments remains clear.

[74] *Ibid.*, p. 21. [75] *Interest of England*, pp. 15–18. [76] *Ibid.*, p. 17. [77] *Ibid.*, p. 17.
[78] University College Cork Library, Caulfield collection, UC/RC/PP/8/23. [79] *Ibid.*
[80] *Ibid.*.

Gookin's firm adherence to an anti-military position in parliament emerged in his pamphlets, which repeatedly criticised the perpetration of violence by the army. Describing the harassment and grinding down of the common people by what he called the 'incredible oppression of the Souldiers', he did concede that 'there never was an Army (except of Angels, where the Lord of Hosts was Captain) that had not some that swerv'd from the integrity of the rest', but trenchantly inquired 'who will not believe an English Souldier, rather than an Irish Teige, if the matter should come to dispute[?]'.[81] In the small body of his correspondence with Thurloe which has survived, he also expressed his disquiet about military hegemony. Opposing the military party in a 1657 vote (against the bill for decimating the cavaliers) he articulated a philosophical basis for his position:

that which makes me feare the passing of the bill is, that therby his highness government will be more founded in force, and more removed from that natural foundation, which the people in parliament are desirous to give him; supposing therby hee will become more theirs, than now hee is, and will in time find the safety and peace of the nation to be as well maintained by the lawes of the land, as by the sword.[82]

This passage recalled the pointed terms in which in 1650 Andrew Marvell was praising Cromwell, then poised between his Irish and Scottish military campaigns, for his alleged amenability to the people's mandated representatives:

> Nor yet grown stiffer with command,
> But still in the Republic's hand:
>> How fit he is to sway
>> That can so well obey.
> He to the Commons' feet presents
> A kingdom, for his first year's rents:
>> And what he may, forbears
>> His fame, to make it theirs:
> And has his sword and spoils ungirt,
> To lay them at the public's skirt.[83]

Gookin, then, by contrast to Lawrence's projected separation of castes, envisaged the future of the country as one of ongoing assimilation of Irish manners and culture by English ones, and concomitantly of Catholic by Protestant belief and practice. He differentiated this conquest from former ones by the engagement of the whole 'Nation of England' in it, as opposed to the partial nature of 'former Conquests'. Furthermore, in the past many English were tenants to Irish proprietors, the Irish were 'the

---

[81] *Author and Case*, p. 16.   [82] Thurloe, *State Papers*, V, p. 20.
[83] 'An Horatian Ode upon Cromwell's Return from Ireland' in *Andrew Marvell*, ed. Frank Kermode and Keith Walker (Oxford, 1990), p. 84.

chiefly estated', and lawyers, jurors and members of the parliament were Irish. He adverted also to language use: 'The frequent use of the Irish Language in all commerce, and the Englishes habituating themselves to that Language, was one great means of Irishifying the English Colonies; But now the Language will be generally English; and if the Irish be mingled with the English, they will probably learn and be habituated to the English Tongue'.[84] The thorough nature of this latest 'conquest', then, would in his sanguine view tip the balance decisively towards the establishment of hegemony of the English interest and Englishness in culture, language and way of life. He contested Lawrence's whole argument about 'cohabitation' being the cause of the rebellion, pinpointing instead those courses of action, neglected up to 1641, which could have averted it: care taken for spreading the Protestant religion, educating 'their gentry in civility', suppressing their language, and so forth. In places anticipating the tone of a Prendergast inveighing against English inhumanity, he recruited to his viewpoint Sir John Davies, complete with page-references, on how the English in effect made rebellion inevitable by 'seating themselves in the rich plains, and driving the Irish to mountains and barren lands'.[85]

When at one point he directly broached the thorny question of future security for planters, it was in order to argue that while transplantation might help prevent unpleasant surprises to come, yet it did not constitute any kind of permanent solution: or as he put it in a vivid phrase: 'tis too narrow a plaister to cover the sore of Ireland'.[86] If safety were the only consideration, he drily added, then a safer way yet 'was to knock them all on the head, that will make them sure, and us safe for certain'.[87] The necessity of taking a longer view was far more evident to Gookin than to his opponent. Yes, transplantation or wholesale extermination would be ways of making the English safe, but there may be other, preferable alternatives. 'Our old doting Ancestors thought Communion one of these wayes';[88] and, ignoring their alleged 'degeneration', he appealed to the most dignified historical precedents to support their view: 'Where had been our Empire (sayes *Seneca*) if wholsom Providence had not mixed the conquered with the Conquerours? And *Livy*, The State of Rome was advanc't by receiving their enemies into them.'[89]

These ideas of 'Communion' and 'receiving their enemies into them' were instances of an important element in Gookin's thinking, and a highly unusual one. Certainly this vision of a long-term assimilation of Irish into English preserved intact the structure of a dominant and a submissive party, but it was also notably free of the fanatical quasi-compulsion to

[84] *Great Case*, p. 20.   [85] *Argument*, pp. 38–9.   [86] *Author and Case*, p. 39.
[87] *Ibid.*, p. 39.   [88] *Ibid.*, p. 40.   [89] *Ibid.*, p. 40.

keep the Irish away as something foul, a contaminant to English being, which was produced in and by the 1641 atrocity literature and persisted in so many other writings from 1642 onwards.[90] Gookin repeatedly rehearsed this trope of absorbing, often with an eloquence which would seem to mark conviction, and using powerful metaphors. Even allowing for the untypicality and, on the national scale, unreliability, of his perception of the relative strengths of Irish and English (an insight which was probably the product of his own breeding in Munster), his line of argument was striking. First he noted the currently abject condition of the Irish:

they were strong, they are weak; they were numerous, they are consumed by Sword, Pestilence and Famine; they were hearty, they are out of courage; they were rich, they are poor and beggarly; they had Souldiers, they are left naked; they had Cities, strong-holds, they have now but cottages to put their heads in; they had civil power, they have lost it; they had Priests to harden them, they are banished; the Tables are just turned; the English are what the Irish were; rich, high, powerfull, *etc.* the *Irish* are what the *English* were, poor, few, *etc* . . . What can they do? What may they not be made suffer? (Italics in original)[91]

This passage was presumably a further attempt to persuade the opposition that to refrain from large-scale transplantation would not carry unacceptable risks. Gookin's emphasis on the power previously wielded by the Irish may be read in two ways: either it was a disingenuous move by which he sought his audience's assent to a moderate line of action by reinforcing their assumptions about the 1641 rebellion, or it may be attributed to his own rather unrepresentative background in Munster. The final question, however – 'What may they not be made suffer?' – brings the reader sharply up against the responsibilities of rule and to a central concern in Gookin's thinking, namely the problem of discerning what was appropriate action by the English in relation to the defeated collectivity of the Irish nation. Following on this chilling reminder of the currently abject state of that nation, he went on to open out the view to the positive future which may be brought about, to the benefit of both groups as he saw it, if only extreme action was refrained from: 'they are few, the *English* many; we may overspread them, and incorporate them into our selves, and so by an

---

[90] The large body of recent writing in literary criticism and cultural studies on the development of a bounded selfhood – in Norbert Elias's phrase, *homo clausus* – in the early modern period, and its close connections with the development of various colonialisms, illuminates the function of these tropes in Gookin's mentality. See in particular Stallybrass and White, *The Poetics and Politics of Transgression* and, on colonial discourse theory in general, the writings by Stephen Greenblatt, Tzvetan Todorov, José Rabása, Homi Bhabha, Peter Hulme and Benita Parry cited in the bibliography to that volume. There has not yet been enough application of these or other theoretical perspectives to Anglo-Irish writings outside the specifically literary canon: for some discussion of this see the essays by Patricia Coughlan cited in the bibliography.

[91] *Author and Case*, p. 41.

onenesse take away the foundation of difference and fear together; we may breed up their youth, habituate them to our customs, cause a disuse of their Language: we have opportunities of communicating better things unto them, and probabilities they may be received'.[92] The word 'incorporation' with its implicit idea of arriving at the one body suggested an ultimate total fusing of English with Irish; Gookin presented this as a benign condition, removing 'difference' and 'fear' together. There is, however, no gainsaying the fact that the metaphor he used at this point, stripped of the beneficent eucharistic overtones of the earlier term 'Communion', was one based on cannibalism ('incorporate them into ourselves'), in which the English were perceived as not merely 'overspread[ing]' the Irish, but consuming them entirely so that ultimately only a single identity remains.[93] Ultimately, then, his careful reflections on viable moral stances did not extend, any more than those of his contemporaries, to anything which might be called cultural relativism towards the colonised.

IV

Twenty years later, in Massachusetts, questions of colonial relationships with earlier inhabitants were again being explored by Vincent Gookin's first cousin Daniel, his elder by seven years. Daniel was first a Virginia planter, from 1630 till 1644; then after his Puritan conversion he moved to New England, where he lived, first in Boston, then in Cambridge, till his death in 1687. Daniel was a prominent member of the Bay Colony, elected annually from 1652 to the office of 'assistant'. In 1656 he became 'superintendent' of all the Indians who had submitted to the Massachusetts government and discharged the civil aspects of the religious mission of his friend John Eliot, then working apace at the conversion of the Native American population. Daniel's surviving writings consist of two texts, both unpublished in his time: the *Historical Collections . . . of the Indians in New England* (c. 1674) and *An Historical Account of the Doings and Sufferings of the Christian Indians in New England in the Years 1675, 1676, 1677* (1677).[94] These writings, which have their own place in the

---

[92] *Ibid.*, pp. 40–1.   [93] *Ibid.*, p. 40.
[94] Both unpublished in Gookin's time. *Historical Collections* is printed in *Massachusetts Historical Society Collections*, 1 (Boston, 1792), pp. 141–226, and *Historical Account* in *Archaeologia Americana: Transactions and Collections of the American Antiquarian Society*, 2 (Cambridge, MA, 1836); facsimile reprint in *Research Library of Colonial Americana* (New York, 1972), pp. 425–534. Also see Jill Lepore, *The Name of War: King Philip's War and the Origins of American Identity* (New York, 1998), which is an outstanding recent account of the historical and ideological context and has a very full analytic bibliographical essay. Louise A. Breen discussed Daniel Gookin in an unpublished 1997 conference paper, 'Praying with the Enemy: Daniel Gookin and the Perils of Intercultural Mediatorship in Colonial Massachusetts', abstracted at <http://www.ucl.ac.uk/history/abstract.htm>.

historiography of early colonial America and belong primarily in that context, will not be examined in detail here.[95] It is important to acknowledge all the objective divergences – anthropological and geographic, to mention only two – between the two theatres of discourse. Nevertheless striking parallels emerge between the underlying complexion of Daniel's and Vincent's thinking when it is considered as part of the subjective mentality of the colonial settlers. Both cousins may, after all, be counted members of a more or less Puritan elite engaging with the Irish and the American settlements and plantations and sharing a governing ideology.

If, as it is not unreasonable to suspect, there was an inter-influence of each upon the other, how might this have come about? No information about contact between the families during the earlier decades of the century, whether in County Cork or in Kent, appears to have survived, though Sir Vincent did bring up his family in Ireland.[96] But Daniel the younger visited England several times: in 1639 for his marriage; in July 1650 when he stayed a few months; and, significantly, in 1655 when he was there from at least July until early November. It is reasonable to assume that during this visit he could have read his cousin's two pamphlets, published in January and May respectively. Furthermore, Daniel, like Vincent on occasion, was in direct contact with Cromwell and had his distinct approval. Certainly after the unexpected and indeed unplanned capture of Jamaica that summer he was appointed as commissioner to persuade New England settlers to colonise the new acquisition. This proved a mixed blessing: Daniel's correspondence with Thurloe shows that his best efforts could not overcome the extreme reluctance of his fellow settlers in the Massachusetts area to remove to an island they believed was subject to Spanish harassment and to an unhealthy climate, and the plan failed.[97] After a prolonged residence at Dunkirk during 1657–8, Daniel returned to America for good, where he resumed his office as superintendent of the Indians, and continued so till his death. In 1674 he wrote the better known of his two treatises, the *Historical Collections*, which was overtaken by an historical irony in the form of the outbreak of 'King Philip's War', a cataclysmic set of events which among other things

---

[95] Neither do I propose to elide the differences between the historical situations of Munster in the 1650s and Massachusetts in the 1670s, or naively to equate the colonial project of the Bay Colony with the drive to establish once and for all on a secure footing the centuries-old English interest in Ireland. Nor can much ground for comparison be found between the way of life of the Native American nations and that of the Irish in the mid-seventeenth century; James Muldoon's often-cited 'The Indian as Irishman', *Essex Institute Historical Collections*, 3 (1975), pp. 267–89, while suggestive, in my view overstates the parallels which can be found between the two situations.

[96] *Cal SP Ire, 1647–1660*, p. 185.

[97] See Thurloe, *State Papers*, IV, pp. 449, 509–10; V, pp. 6–7, and J. H. Andrews, *The Colonial Period in American History* (4 vols., New Haven, 1934), I, p. 499.

swept away much of the work of converting and 'civilising' the Native American peoples of the region which had been so diligently pursued by Eliot for decades before. After the war his colleagues in the Massachusetts colony excoriated Gookin for his over-sympathetic attitude to the Indians, and temporarily removed him from his official functions. In *An Historical Account of the Doings and Sufferings of the Christian Indians*, however, he sought to defend this group against the vilification by the settlers of all Native Americans. In it he doggedly recorded instance after instance of their mistreatment during the war because of a mixture of prejudice, war hysteria, and expansionist greed among many of the English. This included the forcible resettlement of the inhabitants of most of the 'praying towns' – transplantation by any other name – on Long Island and Deer Island, where they risked death from starvation and exposure; to Gookin's mind they were being made to 'pass into the furnace of affliction'.[98] He was clear-sighted about what might be called the popular paranoia prevailing in the colony in the war months: of the Boston trial for murder, instigated by the outstandingly brutal Samuel Moseley in August 1675, of fifteen Christian Indians (all but two of whom were ultimately acquitted and freed), he noted: 'the clamours of the people were very great upon this occasion, and all things against those praying Indians accused (as one of the most intelligent of the magistrates said) were represented as very great, as things appear in mist or fog'.[99]

The first text, *Historical Collections*, was part-ethnography, part-enthusiastic charting of Eliot's work at conversion, part-project for bringing 'civilisation' to the Native Americans. The lists of praying towns with the numbers of their population and the detailed accounts of Eliot's preaching and catechising, while a useful early source of information, were not, however, the work's main claim to distinction. The points in both texts where Daniel Gookin was at his most compelling were rather the discursive exploration of his sense of what the appropriate English relation to the indigenous peoples might be, and ultimately of how productive co-existence might be achieved. Here the parallels with Vincent's thought are most apparent. Each man wrote from a convinced Protestant viewpoint about the pervasive, indeed governing inspiration of Christian faith and adherence (whatever their differences may have been about church government in practice, as between congregationalism and presbytery). Likewise each was, of course, unquestioning about the benefits of

---

[98] *Historical Account*, p. 497. For the fullest references to the forced removals, see especially *Historical Account*, pp. 468–9, 485.
[99] *Historical Account*, p. 459. See Lepore, *The Name of War*, pp. 137–8; one was the skilled artisan called by the English 'James Printer', trained by Eliot, who had printed his various volumes of proselytising literature.

English rule and authority in the milieu in question, and likewise each merged economic motives with spiritual ones. Daniel advocated the Indians' enlightenment by being shown the true way to civility and a Christian way of life, and there was, of course, no doubt in his mind about the hierarchy between the two cultures. He also showed, though to a muted degree by comparison with the likes of William Bradford, a familiar Puritan and bourgeois unease with the carnivalesque and communally participatory qualities of Native American culture. Instances of this are the potlatch custom where on certain occasions 'a man giveth away all that ever he hath', and with the 'great vehemency they use in the motion of their bodies, in their dances'.[100]

So much would not distinguish either cousin from most of the normal views of the period. But they were also alike, and both different from dominant attitudes in their respective milieux, in being prepared to hold up an ultimate assimilation as the model and goal for the future development of their societies. Daniel also adduced some prudential considerations for building up the converted Indians' communities not far away, but right at the outskirts of English towns where they might have provided a 'wall' and preliminary defence against attack upon the colony's centres by hostile nations. His sad narrative of this and that injustice and atrocity in the *Historical Account* was pervaded by declarations, derived from scripture, of what was due to this group of what he and Eliot saw as newly enlightened souls. He perceived them as sharers in the Christian revelation who had been faithful allies of the English, assisting them as guides, trackers and spies.[101] Thus 'a covenant, though made with the Gibeonites, is a very binding thing, and the breach of it sorely punished by the Lord, as may appear in 2 Sam.xxi.1,2,3'.[102] But a secular discourse of civilly based rights was strikingly predominant even in his post-war writing; the following, arguing against the wartime practice of summary removal from their habitations of those against whom no crime had been proved, was a typical instance of the deployment of such discourse: 'the General Court hath granted those Indians lands and townships, and thereby confirmed and settled them therein as the English; so that, besides their own natural right, they have this legal title, and stand possessed of them as the English are'.[103]

Further, there is intriguing evidence of tensions within his own think-

[100] *Historical Collections . . . of the Indians*, p. 153. Also see Andrew Parker, Mary Russo, Doris Sommer and Patricia Yaeger (eds.), *Nationalisms and Sexualities* (New York, 1992).
[101] James Drake, 'Restraining Atrocity: The Conduct of King Philip's War', *New England Quarterly*, 70 (1997), pp. 33–56, usefully places Gookin's positive views in the context of others' very different attitudes. On a minor point, it does not seem accurate in attributing to him 'a military background in England'; his military title refers to his service in the town militias of the colony.   [102] *Account*, p. 468.   [103] *Ibid.*, p. 469.

ing about the status of the English in Massachusetts, anxieties which reveal a reflectiveness and capacity for compunction characteristic also of Vincent's thought. So at different moments he acknowledged the expansionist drive of the English as 'a growing and potent people, comparatively to the Indians'[104] and, albeit under the sign of Christian conversion, recalled the 'promises made to Jesus Christ' that 'God will give him the heathen for his inheritance, and the uttermost parts of the earth for his possession'.[105] Yet elsewhere he admitted, with a kind of rueful delicacy, that 'the Indians here [in the English town of Marlborough] do not much rejoice under the English men's shadow, who do so overtop them in their number of people, flocks of cattle, etc., that the Indians do not greatly flourish, or delight in their station at present'.[106]

He specifically advocated close proximity between the English and Indians as the best way forward: 'that they may cohabit together, without which neither religion nor civility can well prosper'.[107] By the founding of a free school for both to attend at Okommakamesit (*alias* Marlborough), 'the Indians will be able to converse with the English familiarly; and thereby learn civility and religion from them'.[108] The momentous implications of this idea of shared education were evidently not lost upon him. If as a result the Indians would henceforth be able 'to converse with the English familiarly', that 'approved experiment' which was here specified as a linguistic one, would also enable the colony to change the speech of this 'barbarous people' into that of the 'more civil and potent nation that hath conquered them'.[109] Finally, the consequences of denying the Indians such civil conversation (to coin a phrase) were, he said, all too evident at the other side of the Atlantic:

And I incline to believe, that if that course had been effectually taken with the Irish, their enmity and rebellion against the English had been long since cured or prevented, and they better instructed in the Protestant religion; and consequently redeemed from the vassalage and affection to the Romish see; who have by this means kept the greatest part of them in ignorance, and consequentially in brutishness and superstition to this day.[110]

V

In conclusion, should the writings of Vincent and Daniel Gookin be judged as instances of political thought, however small scale and particular in their scope? Certainly, in Vincent's case, it is necessary to make allowance for all the practical circumstances underlying the composition

---

[104] *Historical Collections . . . of the Indians*, p. 179.   [105] *Ibid.*, p. 223.
[106] *Ibid.*, p.185. There is a scriptural allusion to David rejoicing under the shadow of Christ.
[107] *Ibid.*, p. 179.   [108] *Ibid.*, p. 220.   [109] *Ibid.*, pp. 220, 221.   [110] *Ibid.*, p. 222.

of his two pamphlets: his wish to strike a blow against the military party for reasons of interest as well as political belief; his need (and that of his whole class) for the labour of the Irish common people to sustain the profitability of their estates; his conscious political role in building up an image of the Old Protestants as judicious and reasonable men to whom much could be entrusted; and his own active and paid function in the sharing out of the very land acquired by means of the expropriation of Catholic proprietors. But, perhaps paradoxically, the more detailed the analysis one makes of the background of the pamphlets, the greater the risk of losing sight of the degree of reflectiveness and even of moral insight or humane impulse shown by both Gookins.[111] In the case of Vincent in particular, he should not be seen as what Memmi called 'the colonist who refuses', because of course he evidently cannot be said to have refused.[112] But out of the extreme moment when the Irish transplantation policy, in all its barbarity, was being urged upon those in power, he defined and elaborated a position from which that inhumanity could be apprehended. The presence of pragmatic motives and social interests should not obscure the true note of reflection upon how settler and old inhabitant were, in some necessary future and in some sense, to learn to live together. Neither, in Daniel's case, should the ideological boundaries of his origins and of his religious belief, or the stake he too held in the Bay Colony, obscure the value he insistently placed upon willingness to accept Native Americans, once Christian, as fellow human beings, in all their vulnerability and in all their ultimate potential as fellow citizens.

---

[111] *Pace* the usual view hitherto taken among historians, of which a typical example is Ivan Roots' remark that '[t]he Old Protestants set out to mitigate the policy of "Hell or Connaught" not because of any squeamishness about the hardship it inflicted upon the natives' but because of their economic need of 'a cheap labour force': 'Union and Disunion in the British Isles 1637–1660' in Roots (ed.), *'Into Another Mould': Aspects of the Interregnum* (Exeter, revised and expanded edition, 1998), p. 18.

[112] Albert Memmi, *The Colonizer and the Colonized*, trans. Howard Greenfield (London, 1957, repub. 1990), pp. 84–110.

Recasting a tradition: William Molyneux and
the sources of *The Case of Ireland . . . Stated*
(1698)

Patrick Kelly

There are substantial reasons for regarding William Molyneux's *The Case
of Ireland's Being Bound by Acts of Parliament in England and elsewhere
Stated*, published in 1698, as the most significant Irish political pamphlet
of the seventeenth and eighteenth centuries.[1] Though it never achieved
the enduring literary fame of Jonathan Swift's *Drapiers Letters* (1724),
through its nine reprintings to 1782 Molyneux's *Case* enjoyed a continuing
political vitality down to the time of the debates over Union with Britain in
1800 that none of the other frequently republished political writings of the
time, such as William King's *The State of the Protestants of Ireland, under the
Government of the Late King James* (1691), could aspire to.[2] Moreover *The
Case of Ireland* also attracted attention in the early stages of the American
Revolution, for its relevance to the general question of the relations
between England and its dependencies. A notable factor in ensuring the
continuing influence of Molyneux's *Case* was the belief that the book was
publicly burnt by order of the English parliament in 1698, a claim first
aired in 1719 and put into widespread circulation by the Dublin radical
Charles Lucas in 1749.[3] Although modern interest in Molyneux's *Case* has
largely focused on its fortunes in the eighteenth century as the *fons et origo*
of a tradition of resistance to the claims of the English parliament to legislate for Ireland, its relation to earlier political discourse in seventeenth-
century Ireland has not been ignored. Three-quarters of a century ago
Charles H. McIlwain indicated its debt to the controversy over English
parliamentary authority in Ireland in the early 1640s, particularly to a

---

[1] This chapter draws on material collected for the preparation of a critical edition of
Molyneux's book, to be published by the Irish Legal History Society. Citations from *The
Case of Ireland* are taken from the 1977 reprint (Cadenus Press, Dublin, with introduction
by J. G. Simms), with references to its page numbers (generally given in brackets in the
text).
[2] For the *fortuna* of *The Case* in the eighteenth century, see Patrick Kelly, 'William
Molyneux and the Spirit of Liberty in Eighteenth-Century Ireland', *Eighteenth-Century
Ireland: Iris an dá chultúr*, 3 (1988), pp. 133–48.
[3] There is no record of the decision to burn the *Case* in the 1698 *Commons Journal*, nor any
contemporary reference to its taking place. However, the book was severely censured by
the English House of Commons. See further pp. 104–5 below.

paper entitled 'A Declaration setting forth how, and by what Means, the Laws and Statutes of England, from Time to Time, came to be of force in Ireland'.[4] The extent of this debt was further revealed by Caroline Robbins in *The Eighteenth-Century Commonwealthman*, who pointed out that substantial sections of the pamphlet were directly taken from 'A Disquisition touching that Great Question Whether an Act of Parliament made in England shall binde the Kingdome and people of Ireland without theire Allowance and Acceptance of such Act in the Kingdome of Ireland', written by Molyneux's father-in-law, Sir William Domville.[5] Since then it has become apparent that there is a vast amount of information on the circumstances leading to the publication of *The Case of Ireland*, in terms both of the broad political context and of the actual circumstances surrounding its composition, and the immediate reaction to it, especially in the English parliament. This chapter explores how these various influences helped determine Molyneux's decision to produce a defence of the legislative independence of the Irish parliament, shaped the way he went about constructing this defence, and subsequently precipitated the reaction to it in the English parliament.

I

For an answer to the question why Molyneux was led to publish on the topic of Ireland's legislative independence of the English parliament one must turn to *The Case of Ireland*. In The Preface to the Reader Molyneux noted that three public issues – namely, English determination to restrict the export of Irish woollen cloths; the appeal in the bishop of Derry's case before the English House of Lords; and the issue of what was to happen to the lands forfeited from the Irish Jacobites – had led him (though without any particular concern with these issues other than as an Irish member of parliament and property-owner) to seek to set the English parliament right as to the nature of its powers in Ireland. This disclaimer, not dissimilar to those with which Molyneux's friend John Locke prefaced some of his works, is intended more to convince the reader of the author's good faith and objectivity than to set out the truth. For Molyneux was indeed implicated, though perhaps not in terms of direct financial interest, in all three of these matters. Most pertinent was his role in assisting Bishop William King of Derry in the preparation of his case with the Irish Society of London (the city company which managed the Londonderry

[4] C. H. McIwain, *The American Revolution: A Constitutional Interpretation* ([1923]; reprint, New York, 1958), chapter 2, especially pp. 33–46.
[5] Caroline Robbins, *The Eighteenth-Century Commonwealthman* (Cambridge, MA, 1959), p. 140.

plantation) over fishing rights and land-property near Derry.[6] After losing his case in the Irish Court of Chancery, King had appealed to the Irish House of Lords that duly found in his favour in the autumn of 1697. The Society then turned to the English House of Lords, challenging the competence of the Irish Lords to hear appeals from the Irish Court of Chancery. When the case opened before the English Lords in January 1698, the counsel for the Society stated that the central question was 'the nature of the Irish parliament', an issue which soon appeared to be merely rhetorical, as the English Lords peremptorily refused to hear the plea from the bishop's counsel to examine whether it had the right to hear appeals from Ireland, and proceeded as if the matter were simply self-evident.[7]

The tensions revealed by the bishop of Derry's case were symptomatic, however, of more general strains in Anglo-Irish relations reaching back to the 1688 Revolution and the Jacobite War.[8] Although, in the first flush of confidence after the battle of the Boyne in 1690, William had consulted the Anglo-Irish colonists over the terms offered in the Declaration of Finglas, they had had no voice in the final treaty negotiations at Limerick and signally failed to appreciate the strategic demands of the European war that had led William to make extensive concessions to the garrison. The ill-will generated by this exclusion persisted down to the Irish parliamentary session of 1697, and was manifested in the refusal of the Irish parliament to confirm the Treaty of Limerick in 1692 and 1695, only finally doing so in a truncated fashion in 1697. Two significant new developments in Irish political life emerged after 1692. The first was the increased regularity with which sessions of the Irish parliament were now held – in contrast to the single parliament of 1661–6 in the three decades from the Restoration to the Revolution. The second was the emergence of a more confrontational attitude towards the Dublin administration and the English government manifested in a (supposed re-)assertion of constitutional rights by the colonists, notably in the so-called 'sole right' claim that only the Irish Commons had the right to initiate tax proposals, that surfaced in each session from 1692 to 1697. The men behind this new aggressiveness were for the most part former exiles in London during the Jacobite War, whose outlook had, at least to some extent, been shaped by what they had witnessed in the Convention and early sessions of the 1690–5 English parliament. One may further speculate that these tensions

---

[6] See list of precedents relating to the appeal compiled by Molyneux and King in early 1698 in Archbishop Marsh's Library, Dublin, MS Z 3 2.5 (77). Moreover, the manuscript drafts, in TCD, MS 890, show that Molyneux antedated *The Case of Ireland* from 26 March to 8 February 1698, the date when Lord Chancellor Somers finally laid these precedents before the House.   [7] HMC, *House of Lords MSS, 1697–99*, pp. 16–24.

[8] For the general background, see Patrick Kelly, 'The Irish Woollen Prohibition Act of 1699: Kearney Revisited', *Irish Economic and Social History*, 7 (1980), pp. 24–39.

over English authority in Ireland were exacerbated by the fact that no constitutional debate took place in Ireland at the time of the Revolution, as it had done in England and Scotland. Moreover, the fact that issues such as the English parliament's power to legislate for Ireland, the questions of legal appeals to England, and the status of Poynings' Law had been raised in James' Dublin parliament of 1689 (illegal in English eyes), made it difficult for the Protestant colonists to raise them after 1691 without leading to accusations that they were no different from the defeated Jacobites.[9]

More overt and immediate than these underlying constitutional tensions was the controversy which had erupted in England some two and a half years previously over competition from Irish woollen exports, and developed into a party political issue at the end of 1697. This in turn sparked off a pamphlet debate which provided the immediate context for the appearance of Molyneux's *Case*. The strains imposed on the English economy as a result of the war against France begun in 1689, especially the credit crisis provoked by the transfer burden imposed by payments to Europe, had brought the English woollen export industry (one of the main pillars of the country's economy) into severe difficulties by 1694. These were to deepen with the currency crisis of 1695–7 and the adverse harvest conditions of those years, especially in the woollen manufacturing areas of the west of England whose products were most directly in competition with Irish exports. In such circumstances the remarkable recovery of the Irish woollen industry by the mid-1690s appeared particularly threatening. Calls for its suppression began in 1695, notably with the publication of the Bristol writer John Cary's *Essay on the State of England in Relation to its Trade, its Poor, and its Taxes* . . .[10] Proposals were made for replacing the Irish woollen industry by a linen manufactury, and when the subject was taken up by the Board of Trade in late 1696 Locke sought information from Molyneux on the potential for developing linen in Ireland – a suggestion to which Molyneux responded with enthusiasm. However, when parliament assembled in December 1697 for the first session after the Nine Years War, the Irish woollens issue rapidly became transformed from a commercial question to one of party politics. The call for the destruction of the Irish woollen industry was taken up by the Tory

[9] Particularly in relation to the 'Act declaring, That the Parliament of *England* cannot bind Ireland [and] against Writs of Error and Appeals . . . into England'; text in Thomas Davis, *The Patriot Parliament*, ed. Sir Charles Gavin Duffy (2nd edn, Dublin, 1893), pp. 43–8.

[10] Cf. the letter to Cary from the Bristol MPs Yates and Dale, December 1695: 'We cannot think anything will hinder Ireland's increase in the Woollen Manufacture so much as by . . . reduceing that Kingdome to the terms of a Colony': P. McGrath (ed.), *Merchants and Merchandise in Seventeenth Century Bristol* (London, 1955), p. 167.

magnate Sir Edward Seymour, both as a means of re-establishing his political base in the important clothing town of Exeter and as part of a broader campaign against the Junto ministry, the key Commons supporters of whose leading figure, Lord Chancellor Somers, Edward Clarke and Sir Walter Yonge, represented clothing interests in Somerset and Essex.[11]

Associated with the launching of Seymour's campaign was the publication of a short but violently-worded pamphlet, entitled *A Letter from a Gentleman in the Country, to a Member of the House Commons; in Reference to the Votes of the 14th Instant.*[12] This not only listed a series of areas in which Irish competition threatened English trade but broke new ground in attacking the Anglo-Irish on a variety of political fronts. Among its more intemperate claims was that Ireland was a nursery for 'Popery and Slavery', and that the 'extraordinary . . . Discipline' which the English there had to exercise to restrain the Irish from rebellion ' . . . was designed to breed up Instruments for Arbitrary government in *Ireland* to introduce it here'. England had thus good reason 'to enquire into the dispose and manage of the Trade of that Kingdom, which hath lost this Nation so much Blood and Treasure to recover after 32 Rebellions', continuing:

> But that which I think the most unaccountable of all is, that we suffer them to *hold parliaments, settle Estates, pass Attainders, Regulate our Trade, Pardon their own Rebellions,* that we have paid for. This could be done by nothing but Irish Assurance, nor endured by any but English Conquerours, for so I hope they will yet allow us to be, if not, that your House will take a course to make them remember it.

In the light of this, it was scarcely surprising that among the concluding proposals for regulating Irish trade, the author slipped in a call for the abolition of the Irish parliament: 'That they hold no parliaments, but be governed by the parliament Laws of England'.[13]

The publication of this pamphlet evoked a prompt reply from the Irish merchant and Member of Parliament Sir Francis Brewster, which was shortly followed by several other pamphlets for and against the Irish woollen industry, most of which also alluded to the political relations

---

[11] As such, it certainly paid off. Seymour and his associate Sir Bartholomew Shower were triumphantly returned for Exeter in the 1698 election. Shower was an important figure in both the woollens campaign and the bishop of Derry's case, appearing as counsel in the House of Lords for the Irish Society as well as for the promoters of the woollens bill. He subsequently published a report of the 1698 bishop of Derry appeal in *Cases in Parliament Resolved and Adjudged upon Petitions, and Writs of Error* (London, 1698), pp. 78–83.

[12] The votes were for leave to Sir Edward Seymour to bring in a bill prohibiting the export of Irish woollens, and for setting up a Committee to consider the trade of England and Ireland: *Commons Jnl, Eng*, XII, p. 7.

[13] See text of *Letter* in Patrick Kelly, 'A Pamphlet Attributed to John Toland and an Unpublished Reply by Archbishop William King', *Topoi*, 4 (1985), pp. 84–6.

between England and Ireland.[14] Amongst those to prepare a reply to the *Letter* was Bishop King of Derry, angered both by the writer's ignorance of Irish economic conditions and by his call for the abolition of the Irish parliament. Informants in England had told King that the author of *A Letter from a Gentleman* was none other than John Toland, a suggestion which the bishop found convincing, though he was also prejudiced against Toland as the author of *Christianity not Mysterious* (which had been burnt by the Irish parliament in September 1697). Two decades later when King's friend Lord Molesworth proposed using Toland's pen to attack the bill which eventually became the Declaratory Act of 1720, asserting the now British parliament's claim to legislative superiority over Ireland, King again revealed his deep distrust of Toland and the latter's ignorance of Irish conditions.[15] Molyneux's *Case of Ireland* can also be seen as a response to *A Letter from a Gentleman*; three specific references seemingly respond directly to arguments raised in the work.[16] Indeed the provocative language suggests the *Letter* was a deliberate act of coat-trailing intended to provoke a defence of the Irish parliament, such as Molyneux was imprudent enough to supply.[17]

Before turning to the contents of Molyneux's pamphlet, let us look for a moment at its author, this William Molyneux who, 'seeing all Others silent', ventured 'to Expose my own Weakness, rather than be wanting at this time to *my Country*'.[18] William Molyneux (1656–98) was a wealthy Irish lawyer and minor landowner, best known as the author of a recent textbook on dioptrics, who had spent the period of the Jacobite War as an exile in England, and whose main claim to fame in the eyes of posterity, other than as the author of *The Case of Ireland*, was the correspondence with John Locke, on which he had embarked in 1692.[19] This friendship left its mark on the development of Locke's *Essay concerning Human Understanding* in its second (1694) and third (1695) editions, particularly

[14] Among the more important titles were [? Francis Annesley], *Some Thoughts on the Bill Depending before the . . . House of Lords for Prohibiting the Exportation of the Woolen Manufactures of Ireland into Foreign Parts* (London, 1698), and [Sir Francis Brewster], *A Discourse of Ireland and the Different Interests thereof* (London, 1698).
[15] King to Molesworth, 10 and 20 September 1720, TCD, MS 750/6/117–9. Toland's eventual contribution, *Reasons Why the Bill for the better Securing the Dependency of Ireland, should not Pass* (London, 1720), drew heavily on Molyneux's *Case*.
[16] *The Case of Ireland*, pp. 24, 33, 112.
[17] Cf. Methuen's comment of 14 April 1698, that the woollen bill might be stopped in the English Lords 'if the Zeal and Diligence of the Gentlemen of Ireland do not hinder who are every day publishing books and papers not suiting with this Climate', BL, Add. MSS 61,652, f.14.
[18] *Case of Ireland*, p. 24. For Molyneux's life, see J. G. Simms, *William Molyneux of Dublin* (Dublin, 1982).
[19] Subsequently revealed to the world through its publication in *Some Familiar Letters between Mr Locke and Several of his Friends* (London, 1708).

with reference to the perceptual problem relating to the possibility of a blind man recovering sight being able to distinguish visually between objects, which he had previously identified by touch: 'a Problem of that very Ingenious and Studious promoter of real Knowledge, the Learned and Worthy Mr. *Molineux* . . . whom I am proud to call my Friend'. He had also sat in the unsuccessful Irish parliament of 1692 as member for the University of Dublin, a seat which was virtually in the Irish adminis- tration's gift and whose occupant could not have been other than well regarded by the authorities. Re-elected in 1695 Molyneux, now promoted to one of the lucrative masterships in Chancery, emerged as an active House of Commons man, serving on committees and acting as a go- between with the House of Lords. Though he purported to be a reluctant lawyer, preferring the pursuit of natural science as his 1694 autobiogra- phy informs us, he was actually well informed and meticulous. His sub- stantial law commonplace book was known to the eighteenth-century biographer John Birch, and in 1693 Molyneux had compiled an extensive indexed table of precedents from the journals of the Irish Commons.[20] Nothing he had done before 1698 suggested, however, that Molyneux was in any way an opponent of authority. Indeed the whole tenor of *The Case of Ireland* supports the view that Molyneux genuinely believed that the Anglo-Irish conflict could be resolved by rational argument, and he was subsequently much abashed by the violent reaction of the English parlia- ment. That such should have been the case brings out the fact that for all his eminence in the Irish official world and his standing in the republic of letters, there was something a little naive, perhaps even lightweight, about William Molyneux. Even this hitherto unexpected act of courage in setting his name to this challenge to the mighty English parliament was undertaken with little appreciation of the risks involved.[21]

II

Not only the subject matter of the book but also the manner in which Molyneux has chosen to present it are clearly indicated by the title of *The Case of Ireland's Being Bound by Acts of Parliament in England ... Stated*. In much the same way that other late seventeenth-century writers decided to present their material in the form of a dialogue or a letter, Molyneux opted for an extended version of the printed 'State of the Case' document

[20] BL, Add. MSS 4223. ff. 35–8; TCD, MS 622.
[21] The manuscript drafts show that Molyneux made considerable efforts to remove possible causes of offence from his text, though he failed to appreciate quite how objectionable remarks like his comparison of 'the Breaking of [Ireland's] Constitution' to the 'breaking of the Edict of Nantes' (p. 131) must have appeared in England.

that exists in such numbers for legal proceedings at this period, and which he must presumably have drawn up in his legal practice. The genre, however, does not make for easy reading, since it involves dealing in turn with a series of specific objections to the case for Ireland's legislative independence. Moreover this form of presentation serves to obscure the main themes of the book, which get dealt with piecemeal under a variety of headings rather than discussed systematically. These issues would seem to be: the question of conquest in its various ramifications as applicable to post-Revolution Ireland; the necessity of consent as the basis for legislation; and the definition of the constitutional relationship between England and Ireland in terms of what we might describe as a dual monarchy, under which Ireland owed allegiance to the king of England but only in his inextricably linked capacity as king of Ireland, so that in consequence the English government, and above all the English parliament, has no authority in Ireland.

To understand how Molyneux makes use of the various sources deployed in writing *The Case of Ireland*, it is helpful to begin by considering the structure of the book, as laid out at the start of the pamphlet. Following a rhetorical appeal to the English parliament's sense of justice, Molyneux sets out to examine 'the *Right* which *England* may pretend to, for Binding us by their Acts of Parliament' in terms of 'the *Imaginary Title of Conquest* or *Purchase*, or on *Precedents* and *Matters of Record*' (p. 25), under six headings, as follows:

(1) the circumstances of Ireland's original annexation to the English crown under Henry II, 'such as our best Historians give us',
(2) whether Henry's expedition, or any subsequent suppression of rebellions in Ireland, properly constitutes a '*Conquest*' of Ireland,
(3) what title the conquest of Ireland (had there actually been one) would convey to England,
(4) what subsequent concessions have been made to Ireland by her English rulers by way of grants of laws and liberties, and the introduction of English forms of government,
(5) various precedents, and the opinions of jurists on the matter,
(6) a summary of the main arguments for and against the legislative independence of Ireland, with some general conclusions on the case (pp. 25–6).

Though these headings indicate the search for legal and historical precedents as the chief basis of the case for Ireland's legislative independence, Molyneux also devoted considerable attention to arguments based on natural right. After initially representing himself as Ireland's advocate before the English parliament, he went on to claim that he argued 'the Cause of the whole Race of *Adam*: . . . [for] *Liberty* seems the Inherent

Right of all *Mankind*' (p. 24). Indeed commentators have seen Molyneux's significance in the development of Irish political writing as lying precisely in his progression beyond traditional arguments from precedent to those derived from natural right (an approach held to derive largely from Locke's *Second Treatise of Government*).[22] Yet too much should not be made of the distinction between natural law and reason on the one hand and common law and precedent on the other (what Molyneux contrasts on p. 115 as '*Reason*' and '*Record*'). Sixteenth- and seventeenth-century lawyers relied heavily on reason and equity, and though the former generally indicated the artificial reason of the law, arguments based on natural law could still be deployed in English (and presumably Irish) courts even in the later seventeenth century.[23] In *The Case of Ireland* common law and natural law arguments, although occasionally contrasted, usually serve to corroborate each other.

The crucial evidence in seeking to understand how Molyneux came to present his case for Irish legislative independence lies in the surviving manuscripts of the pamphlet, now among the Molyneux papers in the library of Trinity College, Dublin. These consist of the holograph and a faircopy in the hand of an amanuensis, both of which have been heavily emended and added to by Molyneux himself.[24] Though earlier commentators dismissed the faircopy as of little apparent interest, it was in fact the actual copy used by the printer in setting the book, 'cast off into formes' for this purpose, and constituting the unique known example of such a printer's copy from the age of the handpress in Ireland.[25] Behind these manuscripts dating from the composition of *The Case* in 1698, however, lie the two unacknowledged mid-seventeenth-century legal papers identified by McIlwain and Robbins, namely William Domville's 'A Disquisition touching that Great Question Whether an Act of Parliament made in England shall binde the Kingdome and people of Ireland without their Allowance and Acceptance of such Act in the Kingdome of Ireland' and 'A Declaration setting forth how, and by what Means, the Laws and Statutes of England, from Time to Time, came to be of force in Ireland'. The first of these had been written at the time of the Restoration

[22] Cf. Denis Donoghue's Afterword to the 1977 edition of *The Case*; Simms, *William Molyneux*, p. 104.
[23] See, for example, Keith Thomas, 'Age and Authority in Early Modern England', *Proceedings of the British Academy*, 62 (1976), p. 222.
[24] TCD, MS 890, ff. 66–155, and ff. 156–246, respectively.
[25] The printer's copy is in the hand of an amanuensis who had worked for Molyneux from the early 1690s, and was also the scribe of Molyneux's compendium of the Journals of the Irish House of Commons (TCD, MS 622). See further, Patrick Kelly, 'The Printer's Copy of the MS. of William, "The Case of Ireland's Being Bound by Acts of Parliament in England, Stated", 1698', *Long Room*, 18–19 (1979), pp. 6–13.

by Molyneux's own father-in-in-law, apparently clarifying the legislative relations between England and Ireland for the benefit of the Irish Convention which presided over the implementation of the recall of the Stuarts in Ireland.[26] The earlier Declaration was a succinct statement of the Irish parliament's independence of Westminster written in 1643, which had been the subject of an inquiry before both Houses of the Irish parliament in April 1644. The attribution to Bolton occurred in a letter from Molyneux's brother-in-law, John Madden, to the Irish non-juror Henry Dodwell in 1700, identifying the Declaration as what Molyneux had used as the basis for his 'defence of our Irish libertyes'.[27] Although the eighteenth-century publisher of the Declaration, Walter Harris, rejected Bolton as its author on the grounds that the work represented too Catholic a stance for Charles I's Protestant lord chancellor, suggesting instead Patrick Darcy on the basis of parallels with the latter's *Argument* of 1641,[28] it seems reasonable to assume that William Molyneux would, like his brother-in-law Madden, have known the Declaration as the product of Bolton's pen. However, since Domville would seem to have made use of the Declaration in preparing his own paper in 1660, it is not always easy to be certain to which of the two sources Molyneux is immediately indebted for a particular point.

Molyneux began work on what eventually turned into *The Case of Ireland* by having a copy of Domville's Disquisition transcribed for him by the amanuensis who subsequently prepared the printer's copy of *The Case*.[29] Since this copy is a somewhat modernised version of an earlier scribal copy of the Disquisition to which Molyneux already had access,[30] it may well be that Molyneux originally envisaged his contribution to the 1698 debate over Ireland's legislative independence of the English parliament as simply publishing an updated version of Domville's Disquisition.

---

[26] See Aidan Clarke, 'Colonial Constitutional Attitudes in Ireland, 1640–60', *Proceedings of the Royal Irish Academy*, 90 section C, 11 (1990), p. 363, and chapter 2 above.

[27] Though Madden's letter no longer survives, the information is provided in Dodwell's reply of 7 December 1700 (TCD, MS 1995–2008, item 741). Positive identification of the manuscript as the Declaration is provided by the phrase: 'The opinions of Hussey and my Lord Cooke were those that gave the author the occasion to write.' Cf. p. 95 below.

[28] Walter Harris (ed.), *Hibernica*: Part II. *Or Two Treatises Relating to Ireland* (Dublin, 1750), Preface. While the attribution to Darcy has recently been strongly reasserted in C. E. J. Caldicott's introduction to his reprint of *An Argument Delivered by Patrick Darcy, Esquire* [1643] in *Camden Society Miscellany*, 21 (London, 1992), pp. 217–18, views identical to those in the Declaration were actually voiced by Bolton as leader of a delegation to Charles I in 1644. While evidence might be adduced against the authorship of both Bolton and Darcy, the issue does not call for further discussion here.

[29] TCD, MS 890, ff. 45–59 (with corrections by Molyneux); this is the version of the Disquisition from which the excerpts included in *The Case* have been taken. Subsequent references are to the original pagination of this MS version.

[30] TCD, MS 890, ff. 1–17 (corrected by Domville).

He must soon have decided that this would not answer the purpose – perhaps because of the volume of English legislation affecting Ireland since the Restoration, or perhaps because he realised that there were important aspects of the matter not sufficiently covered by Domville.[31] That he finally chose not to publish the Disquisition brings up another point of importance in considering the relation between Molyneux and the sources of *The Case of Ireland*, namely the question of discontinuities as well as continuities. What Molyneux chose to discard in the arguments of these sources is from the point of the evolution of a tradition of writing on Anglo-Irish constitutional relations almost as interesting as what he chose to incorporate in his book. Furthermore, the care with which he used and reshaped these sources demonstrates that Molyneux was no mere plagiarist in producing *The Case of Ireland*.[32]

The text that sprang from Molyneux's rejection of the idea of simply publishing Domville's paper evolved as a series of accretions around a core derived from the Disquisition. After sending the work to the printer Molyneux admitted to Locke that he had written in considerable haste, and some of the later additions have certainly been rather clumsily integrated with the earlier material. An important example of such changes of mind is the way in which the original intention of addressing the work to the English parliament (indicated by the rejected title of 'An Humble Remonstrance To the parliament of England In Relation to Ireland. by W: M: of D. Esqr.' preserved in the printer's copy) was superseded by the dedication to King William. Since, as Molyneux told Locke, the dedication had been suggested by unnamed friends in Dublin, other changes may also have originated in the same way.[33]

Domville's Disquisition provided Molyneux with both the main core and the general structure of *The Case of Ireland*. That is, the account of the peaceful submission of the Irish to the 'three first *Kings* of Ireland of the *Norman Race*' (p. 56), and these rulers' reciprocal grant of English laws and customs to the Irish, together with the right to hold their own parliament; the account of English laws from Edward the Confessor to Henry

---

[31] The search for precedents in Bishop King's appeal may have been one of the factors that led Molyneux to expand on Domville. On 5 February 1697/8, King referred to the discovery of an important precedent in the form of the Prior of Llanthony's Case, TCD, MS 750/1/168–70. The account of the Llanthony case in Molyneux's pamphlet (p. 101) has been subsequently interpolated in the holograph.

[32] As tentatively asserted by R. L. Schuyler, *Parliament and the British Empire* ([1929]; reprint, London, 1963), p. 81.

[33] Molyneux to Locke, 19 April 1698; also remarking that if he still had the book in his hands, 'I could considerably amend, and add to it': *The Correspondence of John Locke*, ed. E. S. de Beer (Oxford, 1974), IV, pp. 376–7. Evidence of haste is provided by the fact that in two separate places (pp. 71 and 95) Molyneux speaks of having concluded the subject of the 'Fourth Enquiry'.

III; the re-enactment of various English statutes in Ireland in the later medieval period between the granting of Magna Chart in 9 Hen. 3 and the general re-enactment of the body of English public statutes in 10 Hen. 7; the consideration of various medieval cases relating to Ireland, and much of the final section recapitulating the earlier arguments with various additional points. In all, the material derived from the Disquisition, including both the (extensive) passages reproduced at length and the arguments more loosely based on it, amounts to well over a third of the final text of *The Case of Ireland*. While no acknowledgement is made to the Disquisition, Molyneux, however, mentioned Domville twice by name, first as the one-time owner of the copy of the Irish *Modus Tenendi parliamenta* (p. 44) and secondly as the transcriber of a confirmation of a grant of Liberties and Immunities to the Irish by Edward III (p. 124).

In places the excerpts from the Disquisition were interspersed with additional material added by Molyneux, and some of Domville's ideas have been discarded as no longer applicable. Most notable of the latter is the (by the 1690s) distinctly old-fashioned view which Domville held of the relation between king and parliament in the process of law making, where the king was seen as the active party and the parliament as more or less passively according the consent of the people.[34] Perhaps not surprisingly, Domville's references to Ireland as a conquered country, despite his demonstration that the Irish submitted voluntarily to Henry II, have also been discarded. When discussing what were the laws of England that were granted to the Irish, Molyneux inserted before Domville's specification of 'the Lawes and Customes throughout the whole Realm', what he termed 'the Great *Law of Parliaments*, which *England* so justly Challenges [i.e. claims], and all *Mankind* have a *Right* to. By [which] I mean that Law whereby all Laws receive their Sanction, [?through] *The Free Debates and Consent of the People, by Themselves or their Chosen Representatives*' (p. 58). Molyneux also updated Domville's discussion of certain subjects, as for instance in the case of the Irish *Modus Tenendi parliamenta* where Molyneux uses the Preface to his brother-in-law Bishop Dopping's edition of 1692 to refute the objections of Prynne and Selden to the document's authenticity.[35] Another highly significant development was Molyneux's assimilation of Domville's account of the initial submission and Henry's grant of English law to the language of 'Revolution

[34] 'However the Commons and Lords both of England and Ireland may . . . be both Privys and Partys to the Exercise of the Legislative Power Yet that makes them no sharers in it': Disquisition, p. 27.
[35] Anthony Dopping (ed.), *Modus Tenendi Parliamenta et Consilia in Hibernia* (Dublin, 1692). This reference was of more than theoretical significance, as the entire Irish Modus had been submitted (in manuscript) among the bishop of Derry's precedents for the appeal in the English Lords. Cf. HMC, *House of Lords MSS, 1697–99*, pp. 34–8.

Principles' by terming it 'the *Original Compact*' of the Irish polity (p. 46).[36] This concept of the establishment of English government in 1172 in this fashion as Ireland's original contract was one of Molyneux's most significant legacies for Irish political discourse in the eighteenth century. Its emotional and intellectual appeal was notably reflected in the Irish Lords' 1719 Representation to George I in defence of Ireland's jurisdictional independence, drafted by (the then) Archbishop King.[37]

The most important source on which Molyneux drew to expand on Domville's Disquisition was Bolton's Declaration, though it seems likely that he did not become acquainted with it until he had embarked on his revision of Domville. What principally commanded Molyneux's attention in the Declaration was the way it drew attention to and challenged the ambiguous views of the key legal authority on whom Domville had principally relied to corroborate the claim that Ireland was not a conquered territory and therefore not subject to the English parliament, namely the great jurist and commentator Sir Edward Coke. As well as confirming in the *Institutes* that Henry II not only had granted English laws and customs to the Irish on the occasion of his 1172 expedition but had actually given them a parliament,[38] Coke, as Bolton showed, had elsewhere expressed the quite contrary opinion that Ireland was a conquered territory with all the consequences that flowed from that fact. This embarrassing concession of Irish subordination was to be found in the account of Calvin's Case in Coke's *Seventh Report*, in a dictum referring to Chief Justice Hussey's decision in the Merchants of Waterford's Case: 'that albeit *Ireland* be a distinct dominion from *England*, yet the title thereof being by conquest, the same by judgment of law, might by express words be bound by the parliament of *England*'. Coke then went on to relate a further judgement specifying that appeals in writs of error from the King's Bench in Ireland lay to the King's Bench in England, although King John's original grant of laws to Ireland had not provided for such an appeal mechanism.[39] On this basis, others argued that Ireland's juridical subordination

---

[36] By taking 1172 as the 'original of government' in Ireland, Molyneux avoids having to consider any prior English claims to Ireland by King Arthur, the Saxon rulers, or even William the Conqueror, such as Domville raised, and as were later discussed by William Atwood in his reply to Molyneux, entitled *The History, and Reasons of the Dependency of Ireland upon the Imperial Crown of the Kingdom of England* (London, 1698), pp. 12–16, 38–9.

[37] Cf. *Lords Jnl, Ire*, II, pp. 655–6.

[38] Coke, *The Fourth Part of the Institutes of the laws of England* (1644), caps. 1 and 76.

[39] 'Declaration' in Harris, *Hibernica*, part II (London, 1750), p. 10. Cf. Coke, *La Sept Part des Reports de Sr. Edw. Coke Chivalier, chiefe Iustice del Common Bank* (1608), s.v. Calvin's Case, pp. 17v and 22v–23r. As Bishop King grimly noted (TCD, MS 2331) on the English Lords' rejection of his case, the 1689 Irish Jacobite Parliament had shown greater concern for Irish liberties as regards writs of error and appeals (cf. n.9 above) than the current English parliament.

to the English court in the matter of appeals implied *a fortiore* the legislative subordination of the Irish parliament to that of England.[40] Molyneux's response to Coke's damaging assertions in Calvin's Case called forth some of the strongest language in *The Case*. Though at first spoken of as 'a Name of great Veneration with the Gentlemen of the Long Robe', Coke was subsequently accused of having been so wholly caught up with the Common Law that he was ignorant of '*the Law of Nature and Reason*', was guilty of elementary errors in logic, and was seeking by 'the *bare Assertion* of a Judge [to] bind *a whole Nation*'. 'So that we may observe my Lord *Cook* enormously stumbling at every turn in this Point.'[41] To counteract the view of Ireland as an acquisition by conquest, the Declaration had emphasised the creation of English government in Ireland by King John in 12 John (1210–11) rather than by Henry II's grant at Lismore. For Bolton, as for Domville (and Molyneux), the succession to the Lordship of Ireland passed by way of Henry's donation to John in the parliament at Oxford in 1184: 'by this . . . *Ireland* was most eminently set apart again, as a *Separate* and *Distinct Kingdom* by itself from the Kingdom of *England*' (p. 47). This, together with the papal approval of the 1184 grant, broke the sequence of conquest and established a separate Irish polity that only fortuitously became reunited with the crown of England as a result of Richard I's having no direct heirs.[42] Though this emphasis on John's sovereignty over Ireland deriving from donation implicitly refutes John's alternative title by descent from Richard which Coke in his Report on Calvin's case argued maintained the rights of conquest acquired by Henry II, it was, in Molyneux's hands, to prove somewhat of a Trojan horse. William Atwood in *The History and Reasons, of the Dependency of Ireland upon the Imperial Crown of England, Rectifying Mr Molineux's State of the Case of Ireland . . .* (1698) gleefully seized on the fact that the donation to John in 1184 had been made in parliament to argue that on Molyneux's own admission the English parliament must have been involved in the original settlement of Ireland, since Henry assumed that its consent was required to alienate Ireland to his youngest son. 'Here's a parliamentary and co-temporary Exposition of what this

[40] Though Barbara Black's illuminating 'The Constitution of Empire: The Case for the Colonists', *University of Pennsylvania Law Review*, 124 (1976), pp. 1178–84, shows that Coke was less concerned with demonstrating Ireland's subjection to the English legislature than a first reading of the excerpt suggests, Bolton and Molyneux read the passage in terms made all the starker by Coke's support elsewhere for Ireland's case.

[41] *Case of Ireland*, pp. 95–9. The Declaration's comment (Harris, *Hibernica*, pt II, p. 20) is more restrained: 'although he [Coke] was exceeding well learned, and a great honour and light to the laws of *England*, yet he was in this particular exceedingly mistaken'.

[42] Molyneux must have been unaware of the convincing refutation of this claim as to John's title, independent of the succession through Richard, in the contemporary manuscript reply to the Declaration by Serjeant Mayart (printed in Harris, *Hibernica*, pt II, pp. 25–9).

Gentleman [Molyneux] calls the *Original Compact* between *England* and *Ireland*.'[43] The only other substantial contribution which the Declaration provided to Molyneux was in relation to Irish re-enactments of English Tudor and Stuart legislation from the Reformation to 1640, a period in which there was an enormous range of precedents of re-enacting English statutes, including some which specifically sought to bind Ireland by name.[44]

If Domville's Disquisition and Bolton's Declaration were the main – if unacknowledged – sources on which Molyneux drew in the composition of *The Case of Ireland*, the most clearly indicated source of the book is Locke's *Second Treatise* on the subject of Conquest – a debt which Molyneux warmly acknowledged to 'an Incomparable *Treatise* . . . said to be written by my Excellent Friend, JOHN LOCKE, Esq. . . . [which] the Greatest Genius in *Christendom* need not disown it' (p. 39). Whether Locke would have been so pleased with Molyneux's indiscreet revelation of what was one of his most carefully guarded secrets (despite the subsequently interpolated qualifier 'Whether it be so or not, I know not') may well be doubted.[45] The material on conquest derived from chapter 16 of Locke's *Second Treatise* enabled Molyneux to deal with the third of the questions which he posed at the beginning of *The Case*, namely what title the conquest of Ireland (had there actually been one) would convey to England, in terms of rights over the inhabitants.[46] From this he is able to show that even a just conqueror obtained very limited rights over the property of the conquered, and none over their innocent wives and children, still less any rights over 'those who *Conquered with him*'. Furthermore, Locke provided the key to understanding what commentators have perhaps found the most puzzling allusion to conquest in *The Case*, namely the reference to the majority of the inhabitants of Ireland being 'the Progeny of the *English* and *Britains*' (pp. 34–5). A similar claim in *Second Treatise*, section 177, in relation to the rights of the descendants of the Normans who accompanied William the Conqueror, showed that Molyneux's statement, far from seeking to reduce the significance of the native Irish element in the population (as some commentators would

[43] Although Domville and Molyneux eschewed all reference to the papal donations of Ireland to either Henry or John, the Declaration (*ibid.*, p. 18) evinced no such embarrassment. The staunchly Whig Atwood accommodated the papal donation to John by assimilating it to the *ius gentium* of the medieval period, thus avoiding any taint of relying on 'Popery'. See *Dependency of Ireland*, pp. 35–6 and chapter 11 below.

[44] *The Case*, 68–70. Cf. Declaration (Harris, *Hibernica*, pt II, pp. 9–10).

[45] See further p. 104 below. This divergence of views does not seem to have marred the meeting that took place between Locke and Molyneux in the late summer of 1698.

[46] The previous question as to whether Henry II's expedition, or any subsequent suppression of rebellions in Ireland, properly constituted a '*Conquest*' of Ireland is considered below, pp. 101-2.

have it), established rather that no one was in a position to contradict anybody in Ireland who wished to claim the rights of Englishmen on the basis of descent from the original conquerors.[47] Locke was also subsequently extensively cited (though without acknowledgement) on the fundamental natural law right to consent to legislation, without which people are essentially slaves, and on the purposes for which society and government were originally established.[48] Molyneux's most significant expansion on Locke was his reinterpretation of the natural right of individuals to be governed only by laws to which they have given their consent as conferring a similar right on communities, which means that no nation has a right to dominate another. Locke also perhaps provided Molyneux with the inspiration for the model of the relations between England and Ireland as those between elder and younger brother, though the additional notion of the sovereign as father acting as umpire to protect the rights of the younger, which Molyneux invokes in his dedication to the king, was indubitably Molyneux's own.[49] Finally the objection that the consequence of the power to impose laws without consent will be the imposition of taxation without consent, draws on *Treatises*, II, sections 139–40. However, Molyneux was considerably more outspoken than Locke in asserting that 'To *Tax* me without Consent is little better . . . than *down-right Robbing me*', though he prefaced this claim with a restatement of Locke's famous definition of property, in the form: 'Whatever another may *Rightfully* take from me *without my Consent*, I have certainly no *Property* in' (pp. 129–30).[50]

The use of the extremely varied other sources of *The Case* need not detain us long. In all Molyneux cited over forty different sources, but these are generally drawn on for specific points of detail, sometimes in rather a cavalier fashion.[51] One such instance was the reference to

47 Simms, *William Molyneux*, pp. 105–6, speaks of this 'extraordinary statement . . . [which] apparently relegated the greater part of the population to the category of non-persons'. See also Jacqueline R. Hill, 'Ireland without Union: Molyneux and His Legacy' in John Robertson (ed.), *A Union for Empire: Political Thought and the British Union of 1707* (Cambridge, 1995), pp. 280–1. John Locke, *Two Treatises of Government*, ed. Peter Laslett (Cambridge, 1960), II, p. 178, further claims that generally 'the Conquerers and Conquered . . . incorporate into one People, under the same Laws and Freedom'.
48 Cf. *Case*, pp. 78, 93–4 and 116–17. The second passage synopsises *Treatises*, II, section 4.
49 Cf. *Treatises*, II, section 202.
50 Cf. *Treatises*, II, section 138. Atwood's *Dependency of Ireland*, pp. 207–8, indignantly repudiated the suggestion of the English parliament's taxing Ireland. However, Serjeant Mayart's 1644 answer to the Declaration had not only argued for England's right to tax Ireland, but actually asserted that the English parliament was better placed to decide on Ireland's legislative needs than the Irish (Harris, *Hibernica*, pt II, pp. 77, 108–9), a claim made, however, in the context of the alleged involvement of Irish Catholic Members of Parliament in the 1641 Rebellion.
51 Cf. 'List of works cited . . .' in Simms (ed.), *Case*, appendix C; it is not, however, exhaustive.

William Petyt's *The Ancient Right of the Commons Asserted . . .* (1680) on pp. 53–5, where, despite referring to the recent English controversy over the presence of the Commons in parliament before 49 Henry 3, Molyneux ignored its implications, and simply mined a specific point supporting his argument for the antiquity of parliament in the Irish constitution. Similarly, in his use of William Prynne's *Brief Animadversions on . . . the Fourth Part of the Institutes . . . Compiled by Sir Edward Cooke* (1669) on p. 58, Molyneux deliberately exploited an ambiguous reference to Henry II's holding a parliament in Ireland, while ignoring Prynne's explicit denial of his having done so elsewhere.[52]

One thing, however, that clearly emerges from the detailed consideration of Molyneux's use of sources in *The Case of Ireland* is that, contrary to what is so frequently and confidently asserted, there is not the slightest evidence that Molyneux incurred any debt whatsoever to the mid-seventeenth-century work by Patrick Darcy, entitled *An Argument Delivered by Patrick Darcy, Esquire; By the Express Order of the House of Commons in the parliament of Ireland, 9 Iunii, 1641* (Waterford, 1643). For a start the subject with which Molyneux dealt, namely Ireland's legislative independence of the English parliament, was only a small part of what Darcy considered in his *Argument* (although it did indeed constitute the first of the questions to which he provided replies). There was very little overlap in terms of statutes or cases cited by the two works; for example, in relation to appeals in writs of error to the King's Bench in England, Darcy cited Stafford v. Stafford, where Molyneux cited that of 'one Kelly'.[53] The only case rehearsed by both writers would appear to be Calvin's case, though Darcy referred to it only in an extremely general fashion by contrast with Molyneux's extended discussion of its unwelcome implications, as spelled out in Coke's *Seventh Report*.[54] Even in the instance of the so-called 'missing statutes' from the later medieval period (statutes for which parliament rolls did not survive but which were believed to have been enacted), of which Darcy's recent editor C. E. J. Caldicott makes so much, Molyneux and Darcy cited largely different statutes by way of example. As to the two instances, where they coincided, Molyneux's remarks, far from being a paraphrase of Darcy as Caldicott

---

[52] *Animadversions*, p. 259, denies the existence of parliaments in Ireland before Edward I's reign, mentioning in parenthesis 'except that of King Henry the 2nd aforementioned'. Turning to p. 249 we learn that Prynne actually rejects the claim that Henry held a parliament in Ireland as 'a fabulous untruth'.

[53] Molyneux's source for the Kelly case is an anonymous late seventeenth-century paper, entitled 'That the Legislative Power in Ireland doth belong to the King by the Advice of his Parliament of Ireland, not of his Parliament of England' in the Molyneux Papers (TCD, MS 888/1, ff.127–30), from which he also derives the information on pp. 83–4 on Irish parliamentary representatives in England in the Middle Ages.

[54] *Camden Miscellany*, 31, p. 271. Cf. p. 95 above.

would have it, were a direct citation from an editorial comment in Bolton's pioneering 1621 edition of the Irish Statutes.[55]

III

Lest the discussion of the material in *The Case of Ireland* derived from earlier sources create the impression that Molyneux contributed little of his own to the ideas in the book, it is desirable to speak briefly of the new elements which he himself introduced. Most obvious was the consideration of the implications of England's legislating for Ireland in the post-Restoration period, with rather different ramifications for pre- and post-Revolution statutes. Much of the former was commercial legislation such as the Navigation Acts or Cattle Acts, where Molyneux was able to suggest that Ireland was no more affected than foreign countries like France (pp. 87–8). Yet he claimed that the Restoration land settlement legislation in Ireland revoked the English Adventurers' Act of 1642 purporting to dispose of Irish estates to those who would put up money for the reconquest of Ireland (p. 85).[56] The legislation from 1689 onwards was a rather different matter, particularly the decision of the Convention in choosing a new sovereign for England and thereby actually determining who was sovereign of Ireland – a point subsequently made much of by William Atwood.[57] Even in relation to legislation specifically affecting Ireland, effective rebuttals were hard to find. Molyneux's attempts to explain away the powers that the Convention parliament exercised over Ireland by reference to the impossibility of holding an Irish parliament during the Jacobite war, together with a strained notion of what might be called 'virtual consent' conferred by the agreement of the Anglo-Irish refugees in London in the absence of a formal parliament (pp. 90–2), rang fairly hollow.[58] His handling of these issues was strongly criticised by Bishop King in a letter to Francis Annesley on the publication of *The Case*,[59] and formed the main burden of the objections in Charles Leslie's

[55] Richard Bolton (ed.), *The statutes of Ireland, beginning the 3rd yeare of k. Edward III untill the … 13th yeare of k. James I* (Dublin, 1621), p. 67. Bolton's comment is also referred to in Serjeant Mayart's Answer (Harris, *Hibernica*, pt II, p. 91).
[56] Simon Clement's *Answer to Mr. Molyneux …* (1698), pp. 85–6 would, however, seem to be correct in denying Molyneux's assertion that the Irish legislation repealed the Adventurers' Acts.   [57] *Dependency of Ireland*, Dedication, and pp. 78–81, 91–3, 108–9.
[58] Interestingly Molyneux made no reference to the current dispute over the Irish Parliament's amending part of the English 1696 Act for the Better Security of the Royal Person and Government (the Act following the 1696 assassination attempt on William) in the 1697 session, which roused such anger in England and would be considered by the Commons Committee appointed to examine Molyneux's *Case* in May 1698. See further, 'The Minutebook of James Courthope', *Camden Miscellany*, 20 (London, 1953), pt 3, pp. 47–51, and *Commons Jnl, Eng*, XII, pp. 326–37.
[59] King to Annesley, 16 April 1698, TCD, MS 750/1/232–3.

Considerations of Importance to Ireland: in a Letter to a Member of parliament there upon Occasion of Mr Molyneux's . . . Case of Ireland . . . [?1699]. Ultimately, Molyneux found himself driven back on the rhetorical device of demanding: 'And shall *Proceedings only of Thirty-Seven Years standing,* be urg'd against a Nation to Deprive them of the *Rights* and *Liberties* which they Enjoy'd for Five Hundred Years before, and which were Invaded . . . against their *Consent*, and from that day to this have been constantly complain'd of? Let any English Heart that stands so *Justly* in Vindication of his own *Rights* and *Liberties*, answer this Question' (p. 88). Unfortunately the English parliament proved deaf to such an appeal, and this passage too was among those specifically singled out for condemnation by the House of Commons.

Perhaps more significant than the specific material dealing with the problems posed by English post-Restoration legislation was Molyneux's general recasting of the 'conquest' question, which has been briefly alluded to in considering his debt to Locke. Relying on the feudal theory that territory could only be acquired by conquest or descent, English writers had exploited the inherent ambiguity to claim that Henry II's acquisition of the country had made the Irish entirely subject to his will, as following a military conquest. By defining *'Conquest'* as *'an Acquisition . . . by Force of Arms to which, Force has likewise been Opposed'* (p. 30), and demonstrating from history that the Irish princes' submission was voluntary, Molyneux was able to counter this claim and show that Henry had granted the Irish the same rights and freedoms as Englishmen, including their own parliament. Not surprisingly this definition of *'Conquest'* was also among the passages censured by the English Commons in June 1698. Nor was Molyneux prepared to accept the new concept put forward in the later seventeenth century that territory might be acquired by colonisation or 'plantation', in addition to descent or conquest, a view argued by the counsel for the Irish Society in the bishop of Derry's appeal.[60] He was adamant that Ireland was no mere colony of England, subject to the English parliament on the model of a Roman province. 'Of all the Objections Raised against us, I take this to be the most Extravagant; it seems to have the least *Foundation* or *Colour* from *Reason* or *Record*: Does it not manifestly appear by the *Constitution* of Ireland, that 'tis a *Compleat Kingdom* within itself?' (p. 115).

This extended consideration of 'conquest', under which Molyneux also rejected the notion that the English parliament has somehow or other 'purchased' Ireland by paying for the suppression of rebellions there (pp. 112–14), brought in the third element in the disclaimer in the Preface to the Reader, namely the issue of forfeited estates. In the late 1690s

---

[60] Shower, *Cases in Parliament*, p. 80.

conquest was not merely a matter of historical precedent determining whether Ireland was a free country (p. 30), nor simply of relevance to the English debate over allegiance to William and Mary that had led to the condemnation of Bishop Burnet's *Pastoral Letter* in 1692 (p. 33). In Irish terms, the implicit question raised by conquest was whether as participants in the reconquest of Ireland in 1689–91 the two Houses of the English parliament had the right to determine what should happen to the forfeited estates of the Jacobites. This had been an issue immediately following the war, when it was raised in the English House of Commons early in 1693, but though the view had been expressed that the forfeited estates should go towards paying for the costs of reconquering Ireland, nothing had been done and William had disposed of them himself, partly in grants to foreign favourites and English ministers.[61] The Irish forfeitures issue, along with grants to Portland and Somers in England, was seen as a further means of attacking the Whig Junto. Since many of William's grants had been sold on, or leased, to bona fide Anglo-Irish purchasers, the question of a possible resumption by an English Act of parliament was extremely topical.[62]

The other main area in which Molyneux innovated was in his dual monarchy model for the relations between England and Ireland, an archetype which has been taken as indicating a failure on Molyneux's part to realise the implications of the transfer of sovereignty in England to the king in parliament brought about by the Revolution settlement, especially in the Bill of Rights and the new coronation oath. Given Molyneux's reliance on the significance of Poynings' Law in defining the constitutional relations between England and Ireland, there is a case for seeing his dual monarchy model as intended not so much as a description of the actual constitutional relations between England and Ireland but rather as a normative statement that sought to reject the implications for Ireland of the changed relations between king and parliament in England effected by the Revolution: '*Ireland*, tho' Annex'd to the Crown of *England*, has always been look'd upon to be a *Kingdom Compleat within itself*, and to have all Jurisdiction to an *Absolute* Kingdom belonging, and Subordinate to no Legislative Authority on Earth' (p. 103).[63] As Molyneux remarked on p. 38 in relation to his discussion of the rights of conquest, 'But we Enquire not now, what is the *Practice*, but what *Right there is to do so*.'

---

[61] Molyneux had been nominated a Commissioner for Forfeitures in 1692, though he denied that he had ever acted in this capacity; Simms, *William Molyneux*, p. 93.

[62] An English Act of Resumption affecting Ireland was passed in 1700. The prolonged and bitter clash between the English Lords and Commons over its terms in April 1700 brought about the final collapse of the Junto with Somers' dismissal for the Lord Chancellorship: Henry Horwitz, *Parliament, Policy and Politics* (Manchester, 1977), pp. 262–70.   [63] This extract was also subsequently censured by the English Commons.

Molyneux's seeming purpose was to establish the rights of the Irish constitution with regard to legislation by the English parliament, even if these
could not be immediately asserted. Such an understanding was subsequently advanced by Archbishop King in the renewed 1719–20 conflict
over the jurisdictional independence of the Irish parliament, arising out of
the Annesley case. Discussing the English parliament's probable reaction
to the Representation which the Irish House of Lords had addressed to
George I, setting forth the rights of the Irish constitution, King wrote to
the Irish peer Lord Southwell: 'Whatever the consequence I think it fit to
put it to an issue . . . and our claim will remain upon record, and tho' over-
borne at present . . . may serve instead when more favourable circumstances happen.'[64]

IV

The earliest reference to the appearance of *The Case* occurred in a letter of
16 April 1698 from Bishop King to Francis Annesley, an Anglo-Irish
lawyer in London, who was managing his response to the Irish Society's
appeal to the House of Lords. King expressed astonishment at
Molyneux's having produced the book, which he described as inopp or-
tune in its timing, likely to provoke further difficulties with England (particularly with regard to his own case before the Lords), and making
concessions in relation to post-Restoration legislation affecting Ireland
that King felt highly injudicious.[65] King also broached to Annesley in a
somewhat shamefaced fashion the fact that he had promised to obtain
Annesley's help in presenting the book to King William, though he again
had strong misgivings about the effect this might have in London.
Although Molyneux had actually gone as far as to have a special issue
printed for dissemination in London, bearing the imprint of Locke's
London publishers, Awnsham and John Churchill, any question of a
formal presentation to William was dropped. Meanwhile opponents of
Irish interests were reported to be making strenuous efforts in London to
obtain a copy of the book, either to persuade the king to proceed directly
against Molyneux, or to bring *The Case of Ireland* before the English
Commons and have the author punished, or even impeached.
Molyneux's most effective protectors were the Irish Lord Chancellor,
John Methuen, and his old college friend Robert Molesworth, both of

[64] King to Southwell, 8 January 1719/20 (TCD, MS 750/5/ 242–5); on 2 January 1719/20 he
had expressed similar views to Molyneux's son Samuel, implying that what was needed to
assert Irish rights was an expanded version of his father's book (*ibid.*, 238–9).
[65] On the immediate reaction to *The Case*, see Kelly, 'Irish Woollen Prohibition Act', pp.
36–8.

whom sat in the English House of Commons. While Methuen's concerns were perhaps more influenced by a desire to save the compromise arrangements that he had made with the moderates to prevent the passage of the Irish woollens bill through the Lords, his letters to the Irish governor Lord Galway also expressed personal concern for Molyneux, tinged with a certain exasperation: 'being satisfied he had no ill intention, although I must always say that the worst enemy of Ireland could by no way have done us so much mischief'. The best way to protect Molyneux seemed to be to forestall the enemies of the book by presenting it to the Commons himself, which was done with the approval of the king on 21 May. These events and the subsequent proceedings before the English Commons bring out how intensely political the publication of the work turned out to be, and in ways that the author probably never envisaged. From an initial context of the struggle between the government and opposition over Irish woollens at the beginning of the 1697–8 session, the woollens question and Irish matters generally soon became an issue within government, as part of the tensions which opened up, following the ending of the Nine Years War, between William and the Whig Junto. By May 1698 it was the Junto who were determined to proceed against Irish interests despite the sympathy which the king felt for his Irish subjects. Like the Standing Army issue, Irish woollens were a matter on which the Junto turned out to be both ideologically and electorally vulnerable. Somers and his supporters Edward Clarke and Walter Yonge, as we have already seen, were closely linked with West Country and Essex interests determined to destroy the Irish woollens export industry. Several sources indicate the leading role taken by Clarke against Molyneux's *Case*, a particular irony in that this close friend of John Locke had been responsible for originally recommending Molyneux to Methuen at Locke's request in April 1697. Moreover, Locke's rather cryptic reaction to an assurance from Clarke that he would not be dragged into the matter suggests he too had little sympathy with Molyneux's views.[66]

The deliberations of the Committee to which the book was referred resulted in a Commons' Resolution of 27 June 1698 condemning Molyneux's book 'as of dangerous Consequence to the Crown and People of *England*, by denying the Authority of the King and Parliament of *England*, to bind the Kingdom and People of *Ireland*'. This in turn led

[66] The relevant letter from Clarke does not survive, but Locke's reply of 30 May 1698 reads: 'I thank you for the care you promise me to take that I receive no inconvenience by the indiscretion of a man which mightily surprised me. But as there is no fence against other people's folly, so I think nobody is to answer for other people's follies but they themselves', *Locke Correspondence*, VI, p. 410.

to an Address to the king referring to 'the bold and pernicious Assertions' and 'dangerous Positions contained in the said Book'. However, the main thrust of the Address was directed at the Irish parliament's 1697 amendments to the English 'Act for the better Security of the Royal Person and Government', which were interpreted as evidence of a broader desire 'to shake off [Irish] Subjection to, and Dependence on this Kingdom'. While no reference was made to Molyneux personally, William was called on to 'prevent any thing of the like Nature for the future, and the pernicious Consequences of what is past, by punishing and discountenancing those who have been guilty thereof'.[67] Also involved in the Committee's Report had been the earlier singling out of thirty-two passages from *The Case* as particularly 'tend[ing] to the disowning and denying the Authority of the parliament of *England* over *Ireland*'. These varied from Molyneux's formulation of his intention in writing the work ('How far the parliament of *England* may think it reasonable to intermeddle with the Affairs of *Ireland*, and bind us up by Laws made in their House'), to the definition of Conquest as 'an Acquisition of a Kingdom by Force of Arms, to which Force has likewise been opposed', to the suggestion that virtually everybody in Ireland could claim the freedoms of Englishmen on the basis of descent, to the claim that the Irish Restoration land settlement legislation (the Acts of Settlement and Explanation) had set aside the English Adventurers' Act of 1642, to the extract from the 1541 Irish Act establishing Henry VIII's title as king of Ireland, to Molyneux's concluding assertion that ill treatment by the English parliament might drive the Irish 'into Discontent'.[68] This general hostility towards Ireland was reinforced by another Address calling on the king to take the necessary steps to restrict the export of Irish woollens, which reiterated a similar call from the Lords.[69]

V

What has been said demonstrates both Molyneux's unacknowledged debt to earlier writers on the question of Ireland's legislative independence and the extent to which *The Case of Ireland* related to specific aspects of Anglo-Irish relations in 1698. From the point of view of the development of Molyneux's role as the *fons et origo* of the eighteenth-century tradition starting from 1719, the fact that Molyneux deliberately chose to conceal his continuity with the earlier tradition was of considerable importance. The reasons why he should have wished to do so are by

---

[67] *Commons Jnl, Eng*, XII, pp. 331, 337 (27, 30 June 1698). However, no subsequent action was taken against Molyneux.   [68] *Ibid.*, pp. 324–6 (23 June 1698).
[69] *Ibid.*, p. 338; *Lords Jnl, Eng*, XVI, p. 314.

no means obvious; neither the suggestion that he was influenced by the tradition of repudiating any debt to his predecessors along the lines of the great seventeenth-century scientific writers such as Galileo, Bacon and Descartes whom he lauded in his 1694 autobiography, nor the fear of appearing to draw on a tradition that was as much Catholic as Protestant carry much conviction. Molyneux's opting for such an occlusion of the earlier tradition nonetheless created an effective caesura between the political thought of pre- and post-Revolution Ireland. Even when the writings of the earlier seventeenth century became available with the publication of Harris' *Hibernia* in 1749–50 and the republication of Darcy's *Argument* in 1764, these texts (and others published later) seem to have been viewed as items of antiquarian interest rather than as part of a living tradition. The manner in which Molyneux had been taken up from 1719 onwards was too firmly established as a new beginning for his pre-Revolution predecessors to achieve their proper recognition. If to a few members of later generations Molyneux appeared too timid and deferential in his dealings with the English parliament – to Charles Lucas for his dependence on Poynings' Act; to an anonymous scribbler on a copy of the 1770 edition now in the Royal Irish Academy, for the submissive tone which the opening pages of *The Case* adopted towards the English parliament; and to the editor of the 1782 edition, for describing the prospect of Union with Britain 'as an Happiness we can hardly hope for' – for others as late as the early nineteenth century Molyneux still had a radical appeal (rather greater than what his actual views probably justified).[70] In the Belfast celebrations of the first and second anniversaries of the Fall of the Bastille, Molyneux was honoured along with his friend John Locke; Wolfe Tone claimed that Molyneux provided him with the salutary lesson that the root cause of all of Ireland's ills was her connection with England, while as late as 1820 the name 'W. Molyneux' seemed to one anonymous writer the most fitting pseudonym to launch a radical broadside even in England.[71] Indeed, the number of similar claims for the later eighteenth and early nineteenth centuries are such that the 1779 pamphlet which described *The Case of Ireland* as 'the Manual of Irish Liberty' can scarcely be accused of exaggeration.[72]

---

[70] Kelly, 'Spirit of Liberty', pp. 144–5.
[71] Cf. *The Constitutional Mirror*, a broadsheet of *c*.1820, signed 'W. Molineux'.
[72] *The Alarm, or the Irish Spy. In a Series of Letters on the Present State of the Affairs of Ireland ...* (1779), p. 53.

5   Political ideas and their social contexts in seventeenth-century Ireland

Raymond Gillespie

Historians who have examined political ideas in seventeenth-century Ireland have, in the main, adopted one of two approaches to the subject. There have been a number of studies of individuals who were the authors of carefully crafted and articulated systems of political thought. The position of William Molyneux on the vexed problem of Anglo-Irish relations in the 1690s, for instance, has been analysed from a number of perspectives.[1] In other instances, historians have studied the ideas of entire groups of people, usually, as for example with the New English or native Irish, defined on an ethnic basis using the analytic tool of the 'mind set'.[2] While each of these historical approaches is useful they exhibit two main weaknesses. The first concentrates on the ideas of an elite of conscious 'political thinkers' and the second fails to recognise the enormous diversity of political ideas that existed within what appear to be cohesive ethnic groups. In the 1640s, for example, many but by no means all of the native Irish sported royalist sympathies. A minority, including one group in Limerick, called for the creation of a 'free state of themselves as they had in Holland'.[3] Others in 1642 understood the idea of kingship as a re-creation of an older system of lordship, with some in Cavan crying 'God save king O'Reilly' and others in Tyrone declaring that Sir Phelim O'Neill, the leader of the rising, would be king.[4] Ideas about political life and organisation were, in reality, diffuse and readily encountered, not confined to the tracts created by a political or intellectual elite of the seventeenth century. This does not imply that the vast bulk of those who lived in seventeenth-century Ireland meditated daily on forms of

---

[1] For example, J. G. Simms, *William Molyneux of Dublin* (Dublin, 1982); J. R. Hill, 'Ireland without Union: Molyneux and His Legacy' in John Robertson (ed.), *A Union for Empire* (Cambridge, 1995), pp. 271–96.

[2] For example, Nicholas Canny, 'The Formation of the Irish Mind', *Past and Present*, 95 (1982), pp. 91–116; Nicholas Canny, 'Edmund Spenser and the Development of an Anglo-Irish Identity', *Yearbook of English Studies*, 13 (1983), pp. 1–19.

[3] TCD, MS 829, f. 310v.

[4] TCD, MS 832, ff. 102v, 113, 118; MS 834, ff. 57v, 58, 81; MS 835, f. 13; MS 839, f. 6v; MS 836, ff. 57v, 72.

government or had sophisticated abstract or philosophical notions at their disposal for the analysis of political ideas, since clearly they did not. They did, however, have a political vocabulary that defined the nature of the political community and what might, or might not, go on in it.

I

The interpretation of 'political thought' not as the development of articulated philosophical systems or definitions of ethnic identity – although both are important attributes of political ideology – but rather as a socially and culturally based phenomenon raises questions about the nature and role of political thought in seventeenth-century Ireland. Within the Irish social system political thought might be best understood as a series of conceptual maps or sets of symbols through which contemporaries tried to make sense of the events in the political world around them.[5] Each mental map does not have to be seen as totally integrated and thus may have many culs-de-sac and unexplored routes. Nor were these socially constructed maps consulted daily. Rather, when the political perceptions that underpinned accepted configurations of ideas were placed under strain, contemporaries scrutinised those assumptions more carefully to find a way out of their difficulties, either by looking more carefully at the course of the major routeways or by exploring some of the less travelled byways which posed challenges to social self-definition.

The strains to which the varying systems of political ideas were exposed varied a great deal. On the one hand there were large communal strains, such as the crises of the 1640s or the 1680s; while, on the other, more personal pressures emerged under which individuals were forced to clarify their assumptions about the political world. The outbreak of war in Ireland in October 1641, for instance, forced many of the insurgents to consider why they were at war and towards what aim their efforts were directed. Many expressed their positions in the language of kingship. Settlers, who later gave evidence about what they heard rebels say, repeatedly recalled that their captors justified their actions with references to the king's support. They were less specific about what the idea of kingship actually meant to the rebels. Clearly, for many, kingship proved a rather ill-formed concept and where the reality differed from their perception the differences were massaged through the use of rumour, especially the speculation that the king had become Catholic.[6] In other instances internal

---

[5] What follows has been much influenced by Clifford Geertz, 'Ideology as a Cultural System' in his *The Interpretation of Cultures* (London, 1993), pp. 193–233.

[6] For the importance of rumour, Raymond Gillespie, 'Destabilising Ulster, 1641–2' in Brian Mac Cuarta (ed.), *Ulster 1641: Aspects of the Rising* (Belfast, 1993), pp. 112–16.

tensions such as that produced by the crown's ambigious religious position were simply left unresolved. Such political ideas were formulated to be workable, not intellectually tidy. Nevertheless their royalism was genuine and should not be explained away, although at least one Limerick deponent tried to do so in 1642, claiming that 'they [the rebels] then but made use of the king's name for their own ends'.[7] The origins of such popular royalism need to be given more careful consideration.[8]

The closest contact that many of these insurgents had with the sovereign was through the common law processes of the early seventeenth century. The idea of the monarch as a source of all authority was known through such ephemeral documents as proclamations and writs and witnessing the proceedings of the manorial and other courts which used formulations such as 'the king's peace'.[9] There is evidence that at least one man in the 1640s acquired the formal language of politics from the ephemera of government. A letter from Ireland published in London in 1643 recorded that

there was a friar taken in the last expedition unto Connacht about whom was found a collection of all your votes, ordinances and declarations in England, very carefully perused and marked with short marginal notes by him and out of them a large manuscript entitled 'An apology of the Catholics of Ireland . . .' in truth so unhappily penned and with so little variation of language that but for the alteration of Ireland for England and some great persons of this kingdom in the places of some named by you, your clerk would hardly know it from one of your own declarations.[10]

It seems highly likely that the crisis of the 1640s linked these rather vague notions of kingship with the more generalised idea of monarchy articulated by the elite at war in the 1640s.

The same sort of focusing of attention on a specific issue generated by circumstances is also evident in the response of some of the settlers to the outbreak of war in England in August 1642 and the ensuing Irish cessation of hostilities in September 1643. The practical outworkings of this are well known. Murrough O'Brien, Lord Inchiquin, defected to

---

[7] TCD, MS 829, f. 352v.
[8] For elite royalism, Breandán Ó Buachalla, 'James Our True King: The Ideology of Irish Royalism in the Seventeenth Century' in D. G. Boyce, Robert Eccleshall and Vincent Geoghegan (eds.), *Political Thought in Ireland since the Seventeenth Century* (London, 1993), pp. 7–35.
[9] For the importance of the manor court, Raymond Gillespie, 'A Manor Court in Seventeenth-Century Ireland', *Irish Economic and Social History*, 25 (1998), pp. 81–7. This idea is developed further in Raymond Gillespie, 'Negotiating Order in Early Seventeenth-Century Ireland' in M. J. Braddick and John Walter (eds.), *Order, Hierarchy and Subordination in Early Modern Britain* (Cambridge, forthcoming).
[10] *A letter from a Protestant in Ireland to a member of the House of Commons of England* ([n.p., 1643]), p. 5.

parliament and a split emerged between the settler forces and Robert Munro, commander of the Scottish forces, in Ulster. These developments also contained an ideological component. In 1643 two tracts emanated from some settlers in Ireland arguing for a political system rather different from that which had been seen previously. The first – an unpublished text – was prepared as a briefing note for the Irish settler commissioners at Oxford who wanted to ensure that their interests with the king should not be neglected in negotiations with the Confederates.[11] The second was the 'Declaration' often ascribed to Patrick Darcy.[12] However, to judge from its appeal to biblical authority, not present in Darcy's earlier work, it probably comes from a Protestant source.

These tracts argued a position which had been previously expressed by a number of Old English politicians, that Ireland was a separate and distinct kingdom and that the Westminster parliament had no authority to legislate for Irish affairs. The first tract relied heavily on historical arguments for its rationale and the second on legal precedents. From the context of 1643 the logic of this position seems clear. At least some of the Irish settlers feared the intervention of a London Parliament in Irish affairs, as was, in effect, occurring in Ulster. The political and economic impact of this, especially the implementation of the land redistribution implied by the Adventurers' Act of 1642, would have significantly altered the balance of power in Ireland, an occurrence which some of the existing colonial elite wished to prevent. This prompted some settlers to explore a set of political ideas concerning the relationship of the English and Irish parliaments which they had been hitherto unwilling to examine.

The periods of tension that generated new conceptual maps of Irish political ideology were not only experienced communally. Individuals too encountered challenges that helped them reshape their ideas. These, in turn, fed into a wider communal pool of ideological possibilities. In September 1678 Henry Jones, the Church of Ireland bishop of Meath and former Cromwellian governor of Ireland, preached the funeral sermon for James Margretson, the late Church of Ireland archbishop of Armagh, in Christ Church, Dublin. In 1679 he published the sermon, adding to it a brief biography of Margretson and a rebuttal of accusations made against the late archbishop. One of these accusations suggested that Margretson had spent most of his considerable fortune in England. 'Yet is there that', Jones observed, 'what is objected for a crime; that in England he laid out what he had acquired in Ireland and not there rather where he had it.'[13] In

[11] Bodl., Carte MS 13, f. 213.
[12] Printed in Walter Harris (ed.), *Hibernica* (2 vols., Dublin, 1770), II, pp. 9–45. Also see chapters 2 and 4 above.
[13] Henry Jones, *A sermon at the funeral of James Margretson, D. D. Late Arch-Bishop of Armagh and Primate of Ireland* (London, 1679).

the atmosphere of 1679 this proved a highly emotive subject, for the relationship between the English and Irish Exchequers was a topic for debate. The growing prosperity of Ireland in the later seventeenth century had led to secret subventions being made to Charles II.[14] Moreover, the legislative framework being used for the extension of English control in the West Indies in the 1670s was based on Poynings' Law in Ireland, hence emphasising the colonial relationship of Ireland and England.[15] The subtext of this debate was clear, if as yet not very well articulated in Ireland. It concerned the respective rights of the English and Irish parliaments. The Cattle Acts of the 1660s and the Navigation Acts, passed between 1651 and 1681, had all laid out the claim of the English parliament to legislate for Ireland. However, the Irish parliament, despite the best efforts of the duke of Ormond, did not meet between 1666 and 1692. Consequently its theoretical sense of its role remained poorly developed. Certainly at Margretson's funeral Jones, normally a pragmatist, had no alternative but to formulate a political response and replied by stressing the fact that Margretson had spent £10,000 in Ireland. Forced to justify why Margretson had invested so heavily in England, Jones defended him by asking were 'not his considerations prudent and provident', since a rebellion on the scale of that of the 1640s might happen again.[16] Thus Jones' personal experience of having to defend his former colleague's action, combined with his recognition of the dangers of Ireland as colony, prompted his formulation of a political idea about the respective importance of England and Ireland. Though not a 'political thinker' he did have to consider political ideas when they appeared in particular circumstances.

II

These examples suggest that political sentiments in seventeenth-century Ireland were more contingent and fluctuating than the world of elite treatises might suggest. Crises, both communal and personal, in assumptions about the way in which the political world worked required the formulation of new ideological maps to negotiate difficulties. Political ideas were reworked to provide new models for the way in which the world might make sense. However these novel formulations did not suddenly materialise. There was considerable cross-fertilisation between different interest groups. In some instances native Irish at a comparatively low level in the

---

[14] Sean Egan, 'Finance and the Government of Ireland, 1660–85' (PhD thesis, Trinity College Dublin, 1983). Also see chapter 10 below.
[15] *Cal SP Colonial, 1669–74*, p. 545; *Cal SP Colonial, 1677–80*, pp. 67, 158; *Cal SP Domestic, 1676–7*, p. 587; *Acts of the Privy Council, Colonial, 1613–80*, pp. 745, 817.
[16] Jones, *A Sermon*, pp. 41–2.

social order would borrow ideas of kingship from newcomers. Similarly, by the 1660s some settlers could take from the political formulation of Ireland as a distinct kingdom expressed by Patrick Darcy in the 1640s. The formation of political ideas is therefore inseparable from the social context in which they circulated: ideas encountered in other milieux were applied as circumstances required. To understand how this process may have worked it is necessary to consider what is probably the most significant development of early modern Ireland, the emergence of a politically significant 'textual culture'.

Early modern Ireland did not see a sudden transformation from a world dominated by oral tradition to one dominated by the written word. The strong manuscript tradition of sixteenth-century Ireland continued into the eighteenth century. Nor was eighteenth-century Ireland bereft of a powerful oral tradition. Rather the seventeenth century saw a shift in the balance between oral and written in the way in which the business of the everyday world was conducted. The emergence of the lease, for example, as a way of regulating landholding was of fundamental importance in familiarising all the inhabitants of seventeenth-century Ireland with the authority of the written word. The spread of the common law system and governmental control through printed proclamations were other mechanisms promoting a textual culture. The inhabitants of seventeenth-century Ireland could not necessarily read the contents of those documents, although by the end of the century many could. Just how many could do so it is impossible to say. On some Irish estates in the 1680s up to 80 per cent of leaseholders, representing the 'middling sort', could sign their names and in Dublin the skill seems to have been even more widespread.[17] Reading was acquired before writing and hence many who could not write could read; on the basis of signature literacy figures this suggests a high level of reading ability. Whether the inhabitants of seventeenth-century Ireland had acquired the technical expertise of reading or not, they became familiar with the importance of the written word whether heard or read. At times of crisis the processes of reading and writing formed foci for fears and discontents. In 1679, for instance, Sir William Petty reported that, in response to the political crisis, there were in Dublin

several clubs and meetings to draw up advices to be sent to England upon that account. I myself have just now finished a couple of sheets but am unresolved

---

[17] Raymond Gillespie, 'The Circulation of Print in Seventeenth-Century Ireland', *Studia Hibernica*, 29 (1995–7), pp. 32–3; T. C. Barnard, 'Learning, the Learned and Literacy in Ireland, c.1660–1760' in T. C. Barnard, Dáibhí Ó Cróinín and Katharine Simms (eds.), *'A Miracle of Learning': Studies in Manuscripts and Irish Learning* (Aldershot, 1998), pp. 220–1.

what to do with them . . . and yet I verily believe that the coffee houses hath been very prolific, and so I believe this paper will be, so soon as other men can vent it as their own.[18]

One consequence of these developments was that individuals of diverse backgrounds became more familiar with the importance of the written word. One rebel in County Down in the early 1640s, for instance, allegedly told a man before he killed him that 'he shall never write a *mittus* to send me to Down gaol again'.[19] The rebel was probably illiterate but he knew how a legal process, defined by the written word, worked and the terms associated with it. If those native Irish who were in arms in late 1641 had borrowed their ideas of kingship from the written formulae of the common law, then Sir Phelim O'Neill's use of a document, albeit forged, supported their contention.[20] To judge from reports of the way that the forged royal commission was used, its wording was irrelevant but the fact that it was a sealed document carried weight. One illiterate woman, Gertrude Carlise from Tyrone, was impressed at being shown 'a seal which they [the rebels] said was the king's seal to a commission warranted them to do the same'. The Catholic bishop of Derry in 1643 reportedly admitted that the document was forged to encourage not the gentry into rebellion but the 'common sort of people'. He added that the power of the written document 'induced and lead them into those forward actions and cruelties'.[21] From a different perspective the destruction of Bibles by the native Irish in the 1640s implies a sense that those written words, as a way to God, remained problematic: hence one comment by the insurgents that 'this book hath bred the quarrel'.[22] What was written, and communicated either in manuscript or print, critically shaped ideas. Some might well be able to read what was written and they in turn would read it to others. The act of reading proclamations aloud, as well as their printing, was important in their diffusion.

The evolution of late seventeenth-century political ideas in Ireland was not dependent on some pre-existing ethnic groupings but evolved from micro-societies which were arranged around the interpretation of texts. Such explanations were revised when a crisis forced a reconsideration of the way in which those micro-societies operated. Both the social dimension and the attitudes of individuals were important in the formulation of political thought. The community defined by those ideas could

---

[18] Marquis of Lansdowne (ed.), *The Petty–Southwell Correspondence* (London, 1928), p. 73.
[19] TCD, MS 838, ff. 117v.   [20] Gillespie, 'Destabilising Ulster', p. 114.
[21] TCD, MS 839, ff. 32, 45v.
[22] Gillespie, 'Destabilising Ulster', pp. 115–16. These attitudes have been more fully examined in Raymond Gillespie, *Devoted People: Belief and Religion in Early Modern Ireland* (Manchester, 1997).

accommodate different shades of political thought within ethnic groups and between them. The remainder of this chapter will consider the sorts of texts which both shaped and defined the political textual communities of late seventeenth-century Ireland. For convenience we will consider the texts within a manuscript tradition, the role of print, the interpretation of some texts on the stage, and finally the interacting roles of manuscript, print and theatre in the creation of rituals by government to shape political ideas.

Perhaps the most important, yet the most restricted, text used in shaping political ideas was that in manuscript. It was restrictive because scribal publication limited the number of copies of texts that could be produced. It was important because of the strong authorial presence that acted as a bridge between an oral world and one that valued writing.[23] For this reason many of the manuscript political tracts of the 1640s were couched in a dialogue form. In these written tracts two sides of an argument could be put and the issues then resolved in favour of one side. Such dialogues included discussion between two imaginary councillors, between figures drawn from classical mythology or, in one case, between a cross (or crucifix) and a gibbet.[24]

Manuscript publication was not always so carefully thought out as to produce a coherent argument and at least some of the importance of this genre derives not from the detail of the argument but from the form. A few played on well-known forms to invert their normal meaning. In 1662 the departure of the assize judges from Derry served as a signal for the spreading of manuscript 'libels', probably by Presbyterians, including one large one which was set up in the manner of a proclamation.[25] In other cases popular rituals were played on for popular effect. In the late 1680s objections to the innovations of James II appeared nailed to the door of Christ Church Cathedral in Dublin in the form 'to publish the bans of matrimony between that church and the see of Rome bidding any that could forthwith to show cause why they should not be joined together'.[26] Most of these texts have now disappeared so it is impossible to know what they said. It is highly unlikely that they contained coherent statements of political ideology. They probably did contain a series of

[23] The importance of scribal publication is highlighted in Harold Love, *Scribal Publication in Seventeenth-Century England* (Oxford, 1993).

[24] For example, Bodl., Carte MS 2, f. 326v; MS 4, ff. 241–7v; Aidan Clarke (ed.), 'A Discourse between Two Councillors of State, the One of England, and the Other of Ireland (1642)', *Analecta Hibernica*, 26 (1970), pp. 159–76.

[25] Bodl., Carte MS 45, f. 117.

[26] *Ireland's lamentation: being a short, but perfect, full and true account of the situation, natural constitution and produce of Ireland* (London, 1689), p. 12. For another 'libel' nailed to the door of Christ Church, Dublin in 1688, Andrew Clark (ed.,) *The Life and Times of Anthony Wood, Antiquary of Oxford, 1632–95* (4 vols., Oxford, 1891–5), III, p. 255.

poorly articulated political sentiments argued with a powerful authorial voice and a point of contact with a wider world.

Potentially, the printing press offered a great deal of scope to those who wished to put their political thoughts into wider circulation. However in practice this was not true. James Verdon, the rector of East Dereham in Norfolk, touring Ireland in 1699 observed: 'Moreover they have a printing house which [is] I must own no great glory for them because they seldom print anything but news and tickets for funerals.'[27] Why this should be is unclear. Certainly censorship through the office of King's Printer played a part but as religious groups soon discovered it was easy to find a sympathetic printer who would issue a tract without an identifying name. For some types of political ideas, couched in literary terms to make their meaning ambiguous, Dublin did not provide the social or cultural cachet which London did. The intensely political dramas of Roger Boyle, earl of Orrery, were all published in London. His early novel *Parthenissa*, which agonised about killing kings and the problems of conquest, was produced in London, apart from the first printing of the first part which appeared in Waterford.[28] This meant that much of the demand for print was fed not through the output of the press but by the import of books, mainly from England. This had the important effect of exposing many of those in seventeenth-century Ireland to political ideas from London and enabling them to adapt them for use in Ireland. *The whole duty of man* by Richard Allestree, for example, is a text, first published in 1658, which frequently appears in Irish libraries of the late seventeenth century and which helped to introduce English ideas about duty to the king to a wider Irish world.

The problem with interpreting the world of print in seventeenth-century Ireland is that although a number of library lists exist it is impossible to be sure whether any of the works were ever read by those who owned them. Many people, however, did regard books as important ways of persuading others of their views. When Patrick Darcy fled Dublin in late 1641 he left behind many of his possessions, including his books. Writing to Ormond in January 1642 he urged him to take care of them since 'to serve your lordship and your house was a principal use I made of them'. Later, in 1660 William Petty, the author of the recently published *Reflections upon Ireland*, grumbled at the cost of sending forty-five copies to Dublin but urged John Petty there not to be sparing with them 'if they edify'.[29]

However it is possible to be sure that one text with potentially explosive

[27] BL., Add. MSS 41769, f. 35
[28] Nigel Smith, *Literature and Revolution in England, 1640–60* (New Haven, 1994), pp. 244–6.
[29] Bodl., Carte MS 2, f. 266. BL, typescript listing of Petty papers, vol. 6, 1st series no. 12, Sir William Petty to John Petty, 8 March, 1659/60. I am grateful to Jane Ohlmeyer for this latter reference.

political overtones that appears in all Irish library lists, sometimes in multiple copies, and circulated in a wider world also was continually read: the Bible.[30] From the point of view of political ideas the Bible could be an influential text. The author of the 1643 'Declaration' was prepared to allow that one of the six grounds of his argument was 'the law of God', although Sergeant Samuel Mayart replying to that text was less convinced of its applicability.[31] If the Bible could be influential, its reading for political ideas could be highly problematical. After the trial of the conspirators in Blood's plot of 1663 the trial judge sentencing them told them that the Protestantism which they claimed to uphold was found in scripture and proceeded to demonstrate the point at some length. A week later the conspirators in their gallows speeches replied, also quoting scripture to justify their points of view.[32] It was clear that for political purposes there were many ways of reading the Bible.

In the seventeenth century various Protestant modes of biblical interpretation produced different political ideas. One might read the Bible not as a historical or salvational narrative but typologically, that is as a series of types which could be applied to everyday life. The political application of such activity can be seen in the work of Sir William Temple, the son of the Irish attorney general, Sir John Temple. In his 1672 essay on the origins and nature of government he drew the analogy between the family and the kingdom. 'A family seems to be a little kingdom', he observed, 'and a kingdom to be but a great family.' It followed that as the father was the natural head of a family so a king was the rightful head of a kingdom.[33] To exploit this idea required a typological reading of the creation story in the book of Genesis to see Adam as a type of both Christ and a king.

Such a reading of scripture was clearly highly charged with political possibilities, as the experience of the 1650s suggested. By the 1660s attempts were being made to curtail it in Ireland. The earl of Orrery confessed in 1660

to an aversion from the late custom of our age for every private hand as it serves as one occasion to draw all stories and expressions of scripture into consequence for our lives and the framing of our opinions. I have observed this use to be of mischievous effect and destructive in a great measure to the respect and obedience we owe to civil authority. I revere the scriptures but esteem them given to us for other use than to fortify disputes concerning state affairs out of every part of them.[34]

[30] For further details, Raymond Gillespie, 'Reading the Bible in Seventeenth-Century Ireland' in Bernadette Cunningham and Máire Kennedy (eds.), *The Experience of Reading: Irish Historical Perspectives* (Dublin, 1999), pp. 10–38.
[31] Harris, *Hibernica*, II, pp. 41, 43, 225–6.
[32] Worcester College, Oxford, MS 33, ff. 166–80.
[33] William Temple, *Miscellanea* (London, 1680), p. 68.
[34] [Roger Boyle, earl of Orrery], *The Irish colours displayed, in a reply to an Irish Protestant to a later letter of an Irish Roman Catholique* ([London, 1662]), p. 16.

It was perhaps for this reason that John Dryden's *Absolom and Achitophel*, which relied heavily for its effect on such typological reading of scripture, was the only one of his major political works not reprinted in Dublin. Other ways of reading scripture to defuse its political message were promoted. When the duke of Ormond read scripture he took not a political but a moral message from it. As he reminded the Franciscan Peter Walsh who attempted to convert him to Catholicism in 1686, 'he had taken notice in Scripture, where the day of judgement is set forth, Christ does not interrogate about the manner of believing but about a man's works'.[35] This moral reading also appears in Temple's later political work on popular discontents that held that 'for as every prince should govern as he would desire to be governed if he were a subject, so every subject should obey as he would desire to be obeyed if he were a prince; since this moral principle of doing as you would be done by is certainly the most universally allowed of any other in the world'.[36] The ethical reading of Matthew VII.12 or Luke VI.31 is obvious here. Such a shift in the practices of reading the Bible was only part of a much wider change in the structure of the Church of Ireland in the later seventeenth century, and other texts such as *The whole duty of man* were also involved in this change. How successful it was is difficult to measure. There are some indications that typological reading of scripture was much less common in Ireland by 1700 than it had been a century earlier. Yet it remained part of Bible reading for those Protestants who dissented from the Established church.

III

The world of print in action can be observed in ways other than reading by examining the world of theatre. Here the printed or manuscript text was given an interpretation for a wider audience, some of whom may have been unable to read the text for themselves. Moreover, for those who could read the printed text, another layer was added to the interpretation as provided by the stage. The stage was considered an important means of conveying ideas and cementing social order. Robert Ware in his 1678 history of Dublin lamented the decline of civic pageantry but argued that this had been replaced by the theatre and 'I conceive that the mayor and aldermen ought to compensate such a great neglect of duty by resorting on those days and festivals to the king's theatre in their own person and then causing a general resort of freemen at those times to that place'.[37]

[35] Lord Mountmorres, *The History Of The Irish Parliament, From The Year 1634 To 1666* (London, 1792), p. 299.
[36] Jonathan Swift (ed.), *Miscellanea: The Third Part* (London, 1701), p. 38.
[37] Armagh Public Library, Robert Ware's MS history and antiquities of Dublin (1678), pp. 140–3. For the mayor attending the theatre, Patrick Melvin (ed.), 'Letters of Lord Longford and Others on Irish Affairs, 1689–1702', *Analecta Hibernica*, 32 (1985), p. 40.

Moreover one did not have to enter the theatre to experience plays. It is difficult to overestimate the importance of dramatic texts to the inhabitants of early modern Ireland. Most private libraries contained some play scripts. In the case of the duke of Ormond his library list of 1685 recorded forty-two volumes described as 'plays' in addition to attributed works such as three volumes of Ben Jonson's plays and those by Newcastle. By 1715 his son had sixty-one volumes of 'plays' in the library although seven had been lost. These may have been mislaid but equally probably might have been lent to others which would suggest a circulation of these texts in a wider world.[38] Some highly political dramas such as Henry Burkhead's play about Sir Charles Coote in Ireland, *A tragedy of Cola's furie or Lirenda's miserie*, which was printed at Kilkenny in 1645 and possibly reprinted the following year, were almost certainly never staged. It was more probably published to be read in the same way as the manuscript dialogues described above.

The importance of drama in shaping attitudes was appreciated by contemporaries, and especially by religious groups who regularly used dramatic forms to further their message. The Jesuit school in New Ross, for instance, from 1660 'amused and instructed the people [of the town] by plays' on moral and religious subjects. What the repetoire was is not known. Only one piece, a poem recited at the breakup of the school in 1670, survives.[39] Of course the line between moral behaviour and political ideas of authority was a thin one. In 1666 the earl of Orrery complained that the Jesuits in Cork

did act a play whither a great confluence of people repaired, notwithstanding that Mr John Andrews, minister of the place, did expressly prohibit him [the Jesuit master], because the design of it was to stir up sedition, for the plot was that a pastor having lost his flock by wolves, and other beasts of prey, he was persuaded to teach a school and his scholars helping him to destroy the wolves, he turned pastor to a flock again. This is the fable and in this pastoral he seemed to shew to them his own condition and hopes. The argument was bad, the plot worse, the contempt of authority worst of all.[40]

Drama did not have to be great art to convey a political message. One of the most striking examples of the use of the stage by Irish Jesuits to convey a political message was provided by the play staged by the students in the Jesuit school at Kilkenny in 1644. The action, set in Japan and drawn from Francis Solier's ecclesiastical history of Japan, concerned Titus who

[38] HMC, *Calendar of the manuscripts of the marquis of Ormonde*, NS (8 vols., London, 1902–20), VII, pp. 513–27; PRO, FEC1/877.

[39] W. S. Clark, *The Early Irish Stage* (Oxford, 1955), pp. 70–1; [Luke Wadding], *A smale garland of pious and godly songs composed by a devout man* (Ghent, 1684), pp. 45–9.

[40] Thomas Morrice, *A Collection of State Letters of . . . Roger Boyle, Earl of Orrery* (2 vols., Dublin, 1743), II, p. 74.

was pressurised to abdure his faith by the king of Bungo. Titus and his family remained steadfast and were given signs of Divine care for the elect so that the king granted them not only their lives and estates but also freedom of religion.[41] The agenda of such a play staged at the beginning of negotiations between the Confederation of Kilkenny and the king for a settlement of Ireland seems clear: the religious principles of Catholicism could not be compromised and there was divine sanction for maintaining a religious position.

The political context of the staging of dramatic works certainly had an impact on the absorption of political ideas. It is possible to equate some productions of the Dublin stage with political events. For instance it is probably no coincidence that *Macbeth*, a play about the iniquity of killing kings, was staged at times of political crisis in 1674 and 1682 and Shakespeare's *Henry VIII* with its speech of the glories of the future Queen Elizabeth was presented in the same years.[42] However it is possible to go rather further and to attempt to understand the reception of the texts from the circumstances of their performance. A simple case here is the performance of Orrery's play *The general* in October 1662. The profound political underpinnings of Orrery's drama, especially in the agonising about regicide, is well known and the plot of *The general* fits this model. It reflects the political crisis of 1659 since a usurper king is killed by a loyal general in a duel, thus restoring the true king.[43] It was probably written in the early part of 1661 and sent to the king who, not unnaturally, highly approved of it. Its first performance, however, was not until October 1662 in Dublin as part of a banquet given for 'most of the persons of honour in these parts'.[44] Chief among the 'persons of honour' was James Butler, duke of Ormond, who had arrived in Ireland in July 1662. It was the first meeting between these two men who were to be the two major power brokers in late seventeenth-century Ireland. The encounter had the potential to be explosive since they were of different temperaments. Ormond was a high churchman of Old English background who saw a place for Catholics in the new order if they behaved themselves; Orrery was of a more evangelical cast of mind and saw disloyalty and treachery everywhere. Moreover while Ormond had gone into exile with Charles, Orrery (then Lord Broghill) had remained at home, co-operating with the Cromwellian regime. It was therefore important

---

[41] The text is reproduced in Timothy Corcoran, *State Policy in Irish Education, 1536 to 1816* (Dublin, 1916), pp. 208–11 and W. K. Sessions, *The First Printers in Waterford, Cork and Kilkenny* (York, 1990), pp. 51–3.   [42] Clark, *The Early Irish Stage*, pp. 72–4, 204–5.
[43] For Orrery as 'political' dramatist, Nancy Klein Maguire, *Regicide and Restoration: English Tragicomedy, 1660–71* (Cambridge, 1992), pp. 164–89.
[44] For the circumstances, W.S. Clark (ed.), *The Dramatic Works of Roger Boyle, Earl of Orrery* (2 vols., Cambridge, MA, 1937), I, pp. 27–33.

that the two men should find a common set of political ideas if they were to work together to govern Ireland. It was one of the functions of the performance of *The general*, which already had the royal seal of approval, to begin that negotiation. The themes that Orrery wished Ormond to take from the play had, in fact, been spelt out in a letter to the duke on 23 January 1662 when Orrery had sent him a draft of the play.[45] The speeches were, he claimed, 'of duel, honour, jealousy, revenge, love and envy' and were entirely new. Here the important word is 'honour', the idea of which runs through the play and the means of killing of the usurper in a duel reinforces the idea. Acting honourably, with all the connotations of loyalty and duty which that word held, was to be the key to the way Ireland was governed in the later seventeenth century. In one way the drama proved remarkably successful in that concepts of honour became central in forming political ideas in the later seventeenth century. However, the construction of the idea for Ormond was rather different from that espoused by Orrery. The attempted 'negotiations' quickly foundered in a dispute between the two men.

The role of drama in both reflecting and reshaping political ideas might be further developed. The rise of formal theatre in Dublin from the 1630s, underpinning Lord Deputy Wentworth's plans for the development of Ireland, brought new demand for plays. This was met not only from English sources but also by plays written for the Irish stage by the English dramatist James Shirley and by the home grown Henry Burnell. James Shirley's early efforts for the Irish stage seem to have met with considerable success.[46] His *The royal master*, first performed in 1637 and dealing with the intrigue of court politics and the issues of betrayal and loyalty, met with some critical acclaim. People representing all sides of Irish society from the later confederate Richard Bellings to the later Ormondist William Smith wrote commendatory verses on its appearance.[47] As Shirley moved into more disputed territory and as the administration of Wentworth became more unstable so the political message of the plays became less acceptable to many. *St. Patrick for Ireland*, entered at the Stationers' Company in April 1640 and thus probably produced on the Dublin stage in late 1639 or early 1640, apparently prompted some reaction. From one perspective the image of St Patrick was as a Church of Ireland bishop who wore not only a mitre but also 'lawn that is whiter' (Act III.i). His impeccable Laudian credentials were further suggested by

45 Morrice, *A Collection of State Letters*, I, pp. 76–7.
46 For Shirley's career, A.H. Stevenson, 'Shirley's Years in Ireland', *Review of English Studies*, 20 (1944), pp. 19–28.
47 For the identifications, Sandra A. Burner, *James Shirley: A Study of Literary Coteries and Patronage in Seventeenth-Century England* (Lanham, NJ, 1988), pp. 124–7.

part of a prophecy predicting Patrick in which it is noted 'and in the east his table stand' (Act I.i) in the manner of a Laudian altar.[48] It was this Ireland that received Patrick's blessing and his prophecy in Act V.iii that the government of Ireland would be blessed and the crown flourish: 'the throne you shall leave glorious.'

It may be that profound disagreement with the political argument of *St. Patrick for Ireland* inspired the Dublin lawyer, and later member of the Confederation of Kilkenny, Henry Burnell to compose a reply, *Landgartha*, which he began in January 1640 and which was staged in Dublin on 17 March 1640.[49] One of the dedicatory verses in *Landgartha*, that by John Bermingham, attacked playwrights who used dramatic special effects such as 'flames and fire/ Tempests and whirlwinds' rather than literary skill to achieve their ends.[50] Such theatricality was one of the hallmarks of *St. Patrick for Ireland* which had marshalled songs, special effects and fantastic costumes in an effort to fill the Dublin theatre. If the stagecraft was different in the two plays the political message was likewise contrasting. *Landgartha* centred around a group of virtuous Norwegian women, led by Landgartha, who after the expulsion of the tyrannical king of Sweden by Reyner, king of Denmark, were left in Norway to be 'the law makers to yourselves/ for those, by whom we reign, shall be our guides'. Landgartha was seduced and subsequently betrayed by Reyner who understood too late the nature and reprehensibility of his actions after her loyalty had been displayed in a civil war. The play was not a simple political allegory and there can probably be no exact matching of characters with reality. Briefly in the wedding masque in Act III, a play within a play, the disguise slips and it appears that Reyner is in fact king of 'Brutiane'. A further clue is provided by the reference to the fact that the island kingdom 'derives/ Her name from white rocks, being a little world', a clear reference to Alba or Scotland. It seems that we are to read Reyner as being Charles I who has betrayed those who should make the laws for Denmark, but contemporaries might have understood a betrayal of the Old English who should make the laws for Ireland. In the play the betrayal was sexual but the real life political betrayal of the Old English may have been the Graces. This equation of the women, and in particular Landgartha, with the Old English, which contemporaries were clearly meant to make, enabled Burnell to expound a set of political ideas about

[48] For the text, William Gifford, *The Dramatic Works and Poems of James Shirley* (6 vols., Edinburgh, 1833), IV, pp. 363–443. A more recent edition is J. P. Turner, *A Critical Edition of James Shirley's 'St. Patrick for Ireland'* (New York, 1979).
[49] Henry Burnell, *Landgartha, a tragie-comedy as it was presented in the New Theatre in Dublin with good aplause, being an ancient story* (Dublin, 1641).
[50] Burnell, *Landgartha*, sig. A3v.

how a state should be run, using the example of Landgartha and her contemporaries.

The world constructed by Burnell was free from the factionalism and
intrigue of court politics which so characterised the plays of James Shirley
produced in the court of Wentworth. In Burnell's play terms such as
'vertue' and 'honour' were important. Landgartha's final speech set out a
view of the relations of kings and their subjects in which the former
should 'be merciful in chief to thy subjects/ to allure their hearts by love:
that being the tye/ that will hold strongest; never can be broken/ Unless by
fools or madmen'. If a king 'be just and vertuous and you need not/ Feare
poison, poynards or conspiracie'.[51] Spoken in the aftermath of a civil war,
which may be analogous to the Bishops' Wars in Scotland, this provided
the rules for governing a kingdom such as Ireland in which the women (or
the Old English) were to be the law makers. Such sentiments were clearly
intended to provide rules for the meeting of the parliament of 1640. For
Dublin audiences, therefore, the Dublin stage of 1639–40 might be seen
as producing a dialogue between two differing sets of political ideas, one
articulated by Shirley's *St. Patrick for Ireland* and the other by Burnell's
Landgartha. Both contained sets of political ideas which were diffused
into a wider audience.

From the end of the seventeenth century there are other examples of
Irish theatre which both reflected political ideas and may have helped to
shape them in the minds of some. *Love and a bottle*, by the late seventeenth-century dramatist from Derry, George Farquhar, may have been
first performed in London in 1698 but it was written either in Ireland,
possibly for performance by the Dublin company of which Farquhar was
a member, or on the journey to London.[52] On the surface it is a play
which satirises the Anglo-Irish settlers who seem to be depicted as
loutish, hard drinking and untrustworthy boors as represented by
Roebuck who is the first character the audience encounters. It only gradually becomes clear during the play that Lovewell, described as 'sober and
modest' is Anglo-Irish also and he eventually marries the heroine
Lucinda. The entertainment at the smart wedding is shown as Irish in
form. The play is thus as much a satire on the stage image of the Anglo-
Irishman as it is a presentation of it. Similar points are made in William
Philips' *St. Stephen's Green or the generous lovers* first performed on the
Dublin stage in 1699, the year following the publication of William
Molyneux's *Case of Ireland*.[53] What Molyneux had tried to propose in a
political text the play presents on the stage. In contrast to the work of

[51] Burnell, *Landgartha*, sig. I4.
[52] S. S. Kenny (ed.), *The Works of George Farquhar* (2 vols., Oxford, 1988), I, pp. 6–9.
[53] William Philips, *St. Stephen's Green or the generous lovers*, ed. Christopher Murray (Dublin, 1980).

Burnell it is set not in a mythical past but in the present, in Dublin – the first play to be so set. The exchange between Vainly and Freelove forces Sir Francis Feignyouth to intervene with the very Molyneux-like sentiment 'I can hold no longer. Why thou worthless contemptible wretch! Do you entertain strangers with your aversion for your country without being able to give one reason for it; and can you give one reason for liking it, which if it were true would make all others abhor it?' (Act III.i.273–8). These sorts of activities by dramatists put into more general circulation the ideas being formulated in other places and for other reasons and helped to increase the number of political options in circulation from which others could make their choices.

IV

The two elements that have been discussed above, the written word either in manuscript or printed form and its enactment and interpretation in dramatic form, can be combined to understand something of the social and cultural context of political thought and how it circulated. The trauma of the 1640s severed the tacit consensus of the early part of the seventeenth century and in the years after the Restoration it was necessary not only to reconstruct, but also to reimagine Ireland. One of the ways in which this expressed itself was in the development of state ritual. In the early part of the seventeenth century the idea of a separate crown of Ireland was little developed or discussed by settlers in Ireland. Dublin was not a centre of court life. Dramatic performance, intended to enhance the person of the lord deputy as representative of the king, was almost nonexistent apart from irregular celebrations of St George's day. Wentworth had gone some way to improving this situation in 1637 with triumphal arches being erected at Limerick when he went there and orations on his arrival at Kilkenny, Carlow and Limerick.[54] The revival of state ritual was given its fullest expression by James Butler, duke of Ormond, who was appointed lord lieutenant of Ireland at the Restoration. In 1662 he entered Dublin in some state accompanied by the city sheriffs and a peal of ordinance and fireworks.[55] In 1665 his entry was even more impressive, with pageants being played along the route of his progress.[56] Three of these have been identified as Ceres attended by four virgins at the Thosel, Vulcan by an anvil with four sleeping Cyclopes at Castle Street and, at the gate of the castle, Bacchus with 'four or five good

---

[54] *Cal S P Ire, 1633–47*, p. 169. For the Kilkenny entrances see Patrick Walters, 'Note of Entries in the Corporation Records, Kilkenny, Relating to a Visit of Lord Viscount Wentworth to Kilkenny, 1637', *Journal of the Royal Society of Antiquaries of Ireland*, 25 (1883–4), pp. 242–9.   [55] BL, Add. MSS 4784, ff. 246v–7.
[56] BL, Add. MSS 4684, f. 253.

fellows'. The imagery here is striking. Ceres was the god representing the
generative power of nature or fertility. Vulcan symbolised power, having
made the chariot in which Phaeton flew to the sun, and with the Cyclopes
he made Zeus's thunderbolts, and Bacchus represented conviviality and
joviality.[57] Such large-scale entrances of lords lieutenant became the
norm in late seventeenth-century Ireland. When Ormond's replacement,
John Robartes, entered Dublin in 1669 the gentry flocked to the city and
the corporation was ordered to provide a suitable reception for the new
viceroy. When Robartes arrived on 23 September he was met by the Privy
Council and the sheriffs and escorted to the city for an entrance accompanied by speeches.[58] All shops in the city were closed, bonfires were lit
and there was considerable revelry and drunkenness.[59] Two days later the
gentry began leaving the city after the swearing in. When the king, James
II, appeared in person in Dublin in 1688 a similar grand-scale event was
organised, with harpists playing on stages in the streets and large throngs
of officials in the city. Women, of rather low life according to one
Protestant commentator, scattered flowers before the king as lilies had
been scattered before Robartes earlier.[60]

The themes that were present in the dramatic entrances recur in the
poetry that was composed for recitation at these formal occasions. The
idea of abundance under Ormond's rule appears in an undated poem on
his arrival in Ireland that declared 'And as our wants so will his bounties
grow/ For of supplies 'tis he has all the springs/ The best lieutenant to the
best of kings.' The image of light associated with Vulcan also appears in a
poem by John Binker to Ormond on leaving the government: 'For as he
conquers darkness so we shall/ Triumph o'er death by Him who conquers
all.'[61] Similar metaphors pepper John Wilson's poem on Arran's appointment as lord deputy in 1682 which was seen as the appearance of a double
sun, one gone east (Ormond's departure to London) and another rising
in the west or Dublin, and this idea of the sun is played on throughout the
poem.[62] The same motifs of the sun and light as characteristics of the lord

[57] The events were reported in *The Newes*, no. 89, 2 Nov. 1665, *Kingdom's intelligencier*, no 18, 6 May 1665 and *Mercurius Publicus*, 2 May 1665.
[58] PRO, State Papers, 63/326/14; *Cal S P Ire, 1669–70*, pp. 2, 3, 4, 6, 6–7.
[59] William Mercer, *A welcom in a poem to his Excellency John, Lord Roberts* (Dublin, 1669), sigs. B4v, C2, C4.
[60] Mercer, *A Welcom*, sig. C4; *Ireland's lamentation*, pp. 26–8; J. T. Gilbert (ed.), *A Jacobite Narrative of the War in Ireland, 1688–91* (Dublin, 1892), p. 47.
[61] HMC, *Calendar of the manuscripts of the marquis of Ormonde*, OS (3 vols., London, 1895–1909), I, p. 114. The volume of poetry described here was not transferred to NLI with the other Ormond papers and its whereabouts is not known.
[62] John Wilson, *To His Excellency, Richard, Earle of Arran . . . Lord Deputy of Ireland. A poem* (Dublin, 1684) printed together with a contemporary manuscript reply in James Maidment and W. H. Logan, *The Dramatic Works of John Wilson* (Edinburgh, 1874), pp. xii–xiv.

deputy reappear in the poetry composed for the formal entrances of Henry, earl of Clarendon, as Irish lord deputy in 1686.[63] Most of these formal addresses survive in manuscript but increasingly from the 1660s they were printed and circulated as broadsheets, possibly as part of the entrance rituals.[64] In some cases they were clearly intended to be memorised and repeated.[65] The poems composed by William Mercer for the arrival of Lord Robartes as lord lieutenant in 1669 used a number of devices such as acrostics to make them even more memorable.[66] The popularity of these events grew and many groups participated by composing poetry for the occasion, including in 1677 a group of admiralty officers who were afraid to let their work go into print.[67] Thus it was possible to combine a whole range of social ways of shaping political ideas. The arrivals of chief governors were marked by the use of the spoken word, the drama of the theatre, the circulation of manuscript and also the world of print, the products of which may have made their way back into the oral culture through later memorisation and recitation.

What the reaction of those witnessing these events was is difficult to establish since few first-hand accounts of participants survive. However one context, that of a quasi-religious experience, frequently appears in the writings of those who witnessed those events. For William Mercer in 1669 the closing of the shops in the city for the entry of Lord Robartes meant 'The boys give blessing to this holy day'.[68] The point was made even more forcefully to a number of Quakers who failed to close their shops on days of important ritual significance such as the king's birthday or 23 October, as they were imprisoned.[69] Something of the emotional power of such quasi-religious events is revealed by the account by Edward Wetenhall, later bishop of Cork, of the announcement of the death of Charles II and the proclamation of James II in 1685. Wetenhall, then in Cork, was awakened by the sound of drums and trumpets and

the same noise which awakened me soon drew together into the city a great multitude out of the adjacent country. And some of the nobility at a distance having

[63] *Upon the arrival of His Excellency, Henry Earl of Clarendon, and his entering upon the Government of Ireland* (Dublin, 1686).

[64] In the early eighteenth century a printing press accompanied Dublin corporation as they rode the franchises striking off and distributing poems: J. W. Phillips, *Printing and Bookselling in Dublin, 1670–1800* (Dublin, 1998), pp. 13–16.

[65] Raymond Gillespie, 'Presbyterian Propaganda' in Kevin Herlihy (ed.), *The Politics of Irish Dissent* (Dublin, 1997), p. 105. One priest in Laois in the 1640s recited to a settler 'seditious verses' about the Bishops' Wars in Scotland which he had probably memorised from a printed broadsheet, TCD, MS 815, ff. 105–5v. Memorisation may explain why the anti-war sentiments nailed to the gate of Kilkenny in the 1640s were cast in verse form; HMC, *Ormonde MSS*, OS, I, p. 105.   [66] Mercer, *A Welcom*, sigs. A4, B1, D4.

[67] Lansdowne, *Petty–Southwell Correspondence*, p. 33.   [68] Mercer, *A Welcom*, sig. C2v.

[69] [William Stockdale], *The Great Cry of Oppression* ([London?], 1683), pp. 221, 235, 239.

received expresses in the night were early with us and the town very full. I never saw in my life, and trust I shall never see again, so vast a number of people in such a medley of passions. They were come together on a business that required joy, and rejoice they did. Yet their love to their late gracious king . . . was so tender that most could not forbear parenthesis of weeping. And some other passions it was plain lay under these, even in the greatest number of the people I could not but observe the variety of the symptoms as I passed through the crowd . . . I cannot deny that I was myself a little transported into the like tenderness and fluctuation of affection which I saw in others.[70]

Such emotional power made these liminal events in which old ideas could be reshaped to fit new contexts.

One effect of these ritual occasions was to mould a new set of relationships between the inhabitants of Ireland and its viceroy. The formulaic themes that seem to have been common to both the drama and the written word, for instance, glorified the Irish chief governor at a point when his authority was in decline under pressure from the London court. He was the fount of power and plenty and thus some of the numinous attributes of kingship were associated with the office that, in reality, was a rather ambiguous one. As William Mercer put in his description of the entry of Robartes, 'Not only subjects but every living thing / this day adore the image of their king.'[71] Dublin became centre of a world rather than a peripheral part of a world in which the focus was London.[72] To create a centre was to presuppose another periphery, in effect to give an identity to Ireland as distinct from being a colony of England. This is close to the argument of William Molyneux's *Case of Ireland*. The pomp of the ceremony was not intended to lay the foundations of a set of political ideas which, when combined with other factors, would give rise to this interpretation, but unintended outcomes are at least as important as those carefully cultivated.

Of course not all political rituals had the cohesive and binding force of those focused on the monarchy, such as proclamations of kings or the entrances of lords lieutenant. Some were intended to confirm and modify the political ideas of specific groups. The celebrations of 23 October, the anniversary of the outbreak of rebellion in 1641, aimed to bind together the 'Protestant interest'. The ways in which it attempted to do this were similar to the techniques used at royal entrances. In this case the liturgy for the religious services approved in the early 1660s provided a frame-

[70] Edward Wetenhall, *Six sermons preached in Ireland in difficult times* (London, 1695), 'Advertisment' to sermon on 'A temper for loyal joy and grief'.
[71] Mercer, *A Welcom*, sig. C2.
[72] For the implications of this for the city, Raymond Gillespie, 'Dublin 1600–1700: A City and its Hinterlands' in Peter Clark and Bernard Lepetit (eds.), *Capital Cities and their Hinterlands in Early Modern Europe* (Aldershot, 1996), pp. 84–104.

work for events. The sermons preached on these occasions became formulaic, based on key texts such as the history of the rebellion by Sir John Temple or less frequently that by Edmund Borlase.[73] Indeed on one occasion in 1679 when the preacher in St Patrick's cathedral attempted to breathe life into his 23 October sermon by quoting Borlase a number of his congregation went to the bookshop to buy a copy afterwards and others borrowed the work.[74] Outside the church, bonfires were normal as well as bell ringing, which made these events flash points, and during the late 1680s the Dublin government attempted to stamp them out since they acted as foci for discontent which might develop into more serious riots.[75] In such ways sectional political ideas were shaped.

V

This chapter has tried to suggest that political ideas in Ireland were not the prerogative of intellectuals such as Patrick Darcy or William Molyneux but had an existence and an appeal much wider than that. Such sentiments existed in a well-developed social context and were continually being reshaped to meet changing social needs. Although not coherently expressed or systematised, they were repeatedly adapted and restated through a wide range of media, manuscript, printed books, broadsheets and the rituals of the theatre. All these were used by different groups to articulate political sentiments and to persuade others of their validity. Those social groups were not necessarily ethnically based but rather were formed around the interpretation of particular texts, such as the Bible or other works. Most people in late seventeenth-century Ireland who regularly encountered political ideas did not spend their days in pondering alternative political systems or ways of thinking. However, when their accepted understanding of how the political world worked underwent a crisis, either communal, as in the 1640s or the 1680s, or personal when they were confronted with a perplexing situation, they looked for new cultural maps to guide them. They built these from observations, many of which were already in circulation. Hence much of the argument of William Molyneux in the 1690s resembles, and was drawn from, Patrick Darcy in the 1640s. In that sense Irish political sensibilities in the later seventeenth century were the product of the circulation of a range of ideas in a social context in which many people took part.

[73] T. C. Barnard, 'The Uses of 23 October 1641 and Irish Protestant Celebration', *EHR*, 106 (1991), pp. 889–920.   [74] BL, Sloane MS 1008, f. 226.
[75] T. C. Barnard, 'Athlone 1685, Limerick, 1710: religious riots or charivaris', *Studia Hibernica*, 27 (1993), pp. 61–75; James Kelly, 'The Glorious and Immortal Memory: Commemoration and Protestant Identity in Ireland, 1660–1800', *Proceedings of the Royal Irish Academy*, 94 (1994), pp. 25–32; HMC, *Ormonde MSS*, NS, VIII, pp. 351, 354.

Part II

Ireland and the Continent

6 Representations of king, parliament and the Irish people in Geoffrey Keating's *Foras Feasa ar Éirinn* and John Lynch's *Cambrensis Eversus* (1662)

Bernadette Cunningham

Irish historians writing in the seventeenth century may have understood less of the workings of early Irish kingship than specialists in early Irish history do today. The kingship of Ireland, however, mattered more to seventeenth-century Old English historians of Ireland than it does to today's specialists. Its history was then no mere academic exercise. Thus, although we may no longer read Geoffrey Keating's *Foras Feasa ar Éirinn*[1] or John Lynch's *Cambrensis Eversus*[2] for the detail of early Irish political institutions, whether pre-Christian or early Christian, we can read those texts to discover mid-seventeenth-century perspectives on kingship, sovereignty, parliament and law in an Irish context. Like their contemporaries throughout Europe, seventeenth-century Irish writers who undertook to write history usually did so with the intention of illuminating the present as much as the past. 'In their selection of subject matter they implicitly conveyed to readers a sense of what was important.'[3]

This chapter examines the ideas of kingship, sovereignty and parliament as portrayed in the historical writings of two seventeenth-century Irish Catholic writers, Geoffrey Keating and John Lynch. Lynch was approximately twenty years younger than Keating and, perhaps crucially, their writings about Ireland's past were separated by the traumas and upheavals of the war in Ireland in the 1640s. Keating's *Foras Feasa ar Éirinn*, completed *c.*1634, was a wide ranging compendium on Irish history, from Adam to the coming of the Normans, drawn primarily from Irish manuscript sources. It was written in Irish in an elegant prose style that ensured its popularity among its readers. Although not printed, it

---

[1] Geoffrey Keating, *Foras Feasa ar Éirinn: the history of Ireland* (*c.*1634). ed. & trans. David Comyn and P. S. Dinneen (4 vols., Irish Texts Society, London, 1902–14).
[2] John Lynch, *Cambrensis Eversus* (St Malo, 1662), ed. and trans. Matthew Kelly (3 vols., Celtic Society, Dublin, 1848–52).
[3] Keith Thomas, *The Perception of the Past in Early Modern England* (London, 1983), p. 3.

was a 'best seller' in manuscript.[4] It was translated into English in the
1630s and into Latin by the 1660s.[5] It continued to be widely copied, borrowed, read and cited through the late seventeenth and eighteenth centuries. In contrast, Lynch's more polemical tract in defence of Ireland's
reputation was written in Latin, and intended for a European, probably
primarily French, audience. It was largely penned in the late 1650s, with
the final touches added after the Restoration of 1660. Though at 250,000
words it was 60 per cent longer than Keating's work, it nonetheless found
a publisher in France in 1662.[6] It appears, however, never to have attained
anything like the same reputation at home that Keating's *Foras Feasa*
enjoyed. Lynch's *Cambrensis Eversus* was not, in any case, intended as a
replacement for Keating's history. Lynch's work was a far less structured,
more polemical tract, which carried the hallmarks of his classical education, but had none of the aura of having emerged from the Gaelic manuscript heritage which permeated Keating's history so completely. It did,
however, bear the intellectual scars of the trauma of having lived through
the mid-seventeenth-century crisis in Ireland.

The two authors are being examined together here because there was a
particularly direct intellectual link between them. John Lynch translated
Geoffrey Keating's *Foras Feasa ar Éirinn* into Latin and it seems likely that
he intended to publish it. One surviving copy of the translation has a
preface by Lynch, which mediates between the potential reader and the
text by placing it in the context of its time and by explaining, if not
entirely excusing, those features which Lynch perceived as the shortcom-
ings of Keating's work.[7] Lynch, who was one of many readers captivated
by the story Keating had to tell and by the way he told it, also cited
Keating's work in his own tract, using it extensively in support of his own
interpretation of Ireland's early history.

I

Geoffrey Keating and John Lynch had much in common. They were both
members of Old English families, descendants of the Anglo-Norman

[4] Over thirty seventeenth-century manuscript copies of the text in Irish are extant. See R. J.
Hayes (ed.), *Manuscript Sources for the History of Irish Civilization* (11 vols., Boston, 1965),
II, pp. 652–9.
[5] The first English translation, by Michael Kearney, is dated 1635; RIA, MS 24 G 16 is a
1668 transcript of that translation. A different translation, probably prepared in the 1670s,
survives in a range of manuscripts including Marsh's Library, MS Z3.1.17; Armagh Public
Library, MS H.III.1; NLI, MS G 293; BL, Add. MSS 4818. The Latin translation is extant
in three copies: RIA, MS 24.I.5; Woodstock Theological Library, Georgetown University,
Washington DC, MS 7; Troyes, Bibl. Muncipale, MS 919. The first printed translation,
The General History of Ireland . . . translated . . . with amendments by D. O'Connor (London,
1723), differs from the two seventeenth-century manuscript translations in English.
[6] [John Lynch,] *Cambrensis Eversus, seu potius historica Fides in Rebus Hibernicis Giraldo
Cambrensi Abrogata* ([St Malo], 1662).   [7] RIA, MS 24.I.5.

settlers in Ireland, an identity that still mattered in seventeenth-century Ireland, although both men were firm advocates of the use of the term *Éireannach* or 'Irish person' to replace the term Old English. We should be careful about assuming this meant that they wished to make common cause completely with the Old Irish. In the case of Lynch in particular, the primary concern was to assert the Irishness of the Old English. This was a necessary step in demonstrating the continuity of the Catholicism of the Old English from the coming of Christianity to Ireland in the time of St Patrick. That such an argument was genealogically implausible did not make it any less important to the construction of Old English identity in the seventeenth century, and Keating's text seemed to offer the framework for the history of Catholic Ireland that the Old English Catholics needed to argue the case successfully.[8]

It is believed that Geoffrey Keating was born *c.* 1580 in the vicinity of Cahir. He was a member of a long-established Munster kin-group of Anglo-Norman ancestry, living in that part of the ancient territory of Decies that lay in County Tipperary rather than Waterford.[9] Given his skilful use of Irish manuscript source material, and his authorship of a number of poems in 'transitional' seventeenth-century style, it seems likely that he had close contacts with the Gaelic Mac Craith school of *Seanchas* in his home neighbourhood. No documented evidence of his early life in Ireland survives; such skeleton biographical details as exist derive principally from a 1722 preface by Thomas O'Sullevane to the *Memoirs of the Marquis of Clanricarde* rather than from contemporary sources.[10] Documented records of Keating's period on the continent remain equally sparse. Writing in 1624 Philip O'Sullivan Beare claimed he held a doctorate in theology from Rheims, whereas an earlier list of 1618–19 associated him with the Irish College at Bordeaux sometime in the period 1603–18.[11] He may well have had links with both places, and certainly the influence of his continental theological education permeated his writings. Keating had returned to Ireland before 1613 and was living in Munster in the 1620s and early 1630s when he wrote his history of Ireland.[12]

John Lynch, an Old English man from a prominent Galway family, was

---

[8] Bernadette Cunningham, 'Seventeenth-Century Interpretations of the Past: The Case of Geoffrey Keating', *IHS*, 25 (1986), pp. 116–28.

[9] Cunningham, 'Seventeenth-Century Interpretations', pp.116–18; Donnchadh Ó Corráin, 'Seathrún Céitinn (*c.*1580–*c.*1644): an Cúlra stairiúil', *Dúchas, 1983, 1984, 1985* (Dublin, 1986), pp. 56–68; R. C. Simington (ed.), *The Civil Survey, A.D. 1654–56* (10 vols., IMC, Dublin, 1931–61), I, *Tipperary*, pp. 306–76.

[10] *Memoirs of the Right Honourable the Marquis of Clanricarde, Lord Deputy General of Ireland* (London, 1722).

[11] T. J. O'Donnell (ed.), *Selections from the Zoilomastix of O'Sullivan Beare* (IMC, Dublin, 1960), p. 22; *Cal SP Ire, 1615–25*, p. 318.   [12] TCD, MS 567, ff. 32–5.

born *c.*1600. Educated first in Galway and subsequently in northern France, at Dieppe, Douai and Rouen, he was ordained a secular Catholic priest at Limerick in 1625 but normally resided in Galway until he left for France in 1652. He held the title of archdeacon of Tuam, but probably more significant for his day to day life was his status as chaplain to Sir Richard Blake, a prominent lawyer and later leading confederate.[13] He probably lived at a house leased by Blake and would have moved in much the same social circles as his second cousin and fellow Galwegian, Patrick Darcy. Lynch spent the last years of his life in exile in northern France, and it was there that he wrote his defence of Ireland to which he gave the title *Cambrensis Eversus.*

Living as an Irish Catholic scholar in a foreign Catholic country, Lynch found it necessary to defend Ireland's reputation in the face of adverse publicity promulgated in particular through the writings of Giraldus Cambrensis. Originally written in the twelfth century, the sometimes scurrilous commentaries on Ireland contained in Giraldus' *Topographia Hibernica* and *Expugnatio Hibernica* had been given a new lease of life among readers of Latin when they were incorporated into William Camden's *Anglica, Hibernica, Hormannica, Cambrica, a veteribus scripta . . .* (printed at Frankfurt in 1602). As Lynch pointed out, people tended to be drawn to stories of remote nations,[14] and particularly to stories of the unusual. Some of the contents of Giraldus' works amply rewarded the curious reader in search of tales of strange peoples. Lynch was aware that reading was forming the opinions of foreigners about Ireland, and he was concerned that the material circulating in France concerning Ireland ridiculed the country of his birth in the eyes of the world.[15] More specifically, being Old English, Lynch was conscious of the reality that foreign readers, reading about Ireland and the national characteristics of the Irish, did not distinguish between the Old English and the native Irish. Thus, even though the comments of Giraldus Cambrensis had referred to the native Irish population of the twelfth century, Lynch in exile found that the work was being read in the seventeenth century as a comment on all those born in Ireland, including the Old English who were of Norman ancestry.[16] Consequently, Lynch sought, like Keating, to defend the reputation of the native Irish as well as the Old English and addressed his Latin treatise primarily to a non-Irish audience.

Although Lynch presented his work in the guise of a refutation of Giraldus, it is clear that there were other writers whose views he wished to

---

[13] A post he held for a period of twenty-four years before 1652. J. F. O'Doherty (ed.), *De Praesulibus Hiberniae* (2 vols., IMC, Dublin, 1944), I, p. ii.
[14] Lynch, *Cambrensis,* II, p. 153.   [15] *Ibid.,* I, p. 221; II, pp. 151–3; III, p. 83.
[16] *Ibid.,* II, p. 153.

challenge. Accounts of the Nine Years War (1594–1603), which presented Hugh O'Neill, earl of Tyrone, as a rebel against the crown, and more recent pamphlet accounts of the war of the 1640s which portrayed Catholics as rebels, were also very much in his mind. He believed that propagandists, hostile to the Catholic nation, had appropriated the history of Ireland. His own polemical writing aimed to defend the reputation of the land of his birth and of the Catholic community of which he was a committed and active member.

The writing of history, in Lynch's view, was a political issue. He praised the work of those scholars who had worked to keep the language and history of Ireland alive. He regarded those like Geoffrey Keating whose scholarship in the Irish language had been in defence of 'the true history of Ireland', as saviours of the Irish past. They had ensured, he asserted, 'that the ancient glory of Ireland should not be entombed by the same convulsion which deprived the Irish of the lands of their fathers and of all their property'.[17] Clearly disturbed by the polemical literature of the 1640s, Lynch viewed the Irish past as ripe for confiscation, and in need of defence from unscrupulous writers. The political agenda of *Cambrensis Eversus* can be seen to have involved more than historical controversy however; it was also a polemical tract promoting a particular Old English agenda.

The form in which Lynch presented his work to the world was as a defence of Ireland's reputation, by reference to her history. The arguments he selected in support of his case illuminated some of the central dilemmas facing the Old English in seventeenth-century Ireland. His construction of the Irish past revealed the essence of his political ideology. The defence which Lynch presented involved him in an analysis of royal power, the nature of sovereignty, the duties of subjects, the role of parliament in an Irish context, the implications of conquest, and the nature of property rights. In passing, he revealed his views on natives and foreigners, and his juxtaposition of medieval and early modern dimensions of this idea gave rise to one of the underlying tensions of the work. Finally and crucially, his work was an essay on the politics of religious toleration.

II

The history of Ireland from creation to the coming of the Normans, written by Geoffrey Keating in the 1620s and early 1630s, was structured around a series of invasions of the island of Ireland culminating in the Norman conquest. This traditional framework of 'takings' of Ireland, drawn by Keating primarily from the *Leabhar Gabhála*, allowed scope to

---

[17] *Ibid.*, II, p. 381; also I, p. 221.

absorb outsiders as central actors in the narrative of Irish history, legitimising their status as contenders for the sovereignty of Ireland.[18] Thus, the
Ireland of Keating's historical imagination absorbed outsiders while
remaining an independent kingdom in its own right, an entity that had
never been subject to any higher authority before the eleventh century.[19]
Keating also emphasised that the Scythians, from whom all the Irish were
descended, had never been subject to any higher temporal power.[20] It was
a theme he returned to several times, and it was repeatedly used by
Lynch. Keating's message here was the antiquity and continuity of the
independent kingdom of Ireland. Citing Giraldus Cambrensis himself
that 'Ireland was, from the beginning free from incursion of any foreign
nation', Keating added: 'It is not so with any other country in Europe.'[21]
For him, the matter appeared as an issue of national pride in a European
context rather than a point of constitutional significance at home.

The second contribution of the Scythians to the heritage of the
kingdom of Ireland, in Keating's view, involved the 'institutes, laws and
ordinances' that originated with them.[22] Following on from this, early
kings were portrayed as judges, implementers and upholders of the law.[23]
Keating attached particular significance to the *Teagasc Ríogh* (Instruction
for Kings), an early medieval tract which outlined 'what a king should
be . . . and how he should rule the people through their laws' (*ag munadh
mar bugh dual do rígh bheith, . . . agus cionnus do smachtfadh na tuatha 'n-a
ndligheadhaibh*).[24] The laws came from the people, and the king was their
guarantor. Thus, in Keating's view, the rule of law dictated the powers of
the king.

According to Keating, the function of revising the law belonged to an
assembly that closely resembled an early modern parliament. The *Feis* of
Tara established by the king was the assembly which instituted laws and
customs and confirmed the annals and records of Ireland.[25] These were
then approved by the Ard Ollamh and inscribed in the *Rolla na Ríogh*
(Roll of Kings) called the 'Psalter of Tara', 'and every custom and record
that was in Ireland that did not agree with that chief book were not
regarded as genuine'.[26] The idea of a written corpus of law, regularly
revised, clearly appealed to Keating's sense of the authority of the written
word. The king's role in relation to law was as facilitator of revision, but
the revision itself was portrayed as the work of a wide-ranging assembly of
nobles, provincial kings and queens, bards, brehons and ollamhs, who sat

---

[18] Cunningham, 'Seventeenth-Century Interpretations'.
[19] Evidence of the independence of the kingdom most regularly cited was the fact that the
Romans had not succeeded in conquering Ireland. *FFÉ*, I, pp. 17, 83, 229.
[20] *Ibid.*, I, p. 229.   [21] *Ibid.*, I, pp. 229–31; 83.   [22] *Ibid.*, I, p. 229.   [23] *Ibid.*, II, p. 155.
[24] *Ibid.*, II, pp. 305, 347; K. Meyer (ed.), *The Instructions of King Cormac Mac Airt* (Dublin,
1909).   [25] *FFÉ.*, II, p. 245.   [26] *Ibid.*, II, p. 251.

in order of precedence in a vast and elaborate hall.[27] It is evident that a seventeenth-century understanding of parliament overlay the way in which these early assemblies were perceived and portrayed.[28]

The political institution of the kingship in pre-Christian Ireland was the element that gave a sense of continuity and coherence to Keating's story of Ireland through the upheavals associated with successive invasions. According to the *Foras Feasa ar Éirinn*, the first high king of Ireland was Sláinghe, one of the Fir Bolg. No particular emphasis was placed on his reign. He was described as one of the five chiefs of the Fir Bolg who led a conquest of Ireland with an army of 5,000. He and his four brothers were initially described as dividing Ireland amongst them whereas later they were portrayed as holding the sovereignty of Ireland in succession to each other.[29] The idea of shared or alternating sovereignty occurs repeatedly in book one of the *Foras Feasa ar Éirinn*. For instance, the three sons of Cearmad Milbheoil of the Tuatha Dé Danann alternated sovereignty every other year (*sealaidheacht flaithis gac re mbliadhan*).[30] On the arrival of the Clanna Mileadh, the most significant invasion in Keating's version of the Irish past, we are told that the sons of Míl initially had joint sovereignty (*comhfhlaitheas*) for a year before Eibhear was killed and Eireamhón then enjoyed full kingship for fourteen years.[31] These stories with their focus on shared sovereignty did not place particular value on a central highkingship but nonetheless the attention of readers was firmly directed towards the idea of the kingdom of Ireland as having a very long history.

In Keating's view of the past there were three distinct epochs of kingship in Ireland. Ireland before the coming of Christianity was the first epoch, firmly brought to a close with the coming of Patrick. The second great era was that of the kingdom of Ireland in the early Christian period down to the coming of the Normans. The final period of kingship began when Henry II of England acquired the sovereignty of Ireland, and Keating devoted particular attention to establishing the legitimacy of the claims of the Norman kings to the sovereignty of Ireland, in the 1170s, but only after he had outlined the stories of earlier kings in considerable detail. Continuity between the Anglo-Norman kingship and the earlier Gaelic kings of Ireland was the crucial innovation in *Foras Feasa ar Éirinn* that distinguished it from the earlier *Leabhar Gabhála* tradition. For an

---

[27] *Ibid.*, III, pp. 37–39.
[28] Katharine Simms, *From Kings to Warlords: The Changing Political Structure of Gaelic Ireland in the Later Middle Ages* (Woodbridge, 1987), p. 77.   [29] *FFÉ*, I, pp. 191–7.
[30] *Ibid.*, I, pp. 109; 223. Their three wives, named Éire, Banba and Fodhla alternated as queens, *FFÉ*, I, pp. 101–3; II, pp. 83–5. In Munster, the descendants of two sons of Oilioll Ólom, Eoghan Mór and Cormac Cas, allegedly took turns every generation in the sovereignty of the two provinces of Munster: *FFÉ*, I, p. 123.   [31] *Ibid.*, II, p. 105.

author of Anglo-Norman descent, and for the entire Old English commu-
nity in seventeenth-century Ireland, that continuity of the kingdom of
Ireland represented an important element in their understanding of
Irishness.

Keating outlined his theory of kingship at the beginning of the second
book of *Foras Feasa ar Éirinn*:

> Now, the reason why one person is made king over tribes and over districts is in
> order that each one in his own principality should be obedient to him, and that
> none of them should have power to resist or oppose him during his sovereignty,
> and to have it understood that it was by God who is Lord and ruler over all that he
> has been appointed king over the peoples to govern them, and hence that they are
> bound to obey him and to bear in mind that it is the same only God who is lord of
> heaven and of earth and of hell that gave him that authority and that it was from
> Him he obtained sovereignty.[32]

At first glance this might seem like an assertion of the idea of the 'divine
right' of kings, but on closer examination this is not so. It was however a
claim that kingship was crucial to the right working of society. Moreover
the king's sovereignty, in the Irish context, as portrayed by Keating, did
not come immediately from God, because the kingship was elective not
hereditary. Before Ireland was Christianised by St Patrick, Keating
recorded, 'it was the learned and those who were most zealous for the
aggrandisement of the public weal that the men of Ireland elected' as
kings. In relation to the early Christian period, Keating identified the
electors as 'the bishops and the nobles and the chroniclers who elected
the kings and lords until the Norman invasion'.[33] Inauguration was
depicted as being politically significant, and Keating felt it necessary to
outline its purpose. In the ceremony of inauguration, a

> chronicler came forward bearing the book called the Instruction for Kings
> [*Teagasc Ríogh*], in which there was a brief summary of the customs and laws of the
> country, and where it was explained how God and the people would reward the
> doing of good, and the punishment that awaited the king and his descendants if he
> did not carry out the principles of justice and equity which the Book of Kings and
> the Instruction for Kings direct to put in practice.[34]

The white wand used in the inauguration ceremony, Keating asserted,
signified equity and justice, truth, and freedom from bias.[35]

Accepting ancient ideas of a sacral kingship, Keating asserted that
during the reign of a good king the whole kingdom prospered. For
instance, during the reign of Eochaidh, last of the Fir Bolg to be king of
Ireland, 'there was no rain nor bad weather . . . nor yet a year without fruit

---

[32] *Ibid.*, III, p. 9.   [33] *Ibid.*, III, p. 11.   [34] *Ibid.*, III, p. 11.
[35] *Ibid.*, III, p. 13. On inauguration ceremonies, see Simms, *From Kings to Warlords*, pp.
21–40; see also Lynch, *Cambrensis*, III, p. 345.

and increase'.[36] Conversely, when the sovereignty of the rightful king was usurped, famine and crop failure followed. Thus the story was told of the serfs and rustic tribes who plotted against Cairbre, king of Ireland, and killed the free tribes of Ireland with the exception of three unborn sons of King Cairbre. The usual prosperity of Ireland did not return until these three had come back and accepted their father's inheritance as kings. Even in this instance, however, it should be noted that the sovereignty of Ireland was not acquired by heredity alone; the sons of Cairbre were asked by the men of Ireland to return and assume sovereignty.[37] Yet it was not Keating's primary concern to analyse the nature of sovereignty. The symbolic message of the story he told focused on the idea of a rightful king, under whom the country would prosper, and the disaster that would befall if that rightful ruler was usurped.

Sovereignty was linked with destiny in the case of Míl, the common ancestor of the Gael, who 'bethought him that Caicher the druid had foretold, long before, to his ancestor Lamhfhionn, that it was in Ireland his descendants would obtain permanent sovereignty'.[38] The scene was thus set for the arrival of the sons of Míl from whom the Gael traced their descent. Sovereignty as destiny was not a regular theme however, nor was its attainment an end in itself. Sovereignty had to be earned from the people, and could be forfeited if a king did not live up to the expectations of the people. 'We do not read in the *seanchus*' Keating wrote, 'that there was ever any king of Ireland from the time of Slainghe to the Norman invasion but a king who obtained the sovereignty of Ireland by the choice of the people, by the excellence of his exploits and by the strength of his hand.'[39]

Keating's description of the ascent of Brian Boru to the position of King of Ireland illustrated central aspects of kingship in an Irish context.[40] Brian Boru obtained the kingdom of Ireland in the eleventh century 'by the strength and bravery of his feats of valour and championship, driving the foreigners and the Danair out of the country'.[41] He was not a usurper, 'for it was not the custom in Ireland that the son should succeed the father in the sovereignty of Ireland, as is plain from the history up to this point, but the sovereignty of Ireland was given to him who was the most powerful in action and exploit'.[42] In Brian Boru's case then, his predecessor, Maolseachlainn, had forfeited his claim, because he had given in to 'luxury and comfort and ease' when he should have been

---

[36] *FFÉ*, I, p. 199.   [37] *Ibid.*, II, p. 241.   [38] *Ibid.*, II, p. 45.   [39] *Ibid.*, III, p. 183.
[40] In some seventeenth-century manuscripts of *Foras Feasa ar Éirinn* the section on inauguration appears not as in the printed text, at the beginning of the early Christian narrative, but rather in connection with the reign of the Dál gCais King, Brian Boru: RIA, MS 24.P.23; University College Cork, Gaelic MS 92; TCD, MS 1394.   [41] *FFÉ*, III, p. 257.
[42] *Ibid.*, III, p. 257.

devoting his energy to expelling foreigners.[43] Because of this the majority of the nobles of Ireland chose Brian Boru to replace him (and those who did not were forced to submit against their will).[44] Military prowess, then, proved the key to winning support of the people and the award of sovereignty. When a rightful king was installed, the whole country prospered and bore fruit.[45]

III

Kingship, in John Lynch's view also, was a central concept. The history of Ireland, he insisted, should be primarily a history of its kings: 'not the names only, but the acts of its kings, should be the principal objects in the narrative of a writer who undertakes to compile the history of a country'.[46] Drawing heavily on Keating, he offered sketches from the lives of the kings of Ireland, down to Ruaidhrí O'Connor, the last high king, in the late twelfth century.[47] Lynch sought to explain the violent nature of many of their kingly exploits: 'It has often been a matter of astonishment to me, and no doubt to others, that of the great number of Irish kings, many if not most of them were cut off by a violent death, and that the successor often hewed his way to the throne over the body of his predecessor.'[48] The approach Lynch adopted was one of normalisation through contextualisation: 'when you find that this inhuman habit of the Irish was common in all contemporary nations, our astonishment ceases; the whole guilt of the atrocious facts cannot be charged against the Irish alone, since most other nations rivalled, if they did not outstrip them in similar barbarities'. He noted that at least fifty Roman emperors died violently, that 'England, our neighbour, supplies examples of atrocity in abundance', and that forty out of 140 Scottish kings died 'before their natural term'.[49] Lynch refrained from any comment on the morality of such activities, and was satisfied to place the whole business in a biblical context. 'Should any

---

[43] *Ibid.*, III, p. 249.   [44] *Ibid.*, III, p. 257.

[45] The three elements of early Irish kingship as analysed by modern Irish scholars – sovereignty, military prowess and fecundity – thus permeate the narrative history of the kingdom of Ireland as presented by Geoffrey Keating and T. Ó Cathasaigh, *Heroic Biography of Cormac Mac Airt* (Dublin, 1977); B. Ó Buachalla, 'Aodh Eangach and the Irish King Hero' in D. Ó Corráin, L. Breatnach and K. McCone (eds.), *Sages, Saints and Storytellers* (Maynooth, 1989), pp. 200–32.   [46] Lynch, *Cambrensis*, I, p. 413.

[47] In his discussion of one of the best-documented pre-Patrician kings, Cormac Mac Airt (+266 AD), Lynch's account was printed as though it were a direct translation of Keating's history, though it was in fact a summary abstract. The points emphasised by Lynch were Cormac's legislative skills, wisdom, hospitality and justice. The account concluded with the story of Cormac's privileged conversion to Christianity and his retrospective Christian burial, Lynch, *Cambrensis,* I, pp. 481–5.   [48] *Ibid.*, II, p. 101.

[49] *Ibid.*, II, pp. 103–5.

nation upbraid Ireland with the infamy of these crimes, a crushing rebuke to the accusation is ever ready in the words of Our Saviour to the Jews, when they clamored for the death of the adulterous woman: "he that is without sin among you, let him first cast a stone at her".'[50]

The story of the pre-Christian kings of Ireland was important because it supported Lynch's claim that Ireland was an independent kingdom. He defended the reputation of these kings, and rejected the idea that they came to power by force of arms alone.[51] Like Keating, he emphasised the eagerness with which the Irish kings embraced Christianity. He offered several stories as evidence of this, such as that of the vision of St Columba who saw the soul of an Irish king ascend straight to heaven, bypassing purgatory on the way.[52] Lynch also examined the institution of kingship, and the traditions associated with it, and did so in a more analytical and theoretical way than is found in Keating's narrative. The anointing of kings, the inauguration ceremony, the wearing of a crown, were all discussed, as well as the process of selection.[53] He stressed that monarchs were freely chosen and that the position was not hereditary. Rather, the king was elected by 'the people of Ireland'. This meant that there were reciprocal obligations between king and subject which worked to secure 'the liberties of Ireland'.[54] Moreover Lynch made important points about the nature of the contract between a king and his people (discussed below, section VI). On the one hand, the idea of a long-established Christian kingdom enhanced Ireland's status in European eyes, and such stories proved a useful counter to the still current accusations of Giraldus Cambrensis. On the other, it was important for Lynch's constitutional arguments on the nature of the kingdom, because it allowed him to argue that the kingdom of Ireland had not been in need of moral reform in the twelfth century. This left the way open to refute stories of papal authority for the Norman invasion.

IV

The evolution of the concept of kingship after the coming of the Normans was a central constitutional issue tackled by Lynch in *Cambrensis Eversus*. He began by specifically rejecting divine right, in the case of Henry II. 'One would imagine, heaven save us, that this Henry was a God that dropped down from the clouds with a "divine" commission.'[55] He followed this with an assertion that 'so far from having a commission from heaven to oppress Ireland, he had none even from earth'.[56] The

---

[50] *Ibid.*, II, p. 107. [51] *Ibid.*, III, pp. 323–5. [52] *Ibid.*, III, p. 305.
[53] *Ibid.*, III, pp. 325–43. [54] *Ibid.*, II, p. 491. [55] *Ibid.*, II, p. 543. [56] *Ibid.*, II, pp. 545–7.

legitimacy of the papal bull on which Henry II's authority was supposedly based was again denied, and the instigator of the Norman invasion, Dermot MacMurrough, was depicted in derogatory terms as an advocate of adultery and rebellion. According to Lynch, Henry II disrupted rather than promoted Irish civility by supporting MacMurrough, 'a man who trampled on the laws and spurned his lawful superiors' and, as a result, the pope could not have relied upon him under any circumstances.[57] Lynch also dismissed Keating's story that one Donnchadh Ó Briain, son of Brian Boru, and king of Ireland, had visited Rome on pilgrimage and had surrendered 'with the consent of all his chieftains, the supreme dominion of Ireland into the hands of the pope'. Lynch maintained that 'the Irish never surrendered the political supremacy of their country to the pope'.[58]

Lynch was careful to assert (for the benefit of his French Catholic readership) that this refutation of the legality of the papal bull was not to be construed as evidence of any Irish disloyalty to the pope. On the contrary, he emphasised the Irish 'inviolable fidelity to the Catholic faith' which they prized more highly than life itself.[59] Drawing on David Rothe's *Analecta Sacra,* he argued that 'of all the countries in Europe subject to heretical kings, there was not one in which a greater number of subjects have persevered in the old faith, and in obedience to the sovereign pontiff than in Ireland'.[60] Lynch even cited the popular support enjoyed by the papal nuncio, Giovanni Battista Rinuccini, in the mid-1640s, noting that this enthusiasm for the papacy had been expressed even though it went against the position of the Supreme Council of the Confederate Catholics of Ireland.[61] Although arguing that the Irish people had never surrendered Irish sovereignty to the papacy, Lynch carefully asserted that 'all their principles in religious affairs were subordinate to the power of the pope'.[62] This clear separation of spiritual from temporal power not only justified Lynch's opposition to the policies of Rinuccini but also formed a central tenet of the political ambitions of the Old English in Ireland.

Lynch rejected Keating's case regarding the process by which the kingship of Ireland passed into the hands of the English crown. Brendan Bradshaw has discussed this in some detail and categorised it as being in the nature of a *translatio imperii.* This term is used to denote the process which began, according to Keating, when a high king, Donnchadh Ó Briain, together with the Irish nobility, entrusted the sovereignty of

[57] *Ibid.,* II, pp. 553–5.   [58] *FFÉ,* III, pp. 291, 347; Lynch, *Cambrensis,* II, p. 623.
[59] Lynch, *Cambrensis,* II, p. 605.
[60] *Ibid.,* II, pp. 613–15; David Rothe, *Analecta Sacra, Nova, et Mira de Rebus Catholicorum in Hibernia . . . gestis* ([Paris], 1616).   [61] Lynch, *Cambrensis,* II, pp. 615–21.
[62] *Ibid.,* II, p. 623.

Ireland to the pope in 1092. This move facilitated the 1155 bull, Laudabiliter, issued by Pope Adrian IV which conferred conditional power on Henry II, specifically requiring him 'to maintain and protect the privileges and liberties of the country' of Ireland. In Keating's view, therefore, the arrival of the Anglo-Normans was not to be regarded as a conquest. It was seen, in Bradshaw's words, as 'the outcome of a process by which Henry II secured acknowledgement of the overlordship conferred on him by Laudabiliter from those on whom it directly impinged, the ecclesiastical and political elites in Ireland.'[63] Approved by the clergy, mediated by John of Salisbury, and by the laity, through the specific invitation of MacMurrough, the military supporters of the Anglo-Norman knights were depicted by Keating as serving the island's legitimate sovereign. The king then arrived in person, to assert his authority over his unruly (Norman) vassals, and the native Irish voluntarily acknowledged the overlordship of the king and were received by him as vassals. By this means, the ancient kingdom of Ireland became a fief of the crown of England, and the native Irish highkingship reached an end.[64]

Lynch's interpretation was quite different. He insisted that through forged papal bulls, 'our countrymen were never brought to trial, much less convicted of any crime, and yet were condemned, most undeservedly, to forfeit their dearly beloved country [*Charissimae Patriae*]'.[65] He reiterated that no foreign power ever held the sovereignty of Ireland.[66] His discussion of the nature of kingship reveals that he viewed it as a crucial issue and that any challenge to Irish sovereignty from an external source, even the papacy, was a very serious matter. It was a subversion of the kingdom of Ireland and a violation 'of rights of immemorial possession'.[67] He emphasised that resistance to any threat of loss of sovereignty was justified, and made it clear that it was the sovereignty of the people that he had in mind rather than any narrower concept of royal sovereignty. Sovereignty, for Lynch, was ultimately vested in the people, who should obey a just king, but were entitled to resist an unjust king by force of arms.[68]

Why did Lynch, a Catholic priest of Anglo-Norman descent, reject the idea of an assignment of sovereignty to the Norman kings via the papacy? First, the theory implied that the Irish had been in need of moral reform, an unhelpful argument in the creation of an image of a holy Catholic country from the coming of Christianity. Second, when the

---

[63] Brendan Bradshaw, 'Geoffrey Keating, Apologist of Irish Ireland' in B. Bradshaw, A. Hadfield and W. Maley (eds.), *Representing Ireland: Literature and the Origins of Conflict* (Cambridge, 1993), p. 176.   [64] Bradshaw, 'Geoffrey Keating', pp. 177–8.
[65] Lynch, *Cambrensis*, II, pp. 451; 469.   [66] *Ibid.*, II, p. 437.   [67] *Ibid.*, II, pp. 443–5.
[68] *Ibid.*, II, pp. 489–93.

kings in question were the Stuarts, rather than earlier English kings, the *translatio imperii* via the papacy was no longer an essential element in the case for the legitimacy of the monarch in an Irish context. The Stuarts could, through their descent, be portrayed as the rightful holders of temporal sovereignty over Ireland, without any reference to the papacy. The Stuart king's legitimacy as Irish sovereign was easily established. The impeccable Milesian genealogy of the Scottish James VI as James I of England, made him entirely acceptable in the role of king of Ireland. Significantly Lynch noted that this idea appealed particularly to the native Irish.[69]

The Stuarts could be portrayed as the legitimate temporal successors of the Irish high kings, in a manner that left the way open for a clear separation of church and monarchy. Crucially, Lynch's argument kept the papacy out of the issue of Irish sovereignty. This in turn allowed Lynch scope to appeal directly to a Stuart king that the Catholicism of the Old English should not be seen as a mark of disloyalty to the monarch in secular matters. The elimination of the supposed constitutional link between the papacy and the monarchy in the matter of the sovereignty of Ireland had become necessary to the Old English case, and Lynch, as an opponent of Papal Nuncio Rinuccini, would have been particularly attracted to such an idea.

V

Having rejected Keating's scenario of a *translatio imperii* as the origin of the Anglo-Norman claim to sovereignty in Ireland, Lynch had to formulate an alternative justification for the authority of the Stuarts as Irish monarchs which safeguarded the legality of Old English claims on land and property in Ireland.[70] Lynch reminded his readers that institutions changed over time, and that the era of the early Christian kings of Ireland was well and truly over. He recalled the scriptural reference to God 'who changeth times and ages and taketh away kingdoms and establisheth them'.[71] This view of a kingdom whose era had passed was forced on him by the need to legitimise the Old English constitutional position. Lynch was prepared to admit a breach in continuity between the early Irish kingdom and the modern era. The problem he faced was that the Milesian genealogy of James VI and I did nothing to support the legitimacy of Old English titles to property in Ireland inherited from their

---

[69] *Ibid.*, III, p. 53.
[70] He argued that O'Brien had been king not of Ireland but of Munster only (and that only Keating claimed otherwise), and that Irish independence had never been surrendered to the papacy.   [71] Daniel II.21; Lynch, *Cambrensis*, III, pp. 43–5.

Norman ancestors. Those property titles rested on the idea that Henry II had indeed acquired legitimate title to Ireland in the twelfth century. Lynch opted for the idea of title legitimised by right of conquest.[72] 'In wars of conquest', he argued, 'might is right. As some customs, though established by crime, yet may be lawfully followed after they have been sanctioned by general and long continued usage, so the supreme power itself, though unjustly acquired, can be justly retained, when it can plead the prescription of long possession.'[73] Sovereignty itself, therefore, claimed by right of conquest, could in Lynch's view be legitimised by the passage of time.

Lynch pointedly extended this argument, based on the idea of long possession, to the title enjoyed by private individuals to their landed property and possessions. 'Private individuals too are not bound to renounce the patrimonies which have been long in possession of their family, though they were originally acquired by the injustice of an ancestor; this principle is acted on every day, and yet neither law nor argument, nor authority is admitted against it.'[74] He realised that he was treading on very thin ice here. Time alone, it could be argued, was all that differentiated the legality of Old English property claims as against those of the more recently arrived New English and even the Cromwellians. Fully conscious of the real threat that had been posed to the property of the Old English from the Commission for Defective Titles and under the Cromwellian confiscations, he had to avoid over-stating his case for the Old English.[75] 'The same usage is more applicable to the transfer of kingdoms and principalities, as they are more easily, more frequently, yes and more justly transferred than the property of individuals', he concluded.[76]

The legitimacy of royal power in Norman Ireland was put into perspective, in Lynch's view, by analogy with the Roman Empire. 'The majesty of the Roman empire itself owed its origin to accumulated crimes.' Yet, 'while it was yet in its infancy, Christ ordered allegiance to be paid to the person invested with the imperial dignity, without any inquiry into the justice or injustice of the right by which it was held. . . . Thereby he gave us to understand that we should obey those who were admitted as undisputed sovereigns, and not question the validity of their title.'[77] A further element of Lynch's historical interpretation of the constitutional position of Ireland related to the status of the Norman kings. He described the limited nature of the authority of English kings in Ireland from the time of Henry II which lasted until the accession of James VI and I. Henry II, and

[72] Ibid., III, pp. 43–5.   [73] Ibid., III, pp. 43–5.   [74] Ibid., III, pp. 43–5.
[75] Aidan Clarke, The Old English in Ireland, 1625–42 (London, 1966), pp. 107–14; R. C. Simington (ed.), The Transplantation to Connacht, 1654–58 (IMC, Dublin, 1970).
[76] Lynch, Cambrensis, III, p. 45.   [77] Ibid., III, pp. 47–9.

his successors, he asserted, recognised only some inhabitants of Ireland as their subjects. The native kings, such as Ruaidhrí O'Connor, he insisted, retained sovereign power and he cited instances where that sovereignty was given *de facto* recognition by the English administration as late as the sixteenth century.[78]

VI

Lynch recognised that the relationship between the sovereign and his subjects involved a contract. King and subjects had each to accept and acknowledge the status of the other. In essence, the sovereignty of the king depended on the willingness of the people to be his subjects. But the king also had to embrace the people as his true subjects – and not as the 'king's Irish enemies' – before he could expect their dutiful allegiance. While his primary concern was to situate the Old English position in its historical context, Lynch made a significant constitutional point on the historical status of the native Irish also. He argued that the wars of the Irish against the English, and particularly the Nine Years War, were not rebellions. 'When a nation wages war against a prince whose authority it does not acknowledge, it must not be stigmatised as rebellious, but as an enemy.'[79] He used Sir John Davies as support for the constitutional argument that sovereignty to be legitimate must be recognised as such by subjects who are acknowledged to be subjects. Thus Hugh O'Neill, earl of Tyrone, had behaved not as a rebel in the Nine Years War but rather as a non-subject, who should have been regarded as having been an enemy from another nation.[80]

Lynch also adapted the argument put forward by Hugo Grotius that legitimate title may be acquired by long possession 'especially when the people tacitly acknowledges it'.[81] He argued that 'wherever there is a treaty, obedience is unquestionably due to the supreme authority. Now nothing can be more certain than that the Irish princes often placed themselves under the protection of the English kings and made some treaties with them.' He claimed that the Irish frequently acknowledged the sovereignty of the king of England 'but they never fully accepted the regular rights and duties of subjects until King James ascended the throne'.[82] Lynch continued that James 'was the cornerstone that made both one on his accession to the English throne. For it was then that the Irish renounced all thoughts of opposition (especially as they believed

---

[78] *Ibid.*, II, p. 525.
[79] *Ibid.*, III, p. 83. Also see T. M. Charles-Edwards, 'A Contract between King and People in Early Medieval Ireland: *Críth Gablach* on kingship', *Peritia*, 8 (1994), pp. 107–19.
[80] Lynch, *Cambrensis*, III, p. 83.   [81] *Ibid.*, III, p. 49.   [82] *Ibid.*, III, p. 53.

that he would embrace the Catholic religion) and willingly acknowledged his authority, because they knew he was descended from the old Irish kings'.[83] This was clearly an issue of contemporary debate because Lynch felt it necessary to rebuke those who ranked Charles II as a foreigner when he could be shown to be descended from the kings of Ireland. He rested his case by reiterating that Grotius had shown that Charles' right to command was, in any case, 'confirmed by long possession'. It was part of Catholic doctrine therefore that 'it is not lawful to rebel against a prince, who has possession of a country and administers its government, though originally he had no right to it, and was guilty of gross injustice in invading and occupying it'.[84] This argument appears to have been designed to have inclusive appeal to all Irish Catholics.

VII

Having asserted that loyalty to the king was an element of Catholic doctrine, Lynch then outlined in detail the dilemma of Irish Catholics whose loyalty to their king had gone unrewarded. They were effectively debarred from office in government, law, the army and the church in their own country 'which was won by the blood of their ancestors'.[85] He apportioned blame not to Charles I but to his evil counsellors. And yet, despite their misfortunes, he asserted, the Irish have remained loyal to the king 'because they were aware these machinations were not to be charged against him but against his officers in Ireland . . . [who] rather like malignant planets, intercepted and diverted the benignant influence of the throne'. He added: 'No cloud can make the sunflower turn from the sun, nor could the cruelty of his officers shake the devotion of the Irish to their King.'[86]

Quoting the passage from Sir John Davies' *Discovery of the True Causes* on Irish respect for the law when justly applied, used earlier by Keating as a conclusion to his *Foras Feasa*, Lynch set the scene for his case for the legality of Irish actions in the 1640s.[87] That the Irish had acted in defence of their king was a commonplace of Old English rhetoric. Lynch believed

---

[83] *Ibid.*, III, p. 53.   [84] *Ibid.*, III, pp. 67, 69.   [85] *Ibid.*, III, p. 71.   [86] *Ibid.*, III, p. 79.

[87] *Ibid.*, III, p. 81. Lynch quoted the passage more extensively than Keating, and translated it into Latin, whereas Keating had cited the passage in English. 'In which condition of subjects, they will gladly continue, without defection or adhering to any other Lord or King, as long as they may be Protected, and Justly Governed, without Oppression on the one side, or Impunity on the other. For, there is no Nation of people under the sunne, that doth love equal and indifferent Justic, better than the Irish; or will rest better satisfied with the execution thereof, so as they may have the protection & benefit of the Law, when upon just cause they do desire it': John Davies, *Discovery of the True Causes why Ireland was never Entirely Subdued* (London, 1612; facsimile reprint, Shannon, 1969), pp. [286–7].

it would have been catastrophic for the Old English to revolt against the king, since the legality of their titles depended entirely on the king's right of conquest.

It would not only be an injustice, but madness, to revolt from princes under whose leadership they formerly acquired and still hold their possessions . . . If they once renounced the protection of their prince, they would be instantly exposed to the arms of two very powerful enemies – namely the English who would be sent over from England to crush the rebellion and the Irish of Spanish descent, who would hail, with rapturous joy, the opportunity of recovering by the sword the possessions which had formerly been wrested from the ancestors.[88]

Discussing the war of the 1640s which he referred to as the Ten Years War, Lynch conflated the native Irish and the Old English into 'the Irish', or the 'natives' (*incolas*), and defined their role as having been in defence of the king against the usurping parliamentarians. Together, they were 'forced to fly to arms in defence of their creed, their king and their country, against their fellow subjects who had no authority over them'.[89] In the light of the earlier discussion on the difference between subjects and non-subjects of the king, the description of the parliamentarians as 'subjects' was intended to turn the tables on them and portray them as rebels for having behaved in a manner that was incompatible with their status as subjects of the king. The parliamentarians had neglected their duties as subjects, an accusation that could not have been made against the Irish in the Nine Years War, because of their status as non-subjects. To emphasise the culpability of the New English, Lynch stated that the perpetrators of crimes in the 1640s had been punished by God for their actions, many soldiers dying of disease and suffering other misfortune. Referring back to the earlier decades of the seventeenth century he recalled the case of the Munster president Sir Henry Brouncker, who, according to Lynch, 'was devoured piecemeal by vermin' in divine retribution for his unjust treatment of the king's subjects in the years immediately following the 1605 declaration against Catholic clergy.[90]

Lynch was prepared to concede that not all the atrocities of the 1640s were committed by Protestants. He admitted some misdeeds among the Catholic Irish, but again attempted to normalise the situation. It was not a rebellion of the whole nation, he repeated; it was a case of people being caught up in a mob situation, where the rule of law was overthrown. He likened events in Ireland to the case of the Bordeaux salt tax riots of 1548, having admitted that 'when once the rein of law and reason is thrown aside the ignorant multitude plunges directly into every excess, and wreaks its vengeance alike on the innocent and guilty'.[91]

[88] Lynch, *Cambrensis*, III, p. 81.   [89] *Ibid.*, III, p. 87.   [90] *Ibid.*, III, p. 101.
[91] *Ibid.*, III, p. 105.

The war of the 1640s, Lynch concluded, was not to be regarded as a rebellion of the whole nation. Those who did take up arms did so because it was 'their wives, their children, their lives, and liberty, which is dearer than life, and their religion, dearest of all which were threatened with ruin. Can it be surprising', he asked, 'that a catastrophe so appalling and indiscriminate should have driven the Irish into a sedition, which so often arose in other countries, from causes comparatively trifling?'[92] He developed the point by stressing that although it was not a rebellion of the whole nation, everyone was punished by parliament. 'All the Irish, not only those engaged in the troubles, but the whole nation, were declared by a vote of parliament guilty of high treason, and condemned to forfeit their property and their lives.'[93] This decision of parliament was against the divine law, he asserted, citing Ezekiel XVIII.10; and also against the laws of man which decreed that 'one man's crime shall not bring others into peril'.[94] The injustice of this parliamentary decision was one of the central concerns of the Old English as portrayed by Lynch.

VIII

Having outlined Old English loyalty to the king, together with a rather weaker assertion of the loyalty of the Old Irish community, Lynch had set the scene to make his case for Irish Catholic representation in parliament. It was the issue he chose to highlight in the dedicatory epistle to Charles II, as well as in the main text of Cambrensis Eversus. Having first rejected the jurisdiction of the English parliament,[95] his grievance was stated as being that 'A parliament was lately held at Dublin, not of natives, according to the custom of our ancestors, but of foreigners, who became our legislators before they were our fellow citizens.'[96] His historical construct, borrowed from Keating's Foras Feasa, had portrayed a harmonious tradition of Irish parliaments, traceable back through the Feis of Tara convened by Irish high kings. This idea of parliament as an indigenous institution where Irishmen regulated their own affairs, under the auspices of their chosen and benevolent sovereign, confirmed mid-seventeenth-century developments which effectively excluded Catholics from parliament in Ireland as an unacceptable usurpation of time-honoured tradition. 'It was galling enough that foreigners should sit in judgement on our lives and properties in the English parliament, but it is far more dreadful to be depending on the mercy of foreigners in the heart of Ireland.' A parliament had met to decide on Irish affairs, in which there

---

[92] Ibid., III, p. 107.   [93] The allusion is to the Adventurers' Act (1642).
[94] Lynch, Cambrensis, III, p. 111.   [95] Ibid., I, pp. 9–11.   [96] Ibid., I, p. 25.

was not 'a single place reserved for the sons, the genuine citizens of the land (*indigenis genuinisque civibus*)'.[97] This was the parliament that assembled in May 1661, effectively an all-Protestant body, in which both Cromwellians and Old Protestants were strongly represented. Its main focus in the first year was the land settlement, as it debated legislation that culminated in the anti-Catholic Act of Settlement (July 1662).[98]

In his address, Lynch reminded Charles II that he was the ruler of a multiple kingdom, and asked for parity with Scotland and England. 'When kings hold several kingdoms under their sceptre, their council is composed of men selected from each, that the interests of all may be secured by their combined deliberations.'[99] Each component of the multiple kingdom, he argued, should have a parliament which represented all the king's subjects in that region. Recognition of the authority of the English king in Ireland did not acknowledge the authority of the English parliament over Ireland.[100] That Catholics were effectively excluded from the Irish parliament meant that it consisted entirely of seventeenth-century newcomers, whether Cromwellians or Old Protestants. Thus the 1661 parliament was, he argued, a body of foreigners.[101] Lynch insisted that the religion of Irish Catholics should not be an obstacle to their inclusion in such a parliament. Their allegiance to the king had been amply proved by their actions not just in the 1640s, but over the previous 300 years. It was not a crime to profess a different religion from the king, and it should not mean political oblivion. 'History', he argued, 'is full of examples of churches flourishing under a king of a different creed', an opinion confirmed by James VI and I, who found that 'the papists were more zealous in their allegiance than many professing Protestants'.[102]

The analysis of recent parliamentary decisions was used to offer Charles II a clear reminder both of the actions of the regicides in England and of traditional Old English Catholic support for the monarch in Ireland. Through these arguments on the proper role of parliament, and the rights of Catholic subjects in a Protestant kingdom, Lynch made the case that the Irish should have 'full liberty', 'the dearest object of our aspirations'.[103] By 'liberty', Lynch explained that he meant the opposite of 'slavery'. Slaves were denied their will, and subjected to wicked rule.[104] The misuse of law was what he saw as undermining liberty. Thus the fraudulent papal bull had 'annihilated the liberty of Irishmen', liberty being 'a thing beyond price'. The just administration of the law, justice being defined by historically legitimate entitlements, was the necessary prerequisite for the liberty of Irishmen.[105]

[97] *Ibid.*, I, p. 29.   [98] *NHI*, III, pp. 423–4.   [99] Lynch, *Cambrensis*, I, p. 69.
[100] Lynch, I, pp. 9–11; III, p. 113.   [101] *Ibid.*, I, p. 25.   [102] *Ibid.*, I, p. 75.
[103] *Ibid.*, I, p. 69.   [104] *Ibid.*, II, p. 491.   [105] *Ibid.*, II, pp. 489–91.

The papal bull which had deprived the Irish of 'their kingdom, their liberty, and their property', was such that the Irish would have been justified in opposing this injustice by force of arms. Lynch cited Cicero, Ovid and other classical authors in support of the principle.[106] He contrasted the halcyon days of early Christian Irish kingship, of reciprocal obligations between king and subject, in which the liberties of the Irish were secure (*tamdieu libertas Hibernos mansit*),[107] with both the Norman and Stuart scenarios. Liberty was guaranteed in early Ireland, he argued, because Irish kings were freely chosen, and could not alienate the kingship, 'the power of electing a successor being vested, not in him, but in the people of Ireland'.[108] 'So long as the reciprocal obligations of king and subject rested on this basis, the liberties of Ireland were secure; for obedience to a king and the enjoyment of liberty are perfectly compatible.'[109] The lack of harmony between king and people since that time, and the lack of just administration of the law, had denied them their historical entitlements in the kingdom of Ireland, had deprived them of their liberty, and had reduced them to the status of slaves.

This view, as expressed by Lynch, was shared by another close reader of Keating's *Foras Feasa ar Éirinn*. Michael Kearney, who translated Keating's history into English in 1635, revised the concluding page of the history for the benefit of its new readers. Kearney, like Lynch, emphasised the need for the just administration of the law which Keating had recommended. The crucial constitutional point from Kearney's view was the failure of the English 'to admit them [the Irish] to the conditions of subjects', and that once that status was achieved, the Irish would 'gladly continue without defection obedient to the King of England'. The king's protection was emphasised here and given precedence over the idea of the rule of law.[110]

Believing that all citizens of Ireland were entitled to the privileges enjoyed by other subjects of the king, the idea of Ireland as a colony registered with Lynch only as a last resort. He saw the Irish and Old English Catholics, and the Old Protestants as all legitimate subjects of the one king in a multiple kingdom. But in coming to terms with the reality of politics in the 1650s he finally conceded that 'we should be perfectly content if the English would even treat us as colonies, which the Romans of old treated as parents their children'. It was the Old English who were his real concern when he exclaimed: 'Many a time I wished that England would extend to the Irish that kindness which grandmothers show to their grandchildren.'[111]

---

[106] *Ibid.*, II, pp. 489–91.   [107] *Ibid.*, II, p. 490.   [108] *Ibid.*, II, p. 491.
[109] *Ibid.*, II, p. 491.   [110] RIA, MS 24.G.16, conclusion.
[111] Lynch, *Cambrensis*, III, pp. 177–9.

IX

The description of Ireland's political life presented by John Lynch in *Cambrensis Eversus* is not without its contradictions and confusions. A core dilemma which Lynch faced in using the past to legitimise current Old English claims to property and political power was that reading twelfth-century Irish history typologically involved as much historical amnesia as memory. The misfortunes of the 'natives' as defined by Lynch in the seventeenth century could not comfortably be equated with those of the twelfth, because of the inconvenient historical reality that many of the 'natives' (*incolas*) of the seventeenth century were the descendants of the 'foreigners' of the twelfth century. Lynch was conscious of the fact that the Old English were now in a very similar position to that of the Gaelic community in the twelfth century, and that the injustices of the current 'conquest' which he opposed were not helpfully seen as 'injustices' in a twelfth-century context.[112] Lynch used several devices to help overcome this difficulty. The term 'native' was used as a way of masking differences between the Old English of the seventeenth century and the native Irish of the twelfth. Just as in the sixteenth-century Irish annals the meaning of the word *Gall* (foreigner) has changed over time,[113] so in Lynch's mind, the word *incola* was just as applicable to the seventeenth-century Old English descendants of the Anglo-Normans as to the Old Gaelic Irish of the twelfth century.

There was also a contradiction inherent in Lynch's case that the Stuart legitimacy depended on their Milesian ancestry, while he insisted at times that Old English ethnicity was to be disregarded. His insistence in the case of the kingship of Ireland that its authority was proven by the fact of its not being hereditary was at odds with his arguments on the legitimacy of hereditary Stuart claims to the throne.[114] The theory of conquest on which Old English property claims rested was not fully consistent with his view that the Cromwellian conquest was intrinsically illegitimate. Only the passage of time separated them. Inspired by Keating's too-plausible, too-coherent history which had integrated the Old English into the story of the origins of the Irish people, Lynch had been drawn into using that history to interpret the present in support of the Old English cause in the mid-seventeenth century. He only gradually came to realise the difficulties inherent in such an exercise. Keating's history had prudently terminated in the 1170s, leaving the past to speak for itself, and allowing the Old English the status of the final wave of settlers in Ireland. Lynch's

---

[112] *Ibid.*, II, p. 489.
[113] B. Cunningham and R. Gillespie, 'Englishmen in Irish Annals', *Irish Economic and Social History*, 17 (1990), pp. 5–21.   [114] Lynch, *Cambrensis*, II, p. 491; III, p. 127.

1650s Old English perspective could no longer leave it at that. By then it was clear that there had indeed been not one but two waves of 'invasion' in the previous hundred years, and in the story of the past from the Old English standpoint in the 1650s, the whole idea of waves of successive invasions (derived from the *Leabhar Gabhála*) was jettisoned. It was a view of the past that had become distinctly unhelpful in a mid-seventeenth-century context.

A core concept which Lynch absorbed from Keating's inclusive history was the idea of *Éireannaigh* or *Hibernos*, meaning those born in Ireland and thereby defined as Irish in the eyes of the world, without any qualification or limitations on that Irishness by virtue of their ancestry. It was a theory that made sense most of all, perhaps, to those like Lynch who looked back on Ireland from overseas.[115] By rejecting ethnicity as an indicator of nationality, Lynch jettisoned a central tenet of medieval European political thought. Yet he clearly had some reservations. Lynch was aware of the centuries-long interaction which had reduced the ethnic distinctions between the native Irish and the Old English in Ireland. He noted the degree of intermarriage, the level of fosterage and nursing of children across ethnic boundaries, the extent to which the two groups had come to share a common language, modes of dress and social behaviour. They were, he said, 'like grafts, which in process of time, assume the form of that tree on which they were engrafted, the English and Irish races have been so united by the social intercourse of 500 years, that long since they are only one people'.[116] Yet, he valued the idea of retaining a distinction between the two kinds of Irishman, and his views in *Cambrensis Eversus* are far more moderate than those expressed in his later controversial publications *Alithinologia* and *Alithinologia supplementum*.[117] 'There are two races of Irishmen in Ireland', he stated, 'one that came from Spain 3000 years ago, the other from England 600 years since.'[118] Earlier, when giving historical illustrations of the traditional hospitality of the Irish, he adapted Keating's history in a revealing way.[119] Keating's preface had referred to the traditional hospitality to foreigners characteristic among the Old English and the Gaeil of Ireland (*i Sean Ghallaibh agus i nGaedhealaigh*

---

[115] The term 'hibernian' was also used in 1612 to denote an Irish Catholic in Barnaby Rich, *A Catholic Conference between Sir Tady Mac Mareall . . . and Patrick Plaine . . .* (London, 1612), p. 27. On earlier uses of the term 'Éireannach' in Ireland, see B. Ó Buachalla, *Aisling Ghéar: na Stiobhartaigh agus an tAos Léinn, 1603–1788* (Dublin, 1996). pp. 73–80.

[116] Lynch, *Cambrensis*, III, p. 147.

[117] [John Lynch], *Alithinologia, sive Veridica Responsio ad Invectam Mendaciis, falaciis calumniis & imposturis foetam in plurimos antistites, proceres & omnis ordinis Hibernos a R.P. R.F.C.* ([St Malo], 1664); *Suplementum Alithinologiae quod partes invectivae in Hibernos cusae in Alithinologia non oppubnatas evertit* ([St Malo], 1667). Also see chapter 7 below.

[118] Lynch, *Cambrensis*, III, p. 81.   [119] *Ibid.*, II, p. 243.

Eirinn). Lynch changed the terminology referring instead to the 'Irish of Milesian and Anglian race' (*Hibernos e Milesio et Anglia Oriundos*).[120] Lynch's dilemma was that he wished the Old English/Anglo-Irish to be regarded simply as Irish, but he was simultaneously reluctant to abandon any distinction between them and the native Irish. He targeted Stanihurst's late sixteenth-century term *Anglo-Hibernici* as being an absurd name, which threatened to 'excite slumbering animosities' and to 'shake to their foundations, the very basis of society'.[121]

Lynch's political case in favour of the Old English rested on the distinction between the recently arrived Protestant, parliamentarian planters who were biased against the king, on the one hand, and, on the other, the Old English whom he construed as 'natives', who both 'by character and hereditary principle [were] inclined to be loyal to the king'.[122] He warned Charles that those who undermined the Old English were ultimately the enemies of Charles himself. 'As the glory or infamy of a father is inseparable from that of his children, so it is with the prince and his subjects. The men who are plotting our destruction are the mortal enemies of your name.'[123] He reminded Charles II that the ancestors of the Old English had laid the foundations of the English king's power in Ireland with their swords, for this conquest was the basis of Old English claims to property in Ireland.[124]

Lynch's Utopia was a kingdom of Ireland ruled by Charles II as its rightful monarch, holding the sovereignty of Ireland by consent of the people; a kingdom in which King Charles had succeeded in giving 'effect to your laws and authority to your courts, restored the lands to cultivation, security to man, and to all the certain possession of their property . . . where foreigners are expelled from our parliament and natives reseated . . . where faith, and justice and equity, are once more enthroned on the judgement seat . . . when the lowly respect but do not fear the powerful, and the powerful takes precedence but does not despise the lowly'.[125] That Utopia had been usurped, in Lynch's view, by foreign parliamentarians who had the interests of neither the king nor the people at heart. It could be regained by the restoration of a harmonious relationship between king and people such as was described by Geoffrey Keating as having prevailed in early Ireland. Then the people would freely entrust the king with the sovereignty of Ireland to act as guarantor of justice and equity, truth and impartiality, for the prosperity of the whole kingdom.

---

[120] *Ibid.*, II, p. 243.   [121] *Ibid.*, III, p. 165.   [122] *Ibid.*, I, p. 45.   [123] *Ibid.*, I, p. 67.
[124] *Ibid.*, I, p. 44.   [125] *Ibid.*, I, p. 79.

7 'Though Hereticks and Politicians should misinterpret their goode zeal': political ideology and Catholicism in early modern Ireland

Tadhg ó hAnnracháin

In November 1645 the newly arrived papal nuncio to the Confederate Catholics of Ireland, Giovanni Battista Rinuccini, declared publicly that the objective of his mission could be reduced to two essential points: to promote fidelity, first to God and religion, and second to the king. This declaration was perfectly in line with the secret instructions that the nuncio had received on his departure from Rome and with the tenor of his correspondence with his superiors while he was in Paris during the summer of 1645.[1] Nevertheless, the nuncio's speech earned him a sharp rebuke from the papal secretary of state, Cardinal Pamfili, who informed him that: 'the Holy See has never wished to approve by positive actions the allegiance, even in civil matters, which is given by Catholic subjects to heretical kings. Whence were such grave difficulties which occurred from the schism of Henry VIII concerning the oaths of allegiance which the kings of England presented by force to Catholics.'[2] The following year, in response to another blunder, he was informed from Rome that papal ministers were forbidden to consent to public declarations 'in which it should appear or could appear that the Holy See approves or assents to an edict of Catholics, even if subjects, in defence of the royalty or person of a heretical king'.[3]

This incident is a telling indication of the difficulty which contemporary Catholic notions of heresy created for the Catholic subjects of

---

[1] 'Instruzioni segrete' in G. Aiazzi, *Nunziatura in Irlanda di Monsignor Gio: Baptista Rinuccini Arcivescovo di Fermo negli anni 1645 à 1649* (Florence, 1844), pp. liii–lvi. That this information was confined to the secret instructions was not insignificant: it has been argued that the public instructions of a diplomat were sometimes designed to be shown publicly; the secret instructions were for the private use of the diplomat only: see Charles Carter, *The Western European Powers, 1500–1700* (New York, 1971), pp. 47–8.
[2] Pamfili to Rinuccini, 20 May 1646, Stanislaus Kavanagh (ed.), *Commentarius Rinuccinianus, de sedis apostolicae legatione ad foederatos Hiberniae Catholicos per annos 1645–9* (IMC, 6 vols., Dublin, 1932–49), II, p. 402; see also *ibid.*, I, p. 653.
[3] *Commentarius Rinuccinianus*, II, p. 405.

Protestant monarchs. Vatican attitudes to the Stuart dynasty had never been particularly hostile. Upon James VI and I's accession to the throne of England, in succession to the excommunicated Elizabeth, Pope Clement VIII addressed a surprisingly cordial letter to the king. This letter went so far as to acknowledge that James had acceded to the throne by the will of God.[4] James' subsequent behaviour disappointed the Vatican authorities but they were still prepared to countenance a marriage between his son and a Catholic princess,[5] to maintain a papal agent to the queen of England during the 1630s,[6] and to contemplate large-scale financial aid to Charles I in the English Civil Wars in return for religious concessions.[7] Yet despite this, an unbridgeable gulf still lay between the Stuart dynasty and the Roman Church because Charles, like his father before him, was a Protestant and as such was probably doomed to hell.

This opinion was not always phrased by contemporary Catholics with the absolute bluntness of, for instance, Peter Talbot's 1657 *Treatise of the Nature of Catholick Faith and Heresie*. However, Talbot's contention in this tract that salvation outside the fold of the Roman Church required a rare combination of luck, goodness, and invincible but not wilful ignorance was powerfully orthodox.[8] This simple fact of the damnable nature of heresy rendered effectively impossible any normalisation of relations between even a moderate Protestant monarch and the Vatican.[9] For the Catholic subject of a non-Catholic king, however, this basic incompatibility created problems that far transcended the merely theoretical. To what extent was it possible for a Catholic to render allegiance to a monarch of a different religion who, in the case of Ireland, claimed to be supreme head or governor of the church, who excluded papal jurisdiction from his dominions and who enjoined attendance at Protestant worship and sacraments?[10]

It was an attempt to answer these questions that provided the impetus for much of the political writing in early modern Ireland. Much of what

---

[4] The text of this letter is available in P. F. Moran (ed.), *Spicilegium Ossoriense: Being a Collection of Original Letters and Papers Illustrative of the History of the Irish Church* (3 vols., Dublin, 1874–84), I, pp. 107–9.

[5] J. J. Silke, 'Primate Lombard and James I', *Irish Theological Quarterly*, 22 (1955), p. 146.

[6] In this regard see Gordon Albion, *Charles I and the Court of Rome* (London, 1935).

[7] V. Gabrieli, 'La Missione di Sir Kenelm Digby alla Corte di Innocenzo X (1645–1648)', *English Miscellany*, 5 (Rome, 1954), pp. 247–88.

[8] Peter Talbot, *A Treatise of the Nature of Catholick Faith and Heresie, with Reflexion upon the Nullitie of the English Protestant Church and Clergy* (Rouen, 1657), pp. 36–8.

[9] The inability of Protestant princes, for example, to accept a papal letter which began 'Dilecto Filio' was not a mere detail but an indication of the limits beyond which the papal diplomatic system could not penetrate: see Oskar Garstein, *Rome and the Counter-Reformation in Scandinavia* (Oxford, 1963), pp. 24–5.

[10] Nicholas Canny, *From Reformation to Restoration: Ireland 1534–1660* (Dublin, 1987), pp. 24, 63–4.

was produced – including the texts discussed here by Peter Lombard, Philip O'Sullivan Beare, Richard O'Ferrall, John Lynch and Conor O'Mahony – was published on the continent of Europe and in Latin. It is difficult to make binding generalisations about such a diverse group of works but a number of preliminary observations are in order. Latin remained the chief academic language of early modern Europe, particularly in clerical circles. However the languages of politics in seventeenth-century Ireland were primarily English and secondarily Irish.[11] On the whole texts written in Latin were aimed at a non-Irish audience and the ones considered here were penned within the territory of a Catholic power. The authors, with the exception of O'Sullivan Beare, were clerics permanently resident on the continent and were naturally sensitive to the official Catholic position on a number of delicate issues. The authorities which they were concerned to placate included the Vatican, the host country and, occasionally, the Stuarts. Thus the political literature in Latin remains an academic (sometimes in the worst sense of the word) discourse, produced by detached though polemical exiles: political writing which had to reckon with the danger of becoming divorced from the political context which it purported to address.[12]

I

On one level, the most simple answer to the question posed above, namely how a Catholic subject reacted to a heretical monarch who persecuted true religion, was to assert that the monarch's assault on the church of God had dissolved the bonds of allegiance. In doing so he or she had legitimised the subject's resistance to heretical tyranny. Such a position was articulated, often for political expediency, by a variety of sixteenth-century Irish 'rebels' including Thomas FitzGerald, James FitzMaurice, Hugh O'Neill and their followers.[13] In 1570, the papal bull, *Regnans in*

[11] One can note for instance the refusal in 1648 of the confederate Supreme Council to accept a document in Latin rather than English from Paul King (*Commentarius Rinuccinianus*, III, pp. 638–9). During the Autumn of 1646, as the marquis of Clanricard and the papal nuncio tried to broker a last-minute agreement near Dublin, it apparently proved impossible to provide Rinuccini with Latin translations of documents (*Commentarius Rinuccinianus*, II, pp. 425–37). English was the natural language of expression in letters penned in response to a quick-moving crisis such as the rebellion of 1641, see for example the Apology of the Anglo-Irish for taking up arms in 1641 (Gilbert (ed.), *Irish Confederation*, I, pp. 246–54.)
[12] In this context see Patrick Corish, 'Two Contemporary Historians of the Confederation of Kilkenny: John Lynch and Richard O'Ferrall', *IHS*, 8 (1952–3), pp. 217–36.
[13] Canny, *From Reformation*, pp. 20, 99, 144–5; see also Micheline Kerney Walsh, '*Destruction by Peace': Hugh O'Neill after Kinsale* (Armagh, 1986); John O'Donovan (ed.), 'The Irish Correspondence of James FitzMaurice of Desmond', *The Journal of the Kilkenny and South-East of Ireland Archaeological Society*, 2 (1858–9), pp. 354–69.

Excelsis, which excommunicated Elizabeth I, provided powerful external endorsement for Catholic rebellion.[14] Yet although not entirely negligible, religion served more as an auxiliary reason for revolt throughout the sixteenth century. As much as anything else, it was a card to play in the quest for external aid against the expanding power of the Tudor monarchy.[15]

The completion of the Tudor conquest, the accession of the unanathemised James VI and I, and peace with Spain produced a new political environment. Theories of justified rebellion against a heretical sovereign largely lost what vogue they had once enjoyed. Only among the substantial Irish communities in exile was the idea of a rebellion in the interests of religion still advocated.[16] For the exiled earls of Tyrone and Tyrconnell this remained the way to interest the papacy and Spain in supporting their efforts to recover their confiscated patrimonies.[17] Militant clerics, such as Florence Conry, also dreamed that intervention from exiles with foreign assistance might revive the fortunes of the Catholic church in Ireland.[18] Even if this never materialised, the insistence that the exiles were the meritorious victims of a failed crusade on behalf of religion served as a key strategy in winning sympathy and support from their continental hosts. In addition, close contact with the culture of the European Counter-Reformation not only served to sharpen the religious zeal of exiles but probably heightened their desire, and that of their children, to dignify their predicament by constructing a narrative of victimisation by heretics.

Prior to the 1640s, probably the most important articulation of this position was Philip O'Sullivan Beare's *Historiae Catholicae Hiberniae Compendium.*[19] This highly coloured history placed religion at the centre of the political turbulence in sixteenth-century Ireland. It was also destined to serve as an important source for future authors: both John Lynch, the Catholic archdeacon of Tuam, and Richard O'Ferrall, the capuchin apologist for the papal nuncio Rinuccini, drew on O'Sullivan Beare to provide ammunition for their differing contentions concerning the merits

[14] Colm Lennon, *Sixteenth-Century Ireland: The Incomplete Conquest* (Dublin, 1994), pp. 315–16. [15] Canny, *From Reformation,* pp. 144–5. [16] See chapter 8 below.
[17] See for example O'Neill and O'Donnell to Paul V, *c.* 1613, in 'Miscellanea Vaticano-Hibernica', *Archivium Hibernicum,* 3 (1914), pp. 302–10; see also their letter to the king of Spain, 9 July 1608, in Micheline Kerney Walsh, *An Exile of Ireland: Hugh O'Neill Prince of Ulster* (Dublin, 1996), pp. 83–4.
[18] See for example Conry to Wadding, 3 August 1627, in Brendan Jennings (ed.), *Wadding Papers,* (IMC, Dublin, 1953), pp. 252–3; Breandán Ó Buachalla, 'Na Stíobhartaigh agus an tAos Léinn: Cing Séamas', *Proceedings of the Royal Irish Academy,* section C, 83 (1983), pp. 97–8.
[19] P. D. O Sullevano Bearro, *Historiae Catholicae Hiberniae Compendium* (Lisbon, 1621). A portion of this work has been published as Matthew Kelly (ed.), *Ireland under Elizabeth* (Dublin, 1850).

of the Old English and Gaelic Irish communities, although O'Ferrall's debt was greater and more obvious.[20] O'Sullivan Beare also served as a vital historical source for the most sustained and intellectually rigorous exposition of Irish Catholics' right to rebellion.[21] This was Conor O'Mahony's *Disputatio Apologetica,* which was written in Portugal in 1645.[22] O'Mahony was an Irish Jesuit, then teaching in the university of Evora, and his text is of interest for two principal reasons: the first is the strength of the case which he presented; and the second is the extremely hostile reception which his work received from the very constituency for which he wrote, namely the Confederate Catholics of Ireland.

In his preface, O'Mahony asserted that all were bound by human, divine and natural law to defend both the Catholic religion and the *patria* in the best manner they could. As an academic, O'Mahony saw his own role as alerting his countrymen to the fact that in Ireland *ius regni* had been usurped by foreign heretics. The task he set himself was to prove this point and to assert that in rejecting the authority of the English monarchs over Ireland, the Irish would not lay themselves open to charges of criminal rebellion, barbarity or treachery.[23] Of interest here was his willingness to use the generic term *Hiberni.* Clearly those whom he addressed by this term were all the Catholics of the island irrespective of their ethnic origin. He warmly approved confederate ordinances designed to outlaw ethnic distinctions and indeed asserted that ten or twenty years' domicile in Ireland conferred on English Catholics the right to be viewed as indigenes.[24] Opposed to this Catholic population was a fairly undifferentiated heretical presence. O'Mahony focused the bulk of his attention on English heretics but, referring primarily to Exodus XXXII and Moses' destruction of thousands of idolatrous Jews, he advocated the expulsion of all non-Catholics from the island.[25] In this way *Hiberni* and *Catholici* become effectively interchangeable terms and the same blurring is evident between *haeretici* and *Angli.*

In order to prove his thesis, O'Mahony first presented what he believed to be the arguments in favour of the English kings' claim to Ireland: first, that Ireland was conquered in a just war; second, that the papal

---

[20] *Commentarius Rinuccinianus,* especially vol. I; John Lynch, *Alithinolgia* (St Malo, 1664) and *Supplementum Alithinolgiae* (St Malo, 1667). Also see chapter 6 above.

[21] James Brennan, 'A Gallican Interlude in Ireland: The Irish Remonstrance of 1661', *Irish Theological Quarterly,* 24 (1957), p. 228.

[22] Conor O'Mahony, *Disputatio apologetica de Iure Regni Hiberniae pro Catholicis Hibernis adversus haereticos Anglos. Accessit eiusdem authoris ad eosdem Catholicos exhortatio* (Lisbon, 1645); for convenience I have chosen to use the edition held in the National Library of Ireland which was reprinted in Dublin during the 1820s, apparently as part of an attempt to impede Catholic emancipation. [23] *Ibid.,* preface and pp. 1–8.

[24] *Ibid.,* pp. 100–1. [25] *Ibid.,* pp. 45, 125.

Laudabiliter conferred the lordship of Ireland on Henry II; third, that
Henry II's lordship and that of his successors was accepted by the three
orders of the kingdom (clergy, nobles and people); and fourth, that by
virtue of centuries of possession a prescriptive right to dominion over
Ireland was acquired.[26] Having presented these four arguments he then
proceeded to attack them. Rather than a just war, he presented the
English invasion as a wrongful incursion to aid the restoration of the adulterous king of Leinster, Dermot MacMurrough, which compounded its
injustice by developing into a general war of aggression. Thus, he suggested that the English kings acquired, not the right of dominion through
this unjust invasion, but an obligation to make restitution to those they
wronged.[27] In terms of the second possible justification of the rights of the
English monarchy, he argued that Laudabiliter, if not an outright forgery,
had been obtained under false pretences and was therefore invalid. Even
if not void from the outset, it became so through neglect of the conditions
under which it had been granted.[28] Of particular interest in this section
was O'Mahony's contention, based on the works of the Jesuit theologians
Bellarmine, Suarez and Molina, that the granting pope had actually
lacked the power to deprive the indigenous Catholic kings of their sovereignty, although he argued that the pope and the Irish people could
deprive a heretic of his dominion.[29]

Like O'Mahony, John Lynch, the archdeacon of Tuam, proved equally
dismissive of Laudabiliter.[30] Lynch, however, differed sharply from
O'Mahony on the question of the acceptance of English royal authority
by the Irish themselves. Certainly, O'Mahony's position was at its
flimsiest here. Referring to O'Sullivan Beare, he argued that Henry II may
have been accepted as the commissioner of the Holy See rather than as
sovereign: if he was approved as king then this acceptance was extorted by
force and therefore void. In advancing this position, O'Mahony was more
concerned with deducing principles from contractual law, relating to
property, theft and marriage, than with advancing political examples. He
paid no attention whatsoever to later historical events which might be
taken to have signalled the acceptance of the sovereignty of English kings
by the Irish population, such as the Kingship Act of 1541 or the Gaelic
Irish acceptance of Surrender and Regrant in the years following.[31]

[26] *Ibid.*, pp. 7–11.   [27] *Ibid.*, pp. 11–18.   [28] *Ibid.*, pp. 18–46.   [29] *Ibid.*, pp. 25, 29, 45.
[30] Indeed, like O'Mahony, Lynch accepted the argument of the solicitor-general of Ireland,
Sir John Davies, that the island had never been fully subdued until the reign of James I,
Alithinolgia, pp. 26–7; *Disputatio*, p. 47; see also Sir John Davies, *A discovery of the true causes
why Ireland was never entirely subdued* (1612); for a modern edition of this text see James
Myers (ed.), *A discovery of the true causes* (Washington, 1988). Also see chapter 6 above.
[31] *Disputatio*, pp. 46–52; concerning surrender and regrant see Brendan Bradshaw, *The Irish
Constitutional Revolution in the Sixteenth Century* (Cambridge, 1979) and Ciaran Brady,
The Chief Governors (Cambridge, 1994).

During the 1650s, another author, the Capuchin Richard O'Ferrall, who sympathised with O'Mahony's arguments (although he had evidently not read his book), turned his attention to these events of the 1540s. O'Ferrall attempted to resolve the problem by indulging his prejudice against the Old English of Ireland, asserting that the parliament which granted the kingly title to Henry VIII was an Old English body that excluded the bulk of the island's population. He then absolved Gaelic nobles like O'Neill and O'Brien who had accepted earldoms from Henry on the grounds that they did so in self-defence and with no intention of opening their territories to English jurisdiction.[32]

O'Ferrall's relatively feeble argument provoked an immediate response from his bitter adversary, John Lynch, who regarded his assertions as a libellous assault on the Old English community. Lynch convincingly outmanoeuvred O'Ferrall on this issue by pointing out the presence of Gaelic Irish magnates at the parliament which conferred the kingship on Henry VIII. He also noted that Gaelic Irish nobles had accepted even Henry's ecclesiastical supremacy during the 1540s.[33] In making this point Lynch, who had not apparently read the *Disputatio*, was training his guns on O'Ferrall alone but his historical examples could also have been used to puncture O'Mahony's thesis. Lynch's further assertion that in the 1613 parliament both Catholic communities heartily endorsed James VI and I's kingship was one which neither O'Mahony nor O'Ferrall appeared equipped to answer.[34] Not surprisingly neither showed any inclination to debate this issue.

Lynch and O'Mahony also traversed similar ground in their various discussions of the English monarch's prescriptive rights in Ireland. To Lynch, the position was fairly self-evident. English monarchs had held Ireland for almost five hundred years. Even goods granted by tyrants or extorted wrongfully from the church were legitimised by one hundred years' possession, so the English claim was irrefutable.[35] O'Mahony's argument proved more complex. The Irish Jesuit was of course writing in Portugal and he had first-hand experience of the Braganza revolt, which had led to the secession in 1640 of Portugal from the dominions of Philip of Spain and a war of independence, which was still continuing as he compiled the *Disputatio*.[36] He was thus fully conversant with the arguments advanced by the Portuguese to deny the Habsburgs their prescriptive rights. Much of the literature in this respect, including António de Sousa's celebrated tract from 1645, *Lusitania Liberata ab iniusto Castellanorum Dominio*, had been written by his own Jesuit

[32] *Commentarius Rinuccianus*, I, pp. 87–98. [33] *Supplementum Alithinolgiae*, pp. 22–3.
[34] *Ibid.* pp. 28–9.
[35] *Alithinolgia*, p. 28; the utility of this approach to Lynch is analysed in chapter 6 above.
[36] Richard Bonney, *The European Dynastic States 1494–1660* (Oxford, 1991), pp. 221–2.

colleagues.[37] Adapting their arguments to an Irish context he pointed out that prescriptive rights were acquired essentially through uninterrupted possession in good faith (defined as the grounded belief that the thing possessed did belong to the possessor) for a specified length of time.[38] He then argued that the English kings satisfied none of these conditions. Possession was denied because of the unjust manner in which title had been acquired: thieves obtained no rights of possession and therefore, he asserted, could not transmit their goods to their heirs. O'Mahony also refused to accept that the English kings had ever dominated the entire island for the required period (one hundred years) and insisted that even their pretended possession was not uninterrupted but rather subject to frequent, legitimate resistance from the Irish.[39]

Taken together, these sections of the *Disputatio* built a formidable case, and O'Mahony's knowledge of theory and his capacity to cite legal authors to support his opinions were impressive. However it was the next section of his book which contemporaries found most disturbing because here, having granted for the sake of argument that the English monarchs once enjoyed sovereignty in Ireland, he argued that the Irish should deprive them of these rights.[40] In this section, O'Mahony displayed the weight of his learning. From a Catholic perspective his choice of authorities to support his case was undoubtedly orthodox if Jesuitical: he relied heavily on Bellarmine, Suarez and Molina (but made no reference to the more conciliatory work of Peter Lombard, the exiled Catholic archbishop of Armagh).[41] According to O'Mahony, kings derived their power not directly from God but in a mediated fashion through the people. The people were bound to obey temporal authority but not to obey commands which ran contrary to God's law.[42] Indeed, because kings were given power for the good of the *res publica* the people retained the right to depose their princes and revoke their authority if they behaved tyrannically. He noted, for instance, that Thomas Aquinas accepted as justified the killing of Julius Caesar.[43] Since the soul was more precious than the body, a tyranny which attacked the spiritual welfare of the people was more deadly than one which merely oppressed its body and wealth: even the pope could

---

[37] De Sousa's text was the final and clinching reference in the list of authorities which O'Mahony cited on this topic: see *Disputatio*, p. 60; the Society of Jesus, in marked contrast to the Portuguese episcopacy, had played a key role in legitimising the Braganza revolt against the Habsburgs. In this regard see Padre Francisco Rodrigues, 'A Companhia de Jesus e a Restauração de Portugal 1640', *Anais da Academia Portuguesa da História*, 1, 4 (1942), pp. 323–425; Joaquim Veríssimo Serrão, *História de Portugal*, vol. IV (Lisbon, 1978), p. 140; C. Hermann and J. Marcadé, *La Péninsule Ibérique au XVIIe siècle* (Paris, 1989), pp. 261–74.   [38] *Disputatio*, pp. 52–60.   [39] *Ibid.*, pp. 61–4.
[40] *Ibid.*, pp. 65–102.   [41] Lombard's position is discussed in more detail below.
[42] *Disputatio*, pp. 68–73.   [43] *Ibid.*, p. 77.

be deposed for heresy.[44] The obvious conclusion therefore was that Irish Catholics would be entirely justified in removing the king, although he noted that up to now the Confederates continued to proffer allegiance to Charles in matters which did not contradict the Catholic faith.[45]

Having concluded his *Disputatio*, O'Mahony added an *Exhortatio* to the Irish people urging them to make use of their power to choose a new monarch. He skilfully invoked Deuteronomy XXII and Moses' injunction to select a native king, noting that the Jews' exclusion of a foreign monarch was to protect against the danger of idolatry or perversion.[46] The two great sins of the chosen people, he argued, were first the freeing of Barabas instead of Christ and second the rejection of their native king, Christ, for a foreigner, Caesar. And so, he extrapolated that the Irish, like other nations, should select a native as king, fearing not the power of heretics but that of God. He also congratulated the Irish on having already killed 150,000 heretics and urged them to eliminate the remainder.[47]

Hardly surprisingly O'Mahony's book engendered enormous hostility in Ireland. In effect, the *Disputatio* challenged the dominant current of seventeenth-century Irish Catholic political thought that stressed the legitimacy of the Stuarts as kings of Ireland.[48] Catholic insistence on this point was regarded as dubious by most Protestants, most famously by James VI and I himself, on whose orders Suarez's *Defensio Catholicae Fidei Contra Anglicanae Sectae Errores* had been burned by the common hangman (a fate which the *Disputatio* shared in Ireland)[49] and for whom even the conciliatory Peter Lombard remained *persona non grata*.[50] For Catholics in the 1640s, the orthodoxy of O'Mahony's case was part of the problem: what it suggested was that James' reading of Bellarmine and Suarez was in fact more credible than that of those Catholics who tried to argue the compatibility of their dual loyalties to king and pope.[51]

[44] *Ibid.*, p. 98.   [45] *Ibid.*   [46] *Ibid.*, pp. 103–4.
[47] *Ibid.*, pp. 118–25. In March 1643 the Irish lords justice alleged that 154,000 Protestants had been killed since October 1641; this figure of the number of Protestant fatalities was, of course, grossly exaggerated.
[48] Breandán Ó Buachalla, 'James Our True King: The Ideology of Irish Royalism in the Seventeenth Century' in G. Boyce, R. Eccleshall and Vincent Geoghegan (eds.), *Political Thought in Ireland since the Seventeenth Century* (London, 1993), pp. 1–35.
[49] This at least was what was reported to Rinuccini in Galway: the author of the book was publicly accused of *lèse-majesté* but the nuncio believed that such a major issue was made of the book in order to foment hatred against Owen Roe O'Neill and also because of the worries which holders of former monastic property had concerning any threat to the legitimacy of the authority from which they had received grants of lands, see *Commentarius Rinuccinianus*, II, p. 769.
[50] Silke, 'Primate Lombard and James I', pp. 41–2; see also below.
[51] See Aidan Clarke, 'Colonial Identity in Early Seventeenth-Century Ireland' in T. W. Moody (ed.), *Nationality and the Pursuit of National Independence* (Belfast, 1978), pp. 57–72.

O'Mahony's willingness to endorse the destruction of heretics, even accepting the inflated figures of Protestant propaganda concerning settler casualties, also threatened to link the Confederates with what they desperately wanted to avoid, namely guilt for the sectarian assaults on Protestants in 1641–2.[52] The *Disputatio* therefore carried the risk of becoming a dangerous hostage to fortune, legitimising Protestant distrust and persecution of Catholics.

For Confederates of Old English extraction, the exhortation to choose a native king had an ominous ring. Despite attempts on both sides of the ethnic divide, of which the Confederate Catholic Association was the most notable, the forging of a common identity for Irish Catholicism in place of distinctions between Gael and Gall, 'meere' Irish and Old English, had proved difficult. Ethnic tensions, particularly between the Old English and Ulster Irish, ran high throughout the 1640s. As Viscount Gormanston admitted to the earl of Clanricard in 1642, his first impression on hearing of the 1641 rebellion had been that the 'Irish' of the north had revived their 'old quarrel' and that their first targets would be their traditional foes, the Old English of the Pale.[53] This was particularly revealing since Gormanston was a staunch Catholic and one of the leaders of the Old English gentry in rebellion.

Fear, suspicion and hatred of Owen Roe O'Neill on the part of Old English Confederates was one of the most corrosive influences within the Confederate Association.[54] The appearance of the *Disputatio*, followed shortly after by the supposed gift from the pope to Owen Roe of Hugh O'Neill's sword, heightened these suspicions considerably.[55] Was it O'Neill's intention, with papal endorsement, to seize the throne of Ireland? The papal claim to Ireland, revived as recently as 1626, was well known in the island,[56] and many suspected, wrongly, that Rinuccini's arrival in Ireland had been to sound out the possibilities of making an open declaration of papal sovereignty. In this context, O'Mahony's

---

[52] In this regard see A[rchivio di] P[ropaganda] F[ide], S[critture] O[riginali Referite nelle] C[ongregazioni] G[enerali], 295, f. 14. Richard Cox, *Hibernia Anglicana: or The History of Ireland from the Conquest thereof by the English to the present time* (London, 1689), described the *Disputation* as 'a most treasonable and scandalous book' (p. 198) and observed that the Catholic clergy never publicly condemned it at the 1666 Congregation in Dublin. Also see Edmund Borlase, *The History of the Irish Rebellion* (London, 1680; Dublin 1743 edn), p. x and chapter 1 above.

[53] Gormanston to Clanricard, 21 January 1642 (Gilbert (ed.), *Irish Confederation*, I, p. 255).

[54] See, for instance, how Robert Talbot attempted to play on Preston's fears of O'Neill in the crisis of 1646: Talbot to Preston (Latin translation), 3 September 1646 (*Commentarius Rinuccinianus*, II, p. 361); see also Muskerry to Clanricard, 17 June 1647 in John Lowe (ed.), *Letter-Book of the Earl of Clanricarde, 1643–47* (IMC, Dublin, 1983), pp. 448–9; Talbot to same, 20 March 1647 (*ibid.*, pp. 269–71).

[55] Bellings' Narrative (Gilbert (ed.), *Irish Confederation*, VII, p. 98).

[56] Albion, *Charles I*, p. 95.

willingness to sink ethnic differences under the common name of *Hibernus* did not win over the Old English landowners who remained aware that they 'could claim noe other pretence of title to their estats than graunts from the crowne of England',[57] and feared expropriation at the hands of a King Owen Roe O'Neill.

Yet the fact that hardly a single voice was lifted in defence of O'Mahony's work requires some explanation. The comprehensive seventeenth-century realignment of Catholic opinion towards stressing the legitimacy of Stuart rule in Ireland was at least partially governed by tactical considerations[58] and resentment of religious persecution flickered underground throughout the 1620s and the 1630s.[59] Although, during the 1640s, the Confederates claimed to be in rebellion on behalf of their prince and his prerogatives, in practical terms they were well aware that they were attempting to extort conditions from him which he had no desire to grant and that there was little hope of achieving their religious goals other than by force of arms.[60] Moreover, the sectarian explosion that accompanied the 1641 rebellion indicated the depth of hostility towards Protestants and the political potential of Catholicism as a rallying cry.[61] For example, one Irish Jesuit gleefully recounted the murder of a Protestant minister by one of Lord Maguire's brothers: having forced the minister to recant his heresy, Maguire then hanged him so that he would die in a state of grace and took his goods as booty.[62] Similarly the reconsecration of a former Augustinian friary attracted a huge and jubilant concourse of Catholic laity.[63]

Moreover, it is difficult to believe that Owen Roe O'Neill and his followers had any philosophical objections to the *Disputatio*. During the 1640s, O'Neill was scrupulously careful in his declarations of fidelity to Charles but he was Hugh O'Neill's nephew and a member of an exile group that had been hoping to ignite a rebellion in Ireland for forty years.[64] During the Confederate era, his troops proudly proclaimed

---

[57] Bellings' Narrative (Gilbert (ed.), *Irish Confederation*, I, p. 19).
[58] Ó Buachalla, 'James Our True King', pp. 11–15. This process was nowhere more obvious than in the case of Peter Lombard, the archbishop of Armagh, who transformed from propagandist for Hugh O'Neill's rebellion to advocate of James' royal right: J. J. Silke, 'Primate Peter Lombard and Hugh O'Neill', *Irish Theological Quarterly*, 22 (1955) pp. 15–30.   [59] See for example *Wadding Papers*, pp. 360, 404.
[60] Gilbert (ed.), *Irish Confederation*, IV, pp. 35–6.
[61] Nicholas Canny, 'In Defence of the Constitution? The Nature of Irish Revolt in the Seventeenth Century' in *Cultures et pratiques politiques en France et en Irelande XVIe–XVIIIe siècle* (Paris, 1991), pp. 23–40; Canny, 'Religion, Politics and the Irish Rising of 1641' in Judith Devlin and Ronan Fanning (eds.), *Historical Studies XX: Religion and Rebellion* (Dublin, 1997), pp. 40–70.   [62] APF, SOCG, 295, ff. 11v–12r.
[63] *Commentarius Rinuccinianus*, II, pp. 272–3.
[64] See Jerrold Casway, *Owen Roe O'Neill and the Struggle for Catholic Ireland* (Philadelphia, 1984), pp. 22–54.

themselves the army of the pope and gave ample proof that any practical demonstration of allegiance to the king was effectively contingent on clerical approval.[65] Had the clerical wing of the Confederates chosen to embrace O'Mahony's position, it seems clear that the Ulster Army at least would have been prepared to support it. But neither the upper echelons of the Irish clergy nor the papal nuncio showed any such inclination. Rinuccini's comments about the book were guardedly neutral.[66] He was personally prepared to face with reasonable equanimity the destruction of royal power in England by parliament but he was bound by his instructions which effectively forbade him to disturb the allegiance of the Irish to the Stuarts.[67] This, no doubt, stemmed from the Vatican's perception that Charles was a moderate Protestant. Thus it would prove more profitable to negotiate secretly with him than to oppose him. More importantly, the Vatican feared the reactions of the Catholic monarchs of Europe if they acted as the patrons of Catholic rebels, even against a Protestant monarch.[68]

The Confederate clergy, for their part, were of course bound by the Oath of Association, which was not just *pro Deo* and *pro patria* but *pro rege* as well, and in 1645 they ringingly denounced a proposition questioning the king's legitimacy.[69] The reasons for Episcopal unanimity on this score were varied. Among the bishops, Thomas Dease appears to have held the position that rebellion was not permissible under any circumstances then pertaining in Ireland. Only the threat of excommunication eventually forced him into the Confederate Association.[70] Dease was however a minority figure within the Irish hierarchy. All its other members were prepared to endorse what the king and his ministers saw as rebellion as a just war in defence of the rights of the Catholic religion.[71] The Confederate pretext was of course that they were in arms in defence of the king's prerogatives. But there was little real clerical concern shown for these. In practical terms, only an utterly defeated or a Catholic king could countenance the church settlement to which the Irish clergy aspired.[72]

But the confederate Oath of Association, which the clergy themselves administered, provided the clergy with all the leverage they needed.[73]

---

[65] See Rinuccini's report on the proceedings of O'Neill (Aiazzi, *Nunziatura*, pp. 223–5).
[66] See Rinuccini to Pancirolo, 1 October 1647 (*Commentarius Rinuccinianus*, II, pp. 769–70).
[67] *Ibid.*, pp. 178–82.
[68] Vatican relations with Catholic powers are discussed in Tadhg Ó hAnnracháin, 'Vatican Diplomacy and the Mission of Rinuccini to Ireland', *Archivium Hibernicum*, 48 (1993), pp. 78–88.   [69] *Commentarius Rinuccinianus*, I, pp. 524–5.   [70] *Ibid.*, pp. 317ff.
[71] *Ibid.*, pp. 320–6.
[72] See *ibid.*, pp. 524–30; Gilbert (ed.), *Irish Confederation*, IV, pp. 260–90.
[73] This oath bound the taker to defend the lives, just freedoms, possessions and rights of all who had sworn the oath: for further details see Tadhg Ó hAnnracháin, 'Rebels and Confederates: The Stance of the Irish clergy in the 1640s' in John Young (ed.), *Celtic Dimensions of the British Civil Wars* (Edinburgh, 1997), pp. 99–100.

Thus the clergy insisted in 1645 that any peace without the retention of churches was untenable and it was on the grounds of perjury that the Supreme Council, which made peace in 1646 without securing this condition, was deposed.[74] The Oath of course was also an oath of allegiance to Charles and in 1645 some Confederates of the peace party tried to argue that this portion should take primacy over its other aspects.[75] The clergy, however, firmly rejected this on the grounds that God's rights always took precedence over the king's.[76] The Oath's superiority as a political tool, therefore, rendered something like the *Disputatio* unnecessary. By virtue of the Oath the Confederate clergy could deny that they were rebels, could conciliate Old English Confederates who were deeply afraid that any change to the English constitution of Ireland would threaten their own position, and yet allow them to demand that Catholicism be elevated to the position of a more or less established church. The Catholic militants among the Confederates, in short, did not need the *Disputatio*. If anything it was an inconvenience in its unnecessary frankness.

II

The ease with which a tract such as the *Disputatio* could mobilise orthodox doctrine did not mean that the Stuart cause was without its Catholic clerical defenders. The first and most notable of these was Peter Lombard, the archbishop of Armagh until 1625. In the first decades of the seventeenth century, Lombard did his best to temper the implications of Jesuit scholarship concerning tyrannicide. On the grounds that James was not a wilful heretic in the manner of Elizabeth, he argued that like a heathen king he was entitled to his subjects' allegiance.[77] To support this he cited a number of scriptural texts including Matthew XXII (Render unto Caesar . . .), 1 Peter II (Submit to every human authority . . . and Honour the king . . .) and Paul Romans XIII (Whosoever resists the authorities. . .).[78] Although Lombard could not deny subjects' rights to depose a tyrant, he insisted that this claim depended on clerical approval and he argued that despite the penal laws against the Catholic religion in Ireland it was not expedient to try to remove James.[79] Consistent with this position was his belief that the king could have not only Catholic subjects but also a Catholic wife (Anne of Denmark had converted prior to 1603) and he was eager to see a dispensation granted for a marriage between Charles and a Catholic princess.[80] In this, one can suggest he was more

---

[74] *Commentarius Rinuccinianus*, I, pp. 524–9; II, pp. 344–6.   [75] *Ibid.*, I, pp. 523–4.
[76] *Ibid.*, I, pp. 524–6.   [77] Silke, 'Primate Lombard and James I', pp. 137–44.
[78] 'Miscellanea Vaticano-Hibernica', p. 283.
[79] *Ibid.*, p. 337; Silke, 'Primate Lombard and James I', pp. 141–3.
[80] Silke, 'Primate Lombard and James I', pp. 144–9.

consistent than the Stuarts themselves: if the king could accept a Catholic wife could he not accept the legitimacy of Catholic subjects?

Lombard's most notable successor was the Galway cleric John Lynch (discussed above and in chapter 6). Lynch also invoked scripture to argue that every king had supreme power in his kingdom: Paul Titus III (Submit to princes and powers),[81] Luke XXI, Job (probably with XXXVI.7 in mind, God allows the righteous to rule as Kings) and Daniel IV.17 (God gives the kingdom of men to whom he chooses).[82] From Tertulianus he argued that kings were under God but above and before all others; and from St Augustine that the power of giving kingdoms came from God. He buttressed his case with historical examples, pointing out that Catholic bishops complied with (*morem gessisse*) thirteen Arian kings in Spain and eight in Italy.[83] He also noted the approval shown by St Augustine for the Emperor Vespasian and by St Athanasius for the Emperor Constantine.[84] That the Catholic Irish owed allegiance to their Protestant king was in his opinion irrefutable.

Lynch, however, was dealing with a more complex situation than Lombard. The turmoil of the 1640s had given birth to the Confederate Catholics. The central problem of this oath-bound association was the old dilemma of allegiance to their Protestant monarch but they also had to resolve critical issues regarding the relationship between Catholic lay and Catholic ecclesiastical authority and the degree of influence which a papal minister could exert in Ireland.[85] The civil war that broke out between different factions of the Confederates in 1648 related directly to their inability to resolve these issues. Lynch was a hot partisan in the interminable debates around these issues. Like Lombard, and unlike O'Mahony, Lynch was not content with blanket definitions of heresy. But where Lombard drew the chief distinction between subjective and objective heresy,[86] Lynch concerned himself more with the differences between Puritans and the king's brand of Protestantism. In his view, Puritans were incomparably worse since they differed in almost everything from the Catholic church, abhorring monarchy and ecclesiastical hierarchy and seeking to create anarchy or democracy in politics; while those who practised '*Protestantismum*' were separated from Rome by only a small number of points.[87] The moderation of his attitude is summed up by his phrase '*regi nostro non proh dolor Catholico*' ['our king, not, alas a

---

[81] *Alithinolgia*, p. 137.   [82] *Supplementum Alithinolgiae*, pp. 23–4.   [83] *Ibid.*, p. 109.
[84] *Ibid.*, p. 122.
[85] See Patrick Corish, 'The Crisis in Ireland in 1648: The Nuncio and the Supreme Council: Conclusions', *Irish Theological Quarterly*, 22 (1955), pp. 231–57, and 'Bishop Nicholas French and the Second Ormond Peace, 1648–9', *IHS*, 6 (1948), pp. 83–100.
[86] Silke, 'Primate Lombard and James I', p. 138.
[87] *Supplementum Alithinolgiae*, pp. 96, 140.

Catholic'] in contrast, for instance, to O'Mahony's simple description of Charles I as *'Carolus Primus haereticus'* ['Charles the First, a heretic'].[88] Lynch's eulogy of Ormond as a man lacking no virtue but true religion was also indicative of a mental attitude which was prepared to shunt religion away from the position which it enjoyed in O'Mahony's schema as an absolute determinant of worth.[89] This distinction between Puritans and Protestants would have made compelling sense to many of Lynch's Irish Catholic contemporaries. In 1642, for instance, an Irish manifesto to Charles insisted that all Protestant sects be excluded from the island except for 'pure' Protestants of the king's own persuasion.[90] As Rinuccini was to demonstrate on his arrival in Ireland, however, Italian attitudes towards heresy were less subtle than Irish.[91]

It has been convincingly argued that pre-Reformation attitudes towards religious difference survived in the Italian peninsula into the seventeenth century. While in other parts of Catholic Europe traditional notions of heresy modulated towards a *de facto* acceptance of other confessions and churches, Italy remained largely immune from pressures towards coexistence.[92] To Italian clerics, the idea of an alternative religious confession was essentially abstract and attitudes were often simplistic. Rinuccini, for instance, continued to confuse the various strands of Protestantism found within the Stuart kingdoms even after his return from Ireland.[93]

This contributed to the divisions that tore the Catholic Confederates apart in 1648. One of the reasons which prompted Rinuccini's resistance to the Inchiquin Truce in 1648 – the point which ignited civil war within the Confederate Association – was his (substantially correct) belief that the proponents of the truce actually preferred to settle with the Protestant Inchiquin rather than to deal with Owen Roe O'Neill's Catholic troops.[94] To Rinuccini, the idea that Catholics could feel more affinity with heretics than with their co-religionists was incomprehensible. There was a note of disbelief in his account of a conversation with an Irish cleric, probably the superior of the Irish Jesuits, Thomas Malone, in 1648. Rinuccini suggested that Owen Roe O'Neill's army should be sent into Munster to protect the province from Inchiquin on the grounds that any Catholic presence was better than ceding the province to heretical domination.

---

[88] *Ibid.*, p. 73; *Disputatio*, p. 10.   [89] *Supplementum Alithinolgiae*, p. 121.
[90] APF, SOCG, 295, f. 6v.   [91] *Supplementum Alithinolgiae*, p. 68.
[92] See Gaetano Catalano and Federico Martino (eds.), *Potestà civile e autorità spirituale in Italia nei secoli della riforma e controriforma* (Milan, 1984), p. 9; A. Dupront, 'Réflexions sur l'hérésie moderne' in *Hérésies et sociétés dans l'Europe préindustrielle* (Paris, 1968), p. 291.
[93] See G. B. Rinuccini, *Il Cappuccino Scozzese* (reprinted Rome, 1863), p. 119.
[94] See Patrick Corish, 'Rinuccini's Censure of 27 May 1648', *Irish Theological Quarterly*, 18 (1951), pp. 322–37.

Malone baldly remarked that this was not always the case.[95] For
Rinuccini, the Catholic credentials of those with such opinions were in
doubt. At the end of his nunciature he denounced what he called the
common sentiment of the 'Ormondite party'. He acidly asked whether
'the followers of the King should not be taken for heretics, but only those
who rebel against the crown, and that in consequence war against the
Puritans is legitimate in so far as they are rebels, and illegitimate immediately when they return to obedience? As if respect for the king alone could
qualify heresies or purge the contagion which falsities inflict on souls.'[96]
Rinuccini, it should be noted, had Irish supporters as well as opponents.
His attitude here was similar to that expressed by O'Mahony and by the
nuncio's arch-apologist, Richard O'Ferrall, in the 1650s and 1660s.[97]
Moreover, it was a mentality that was given chilling practical expression
in the widespread attacks on Protestants in 1641–2.[98]

Thus 1640s Ireland saw two distinct Catholic attitudes towards religious difference jostling for position. One of these, fuelled by economic
discontent and the effective religious mission of the Catholic church in
the previous thirty years, was animated by the belief that participation in
Irish society should be restricted to Catholics. This was symbolised by the
Catholic bishop of Ardfert's offer to the colony of Protestants in Tralee in
1642: if they converted to the Catholic faith he guaranteed that they
would be permitted to stay; if they remained Protestants then they must
depart without their property.[99] The other attitude, more common
among the prosperous, was grounded in Old English traditions. For that
conservative community, loyalty to the king and to Catholicism was part
of a cherished custom. The desire not to sacrifice either aspect of their
inherited identity formed the basis of much of their political ideology.[100]
It was no accident that so much of that thinking was retrospective, looking
for inspiration to the time before the rift between the king and Rome
developed. During the 1640s Confederate constitutionalists were aware
that times had changed and that the constitution itself had to adapt: not
only the reformation legislation but also the statute of *praemunire* would
have to be amended because the king was no longer Catholic.[101] As the
Confederate representatives in negotiations with the lord lieutenant
declared: 'had the constitution of these present times been such as in the

[95] Rinuccini's relation to the pope (Aiazzi, *Nunziatura*, pp. 424–5).   [96] *Ibid.*, p. 432.
[97] *Commentarius Rinuccinianus,* especially vols. I and V; APF, Hibernia, 298, ff. 57–59v.
[98] Canny, 'In Defence of the Constitution?', pp. 23–40.
[99] *Commentarius Rinuccinianus,* I, p. 311.
[100] In this regard consider the responses to the questions posed by the ecclesiastical high
commission for recusancy in Anthony Sheehan, 'Attitudes to Religious Authority in
Cork in 1600', *Analecta Hibernica,* 31 (1984), pp. 63–8.
[101] Gilbert (ed.), *Irish Confederation,* IV, pp. 32–7.

times of our ancestors, when both King and people were Roman Catholics, we should not seek a repeal of any the said laws'.[102] A somewhat plaintive belief in the inherently reasonable nature of their case and regret that 'their goode zeal' could be so misinterpreted featured in Confederate writing. There was resentment too that the Scots were allowed to practise their religion while the Irish were persecuted for adherence to a far more venerable tradition.[103] Another argument that was put to the king was that a policy of coercion had failed to produce the conversion of the Catholic population and that therefore it disrupted the commonwealth to no purpose.[104] What is striking about this point is its sheer simplicity, as if the religious policy of the state was an ordinary political grievance rather than a question of truth and heresy.

This belief that the existing constitutional framework could accommodate differences produced by the reformation formed the context in which the Confederates clung so desperately, and arguably counterproductively, to the idea of negotiation with the king. And it was this reasoning which primed many Irish Catholics against accepting the simple post-reformation dichotomy of Catholic (good) and Protestant (bad) to which a Rinuccini or an O'Mahony subscribed. This backward-looking tradition was also ultimately invoked against Rinuccini, as the Confederate apologists tried to justify their resistance to the nuncio by an appeal to the pre-reformation era, not only with regard to canon law but also in terms of 'the law of the land, as in Catholic times it was practised'.[105] The result with a post-tridentine prelate like the nuncio was to be bitter acrimony and mutual recrimination that continued long after the 1640s.[106]

One particular problem with which the nuncio's opponents had to grapple was the charge that they had betrayed God and the *patria* by a lack of faith and constancy.[107] A belief that God intervened in the world to punish or reward human actions was widespread in Ireland during the seventeenth century.[108] Attacks on Protestants in 1641 were partially motivated by the view among the common people that God had struck on behalf of his people and many were particularly inspired by the belief that a prophecy of St Patrick concerning the liberation of Ireland was being

[102] *Ibid.*, p. 332. [103] APF, SOCG, 295, f. 6.
[104] Gilbert (ed.), *Irish Confederation*, III, p. 307.
[105] Corish, 'The Crisis in Ireland', p. 254.
[106] Corish, 'Two Contemporary Historians', pp. 217–36.
[107] APF, Hibernia, 298, ff. 57–59v; *Supplementum Alithinolgiae*, pp. 143–7.
[108] Nor was this belief confined to Catholics: Canny, *From Reformation*, p. 216; Canny, 'In Defence of the Constitution?'; Canny, 'The Formation of the Irish Mind: Religion, Politics and Gaelic Irish Literature, 1580–1750', *Past and Present*, 95 (1982), pp. 91–116; see also Ó Buachalla, 'Na Stíobhartaigh', especially pp. 107–12.

fulfilled.[109] Nor were such ideas confined to the uneducated. A continentally trained priest, Patrick Roche, wrote in 1641: 'The God of charity hath heard our prayers and hath not stopped his ears to his distressed militants here on Earth: his battle we fight . . . witness our happy proceedings so prosperously so successfully achieved.'[110] Attitudes of this kind had direct implications for political action. For if the God of miracles interceded on behalf of his people, then ordinary calculations of prudence and possibility were subject to revision. The best possible way to attract divine intervention was through faith, by attempting what was pleasing to God even if that appeared unattainable with merely human resources. In February 1646, for instance, Rinuccini urged the Confederate assembly to stiffen their resolve and remember that they 'acted and had acted in the cause of God in which it is not sufficient to weigh matters according to human reasons only but something also is to be relinquished to God and to be entrusted to his aid'.[111] After the battle of Benburb (June 1646), he roundly upbraided the Confederate council, and enjoined them to render thanks to God for their recent miraculous military successes by showing increased faith in divine protection.[112] O'Mahony's *Disputatio* echoed the same position. Those who truly adhered to God's party would triumph. The deeds of Abraham, Moses, Joshua, Gedeon, Samuel, David, Ezechiel and the Maccabees bore testament to this.[113] From St Augustine, he quoted the example of Emperor Honorius who with God's help killed 100,000 of his enemies in one battle without a single casualty. The decline of the eastern Roman empire he ascribed to the loss of the link with Rome while, in his view, history proved that those kings who flourished in the west were faithful sons of the church.[114]

Similar attitudes were found among the Confederate clergy. The bishop of Ferns was convinced in 1647 that 'this summer was made by God to try the hearts and resolutions of Ireland and it will be lost or won this very summer';[115] and this was one of the reasons that he insisted that the disastrous battle of Dungan's Hill be fought in August. Earlier that year, the bishop of Leighlin, Edward Dempsey, adopted similar rhetoric during the debates about the rejection of the First Ormond Peace. According to an account penned by the secretary to the Supreme

[109] APF, SOCG, 295, f. 5v.

[110] *A true copie of a letter sent from Patrick Roch* (London, 1641).

[111] *Commentarius Rinuccinianus*, II, p. 78. This attitude on the part of the nuncio should be seen, I suggest, as a product of his sincere belief, rather than as a display of pious opportunism to cover his dislike of the Ormond Peace.

[112] Rinuccini to the Supreme Council, 25 June 1646 (*Commentarius Rinuccinianus*, II, pp. 228–34). This position is somewhat reminiscent of Lamormaini after the battle of Nördlingen, see Geoffrey Parker, *The Thirty Years' War* (London, 1984), pp. 142–3.

[113] See chapter 8 below.   [114] *Disputatio*, pp. 126–7.

[115] Ferns to Preston, 12 May 1647 (*Cal S P Ireland, 1633–47*), p. 625.

Council, Richard Bellings, Dempsey answered the arguments of those who believed that the Confederates lacked the resources to continue a policy of war by 'citing that text of Scripture, when Christ raised Lazarus from the dead "removete lapidem", wished them to observe, that when our Saviour came to perform that stupendous work, he gave his disciples no other share in it, than of removing the stone. So, said he, perform you that which is within your power, remove the stone, reject the peace, proceed on vigorously, and God will do the rest.'[116] Once the first premise of God's possible intervention was accepted, then such arguments were difficult to counter. Not all accepted them; indeed there was a note of disbelief in Bellings' comment: 'This was the reply given to the premeditated and prudent discourses of many gentlemen, who thought the weight of the subject deserved more particular satisfaction to the arguments concerning it, and those sacred words a more rational interpretation.'[117] But Bellings and his partisans were of course out-voted on the issue.

Not only were arguments like Dempsey's grounded in orthodox religious thinking on the importance of faith but they were well armoured against the charge that the just had not always prevailed in the past. For instance, as O'Mahony pointed out, the oppression of the good by the evil (the example he used was naturally the presecution of the Irish by the English) could be attributed to one of two reasons: either it was a punishment for past sins or it was a test of constancy from God. Among others, the reference here is to the book of Tobit where Raphael told Tobias that, because God had accepted him, it was necessary that he be tried with temptation.[118]

John Lynch's reaction to opinions like this is of interest. Inevitably, he took up cudgels of behalf of those whom he saw calumniated by authors such as Richard O'Ferrall. But Lynch (and indeed Bellings) devoted far more time to attacking the minor premise that the anti-nuncioists had sinned, than the major issue, namely that God intervened according to the rectitude or injustice of a cause. He did argue that disaster was not always a sign of divine displeasure, advancing the idea of St Louis' defeat by the Turks to support his case.[119] He also defended the Supreme Council's action on the grounds of prudence, quoting Hannibal's comment to Scipio that nothing was more uncertain than war and referring (rather riskily?) to examples of where smaller forces had defeated larger ones.[120] The attempt by the Confederate Catholics during the 1640s to gain the 'splendour' of religion was in his view imprudent because they lacked the means to attain this goal.[121] But there were limits

---

[116] Bellings' Narrative (Gilbert (ed.), *Irish Confederation*, VII, p. 5).   [117] *Ibid.*
[118] *Disputatio*, pp. 99–100; Tob. 12,13.   [119] *Supplementum Alithinolgiae*, p. 143.
[120] *Ibid.*, p. 73.   [121] *Ibid.*, p. 5.

to how far Lynch could push this argument because he himself detected the hand of providence in the early years of the Confederate war. The startling victories obtained by the Old English against the tyrannical lord justices in the early 1640s were, in his opinion, a reward for their faith and trust in God.[122]

Lynch also attacked O'Ferrall's bloodthirstiness and his apparent belief that the most meritorious Christians were those who took up arms for their religion. He quoted Lactantius, St Augustine and St Bernard that religion was defended not by killing but by teaching, not by ferocity but by patience, not with swords and shields but by prayers.[123] But again Lynch could not rely on such a position alone because it was simply too radical for contemporary Catholic belief: he also felt it necessary to provide details of Old English crusaders for the faith.[124] Ultimately, in this as in much else, the defence against O'Ferrall became a quarrel about details and interpretation rather than an attack on the religious and philosophical underpinnings of O'Ferrall's argument.

III

In conclusion, it is very clear that there were great disparities in the political attitudes and reasoning of those Catholic exiles who wrote in Latin in the first seven decades of the seventeenth century. What is most striking perhaps is the degree to which such differences could be accommodated within the framework of orthodox Catholic belief. Lombard and O'Mahony, advocating radically different political positions, were drawing on essentially the same Catholic tradition. Lynch was more likely than either to mobilise pagan authors such as Livy, or once he daringly quoted the Protestant Archbishop Ussher (on the duty of passive obedience),[125] but the mainstay of his argument was also securely grounded in Catholic tradition. Catholicism shaped the possibilities of what they could write; but equally what they sought to locate within the Catholic tradition was shaped by the emotional affiliations that they held dear. In that context it seems probable that Stuart and in particular James VI and I's distrust of Catholic loyalty was over-intellectualised. Religious grievance rather than religion itself was arguably the most potent incitement to rebellion against the English state in Ireland, particularly when religious grievance was combined with other resentments of a socio-economic and political nature. However dubious it may have appeared to James, Old English determination to accommodate apparently contradictory

---

[122] *Ibid.*, pp. 193–4.   [123] *Alithinolgia*, pp. 48–9; *Supplementum Alithinolgiae*, p 41.
[124] *Supplementum Alithinolgiae*, pp. 191ff.   [125] *Ibid.*, p. 25.

allegiances was the effective key to such accommodation, a position grounded on a deeper political reality than seems to have been apparent to the philosopher king. By the same token, O'Mahony's virtuoso presentation of Jesuit political thought attracted few takers in Ireland because it conflicted with the cherished beliefs of many Catholics and failed to fit the political needs of others. Ultimately, it was neither the force nor the orthodoxy of his case which determined its reception but its tactical utility.

8   Gaelic Maccabeanism: the politics of reconciliation

Jerrold Casway

It is generally supposed that Irish nationalism and republicanism were late eighteenth-century and French revolutionary by-products. Although this assertion is credible, it would be an oversight to ignore, more than a century before, a fascinating political experiment that was intended to reconcile Ireland's Catholic communities. Owen Roe O'Neill and his northern native officer corps who modelled themselves after the Maccabean 'freedom fighters' of ancient Judea shaped this initiative. This relationship evolved from their classical–biblical education, their heroic–military experiences and the desperation of their exile. Their identification, fostered and articulated by the Irish Franciscan community in Louvain, saw the Maccabean episode as a collegial-republican governing archetype through which the Catholics of Ireland might be defended and conciliated. It was, in its roughest form, an embryonic nationalism and nascent ideology.[1]

The Maccabean role model was not a romanticised contrivance. It became an identity assumed and popularised by Owen Roe O'Neill's generation of disenfranchised native Irish exiles who metaphorically identified their religious and political struggle with the defiance of the Old Testament Maccabees. The Irish affiliation was inspired by the portrayal of Elizabethan Irish colonists as classical Roman bearers of 'civility'.[2] This Elizabethan–Roman precedent of conquest through cultural assimilation was analogous to the campaigns of the Seleucid Greeks in pre-Christian Judea that sparked Mattathias of Modein and his sons to rebellion.

The familiarity of the native Irish with a biblical resistance movement against alien encroachments was not uncharacteristic of this era of religious conflict. Compare the expectations that provoked these two movements: the Seleucid Greek directive to Judean cities 'to follow customs

---

[1] For interesting Scottish parallels see chapter 9 below.
[2] N. Canny, 'The Ideology of English Colonization: From Ireland to America', *William and Mary Quarterly*, 3rd Series, 30 (1973), pp. 588–9.

176

strange [foreign] to their land . . . so that they might forget the law and change their ordinances [observances]',[3] and Richard Stanihurt's 1577 assessment that the Irish 'Ought to be ruled by the same law that the conqueror is governed, to wear the same fashion of attire wherewith the victor is vested, and speak the same language that the vanquisher parleth. And if any of these three lack, doubtless the conquest limpeth.'[4] Opposition to such policies rekindled a Judaic link for the biblically conscious native Irish, who frequently identified their misfortunes with the plight of the ancient Israelites. This association is found in many bardic verses that contrasted the enslavement and suffering of 'Clann Israel' with the problems of Catholic Ireland.[5] In these references Irish suffering was attributed to divine retribution. For instance a poem by an anonymous author, describing the tomb of native Irish chiefs buried in Rome, sounds like a passage from the Old Testament.

> Why should punishment be inflicted
> Most heavily on one race?
> By what justice is Erin cast down?
> Why are her groans unheeded?
> Why are not the Gaels exalted?[6]

Compare this lament to the words of the father of Judas Maccabeus (the 'hammerer'), who bemoaned the fate of Judea and Jerusalem:

> Alas! Why was I born to see this
> the ruin of my people, the ruin
> of the holy city . . .
> Her temple has become like a
> person without honour
> her generous vessels have been
> carried into exile . . .
> All her adornments have been
> taken away . . .
> Why should we live any
> longer? [7]

---

[3] 1 Maccabees I.41; *The First Book of the Maccabees* (New York, 1973), pp. 46–7.
[4] R. Stanihurst, *A Treatise Containing A Plain and Perfect Description of Ireland, 1577*, cited by R. Holinshed, *Chronicles* (London, 1808), VI, p. 5.
[5] Feardorcha O'Meallain, 'In ainman Athara le buaidh' cited by H. O'Muirgheasa (ed.), *Danta Diadha Uladh* (Dublin, 1936), pp. 184–7; Fearflatha O'Gorimh, 'Mo Thruaighe mar taid Gaoidhil' cited by Thomas F. O'Rahilly (ed.), *Measgra Dánta: Miscellaneous Irish poems* (2 vols., Cork, 1927), II, p. 147; Eoghan Ruadh Mac anBhaird, 'Anocht as uaigneach Eire' cited by P. Walsh (ed.), *The Life of Aodh Ruadh O'Domhnaill* (Irish Texts Society, 1957), p. 145; *Disputatio apologetica de Jure Regni Hiberniae, 1645*, cited by Gilbert (ed.), *Contemporary History*, I, p. 6.
[6] 'The Irish Vision of Rome, 1650', cited by *ibid.*, III, p. 191. [7] 1 Maccabees II.1–14.

In search of relief, Mattathias required the 'covenant of our ancestors' and native Ireland looked for leadership, and grieved why 'in Erin we have no Moses?'[8]

These sentiments and associations represent a link between Irish and biblical heroism. As another native poet in 1631 bemoaned in the 'Book of O'Connor Don', the wrath of God was too frequently visited upon this 'great race [of] Maccabeans [the Irish]'.[9] Three decades earlier, the Old English primate of Ireland, Peter Lombard, in his *De Regno Hibernicae, Sanctorum Insulâ, Commentarius*, appealed to Pope Clement VIII to aid the Catholic struggle against Elizabethan England. He argued that the Tudors' misgovernment had surrendered their right to have dominion over Ireland. He spoke of the Irish defence of their faith as '*tamquam redivivi Machabae* [of renewed Maccabees]'.[10] By 1640 this Maccabean affiliation became a rallying model for the disenfranchised native Irish exiles. From contemporary sources, readers were reminded of the 'young Maccabeans fighting for God's cause', 'your Maccabean families', the 'excellent deeds . . . of the valiant Maccabees' and 'our Maccabees'.[11] Owen Roe O'Neill, himself, was referred to as 'your present Maccabean and only champion'.[12] But the general's only extant use of the Maccabean term came during his oration before the battle of Benburb in 1646:

> Know that those that stand before you [Scots and English Protestants] . . . are those that banish you, your Wives and Children from your lands and Houses, and make you seek Bread and Livelihood in strange places. Now you have arms in your hands as good as they have and are Gentlemen as good as they are. You are the flower of Ulster, descended from ancient and Honourable stock of people as any in Europe . . . Maccabeans fighting against their enemy . . .[13]

This speech is remarkably similar to Judas Maccabeus' welcoming address to his summoned kinsmen,[14] or his pre-battle rallying of his soldiers. 'They come against us in great insolence and lawlessness to destroy us and our wives and our children, and to despoil us; but we fight for our lives and our laws. He [God] himself will crush them before us; as for you, do not be afraid of them.'[15] Even the rendering of the Maccabee term to

[8] *Ibid.*, II.20. 'Anocht as uaigneach Eire' in Walsh (ed.), *The Life of Aodh Ruadh*, p. 145.
[9] 'Book of O'Connor Don, 1631' cited by W. Gillies, ' A Poem on the Downfall of Gaoidhill', *Eigse*, 13:3 (1970), p. 208.
[10] P. Lombard, *De Regno Hiberniae, Sanctorum Insulâ, Commentarius*, ed. P. F. Moran (Dublin, 1868).
[11] 'Aphorismical Discovery of Treasonable Faction', Gilbert (ed.), *Contemporary History*, I, pp. 7–8; Unknown to H. Bourke, 19 December 1641, F[ranciscan] L[etters,] K[illiney], D. IV, 67; other random citations are in FLK, D. IV, 67; 'Letter from the Irish Catholic Camp', 4 May 1649, Gilbert (ed.), *Contemporary History*, II, p. 211. Also see chapters 6 and 7 above.   [12] Gilbert (ed.), *Contemporary History*, I, p. 7.   [13] *Ibid.*, pp. 111–12.
[14] 2 Maccabees VIII.4; *The Second Book of the Maccabees* (New York, 1973), p. 66.
[15] 1 Maccabees III.20–2.

Gaelic is curious. Maccabee becomes *macrai*: 'a band of young warriors', or biblically speaking 'children of Holy Innocence', and 'avengers or messengers of God' that reflect Judea's 'stalwart men',[16] her 'valiant Israelites ... devout followers of the law'.[17] What better role model was there for the dispossessed young native Irishmen, who had fled their war-torn homeland in search of careers in Catholic Europe?

I

This Maccabean affiliation developed slowly in the wilderness of exile. Among these alienated young Irishmen there evolved a crusading zeal reminiscent of the Spanish *reconquista* that was directed at the recovery of their homeland and the promotion of their faith. But many of their inspirational sentiments were also drawn from the pronouncements of former leaders like James Fitzmaurice and Hugh O'Neill, who promoted the idea of *et libertate patriae*. The idea of a shared fatherland bonded by the fervour of the Catholic Counter-Reformation bolstered the declining fortunes of provincial and traditional native resistance.[18] This sentiment took root and was nurtured in the Irish regiment in the Spanish Netherlands.

Founded in 1605 by the exiled son of the earl of Tyrone, the regiment became a haven for a new generation of displaced Irishmen.[19] Feared and distrusted by the English and their supporters in post-plantation Ireland, these soldiers were to be insulated and discredited. The Stuart government likened them to the 'frogs of Egypt' and 'poor worms upon the earth'.[20] This disparagement was furthered by a 'divide and conquer' strategy directed at the traditional domestic rivalries among the native and Old English factions. In response to these tactics, the leadership of the native Irish exiles drew upon the unifying measures popularised by Owen Roe's uncle, Hugh O'Neill, the earl of Tyrone. They warned their brethren about England's intentions, and pursued every opportunity to construct a loyal and dedicated cadre to resist English incursions.

In the forefront of this effort were the continentally trained Franciscan clerics, who fuelled the regiment with the righteousness of their cause. Their activities centred on the new Irish College of St Anthony of Padua at Louvain. The dominant spokesmen were Florence Conry, the Catholic

[16] *Ibid.*, IX.14.   [17] *Ibid.*, II.42.
[18] H. Morgan, 'Hugh O'Neill and the Nine Years War in Tudor Ireland', *The Historical Journal*, 36 (1993), p. 23.
[19] J. Casway, 'Henry O'Neill and the Formation of the Irish Regiment in the Netherlands, 1605', *IHS*, 18, 72 (1973), pp. 481–8.
[20] C. Cornwallis to T. Edmondes, 24 June 1605, BL, Stowe MSS 168, f. 50; Lord Salisbury to Edmondes, 20 September 1607, *ibid.*, 169, f. 141v; PRO, SP Flanders, 77/8 II, f. 346v.

archbishop of Tuam, and the college's founder; Dr Eugene Matthews (MacMahon), the Catholic archbishop of Dublin; Dr Robert Chamberlain, the guardian of the Franciscan friary of Louvain; and Conry's military protégé, Sergeant-Major Owen Roe O'Neill of the Irish regiment. This Louvain clique favoured the northern native exiles, but they came to appreciate how greater co-operation with the Old English community could combat English-inspired divisiveness and provincial discord. William Trumbull, the English ambassador to the Spanish Netherlands, best summarised Irish vulnerability when he bragged that all that was needed was 'a final occasion to set them [native Irish and Old English] together by their ears. If there be a little oil of His Majesty liber-ally cast into the fire [provincial discord] I suppose it shall hardly be quenched.'[21] The Irish response for conciliation and unity were the seeds that sowed the concept of Gaelic Maccabeanism.

The most revealing and mature expression of Louvain politics grew out of their attempts to reconcile the Catholic factions for a Spanish-supported Irish enterprise after the outbreak in 1625 of the Anglo-Spanish War. In a document presented to the Spanish king, Conry and his military protégé Owen Roe O'Neill proposed in November 1627 an elaborate campaign and governing scheme that underscored this cove-nanted *patria*. The premise of the document aimed to reconcile the diverse competing factions that would make up this Irish enterprise. Spain's principal concern involved the contested leadership between the two adolescent heirs of the earls of Tyrone (O'Neill) and Tyrconnell (O'Donnell) and the latent distrust of Old English officers. The docu-ment also dramatised how the enterprise could not be attributed to the wary Spanish king. The invasion, it was suggested, should be carried out in the name of both earls. More importantly, the invaders were to sail without affiliated banners and carry out this liberation in 'the name of the liberty of the fatherland of oppressed religion and by establishing as the government a Republic, which should be so called on its flags and in its commissions; and all other public ordinances should be in the name of the Republic and Kingdom of Ireland'. Tyrone and Tyrconnell were each to be called 'captain-generals' of the said republic and kingdom with jurisdiction equally divided between them. This arrangement was to demonstrate that the purpose of the young earls was not to conquer the country for themselves or any prince, 'but for the Kingdom and Republic of Ireland, on account of the oppression, violence and imprisonment inflicted . . . upon [Catholic] consciences, their children, their trade and commerce and their freedom of navigation'. In this kingdom, jurisdiction

---

[21] W. Trumbull to T. Overbury, 16 April 1613, *ibid.*, 77/10 II, f. 286rv.

would be divided according to the different provinces, with each one of the nobles, provinces and principal cities participating in the insurrection sending deputies to the headquarters of the army or the court in order to vote measures and assessments.

In this Catholic republic, the kingdom of Ireland, the interim 'captain-generals' would be advised and counselled by experienced officers and agents with no regard to race. These men would make up a governing council that was intended to oversee affairs until the Irish were capable of governing themselves. The spiritual factor was not ignored. In fact, the pope was expected to give them help and support. It was the intention of the Irish council that the pope should have the continent's Catholic princes tax their clergy for the purpose of financing this religious crusade. The proposal also encouraged the pope to help the republic secure diplomatic recognition from Catholic Europe, and urged the pontiff to excommunicate any Catholic who directly or indirectly worked against this liberation. Finally representatives were to be sent out from Ireland to the Catholic princes of Europe requesting their support and recognition. 'With the government of the Republic established, a general insurrection would be assured, and there would be no need to feel under any obligation either to a stranger or to a native, as Suzerain.'[22]

This unique proposal utilised phrasing that should not be confused with later political terminology. Following Hugh O'Neill's precedent, religion would be the bonding factor underlying the idea of *patria*. The problem is the compatibility of the terms 'kingdom and republic'. The reference to a republic was a transitory one. The sixteenth-century interpretation of *res publica* was a form of commonwealth emphasising public welfare or a free society for the common good, like the liberty of Ireland's Catholic communities. To perceive this term as non-monarchical is to ignore the historical setting and the political perspectives of that era. The republic, alluded to in the document, suggested that power was derived from representations of Ireland's Catholic leaders whose intention was to settle on a suitable unifying ruler, a Catholic monarch. Their interim republican experiment was expected to uphold a Catholic fatherland while not predisposing or alienating support until factional differences were resolved and the country secured. This extraordinary proposal never got past the drafting stage, but the ensuing disappointment inspired Owen Roe O'Neill and a new generation of Franciscan benefactors to rededicate their cause with a biblical precedent of resistance and accommodation – Maccabeanism. The proving of this thesis

---

22 Phillip IV to Infanta Isabella, 27 December 1627, B. Jennings (ed.), *Wild Geese in Spanish Flanders, 1582–1700* (IMC, Dublin, 1964), pp. 228–35.

revolves around three points: the relationship between Maccabean polity and the evolving conciliatory outlook of desperate exiles, Old Testament traditionalism of the Franciscans, and O'Neill's political expectations for his officer corps.

II

Whatever political theory is discernible in the two surviving books of the Maccabees revolves around Mattathias' sons: Judas, the warrior, Jonathan, the politician, and particularly Simon, who was selected as 'high priest' and 'governor-general over [the] . . . people with the right to convene an assembly in that country'. The actual title Simon assumed was 'ethnarch'. This rank was not monarchical, but elective and temporary until a true leader, descended from the house of King David, emerged.[23] According to biblical scholars the original Maccabees did not seek a monarchy because of the messianic requirement of that office. Unfortunately, no other political particulars have survived. But Hellenistic and biblical models influenced the Maccabees, and Judas Maccabeus was fascinated by early Roman republicanism. Judas admired the Roman senate, especially its representative and deliberative capacity. He also marvelled how the Romans 'entrusted their government to one man every year, to rule over the entire country'.[24] But the critical point was the Maccabean acceptance that their fight for Judean freedom took the form of palatine sovereignty, local autonomy within the domain of a larger structure – the Seleucid kingdom.[25] This solution is reminiscent of the political recommendations of the 1627 invasion scheme, and its sponsored independence under papal or Spanish authority. The relationship was not exactly palatine, but it represented a progressive step in exiled political thinking. By 1642 a palatine experiment evolved as the Catholic Confederation of Kilkenny.[26]

The catalyst for this accommodation during the 1630s was the deteriorating conditions for Ireland's Catholics. Motivated by their fear of exclusion, the Old English and native Irish took advantage of the failing political situation in England between the king and his parliament and devised the so-called 'colonel's plot' of 1641. This intrigue involved a general Catholic insurrection co-ordinated with the return of armed Irish Catholic soldiers from the continent. The key difference between this

[23] 1 Maccabees XIV.41–47; *First Book of the Maccabees*, pp. 106–7.
[24] 1 Maccabees VIII.15–16; First *Book of the Maccabees*, p. 75.
[25] 1 Maccabees XIII.36–40; *First Book of the Maccabees*, p. 36. E. Gruen, *Heritage and Hellenism: The Reinvention of Jewish Tradition* (Berkeley, CA, 1998), pp. 1–40.
[26] Also see chapter 9 below.

project and those popularised during the Anglo-Spanish War was the more active participation of the Old English. Their inclusion necessitated native Irish accommodations. The result was the plotters' expressed allegiance to a desperate English monarch, who was willing to concede to Irish Catholic demands. Unfortunately, the 'colonels' plot' became stillborn when Charles I believed he had secured less embarrassing (non-Catholic) allies in Scotland for his campaign against parliament. The collapse of the plot did not deter Owen Roe O'Neill and the northern Irish conspirators. They continued their efforts, and proclaimed that their rebellion in October 1641 was not against the king, but 'in defence and liberty of ourselves and the Irish natives of this kingdom'.[27] In other words, the 1641 plotters rebelled to resecure their lands and religious liberties under the king, or without him, in his name.

The 1641 rebellion gave birth, in the early summer of 1642, to the Kilkenny confederate experiment; an organisational prototype rooted in decades of Franciscan temporising. However, forming a government acceptable to the Irish political nation proved problematic. Somehow the polity of the exiled conspirators had to accommodate the territorial and constitutional expectations of their Old English brethren. The vehicle for this conciliation was proposed by the provincial synod of Armagh, with its pro-Franciscan ties to Louvain and Owen Roe O'Neill. After their meeting in March 1642, their rapprochement evolved into a confederation, whereby the constitutional royalism of the Old English and the embryonic republicanism of the desperate native Irish took form as an elected assembly 'of his Majesty's Roman Catholic subjects of the Kingdom of Ireland'.[28] The motto of the Kilkenny Confederation inscribed on its seal told all: *Pro Deo, Pro Rege, et Patria, Hibernia Unanimis* ('United for God, king, and the Irish fatherland'.)

The suggested unity remained a precarious one and should not be

---

[27] Proclamation of Phelim O'Neill etc., 24 October 1641, PRO, SP Ireland, 63/260/27, f. 135.
[28] P. Corish, 'The Origins of Catholic Nationalism' in *A History of Irish Catholicism* (Dublin, 1968), III, pp. 31–2; D. Cregan, 'The Confederation of Kilkenny' in B. Farrell (ed.), *The Irish Parliamentary Tradition* (Dublin, 1973), p. 103; H. F. Kearney, 'Ecclesiastical Politics and the Counter-Reformation in Ireland, 1618–1648', *Journal of Ecclesiastical History*, 11 (1960), pp. 208–9; Gilbert (ed.), *Contemporary History*, I, pp. 34–6; R. O. Ferrall and R. O. O'Connell (eds.), *Commentarius Rinuccinianus* (6 vols., IMC, Dublin, 1932), I, pp. 314–19. Hugh O'Reilly, the archbishop of Armagh and Irish Primate, presided over the synod. He was acknowledged as the moving force behind the idea of confederation. Although O'Reilly was not a Franciscan, he was probably educated by them and had close ties to Louvain. The archbishop was also a kinsman of Owen Roe O'Neill and was supported in the synod by O'Neill's life-long friend and supporter, the Louvain-educated Eimhear MacMahon, the bishop of Clogher. S. O. O'Mordha, 'Hugh O'Reilly, a Reforming Primate', *Breifne*, 4, 13 (1970), pp. 1–42 and *ibid.*, 4, 15 (1972), pp. 348–52.

overstated. Despite the confederacy's initial proclamation forbidding the use of cultural and political identities,[29] the governing mechanism was undermined by differences within and among these Catholic communities. Many confederates hoped the Kilkenny experiment would be a laboratory for consensual government, a place to settle long-standing religious, tenurial and sovereignty issues. Democratic in structure and aristocratic in personnel,[30] the Kilkenny Confederacy provided a forum and opportunity for a provincial-minded and religiously fractious society to create a Catholic *patria*. To achieve this objective the participants relied on a new national political identity which drew on Florence Conry's 'republican-kingdom', Old English constitutionalism, and the lesson of Maccabean resistance.

Like the 1627 and biblical Maccabean governing schemes, the Confederates were not setting up a true or permanent parliament. Their object was to settle problems and establish through the confederate mechanism a new government that would best serve the interests of Catholic Ireland.[31] Although unitary in nature, the Supreme Council and General Assembly recognised the provincial rights of its constituents. The military organisation of the confederacy and its political base originated on the provincial level. The provinces not only embodied an intermediate jurisdiction that oversaw local county councils; they also represented local needs to the confederate National Assembly.[32] In Ulster, for example, provincial councils met at convenient and centrally located places that were accessible in a war-ravaged countryside.[33] Unlike the 1627 'republican-kingdom' plan, which was generally native Irish and separatist in tone, the Kilkenny Confederation intended to resolve problems among and between Ireland's Catholic communities and the Stuart monarchy. But as Catholic unanimity and faith in the monarchy ebbed, more militant native factions found solace in a secessionist stand expressed in a treatise published in Portugal. Written by a Jesuit, Conor O'Mahony, the *Disputatio Apologetica* (1645) exhorted the Catholics of Ireland to depose heretical and tyrannical monarchs. The author reminded the Irish how the Israelites liberated their land and chose their own king: 'You have splendid leaders in war, well skilled in military science and very brave soldiers . . . Get to work fellow Irishmen and complete the work of your

---

[29] Acts of the General Assembly, October 1642, Gilbert (ed.), *Irish Confederation*, II, p. 80. J. C. Beckett, 'The Confederation of Kilkenny Revisited', *Historical Studies*, 2 (1959), pp. 30–1.   [30] Cregan, 'Confederation of Kilkenny', p.104.

[31] 'An explanation of some of the answers given in behalf of the Confederat Catholiques of Ireland', Gilbert (ed.), *Irish Confederation*, IV, p. 243. Beckett, 'Confederation of Kilkenny Revisited', p. 35.   [32] Cregan, 'Confederation of Kilkenny', pp. 107–8.

[33] For discussion of Ulster provincial councils see J. Casway, 'The Belturbet Council and the Election of 1650', *Clogher Record*, 12 (1986), p. 160.

defence and of your liberty already begun, kill the heretics your enemies and drive them from your midst . . . together with those who support and aid them.'[34] This militant native Irish stance was fallaciously associated with General Owen Roe O'Neill and his northern army supporters. The aged O'Neill, recognising that it was no longer possible to succeed on his own with only foreign succour, distanced himself from O'Mahony's position. The difficulty for O'Neill was that he had invested too much in finding accommodating solutions for his faltering cause in the Confederation and knew that only an accord with English governing authorities could best guarantee the well-being of the disenfranchised native Irish. Without this legitimising recognition, there was no hope that O'Neill and his disciples could secure a future for themselves in the maelstrom of an Irish political settlement. In this setting the ailing O'Neill intended that his young officer corps serve as his Maccabees and fulfil a role anticipated in the 1627 memoranda. If O'Neill was not meant to see the new Ireland, his select cadre would re-establish what he and the Louvain Franciscans had envisioned.

Their resistance plan originated in and was influenced by continental exile politics, particularly the Dutch example of successful revolt, and biblical sources. Residing in the Spanish Netherlands, Owen Roe O'Neill and the Franciscan community at Louvain could not ignore their Protestant neighbours. The Dutch in their campaigns against the Spanish in the late sixteenth century promoted the fatherland idea and frequently compared themselves to the struggling Israelites of the Old Testament. On occasion they saw themselves as Maccabee defenders of their covenant, a pact tantamount to a 'general will'.[35] The question is whether Irish palatinate-republicanism originated in Holland. No direct links favouring Dutch, or even French Huguenots and early Celtic sources exist, but Roman and biblical associations abound. The publicists for the model in question were a new generation of Franciscans who were trained in the best classical civic-humanism traditions at the leading Counter-Reformation universities of Europe.

These seminaries not only promoted Old Testament studies; they also provided common meeting places for Ireland's Catholic factions. This integration was not easy, but Franciscan houses, like the one in Louvain, understood early on the value of Irish harmony.[36] Their successes

---

[34] See chapter 7 above. Bodl., Clarendon Papers, 1647, no. 2664. Gilbert (ed.), *Contemporary History*, I, pp. 667–9. T. O'Fiaich, 'Republicanism and Separatism in the Seventeenth Century', *Leachtaí Cholm Cille* (Maynooth, 1971), pp. 82–5.

[35] M. Walzer, *Exodus and Revolution* (New York, 1985), pp. 79–80. Also see S. Schama, *The Embarrassment of Riches: An Interpretation of Dutch Culture in the Golden Age* (New York, 1987), pp. 51–125.   [36] Corish, 'Catholic Nationalism', p. 29.

affected their influence among the northern Irish lords, who depended on them for political and educational functions. Many of the lessons and values they drew upon came from Old Testament studies, through biblical languages like Hebrew and Greek. Hebraic studies were so important for Irish seminaries that the first Irish College at Salamanca required all theological students to learn Hebrew.[37] But no religious order relied more heavily on the languages and traditions of ancient Judea than the Franciscans, whose biblical focus was stirred by the far-sighted political thinking of John Duns Scotus.

The great thirteenth-century Franciscan theorist found his widest audience in the seventeenth century when '*Scoti Schola numerosior est omnibus aliis simul sumptis*' ['the school of Scotus is more numerous than all the rest put together'].[38] Through the writings of Father Luke Wadding, guardian of the college of St Isidore's in Rome and chief benefactor of the early Irish Catholic Confederation, the thoughts of Duns Scotus invigorated Irish Franciscan thinking. With so much attention given to his spiritual interpretations, Scotus' theories about the state and the origin of the civil power of government have been generally overlooked. The eminent scholar did not favour 'divine right of kings' or the notion that royal power came from God. In Book IV of the *Ordinatio*, Scotus asserted that political authority exercised over non-kinship groups, whether it was under one person or a group, must come from the 'common consent and election on the part of the community'.[39] By this lawful principle, Duns Scotus set out the concept of a precursor 'general will' – a social covenant that bound people together into a political community. Under continental Irish Franciscans, Scotus' political tenets coalesced with Maccabean 'liberation theology'.

The two surviving books of the Maccabees recite a worldly activism of biblical champions, warriors in the cause of religious freedom and national independence. In this quest, Judas and his family promoted themselves as divine instruments, striving to deliver their people from political and cultural oppression. They were revolutionaries, guerrilla fighters and real-life heroes.[40] Set in an apocalyptic milieu, the Maccabees became models for latter-day martyrs and rebels. In a biblical context, Judas and his family signified a heroic shift from the wise scholar

[37] T. Morrissey, 'The Irish Student Diaspora in the Sixteenth Century and the Early Years of the Irish College at Salamanca', *Recusant History*, 14, 4 (1978), pp. 250–1.

[38] F. Bak, '*Scoti Schola numerosior est omnibus aliis simul sumptis*', *Franciscan Studies*, 16 (1956), pp. 144–65.

[39] A. Wolter, *Duns Scotus' Political and Economic Philosophy* (Santa Barbara, CA, 1989), pp. 24, 39–41.

[40] D. Harrington, 'Maccabees' in *The Harper Collins Study Bible* (New York, 1993, revised edn), pp. 1645–8.

and sage to glorified men of action.[41] Incited by their example, and moved by the notions of Scotist-Franciscan political covenants, Archbishop Conry and Owen Roe O'Neill found their standard and archetype for defending their *patria* and reconciling their countrymen.

Another supporting link was the Christian lineage of the Maccabean texts. For Jews, the books of the Maccabees were non-canonical. The Hebrew and Aramaic editions did not survive and the Maccabees re-emerged as part of the Greek Bible tradition, the Septuagint. To Catholics, the Maccabees belong to the canon of sacred scripture.[42] The reasons for this theological descent can only be speculated upon. Politically, when the Hasmonean monarchy was established in violation of Simon Maccabeus' covenant with the people of Judea – the setting up of a king outside of David's line – the accounts and exploits of the Maccabees were censored. Another contributing factor was the militant legacy of the Maccabean movement. For the post-Maccabean Judaic establishment, the 'warrior religion' was seen as dangerous and controversial. It carried with it too many threatening precedents and eventually was excluded from Jewish sacred tradition.[43] How ironic that it fell upon the early Christian church to retrieve the story of these 'freedom fighters' by preserving it in biblical Greek. The conclusions are evident. The Franciscans, with their Scotus political precepts and appreciation for biblical literature, merged these traditions into a bardic 'Clann Israel' association. Stoked by the exigencies of survival and accommodation, the Irish Franciscans and their dependants found in the Maccabean exploits an inspirational rebellion and 'biblical recreation' for Irish Catholic emulation.

Finally there remains the role of Owen Roe O'Neill's native Maccabees during the Irish civil war. In the mind of O'Neill, his Maccabees were to be the military vanguard of the native-confederate cause.[44] Conditioned by the deprivation of exile, and indoctrinated by a generation of polemic agitation, these young men assumed the roles alluded to in the 1627 invasion plan. They returned to their homeland without 'ensigns' or affiliated banners in ships displaying a flag with an Irish harp in a field of green.[45] Like Mattathias and his sons, O'Neill anticipated a role for his protégés in a new Ireland. 'Bred in a nursery of arms'[46] in Catholic Ireland and

---

[41] D. Harrington, *The Maccabean Revolt: Anatomy of a Biblical Revolution* (Wilmington, 1988), pp. 9–13, 48–9, 128–30.

[42] *Ibid.*, p. 13; Harrington, 'Maccabees', pp. 1645–6.

[43] Harrington, *Maccabean Revolt*, pp. 10, 131. Correspondence with Maccabean authority Fr Daniel Harrington, SJ, proved to be most helpful in understanding the character and influence of this biblical phenomenon.

[44] J. Casway, *Owen Roe O'Neill and the Struggle for Catholic Ireland* (Philadelphia, 1984), pp. 66–7.   [45] M. O'Hartigan to L. Wadding, 17 October 1642, FLK, D. IV, f. 849.

[46] Gilbert (ed.), *Contemporary History*, I, pp. 72 and 6–7.

Europe, O'Neill's Maccabees were groomed to lead their province and country into an uncertain future through, or in spite of, the mechanism of the Kilkenny experiment.

Exploratory studies of O'Neill's northern army officer corps reveal that these men were drawn from the leading native families of Ulster and Connacht. Many had at least ten years of service in Europe, were kinsmen to the general, had been victims of the post-flight plantations, were active in the 1641 plotting and served under Owen Roe. Another group of O'Neill's officers had similar characteristics, but lacked foreign service experience. They represented the domestic connection for the 1641 conspiracies. In the tradition of Mattathias of Modein, who passed the torch of resistance to his sons, O'Neill's officers, drawn from the O'Neills, O'Cahans, Maguires, Magennises, O'Reillys, O'Farrells, O'Byrnes, O'Dohertys, O'Hagans, O'Mores, MacMahons, MacDonnells and even non-native Bourkes and Fitzgeralds, made up an aspiring cadre of insurgent liberators, a vanguard of Irish leaders devoted to a Catholic *patria*. Theirs was a nascent nationalism conceived by the necessity and opportunity of the Wars in the Three Kingdoms.

But the biblical age of miracles that fostered the Maccabean story had long ago ended; there would be no relief for their Irish heirs. O'Neill and his Maccabees eventually succumbed to the same forces that defeated their biblical predecessors: factional self-interest, religious divisiveness and expansionist adversaries. In the end, companies of devout Cromwellian soldiers crushed the dreams of an Irish *patria* and O'Neill's Maccabees, just as the legions of Rome stamped out the biblical state of Judea. The diaspora of brethren, separated by nearly two millennia, became the tragic lessons in the history of both peoples. The resulting consequences of each are yet to be resolved.

Part III

Irish political thought and the new British and Irish histories

9 Covenanting ideology in seventeenth-century Scotland

Allan I. Macinnes

The religious and constitutional imperatives of the National Covenant of 1638 justified the Scottish resistance to Charles I which instigated the Wars of the Three Kingdoms. The export of these imperatives to England and Ireland in the Solemn League and Covenant of 1643 initiated the War for the Three Kingdoms. Covenanting ideology, which was the dynamic product of the interaction of political thought and the political process, dominated the British political agenda until 1645 when the emergence of the New Model Army ensured that the English parliament no longer relied on the forces of the Scottish Covenanters. The main covenanting ideologues, who had justified Scottish resistance as the movement of a chosen people, sought not only to rationalise the past but to shape the future through their active participation in the political process. However, the splintering of the covenanting movement, marked by the Engagement of 1648 and the subsequent schism between Protestors and Resolutioners that facilitated the Cromwellian occupation of Scotland in the 1650s, emasculated covenanting as an ideology of power. Nonetheless, the establishment of an erastian Episcopacy in place of autonomous Presbyterianism at the Restoration Settlement revitalised covenanting as an ideology of protest by which the disaffected took to covert conventicling in house and field. Thus the movement became atomised and subjected to rigorous repression and the covenanting legacy became that of sectarian resistance eulogised as the travails of 'the suffering remnant' during the 'killing times'.[1]

The hagiographic historiography of the later covenanting movement has distorted the radical British significance of the early covenanting movement, especially its non-anglocentric contribution to political discourse throughout the Three Kingdoms. The covenanting contribution to this debate has been confounded by three misapprehensions: that the early movement was essentially an aristocratic and conservative

---

[1] D. Reid, *The Party-Coloured Mind* (Edinburgh, 1982); I. B. Cowan, *The Scottish Covenanters, 1660–88* (London, 1982).

reaction;[2] that it persistently promoted political federalism under the guise of religious uniformity;[3] that the early, like the later, movement was predominantly a lowland concern. Thus, the political labelling in vogue from the Restoration era has castigated radicals as extremists and commended conservatives as moderates.[4] Yet covenanting adherence, which was nationwide during the 1640s, was also a marked, if inconsistent, feature in Ulster, where the movement's ideological impact was complemented by political and religious interaction across the North Channel. Such contact served as an Irish bridge between covenanting as an ideology of power and that of protest.[5]

Although the early covenanting movement never moved towards republicanism or a democratic polity, its radicalism was evident in its centralising of power not in aristocratic but in oligarchic hands. Parliamentary committees drawn from the estates of the gentry and burgesses as well as the nobility imposed unprecedented demands on the Scottish localities for ideological conformity, financial supply and military recruitment.[6] At the same time, the radicalism of the centralising oligarchy was manifest not just by its export of a model for revolution, but by its efforts to promote confederation throughout and beyond the British Isles. By institutionalising revolution, the Covenanters sought to promote concentric British loyalties, a projection personified by the leader of the radical mainstream during the 1640s – Archibald Campbell, eighth earl and first marquis of Argyll – as clan chief, Scottish magnate and British statesman.[7] But ready acceptance of a 'British' agenda does not mean the imperial aspirations which James VI and I passed on to Charles I were

[2] R. Rehberg, 'Justification of Resistance in Early Modern Revolutions: A Comparison of the German Peasant War, the Dutch Revolt, and the British Revolution', *International Politics*, 33 (1996), pp. 273–90; M. Lynch, *Scotland: A New History* (London, 1992), pp. 264–6; W. Ferguson, *Scotland's Relations with England: A Survey to 1707* (Edinburgh, 1977), pp. 114–16.

[3] D. Stevenson, 'The Early Covenanters and the Federal Union of Britain' in R. A. Mason (ed.), *Scotland and England 1286–1815* (Edinburgh, 1987), pp. 163–81; K. M. Brown, *Kingdom or Province? Scotland and the Regal Union, 1603–1715* (London, 1992), pp. 81–3; J. Morrill, 'The Britishness of the English Revolution, 1640–1660' in R. G. Asch (ed.), *Three Nations – A Common History? England, Scotland, Ireland and British History, c.1600–1920* (Bochum, 1993), pp. 83–115. Federalism did not enter British political vocabulary until the debates on the Anglo-Scottish of 1707.

[4] M. Goldie, 'Divergence and Union: Scotland and England, 1660–1707' in B. Bradshaw and J. Morrill (eds.), *The British Problem, c.1534–1707: State Formation in the Atlantic Archipelago* (Basingstoke, 1996), pp. 220–45.

[5] Rev. P. Adair, *A True Narrative of the Rise and Progress of the Presbyterian Church in Ireland (1623–1670)* ed. W. D. Killen (Belfast, 1866).

[6] J. R. Young, *The Scottish Parliament, 1639–1661: A Political and Constitutional Analysis* (Edinburgh, 1996).

[7] The house of Argyll was among the first of the political elite in the Three Kingdoms to apply 'British' labels in the wake of the regal union of 1603 and prior to the formal commencement of plantation in Ulster (I[nveraray] C[astle] A[rchives], bundle 63/3; Argyll

sustained by the covenanting movement. On the contrary, the marquis of
Argyll served as a principal architect in transforming regal into confederal
union and imposing this on Charles II, when he was crowned the covenanting king of Great Britain on 1 January 1651.[8]

I

With Scotland's political interests formally subordinated to those of
England after 1603, the religious aspirations of the national Kirk had
become the most distinctive means of promoting Scotland internation-
ally. The Kirk was the only national church in Europe not obliged to tolerate other religious groups in the interests of political expediency. However
the national standing of the Kirk was not unqualified at the outset of
Charles I's reign. Its influence was pervasive throughout the Lowlands
where parishes tended to be relatively small in area and settlements
nucleated. The Kirk's operations in the Highlands, where parishes were
large and communities dispersed, were still at missionary level. Kirk
polity remained a compromise between Presbyterianism and Episcopal
authority, albeit the latter was in the ascendancy. The Kirk had no clear or
unequivocal standard of worship, but its doctrine remained staunchly
Calvinist. The Arminian challenge, first aroused within the Dutch
Reformed Kirk before spreading to the Church of England, had gained
no foothold in Scotland before the death of James VI and I in 1625.

Arminianism accepted Calvinist orthodoxy with regard to original sin
and justification by faith, but rejected its absolute belief in predestination
which offered salvation only for the elect and eternal damnation for the
reprobate. Hence, the Calvinist teaching that the grace of God was irresistible for the elect, who as the true believers could not fall from grace,
was renounced in favour of universal atonement. This precept offered salvation to every individual prepared to repent his or her sins. For the
Arminian, therefore, the assurance of salvation was freely available for all
believers but conditional on human endeavour. For the Calvinist, who
believed in absolute and exclusive salvation for the elect, belief in free
will was an unwarrantable limitation on the sovereignty of God.[9]
The Reformed Kirk, however, was concerned not only to promote the

Transcripts, VIII (1607–10), nos. 114, 256; IX (1611–19), no. 163; S[cottish] R[ecord]
O[ffice], Breadalbane Collection, Gifts and Deposits 112/1/378). Material collated from
Inveraray Castle was generously funded by a Major Research Grants Award from the
British Academy.
[8] A. I. Macinnes, 'Politically Reactionary Brits? The Promotion of Anglo-Scottish Union,
1603–1707' in S. Connolly (ed.), *Kingdoms United? Great Britain and Ireland since 1500*
(Dublin, 1998), pp. 43–55.
[9] J. MacLeod, *Scottish Theology* (Edinburgh, 1974), pp. 28–9; A. L. Drummond, *The Kirk
and the Continent* (Edinburgh, 1956), pp. 110–11.

salvation of the elect, but to identify the national interest with a dutiful dedication to the godly life: that is, every member of every congregation striving to attain a state of grace as the precondition for election must adhere systematically to a Calvinist code of ethics for everyday conduct. Doctrinal precepts, moreover, underwrote the international responsibilities of the Kirk that retained a watching brief over the fate of Protestantism in general and of Calvinist minorities in particular. This special concern was intensified by the course of the Counter-Reformation and the political alignments brought about by the Thirty Years War (1618–48). For militant Catholicism, allied to the autocracy of the Spanish and Austrian Habsburgs, was ranged against and initially triumphed over Protestants and particularist interests within the Holy Roman Empire.[10]

Albeit the actual profession of Catholicism was a minority pursuit in Scotland, Kirk-inspired fears of Counter-Reformation, coupled to James VI's decided preference for an erastian Episcopacy in the Kirk, prompted militants to combine locally in covenants. Banding together for the purposes of local government or political alliance was a socially established practice in Scotland by the sixteenth century and, indeed, had been adopted specifically for religious purposes at the Reformation. Yet, the description of a religious band as a covenant only gained common currency after 1590, as the result of the reception from the continent of federal theology, which gave tangible force to man's absolute dependence on God for salvation.[11]

Covenant, or federal theology, which the Scots shared with evangelical Protestants from Transylvania to New England, emphasised the contractual relationship between God and man rather than the stark Calvinist reliance on election by divine decree. Predestination and thereby man's ultimate dependence on divine grace was not denied. The true believer proved his or her election by covenanting with God, not by exercising his or her free will to chose salvation. Participation in the covenant did not determine election, but merely realised the predetermined will of God. Divine grace moved man to covenant. But once man had so banded himself to God he was assured of election.[12] In Scotland, as in New

[10] G. Marshall, *Presbyteries and Profits* (Oxford, 1980), pp. 74–7, 103–7; A. I. Macinnes, 'Catholic Recusancy and the Penal Laws, 1603–1707', *Records of the Scottish Church History Society*, 23 (1987), pp. 27–63.
[11] S. A. Burrell, 'The Covenant Idea as a Revolutionary Symbol: Scotland, 1596–1637', *Church History*, 27 (1958), pp. 338–50; J. Wormald, 'Bloodfeud, Kindred and Government in Early Modern Scotland', *Past and Present*, 87 (1980), pp. 54–97.
[12] Marshall, *Presbyteries and Profits*, pp. 107–12; MacLeod, *Scottish Theology*, pp. 85, 219; P. Miller, 'The Marrow of Puritan Divinity' in G. M. Walker (ed.), *Puritanism in Early America* (Toronto, 1973), pp. 54–7.

England, the idea of the covenant was popularly translated in the early seventeenth century not simply as an elaboration of God's compact with the elect, but as a means of revealing God's purposes towards his people. The practical vitality of the covenant was derived from the expansion of the concept to cover works as well as grace, whereby banding for spiritual purposes was allied to spiritual assurance. The covenant gave tangible forms to the cardinal precepts of the Reformed Kirk's Confession of Faith: specifically to the assurance of salvation of which all members of congregations should be persuaded and to the necessity of doing good works for the glory of God, for confirmation of the elect and as an example to others.[13] At its most potent, the covenant could be interpreted as a divine band between God and the people of Scotland. Such a covenant had a comprehensive rather than a sectional appeal, for Scottish society as a whole not just the political nation of nobles, gentry, burgesses and clergy.[14] Covenanting was still a minority activity for Presbyterians in the opening decades of the seventeenth century, however. After the exhortation of the Kirk's General Assembly for a mutual band between ministers and their congregations in 1596, no national renewal occurred until 1638. In essence, covenanting was a religious alternative that kept alive evangelical dissent under erastian Episcopacy.[15]

In return for a guarantee that James VI and I would attempt no further liturgical innovations, the Scottish Estates in 1621 had ratified the Five Articles, whose most controversial aspect was that all members of congregations were required to kneel when participating in communion. The ensuing reluctance of the bishops to publicise nonconformity by prosecution had enabled Presbyterian laity, with the connivance of sympathetic ministers, either to absent themselves from communion or to refrain from kneeling. A more radical development was the covert growth of praying societies, known as conventicles, which sought to sustain the purity of the Reformed Kirk by private meetings for collective devotion. By 1625, conventicling circuits established for preaching and administering nonconforming communions had spread from Edinburgh to Fife, and to south-west and west-central Scotland. When Charles I and the Arminian-inclined William Laud – first as bishop of London then as archbishop of

---

[13] Cf. SRO, Paisley Presbytery Records, 1626–47, Charters 2/294/2, f. 4.

[14] S. A. Burrell, 'The Apocalyptic Vision of the Early Covenanters', *SHR*, 43 (1964), pp. 1–24; A. H. Williamson, *Scottish National Consciousness in the Age of James VI* (Edinburgh, 1979), pp. 64–85. In using the concept of the covenant to propagate gospel truths among their congregations, the evangelicals were able to draw upon the dominant ideal of a national Kirk as well as the prestige and social influence all ministers acquired from the reformed emphasis on the preaching of the word.

[15] J. A. Aikman, *An Historical Account of Covenanting in Scotland from 1556 to 1638* (Edinburgh, 1848), p. 65.

Canterbury – imperiously promoted religious uniformity throughout the Three Kingdoms, the maintenance of spiritual assurance among militant Presbyterians was due in no small measure to these circuits.[16]

Although more noted as a receptacle for rather than as a shaper of covenanting ideology in the seventeenth century, the formative role of Ulster should not be understated with regards to conventicling. Popular support for nonconforming Presbyterianism, especially in the south-west of Scotland, was enhanced by the re-export of evangelical fervour from Ulster, most notably by the occasional sorties of such exiled Scottish Presbyterians as Robert Blair and John Livingstone, ministers in the diocese of Down. Praying societies had been imported by Scottish colonists during the 1620s. Sympathetic ministers had been attracted from Scotland by the determination of colonists to preserve a Presbyterian presence within the Episcopal framework of the Church of Ireland. However, this small but zealous Presbyterian vanguard composed less than a tenth of the Protestant ministry in Ulster. The vulnerability of their position to a concerted attack by Irish and Scottish bishops was demonstrated by the suspension of Blair and Livingstone in 1631, for participating in revivalist meetings organised as conventicling communions on both sides of the North Channel. This Presbyterian vanguard was acutely exposed by the Episcopal offensive that concerted with the first imposition by the Court of Laudian directives for religious uniformity: that is, the ecclesiastical canons that terminated the independence of the Church of Ireland from November 1634. Within twenty months, not only had Blair and Livingstone been excommunicated, but their Presbyterian associates had been deposed for their refusal to conform to Anglican standards. Blair and Livingstone, other vanguard ministers and prominent conventiclers from both Ulster and Scotland decided to seek release 'from the bondage of prelates'. In September 1636, around 140 nonconformists embarked from Ulster for New England. Although their ship neared Newfoundland, tempestuous weather forced their return to Scotland by November; a reversal interpreted as divine intervention. God had made evident 'that it was not his will that they should glorify him in America, he having work for them at home'.[17]

[16] D. Stevenson, 'Conventicles in the Kirk, 1619–37', *Records of the Scottish Church History Society*, 18 (1972–4), pp. 99–114; *Autobiography of the Life of Mr Robert Blair*, ed. T. McCrie (Wodrow Society, Edinburgh, 1848), pp. 117, 136–8; *Select Biographies*, ed. W. K. Tweedie (2 vols., Wodrow Society, Edinburgh, 1845–7), I, pp. 134–40, 150–1.

[17] J. S. Reid, *The History of the Presbyterian Church in Ireland* (3 vols., Edinburgh, 1834), I, pp. 94–8, 105, 110–1, 119–22, 130–7, 168–9, 173–8, 182–9, 201–5, 225–34; *Autobiography of Mr Robert Blair*, pp. 57–9, 64, 71, 84–6, 90–1, 101–6, 128–9, 136–7, 142–8; *Select Biographies*, I, pp. 134–5, 141–8, 152–7, 344; J. Row, *The History of the Kirk of Scotland 1558–1637*, ed. D. Laing (Wodrow Society, Edinburgh, 1842), pp. 390, 397–8; Adair, *The*

The influx of Ulster nonconformists to the south-west of Scotland, which coincided with the imposition of the Scottish version of the *Book of Canons*, served to harden the resolve of conventiclers to resist further liturgical innovation as authorised by Charles I in the *Service Book*. Despite the vehemence of their language towards the bishops and their conviction that the political nation should atone for past sins and oppose the promotion of religious uniformity, the conventiclers were catalysts for – rather than instigators of – revolution. In essence, they were a pressure group organised covertly throughout the Lowlands by 1637. Collective as well as personal discipline was maintained by periodic fasting; godliness was cultivated nationally as well as individually. Their militant sense of righteousness reinforced their assurance that they were God's elect on earth. However, not all nonconforming Presbyterians were committed conventiclers. Moreover, the eclectic image of the conventiclers, not dissimilar to that of the Puritans in New England, exposed them to charges of separatism.[18]

For their part, the conventiclers were not convinced that the nobles, as leaders of the political nation disaffected with the authoritarian rule of Charles I, were intent on the pursuit of godliness. Samuel Rutherford, a noted critic of Episcopacy, the Five Articles and Arminianism, was banished from his parochial charge in the south-west during the summer of 1636 for his nonconformity and conventicling associations. Writing from exile in Aberdeen as the opposition to Charles I focused on the imminent publication of the *Service Book* in the spring of 1637, Rutherford cautioned against political confrontation in the name of religion: 'I am not of that mind, that tumults or arms is the way to put Christ on His throne.' The dissatisfied leadership was no less wary of too close an association with conventiclers that would attract official surveillance of their planned

---

Presbyterian Church in Ireland, pp. 16–51. Nonconforming Presbyterians from Scotland found a conducive, if challenging, doctrinal home in Ulster. From 1615, the Church of Ireland was governed by 104 Articles which were not only thoroughly Calvinist, but rigorously predestinarian, accommodating to conscientious scruples with Episcopacy and unequivocally anti-Catholic in identifying the Papacy with Antichrist. Moreover, the prevailing perception of apocalyptical history was pessimistic, as befitting a planted society surrounded by displaced and antipathetic Irish Catholics. In marked contrast to Scotland, where confidence in the ultimate victory of the godly over Antichrist inspired the covenanting movement, Protestants in Ireland were primarily aware that in the last few days Antichrist was at its strongest and the godly were threatened with their greatest sufferings and persecution (A. Ford, *The Protestant Reformation in Ireland, 1590–1641* (Frankfurt am Main, 1987), pp. 194–242).

[18] *Letters of Samuel Rutherford*, ed. A. A. Bonar (2 vols., Edinburgh, 1863), I, pp. 75, 109, 156, 160, 167–71, 195, 200, 211–14, 228–35, 285–6, 370–6; *Diary of Sir Archibald Johnston of Wariston, 1632–39*, ed. J. M. Paul (Scottish History Society, Edinburgh, 1911), pp. 250–64; *The Memoirs of Henry Guthry, Late Bishop of Dunkeld*, ed. G. Crawford (Glasgow, 1747), pp. 78–80.

opposition to the *Service Book*.[19] Nonetheless, the disaffected leadership came to appreciate the ideological advantage of such an association. For the conventiclers were foremost among nonconforming Presbyterians advocating communal banding in covenants as the alternative religious standard to liturgical innovations. The covenant of grace and works not only assured the righteous of their temporal as well as their spiritual calling, but affirmed the special relationship between God and Scotland whose people were heirs to ancient Israel as His covenanted nation. Thus, covenanting in Scotland was a manifestation of the divine band between God and the Scottish people. The godly were bound to seek the reformation of an errant Kirk whose present corruption under 'the tyranny of prelates' was attributable 'to our breach of the covenant, contempt of the Gospel and our defection from the truth'. By March, the godly were being charged to prepare for the coming of Christ, 'The Great Messenger of the Covenant'.[20]

Such purveying of apocalyptic visions undoubtedly added a sense of divine imminence to the political scene. But covenanting adherence in Scotland was not so much a decisive cause of revolt against Charles I as a means of communicating symbolically a fundamental ideological message: that opposition to the royal prerogative in defence of religious and civil liberty was divinely warranted. By identifying their cause with the covenant of grace and works, the disaffected availed themselves of the seventeenth-century equivalent of liberationist theology. At the organisational level, the covert and disciplined nature of conventicling enabled the disaffected leadership to prepare discreetly, but systematically. At the same time, the appearance of spontaneity was preserved when open demonstrations were mounted against the imposition of the *Service Book*, first in Edinburgh and then in Glasgow in the summer of 1637.[21]

II

The riots against the *Service Book* in Scotland's two major cities presaged a 'crisis by monthly instalments'. Nationwide petitioning reinforced by mass lobbying, directed initially against the imposition of liturgical innovations, was extended to attack prerogative courts and to decline the

[19] *Letters of Samuel Rutherford*, I, pp. 59, 69, 102, 107, 117, 134, 148–9, 159, 167.
[20] *Ibid.*, pp. 103–5, 111, 163, 214, 274, 277; *Autobiography of Mr Robert Blair*, pp. 130, 150; *Diary of Sir Archibald Johnston of Wariston, 1632–39*, pp. 206, 250, 256–9, 262.
[21] J. B. Torrance, 'The Covenant Concept in Scottish Theology and Politics and its Legacy', *Scottish Journal of Theology*, 34 (1981), pp. 225–43; G. D. Henderson, *The Burning Bush: Studies in Scottish Church History* (Edinburgh, 1957), pp. 65–70; A. H. Williamson, 'The Jewish Dimension of the Scottish Apocalypse: Climate, Covenant and World Renewal' in Y. Kaplan, H. Mechoulan and R. H. Popkins (eds.), *Menasseh Ben Israel and His World* (New York, 1989), pp. 7–30.

authority of the bishops in Kirk and state.[22] David Dickson, an Ayrshire minister sympathetic to conventicling and notably supportive of the Presbyterian vanguard expelled from Ulster, drafted the National Supplication of 17 October, which first served public notice against breaches of the covenant between God, crown and people. The disaffected must suffer 'the ruin of our estates and fortunes' or endure divine retribution for 'breach of our covenant with God, and forsaking the way of true religione'. The disaffected leadership were thus empowered to elevate their divine obligation to supplicate above their duty to obey royal proclamations to disperse.[23]

Grass roots petitioning and mass lobbying in Edinburgh were initially organised on an informal basis among the constituent Estates of the political nation. From November, however, co-ordination was effectively directed by the Tables, each Estate composing a Table with representatives from the other three joining the nobles to form a revolutionary executive which was constituted formally as the Fifth Table at the outset of December. The operation of a provisional government under the direction of the Fifth Table was acknowledged publicly in the week before the National Covenant was promulgated on 28 February 1638. This written Scottish constitution was drawn up by Archibald Johnston of Wariston, an Edinburgh lawyer of undoubted personal piety, also a conventicler zealously committed to the triumph of Presbyterianism. Possibly a manic-depressive and certainly an insomniac of prodigious energy, Wariston had readily penned rebuttals to royal proclamations against the disaffected element that called for fundamental checks on the prerogative by drawing selectively on biblical sources, Roman law commentaries and parliamentary precedents. In pressing the necessity for free constituent assemblies to redress past and prevent future excesses of royal authoritarianism, he was assisted by Alexander Henderson, a minister from Fife with limited sympathy for conventicling, who had masterminded the riots against the *Service Book* and co-ordinated the appeals through the pulpit for nationwide commitment.[24]

The National Covenant was a revolutionary enterprise binding the Scottish people by social compact to justify and consolidate revolt against absentee monarchy. Its moderate tenor, coupled with its conservative format and appeal to precedents, has belied its radical intent. All four

[22] D. Stevenson, *The Scottish Revolution, 1637–44* (Newton Abbot, 1973), pp. 64–79.
[23] D. H. Fleming, *Scotland's Supplication and Complaint against the Book of Common Prayer (otherwise Laud's Liturgy), the Book of Canons, and the Prelates, 18th October 1637* (Edinburgh, 1927), pp. 59–62.
[24] A. I. Macinnes, *Charles I and the Making of the Covenanting Movement, 1625–1641* (Edinburgh, 1991), pp. 158–73; D. Stevenson, *King or Covenant? Voices from Civil War* (East Linton, 1996), pp. 151–73.

Tables having approved the finalised version before subscriptions commenced, its appearance of unanimity was not deceptive. The National Covenant deliberately maintained a studied ambiguity not just to attract support from all classes and from every locality, but primarily to avoid specific imputations of treason.[25] It was not a private league of rebellious subjects nor an aristocratic reaction against Charles I, but a nationalist manifesto asserting the independence of a sovereign people under God. The explicit intent of the Fifth Table was to propagate a tripartite public band embracing God, crown and people, 'for the maintenance of religione and the King's Majesteis authority, and for the preservatione of the lawes and liberties of the kingdome'. Accordingly, the National Covenant can be split into three parts demonstrating the present cause, the dual imperatives and the fundamental priorities of public banding.[26]

The first component rehearsed the Negative Confession of 1581 in association with a detailed, if selective, series of parliamentary enactments perpetrated to maintain the 'true religion and the King's Majesty'. The radical implications of this part was that loyalty to the crown was conditional on expunging idolatrous, superstitious and popish practices from the Kirk; protecting the purity of the reformed tradition; and upholding the rights of the people to be governed according to the common laws of the realm as grounded in statute. The selection of the parliamentary statutes reveals the radical astuteness of the Fifth Table. Precedents for the removal of erroneous doctrines and prejudicial practices culminated with the collation and codification of the penal laws against Catholic recusants in 1609. The urgency of an uncompromising Protestant crusade to ward off the unabated threat from the Counter-Reformation was thus pressed.[27]

The true religion 'now received and preached' was Protestantism that accorded with the Negative Confession of 1581 – that is, prior to the readmission of bishops in the Kirk (1606–10), to the insinuation of the Five Articles (1618–21) as to the recent liturgical innovations (1636–7). Thus, an attack on Episcopacy was contained with the resolve of the Tables to sweep away all innovations, not just religious, which had threatened

[25] J. Leslie, earl of Rothes, *A Relation of Proceedings Concerning the Affairs of the Kirk of Scotland, from August 1637 to July 1638*, ed. J. Nairne (Bannatyne Club, Edinburgh, 1830), p. 211; P. Donald, *An Uncounselled King: Charles I and the Scottish Troubles, 1637–41* (Cambridge, 1991), pp. 66–7.

[26] Rothes, *A Relation of Proceedings*, p. 90; *Acts of the Parliaments of Scotland*, ed. T. Thomson and C. Innes (12 vols., Edinburgh, 1814–72), V (1625–40), pp. 272–6; *A Source Book of Scottish History*, ed. W.C. Dickinson and G. Donaldson (3 vols., Edinburgh, 1961), III, pp. 95–104.

[27] *Ibid.*, III, pp. 95–100; J. H. S. Burleigh, *A Church History of Scotland* (London, 1973), p. 218; D. Stevenson, *The Covenanters: The National Covenant and Scotland* (Saltire Pamphlets, Edinburgh, 1988), pp. 35–44.

national independence and the subjects' liberties since the union of the crowns. Precedents respecting the vital importance of the 'fundamental lawes' of the kingdom drew chiefly on the legislation of the parliament called to discuss an incorporating union with England in 1604, when James VI and I had been cautioned against breaches of fundamental law. Innovations prejudicial to parliamentary authority were deplored 'as this Realme could be no more a free Monarchy'. This appeal to constitutional tradition masked a radical intent to vest sovereignty in the king-in-parliament at the expense of the royal prerogative. The statutory limitations imposed on monarchy were accepted formally in the solemn oath taken not only by Charles I on being crowned king of Scots in 1633, but by 'all Kings and Princes at their Coronation and reception of their Princely Authority' to preserve the 'true Religion, Lawes and Liberties of this Kingdome'. Moreover, religion and royal authority were so linked that it was impossible to be loyal to the crown without being loyal to the true religion.[28]

The second component of the National Covenant elaborated the concept of a twofold contract on which the whole life of the Scottish kingdom should be based. This contract encapsulated the dual imperatives of covenanting by drawing on historical and political as well as biblical precepts. Opposition to the divine right of kings and absolute monarchy was inspired as much by the monarchomach ideology of French Huguenots and, to a lesser extent, of Dutch Calvinists as by the legacy of resistance to an ungodly monarch that was espoused by John Knox at the Reformation and rationalised in its aftermath by George Buchanan.[29] The religious covenant was a tripartite compact between the king and people to God to uphold the purity of 'the true reformed religion'. Whereas obedience to God was unconditional and irresistible, the people's obligations to the king were limited and conditional. If the king betrayed his people to God, the people had a positive duty to resist avoiding divine retribution. In short, the religious covenant replaced the Israelites with the Scots in the role of the chosen people. Operating within the framework of this religious covenant was a constitutional contract between the king, on the one hand, and the people, on the other, for maintenance of good and lawful government and a just political order. If the king failed to uphold the fundamental laws and liberties of the

---

[28] *A Source Book of Scottish History*, III, pp. 98–100; Brown, *Kingdom or Province?*, pp. 113–14.

[29] G. H. Sabine, *A History of Political Theory* (London, 1968), pp. 375–85; R. G. Cant, 'Scottish Libertarianism in Theory and Practice, 1560–1690', *Proceedings of the Conference on Scottish Studies*, 3 (Norfolk, Va, 1976), pp. 20–31; J. H. Burns, *The True Law of Kingship: Concepts of Monarchy in Early Modern Scotland* (Oxford, 1996), pp. 122–52, 185–221.

kingdom or sought to subvert his subjects' privileges or estates, the people were entitled to take appropriate remedial action, action that included the right to resist.

Although subscribers were obliged merely to forbear rather than condemn innovations in worship, final determination of the acceptability of all ceremonies, as of the current corruptions in ecclesiastical government and the exercise of civil power by bishops and their adherents among the clergy, was to be left to 'free assemblies, and in parliaments'. The pursuit of constitutional redress was not to be subject to the censorious royal management evident in the coronation parliament of 1633.[30] The Fifth Table intended both to secure the redress of pressing grievances between Charles I and his Scottish subjects and to effect a permanent check on absentee monarchy to safeguard the religious and constitutional imperatives of covenanting. The fundamental ordering of priorities between crown and people was underscored by the third and most revolutionary component – the oath of allegiance and mutual association.

Allegiance to monarchy followed allegiance to God. The oath required the subscribers to swear that they would 'to the uttermost of their power, with our meanes and lives, stand to the defence of our dread Soveraigne, the Kings Majesty, his Person and Authority, in the defence and preservation of the foresaid true Religion, Liberties and Lawes of the Kingdome'. This commitment was conditional. In so far as he accepted the religious and constitutional imperatives of the National Covenant, the king was to be defended. The oath went on to require mutual assistance among subscribers 'in the same cause of maintaining the true Religions and his Majesty's Authority, with our best counsel, our bodies, meanes and whole power, against all sorts of persons whatsoever'. The oath was thus a positive act of defiance in reserving loyalty to a covenanted king.[31]

There was no necessary incompatibility in promising to defend royal authority while simultaneously promoting policies contrary to the professed interests of Charles I.[32] For the revolutionary essence of the National Covenant was its ordered priorities: 'the true worship of God, the Majesty of our King, and peace of the Kingdome, for the common happiness of our selves, and the posterity'. Integral to the permanent

[30] *A Source Book of Scottish History*, III, pp. 100–2; W. Scott, *An Apologetical Narration of the State and Government of the Kirk of Scotland since the Reformation*, ed. D. Laing (Wodrow Society, Edinburgh, 1846), pp. 330–42; Row, *The History of the Kirk of Scotland*, pp. 357–66, 376–81.
[31] Rothes, *A Relation of Proceedings*, pp. 90–2, 96–8, 100–2; *A Source Book of Scottish History*, III, pp. 102–4; D. Mathew, *Scotland under Charles I* (London, 1955), p. 256.
[32] I. B. Cowan, 'The Covenanters: A Revision Article', *SHR*, 47 (1968), pp. 38–40; E. J. Cowan, *Montrose: For Covenant and King* (London, 1977), pp. 46–7; Stevenson, *The Scottish Revolution*, p. 85.

achievement of constitutionalism in Kirk and state was the crucial distinction between the office of monarchy and the personal conduct of the king. Resistance to Charles I was in the long-term interests of monarchy and people if the kingdom was to be restored to godly rule. Within a broader European perspective, the propagation of this distinction by the Fifth Table avoided recourse to republicanism in resisting absentee monarchy.[33]

The National Covenant was the culmination of thirteen years of political frustration induced by the absentee rule of Charles I. Yet, Charles was the legitimate heir of the royal house of Stuart, not a usurper. There was no question, therefore, that the people's right of resistance vindicated tyrannicide by the private citizen. Instead, the oath of allegiance and mutual assistance upheld the corporate right of the people to resist a lawful king who threatened to become tyrannical. Such resistance was to be exercised by the natural leaders of society, not the nobles exclusively but the Tables as the corporate embodiment of the inferior magistrate and of civic virtue. In effect, the revolutionary oath required the subscribers to recognise the Tables – not just empirically as the provisional government, but as the divinely warranted custodians of the national interest.[34]

III

Within three years of the publication of the National Covenant the Tables, as the revolutionary embodiment of the covenanting movement, had accomplished by persuasion and coercion a thorough transformation of government within Scotland. While no attempt was made to replace the Stuart monarchy in Scotland, Charles I had no alternative but to accept permanent checks on the royal prerogative in Kirk and state. He was also obliged to recognise that adherence to the National Covenant replaced acquiescence in the dictates of absentee monarchy as the vital prerequisite for the exercise of political power north of the border. In turn, the covenanting movement served as a model for terminating the personal rule of Charles I in the other two kingdoms.[35]

As well as equipping the Tables with the rhetoric of defiance, the

---

[33] A. Campbell, marquis of Argyle, *Instructions to a Son, containing rules of conduct in public and private life* (London, 1661), pp. 30–6; H. Kamen, *The Iron Century: Social Change in Europe, 1550–1660* (London, 1968), pp. 326–30, 362–7.

[34] Sabine, *A History of Political Theory*, pp. 382–3; Burns, *The True Law of Kingship*, pp. 204–9.

[35] Macinnes, *Charles I and the Making of the Covenanting Movement*, pp. 183–213; J. Morrill, *The Nature of the English Revolution* (Harlow, 1993), pp. 252–72; Tadhg ó hAnnracháin, 'Rebels and Confederates: The Stance of the Irish Clergy in the 1640s' in J. R. Young (ed.), *Celtic Dimensions of the British Civil War* (Edinburgh, 1997), pp. 96–115.

National Covenant provided the political will to effect revolution. In the week following its issue in Edinburgh, copies of the National Covenant were prepared for subscription in all leading towns and cities, universities and rural parishes. Subscription was initially intended to be confined to communicants. But, carried along by popular enthusiasm and concerted propaganda from the pulpits spearheaded by Alexander Henderson, stress was laid on covenanting as the manifestation of the willingness, the holiness and the multiplication of the Scots as the chosen people. The practice was changed. Communion became available only to the covenanted. Such implacable resolve left little scope for neutrality. Earthly vengeance as well as divine retribution awaited those not moved to covenant with God. At the same time, reprints of heroic epics recalling the feats of William Wallace and Robert the Bruce, during the Wars of Independence against England in the late thirteenth and early fourteenth century, helped sustain the link between popular nationalism and covenanting ideology.[36]

The political will to effect revolution found initial expression in the Presbyterian Reformation accomplished at Glasgow by the onset of winter in 1638, in a General Assembly whose composition, agenda and procedures were stage-managed by the Fifth Table. The accomplishment of Presbyterianism by constitutional defiance made inevitable the Bishops' Wars of 1639–40, which provided a practical demonstration of the coactive power that justified resistance to Charles I. According to Samuel Rutherford, the Tables were obliged to hold the crown to the dual imperatives of the National Covenant in the interest of the monarchy if not of Charles personally: that is, the king *in abstracto* if not *in concreto*.[37] The radical mainstream of the covenanting movement consistently maintained this coactive power to justify resistance in both the First and Second Bishops' Wars. The king was portrayed as a misinformed absentee prepared to deploy papists, rebels and mercenaries to invade Scotland. In the spring of 1639, ministers advocated recourse to arms from the pulpit following precepts drawn up by Alexander Henderson. An essential distinction was maintained. On the one hand, subjects rising or standing out against law and reason that they may be free from their obedience to their king were not justified. On the other, the Scottish people, 'holding fast their alledgence to their soveraine and

[36] A. Henderson, *Sermons, Prayers and Pulpit Addresses*, ed. R. T. Martin (Edinburgh, 1867), pp. 9–30; Rothes, *A Relation of Proceedings*, pp. 79–80; *Diary of Sir Archibald Johnston of Wariston, 1632–39*, pp. 351–2, 361, 366; J. Gordon, *A History of Scots Affairs, 1637–41*, ed. J. Robertson and G. Grub (3 vols., Spalding Club, Aberdeen, 1841), I, pp. 39–47; Reid, *The Party-Coloured Mind*, pp. 6–10, 37–78.
[37] S. Rutherford, *Lex Rex: The Law and the Prince* (Edinburgh, 1848), pp. 56, 143–8, 199.

in all humilitie supplicating for Religioun and justice', were obliged 'to defend themselves against extreame violence and oppression bringing utter ruin and desolation upon the kirk and kingdome, upon themselves and their posteritie'. These arguments to defend Scotland in 1639 were reiterated in 1640 to justify the covenanting army's invasion of England, now propagated as an offensive posture for defensive purposes.[38]

Because the justifiable exercise of coactive power entailed permanent checks on monarchy, the radical mainstream of the covenanting movement interpreted the role of the political Estates as not just to participate in but to control central government. The political Estates were the trustees of the national interest on behalf of the people. The king was merely the trustee of the political Estates, who executed their power to make law. In the eyes of Argyll, the foremost and most formidable Scottish politician of the 1640s, limited monarchy was a non-negotiable, constitutional imperative.[39] More immediately, the centrality of the Estates to the political process, 'when religion, laws, liberties, invasion of foreign enemies necessitateth the subjects to convene', warranted the formation of the Tables in 1637, their holding of conventions throughout 1638 and 1639 and, ultimately, the formal establishment of the Committee of Estates as the executive arm of government in the parliament of 1640.[40]

Ostensibly on account of the imminent danger of invasion by royalist forces, a Committee of Estates was constituted with comprehensive powers to govern the whole kingdom. The Committee, which consisted of forty members drawn from the Estates of the nobility, gentry and burgesses, was split into two sections. Equal numbers of each Estate either remained in Edinburgh to sustain central government or accompanied the army whose movements were not restricted to Scotland – a clear indication that the Covenanters were prepared to take the war to the Royalists in England. Each section governed autonomously, save for the declaration of war and the conclusion of peace, which required the assent of the whole Committee.[41]

The establishment of the Committee of Estates represented a classical, if corporate, alternative (reminiscent of the consular system of ancient Rome) to the exercise of executive power by a monarch who was patently untrustworthy, palpably reluctant to make lasting concessions and

---

[38] N[ational] L[ibrary of] S[cotland], Wodrow MSS, quarto xxiv, f. 165; E[dinburgh] U[niversity] L[ibrary], Instructions of the Committee of Estates of Scotland, 1640–1, Dc.4.16. f. 1.   [39] Argyle, *Instructions to a Son*, pp. 134–43.
[40] Rutherford, *Lex Rex*, pp. 98–9, 222–3; J. Coffey, 'Samuel Rutherford and the Political Thought of the Scottish Covenanters' in Young (ed.), *Celtic Dimensions of the British Civil Wars*, pp. 75–95.
[41] *Acts of the Parliaments of Scotland*, V, pp. 282–4 c.24; Gordon, *A History of Scots Affairs*, III, pp. 181–4.

resolutely intent on reversing all constraints on the royal prerogative. Although the Committee can be viewed as 'a temporary expedient' in so far as its powers were finite – until a settlement was reached with the king or until the next plenary session of parliament – there was no feasible prospect of Charles I accepting the National Covenant. Accompanying legislation would suggest that the covenanting leadership was intent not only upon legitimising its past exercise of executive power, but upon authorising its future exercise. Decisions of the Tables whether in conventions or by committee over the last thirty months were ratified retrospectively. The scope of treason was extended to all who advised or assisted policies destructive of the covenanting movement. Local government, restructured from the outset of 1639 through committees established within the shires and within the bounds of every presbytery, was consolidated as the principal agency for the imposition of ideological conformity as well as financial supply and military recruitment.[42]

This restructuring of local government to carry out the central dictates of the covenanting leadership had led to the formation of Europe's second professional army (after Sweden), a force which decisively won the Bishops' Wars. The covenanting movement thus asserted and retained the political initiative in Britain from the outset of the peace negotiations which commenced at Ripon in October before transferring to London in December 1640. Having instigated the summons of the Long Parliament in England, the Committee of Estates insisted upon English parliamentary participation in the peace negotiations that were eventually brought to a conclusion in August 1641. In the interim, Scottish commissioners were invited by the English parliament to instigate the prosecution that resulted in the judicial execution that May of the lord deputy of Ireland, Thomas Wentworth, earl of Strafford. The lord deputy's role in enforcing the expulsion of the Presbyterian vanguard from Ulster was incidental to an impeachment process in the House of Lords that was based on his persistent advocacy of war rather than a negotiated settlement with the covenanting movement. A complementary consideration was his imposition of the notorious 'black oath' on Scottish settlers during the First Bishops' War; a loyalty test which demonstrated that the Ulster Scots, regardless of their covenanting affiliations, were not trusted at the Stuart court. Conversely, Stafford's heavy-handed action, coupled to his recruitment of Irish Catholics into the army he was building up for Charles I in anticipation of the Second Bishops' War, had forced settlers, who had decided to remain rather than return to Scotland,

---

[42] *Acts of the Parliaments of Scotland*, V, pp. 280–2 c.23, 285–7 c.26–33; NLS, Salt and Coal: Events, 1635–62, MS 2263, ff. 73–8.

to identify with the covenanting movement in order to retain their plantations in Ulster. Their prospects for preservation were, in turn, enhanced
by Presbyterian solidarity across the North Channel.[43]

Scottish participation in the prosecution of Strafford demonstrated the
main thrust of the negotiating agenda between the Covenanters and the
English parliament was not necessarily the attainment of unity in religion
and uniformity in church government.[44] In keeping with their desires to
strengthen the bond of union between both kingdoms professed since the
first sustained appeal to British public opinion in the prelude to the
Bishops' Wars, the covenanting leadership aimed to secure a lasting alliance by a defensive and offensive league: that is by confederation – not
incorporating – union between Scotland and England. The only institutional innovation was to be the appointment of parliamentary commissioners in both kingdoms, charged to conserve the peace and redress any
breaches in the intervals between parliaments. In ratifying the Treaty of
London, the English parliament reserved its right to determine the nature
of the English reformation, but duly conceded that the waging of war and
the stopping of trade within the king's dominions required parliamentary
approval in both countries. Prompt bestowal of royal assent was interpreted as Charles I's formal acknowledgement of the sovereign and independent power of the Scottish Estates as a 'free parliament', recognition
that laid to rest the spectre of provincialism which had haunted the nation
since the regal union. The Covenanters were not exclusively concerned
with such a bipartisan approach, however. At the same time as the
Scottish commissioners were presenting their proposals for union to their
English counterparts, the Committee of Estates at Edinburgh actively,
but fruitlessly, promoted a tripartite confederation that would involve the
Estates General of the United Provinces.[45] Once the Treaty of London
was concluded, the commander of the Scottish forces, General Alexander
Leslie, a former field-marshall in the Swedish army, had initiated
repeated, but unrequited, approaches to Axel Oxenstierna, the Swedish
Regent, who had actually sponsored the Scottish revolt against Charles I,

[43] J. Rushworth (ed.), *Historical Collections* (8 vols., London, 1680), I, pp. 70–1, 133–4,
722–7, 749–50; M. Perceval-Maxwell, 'Strafford, the Ulster Scots and the Covenanters',
IHS, 18 (1972–3), pp. 525–51; Adair, *The Presbyterian Church in Ireland*, pp. 57–68.
[44] B. P. Levack, *The Formation of the British State: England, Scotland and the Union, 1603–1707*
(Oxford, 1987), pp. 110, 130–1; C. L. Hamilton, 'The Anglo-Scottish Negotiations of
1640–41', *SHR*, 41 (1962), pp. 84–6.
[45] EUL, Instructions of the Committee of Estates, Dc.4.16, ff. 101, 105; NLS, Wodrow
MSS, folio lxxi, f. 63; *Acts of the Parliaments of Scotland*, V, pp. 335–45 c.8; *The Memoirs of
Henry Guthry*, pp. 96–7; *An Honourable speech made in the Parlament of Scotland by the
Earle of Argile . . . the thirtieth of September 1641. Touching the prevention of nationall dissen-
tion, and perpetuating the happie peace and union betwixt the two kingdomes, by the frequent
holding of Parlaments* (London, 1641).

to promote an alternative confederation involving Sweden, the Scottish Covenanters and the English parliamentarians.[46]

IV

Charles had ratified the Treaty of London prior to his departure to Scotland in the hope of detaching the covenanting movement from its alliance with the English Parliamentarians. This mission proved forlorn. Although its mandate had technically expired with the summoning of parliament, the Committee of Estates continued to control proceedings on behalf of the radical mainstream. Parliament secured an effective veto over the executive and judiciary when Charles gave a binding commitment that officers of state, privy councillors and lords of session would henceforth be chosen with the advice and consent of the Scottish Estates. Charles had no alternative but to accept permanent restrictions on the royal prerogative that fulfilled his own prophecy, in the spring of 1638, that the triumph of the covenanting movement would leave him no more power than the doge of Venice. Although the Committee of Estates was not formally resuscitated, its past role as the national government was not only approved but continued through the creation of interval committees: that is, diverse financial, ecclesiastic, diplomatic and judicial committees that were to endure, if necessary, until the next parliamentary session scheduled for June 1644.[47]

The outbreak of the Irish rebellion facilitated the entrenchment of the centralised oligarchy controlling the covenanting movement. News that the Irish Catholics had risen in Ulster under Sir Phelim O'Neill was actually conveyed to the Scottish Estates by Charles in late October, along

---

[46] *Rikskanseleren Axel Oxenstiernas Skrifter och Brefvexling*, II, 9 (Kingl. Vitterhets Historie och Antiquitetsakademien, Stockholm, 1898), pp. 486–8; *Kong Christian den Fjerdes Egenhaendige Breve*, ed. C. F. Bricka and J. A. Fredericia (8 vols., revised edn, Copenhagen, 1969–70), V, pp. 142–4. Oxenstierna's motives for discretely backing the Covenanters with men, money and arms was partly confessional – Protestant solidarity between Calvinists and Lutherans – but primarily pragmatic. He feared that an alliance between Christian IV of Denmark and Charles I could lead to Habsburg support not only against Scotland but also Sweden. I am indebted for this information to my two former graduate students Steve and Alexia, whose innovative work on early modern, Scottish–Scandinavian relations is set out in S. Murdoch, 'Scotland, Denmark-Norway and the House of Stuart, 1603–60: A Diplomatic and Military Analysis' (unpublished PhD thesis, University of Aberdeen, 1998) and A. Grosjean, 'Scots and the Swedish State: Diplomacy, Military Service and Ennoblement, 1611–60' (unpublished PhD thesis, University of Aberdeen, 1999).

[47] G. Burnet, *The Memoirs of the Lives and Actions of James and William, Dukes of Hamilton and Castleherald* (London, 1687), pp. 46, 184–7; *Acts of the Parliaments of Scotland*, V, pp. 391–6 c.76–7, 400–3 c.85, 404–5 c.87–8, 408–9 c.92, 505–7 c.89; SRO, Supplementary Parliamentary Papers, PA 16/3/5/3.

with an invitation for armed intervention by the Covenanters to protect the plantations. However, the covenanting leadership proved unwilling to intervene without the consent of the English parliament. At the same time, the Irish rebellion enabled the Covenanters to sustain rather than scale down their military forces. The Scottish Estates duly offered the services of 10,000 troops to the English parliament at the outset of November. Irish fears of Scottish military prowess meant initially that Scottish colonists were subject to relatively fewer reprisals and depredations. Nonetheless, indiscriminate reports of the 'cruel outrages' of the Irish rebels and the 'pitiful estate of the British in Ireland', afforded Charles an excuse to return south to gain the backing of the English parliament. His endeavours to secure covenanting commitment without waiting for the consent of the English parliament, in blatant disregard for the Treaty of London, had used up his last reserves of political goodwill with the Scottish Estates.[48]

Scottish military involvement in Ireland demonstrated that effective power continued to be vested in the radical mainstream of the covenanting movement. The specific terms for armed intervention were referred to and resolved by the inner circle of radicals commissioned to continue negotiations with the English parliament. Faced with the regrouping of a conservative element within the covenanting movement around James Hamilton, duke of Hamilton, the radical mainstream's interlocking control of the interval committees ensured that the covenanting army intervened on the side of the Parliamentarians not of the Royalists after civil war broke out in England. Radical control led to the summoning of a Convention of Estates – an effective substitute for the parliament which Charles I refused to call. Ostensibly required to supply the covenanting army in Ireland and review the arrears of financial reparations, the brotherly assistance due from the English parliament under the Treaty of London, the Convention was managed adroitly during the summer of 1643. A formal alliance for armed assistance on the basis of the Solemn League and Covenant was cemented on 26 August.[49]

In exporting Scottish constitutional fundamentalism as well as

<hr>

[48] Sir J. Balfour, *Historical Works*, ed. J. Haig (4 vols., Edinburgh, 1824), III, pp. 64, 92, 125, 128–30, 134–5, 143–6; *The Letters and Journals of Robert Baillie*, pp. I, 396–7; D. Stevenson, *Scottish Covenanters and Irish Confederates* (Belfast, 1981), pp. 43–5, 95–102; N. Canny, 'What Really Happened in Ireland in 1641?' in J. H. Ohlmeyer (ed.), *Ireland: From Independence to Occupation, 1641–1660* (Cambridge, 1995), pp. 24–42.

[49] A. I. Macinnes, 'The Scottish Constitution, 1638–51: The Rise and Fall of Oligarchic Centralism' in J. Morrill (ed.), *The Scottish National Covenant in its British Context 1638–51* (Edinburgh, 1990), pp. 106–33; Young, *The Scottish Parliament 1639–1661*, pp. 54–112. *The proceedings of the Commissioners appointed by the Kings maiesty and Parliament of Scotland ...* (London, 1643).

religious revelation to England and Ireland, the Solemn League and Covenant represented a British endeavour to achieve common spiritual and material aims while maintaining distinctive national structures in church and state. In terms of ecumenical congruence, the Solemn League and Covenant was propagated as the necessary application of the covenant of works to that of grace in order to achieve religious reformation in all Three Kingdoms. In terms of political congruence, the coactive power to resist the crown was specifically exported in clause three, which incorporated the covenanting oath of allegiance and mutual association, 'That the world may bear witnesse with our consciences our Loyalty, and that we have no thought or intentions to diminish he Majesty's just power and greatnesse.'[50] Despite the perceptive insight that civil war in the 1640s was not so much a war between as a war among the Three Kingdoms,[51] the Solemn League and Covenant signposted a British commitment to the war for the Three Kingdoms in which the covenanting movement was now formally internationalised through confessional confederation.

Confederation for confessional and constitutional purposes had been reinvigorated in early modern Europe, first by the Protestant Estates in Moravia, Austria and Hungary against imperial power in 1608, followed by that against territorial integration in Bohemia, Moravia, Silesia and the two Lusatias in 1619.[52] By 1630, an itinerant Scot, John Dury, had emerged as the principal protagonist of confessional confederation in northern Europe. A cleric licensed by the Church of England and claiming support from the Protestant hierarchy in all three kingdoms, Dury claimed to be acting for the *Ecclesiastes Britannus* in seeking an accommodation between Calvinists and Lutherans against Habsburg imperialism. Ancillary to this accommodation was the prospect of restoring to the

---

[50] *Acts of the Parliaments of Scotland*, VI (i) (*1641–47*), pp. 41–3, 47–9; *A Source Book of Scottish History*, III, pp. 24–5, 128–31; A. Henderson, *A Sermon preached to the Honourable House of Commons . . . December 27 1643* (London, 1644); T. Mocket, *A View of the Solemn League and Covenant, for reformation, defence of religion, the honour and happyness of the king, and the peace, safety and union of the three kingdomes . . .* (London, 1644). In effect, the Solemn League and Covenant represented an extension of confessional confederation in keeping not only with an apocalyptic world reordering, but also with the ecumenical governance of the true Reformed Kirk as specified in the Melvillean, Second Book of Discipline of 1578 and subsequently reaffirmed in the Form of Church Government issued in 1645 by the Assembly of Divines at Westminster.
[51] J. Pocock, 'The Atlantic Archipelago and the War of the Three Kingdoms' in Bradshaw and Morrill (eds.), *The British Problem*, pp. 172–91.
[52] G. Schramm, 'Armed Conflict in East-Central Europe: Protestant Noble Opposition and Catholic Royalist Factions, 1604–20' and I. Auerbach, 'The Bohemian Opposition, Poland-Lithuania, and the Outbreak of the Thirty Years War' successively in R. J. W. Evans and T. V. Thomas (eds.), *Crown, Church and Estates: Central European Politics in the Sixteenth and Seventeenth Centuries* (London, 1991), pp. 176–225.

Palatinate the exiled family of Elizabeth Stuart, the 'Winter Queen' of Bohemia and sister of Charles I. The main intellectual backing Dury received and acknowledged from within the British Isles came from the Aberdeen doctors, whose irenecism was both opposed to and rejected by the militant Presbyterianism of the covenanting movement. Nonetheless, Dury had won substantive endorsement from Sweden by May 1638, notably from the family of Regent Oxenstierna. This confessional support coincided with Oxenstierna's military and diplomatic backing for the covenanting movement. By 1642, Dury earnestly lobbied the General Assembly of the Kirk for bilateral confederation with Sweden.[53] Confederation, however, became politically compromised and conspiratorially tinged that same year when the Irish rebels constituted themselves as the Catholic Confederation. Among British Protestants, the political and confessional aspirations of the Irish Catholics were deemed clandestine and nefarious by the deliberate confusion of confederation as a legitimate association with confederacy as an illicit conspiracy. This polemical interchange of confederation and confederacy subsequently bedevilled the endeavours of the Covenanters, particularly under the radical leadership of Argyll, to reconfigure British politics through the Solemn League and Covenant.[54]

Conspiratorial aspersions notwithstanding, the association of a solemn league with a perpetual confederacy had been explicitly laid out in the incorporating articles of the United Colonies of New England, subscribed by four Puritan plantations for common defence against the Dutch, the French and the Indians in May 1643 – three months before the

[53] Dansk Rigsarkivet, Copenhagen, Tyske Kancellis Udenrigske Afdeling, Alm.Del. I, no. 141, Breve med Bilag fra engelsk Praest Johannes Duraeus, 1634–39; J. Dury, Epistolae Pace Ecclesiastica, BL, Sloane MSS 654, ff. 216–17; J. Dury, *A Summary Discourse concerning the work of peace ecclesiastical, how it may concurre with the aim of a civill confederation amongst Protestants* . . . (Cambridge, 1641).

[54] Cf. *By the Ecclesiasticall Congregation of both Clergies, secular and regular of the Kingdom of Ireland* . . . (Waterford, 1646); *A declaration made by the Rebells in Ireland against the English and Scottish Protestants, Inhabitants within that kindgome. Also a treacherous oath . . . lately contrived by the Confederate Rebells in a Council held at Kilkenny* (Waterford, reprinted London, 1644); *The bloody diurnall from Ireland being papers of propositions, order, and oath, and severall bloody acts, and proceedings of the Confederate Catholics assembled at Kilkenny* (Kilkenny, reprinted London, 1647); *A great discoverie of a plot in Scotland, by miraculous means* (London, 1641); *The mysterie of iniquity, yet working in the kingdomes of England, Scotland, and Ireland, for the destruction of religion truly Protestant* (London, 1643); C. Walker, *Relations and observations, historicall and politick, upon the Parliament, begun anno Dom. 1640. . . Together with An appendix to The history of Independency, being a brief description of some few of Argyle's proceedings before and since he ioyned in confederacy with the Independent junto in England* . . . (London, 1648); *A brief narrative of the mysteries of State carried on by the Spanish faction in England. . . Together with a vindication of the Presbyterian party* (The Hague, 1651).

Anglo-Scottish treaty.[55] Despite nonconforming associations through the failed migration of conventiclers from both sides of the North Channel seven years earlier, any ideological connection between these Puritan provinces and the constitutional development of confessional confederation by Scottish Covenanters was purely coincidental. Nonetheless, the impact of Ulster on covenanting ideology is particularly important at this juncture. The return of planters in the wake of the Irish rebellion in 1641 had given British resonance to covenanting ideology. Although repatriated Ulster Scots were not among the leading covenanting ideologues, their migratory presence served as a continuous reminder of the Catholic threat not only from Ireland, but also from the Counter-Reformation. At the same time, repeated overtures to the General Assembly of the Kirk to assist and relieve the Presbyterian remnant in Ulster tangibly reinforced apocalyptic beliefs that covenanting commitment to the pursuit of British union was not just a fundamental issue of confessional confederalism, but the first eschatological step towards universal reform.[56]

The traffic of migrants across the North Channel was not all one way, however. The number of ministers supplied or returning from Scotland outstripped those remaining during the 1640s. The arrival of the ten regiments which composed the covenanting army in May 1642 had provided the opportunity not only to retrench but also to consolidate Presbyterianism in Antrim and Down. While not every regiment had a kirk session on arrival, the ministers serving as chaplains along with leading officers serving as ruling elders had formed a Presbytery of Ulster within a month. This Presbytery gradually took in civil charges in parishes occupied by the army, provided the local ministers and gentry eligible for eldership purged themselves of past acceptance of the 'black oath'. A fresh injection of young and unplaced ministers, coupled to the licensed imposition of the Solemn League and Covenant in Ulster from March 1644, provided the impetus for the expansion of Presbyterianism into the counties of Derry, Donegal and Tyrone. Within Scotland, the special watching brief exercised by the Kirk over Ulster was endorsed by the Committee of Estates, which had been restored on the same day that the Solemn League and Covenant was issued and remained the national nucleus of the centralised oligarchy running the movement for the next eight years. In the spirit of confederation, the English parliament also

[55] R. S. Dunn, J. Savage and L. Yeandle (eds.), *The Journal of John Winthrop, 1630–1649* (Cambridge, Mass, 1996), pp. 429–40; H. M. Ward, *The United Colonies of New England, 1634–90* (New York, 1961), pp. 49–59.
[56] A. Williamson, 'Scotland, Antichrist and the Invention of Great Britain' in J. Dwyer, R. A. Mason and A. Murdoch (eds.), *New Perspectives on the Politics and Culture of Early Modern Scotland* (Edinburgh, 1982), pp. 34–58.

supported the Kirk's position. Accordingly, the Presbytery of Ulster served as ideological guardians of the covenant against civil abuses by an army suffering from shortage of provision and pay as against sectaries, Anabaptists and malignant influences still prepared to conform to the 'black oath'.[57]

However, the decisive defeat of the covenanting army by the forces of the Irish Catholic Confederation at Benburb in June 1646 peremptorily ended this working accommodation. Albeit the covenanting army still remained the dominant military presence in the province, the Presbytery of Ulster was on the defensive as a supplicant for, rather than the guardian of, ideological purity. Simultaneously, despite the initial success of armed intervention in England and the compulsory subscription of the Solemn League and Covenant in all three kingdoms, the British influence of the covenanting movement had been further weakened by the outbreak of vicious and debilitating civil war at home. A disaffected Covenanter who had switched his allegiance to the royalist cause, James Graham, marquis of Montrose, ran a brilliant guerrilla campaign in 1644–5 assisted by Alasdair MacColla and forces from Ulster sponsored by the Catholic Confederation. When MacColla split from Montrose in the summer of 1645 in order to maintain a bridgehead with Ireland on the western seaboard, Montrose's Scottish forces were crushed by contingents of the covenanting army withdrawn from England.[58] Nonetheless, MacColla held out until the summer of 1647. In the interim, the intensity of campaigning and the resultant territorial devastation caused the covenanting movement to propagate an Act of Proscription. Conservative elements, who were suspected of being sympathetic to the campaigns of Montrose and MacColla, were purged from public office. Punitive fining compounded by sequestration destroyed all prospect of re-establishing the national consensus behind the movement.[59]

---

[57] H. Scott (ed.), *Fasti Ecclesiae Scoticannae* (revised edn, 8 vols., Edinburgh, 1915–28, 1950), VI, pp. 526–33. Adair, *The Presbyterian Church in Ireland*, pp. 69–134; *A Full Relation of the late expedition of Lord Monroe, Major-Generall of all the Protestant Forces in the Province of Ulster* . . . (London, 1644); Stevenson, *Scottish Covenanters and Irish Confederates*, pp. 103–64, 191–236. It was arguably as much out of respect for this confederal accommodation as for the British integrity of the *ius imperium* of Charles I that the occupying covenanting army had made no attempt to impose their centralised committee structure on Ulster or even to annex the province pending fulfilment of parliamentary promises for supply and brotherly assistance.

[58] M. Napier (ed.), *Memorials of Montrose and His Times* (2 vols., Maitland Club, Edinburgh, 1848–50), I, pp. 254–5, 264–316, 319–63 and II, pp. 175–9; Cowan, *Montrose*, pp. 96–101, 108–22; A. I. Macinnes, *Clanship, Commerce and the House of Stuart, 1603–1788* (East Linton, 1996), pp. 88–121.

[59] *Acts of the Parliaments of Scotland*, VI (i), pp. 503–5 c.102, 549–50, c.160, 567–70 c.195, 580 c.210; SRO, Supplementary Parliamentary Papers, PA 14/3 ff. 501–7.

V

Conscious that civil war and ideological schism were undermining the capacity of the covenanting movement to determine the British political agenda, Argyll made his celebrated speech to the Grand Committee of Both Houses on 15 June 1646, an address to which the chimera of federalism has been attributed.[60] As the leader of the radical mainstream within the movement, Argyll had been instrumental in setting up the one British institution arising out of the Solemn League and Covenant – namely, the Committee for Both Kingdoms, which had been conceived in June 1644, not as a federal executive but as a confederal body to channel diplomatic dealings between the Covenanters and the Parliamentarians. Voluminous attention has been focused on English intransigence, internal divisions between the New Model Army and parliament and on tensions between the Parliamentarians and Covenanters. However, the covenanting oligarchy was itself divided over continued intervention in England. Following the defeat of Montrose in Scotland and prior to the complication of Charles I handing himself over to the covenanting army in England, radicals on the Committee of Estates had actively campaigned for the Covenanters to extricate themselves from the English Civil War and align with Sweden against Christian IV of Denmark; a manoeuvre to counter continuing Danish support for Charles and, more importantly, open up trade through the Baltic Sound.[61] Argyll steadfastly maintained the covenanting imperative of confederal action, while affirming the move from regal to complete union as a visionary ideal. Thus, the English parliament should not unilaterally make peace with Charles I and the confessional politics of the Solemn League immediately required that the Scottish armies in England and Ireland be promptly supplied.[62]

Notwithstanding the patent mistrust engendered by Charles I who had foisted himself on the covenanting army after his flight from Oxford in May 1646, financial rather than ideological considerations primarily moved Argyll and the radicals to transfer the king from their custody to the English parliament for a fee of £400,000 sterling in January 1647. This move, on top of radical endeavours to purge the covenanting oligarchy,

---

[60] M. Lee Jr., 'Scotland, the Union and the Idea of a General Crisis' in R. A. Mason (ed.), *Scots and Britons: Scottish Political Thought and the Union of 1603* (Cambridge, 1994), pp. 41–87.

[61] Dumfries House, Loudoun Papers, 'Green Deed Box', bundle 1; Huntington Library, Loudoun Scottish Collection, box 5, LO 8056–7, box 30, LO 10336; Young, *The Scottish Parliament*, pp. 103–4, 132.

[62] *The Lord Marquess of Argyle's Speech to A Grand Committee of Both Houses of Parliament* (London, 1646).

revived the conservative element under Hamilton, who covertly concluded the Engagement with Charles I to defend and restore monarchical authority. The Engagement, which came into force in 1648, was the first calculated effort, on the part of the Scots, to promote incorporating union as prescribed by James VI and I in the wake of the regal union. Charles was not obliged to subscribe the covenants. Ideological imperatives were further diluted by the stipulation that the king impose Presbyterianism on England for no more than a trial period of three years. This effective abrogation of the coactive power over monarchy was intolerable to the radicals, who claimed that the Engagers were reputedly 'so taken up with a king that they prefer a king's interest to Christ's interest'. The Engagement not only conceded that the Covenanters had lost the political initiative within the British Isles, but also represented a reactionary effort to reassert aristocratic dominance over Scotland. Armed intervention in the Second English Civil War ended disastrously at Preston that August.[63]

Conservative manipulation of the centralised committee structure to compel support for the Engagement led, in the west of Scotland especially, to a recrudescence of petitioning on a scale unprecedented since 1637, against ungodly deviations from religious and constitutional fundamentals. The reaction of the conservative element was to extend the scope of treason for party advantage and impose martial law on recalcitrant localities. A rising of the predominantly unfranchised, but disaffected, in the shires of Ayr and Lanark was vigorously suppressed at Mauchline Moor on 12 June 1648.[64] However, once the news of Preston filtered back to Scotland, the radicals staged a successful revolt which commenced with the Whiggamore Raid on Edinburgh in September and culminated, with armed support from Oliver Cromwell, in a renewed policy of exclusion from public office.[65] Although the Engagers were assured of their lives and property in return for disbanding their army, the rigorous application of the Act of Classes passed by the reconvened Scottish Estates on 23 January 1649 entrenched schism within the movement. While the Kirk gained a right of veto over office holding, the General Assembly remained a supplicant not a director in shaping of

[63] J. Kerr (ed.), *The Covenants and the Covenanters* (Edinburgh, 1896), p. 355; *A Source Book of Scottish History*, III, pp. 134–9; A. I. Macinnes, 'The First Scottish Tories?', *SHR*, 67 (1988), pp. 56–66.

[64] *Acts of the Parliaments of Scotland*, VI (ii), (1647–60), pp. 17 c.39, 86 c.155, 106–7 c.204–5, 108 c.208, 691–2; *The Letters and Journals of Robert Baillie*, III, pp. 444–50; Young, *The Scottish Parliament*, pp. 189–214.

[65] Burnet, *Memoirs of the Dukes of Hamilton*, pp. 365–78; *The Memoirs of Henry Guthry*, pp. 283–304; D. Stevenson, *Revolution and Counter-Revolution in Scotland, 1644–1651* (London, 1977), pp. 115–34.

public policy. The ideological principle underlying the Act of Classes was that acquiescence in the directives of the covenanting movement was insufficient. Those seeking public office had to demonstrate a positive commitment towards radicalism.[66]

The politics of exclusion were almost immediately overtaken by news of Cromwell's staged execution of Charles I on 30 January 1649. The reaction of outrage in Scotland and the prompt proclamation of Charles II on 5 February, not just as king of Scots but as king of Great Britain, was a reassertion of the international identity of the house of Stuart within the context of confederal union. The subsequent patriotic accommodation of radicals, conservatives and former Royalists, which was consolidated by the coronation of Charles II as king of Great Britain on 1 January 1651, confirmed this identity in fundamentalist terms. Robert Douglas, the Edinburgh minister who preached for two hours at the coronation, reminded Charles II that his compulsory subscription of the Covenants was to deny absolutism, for 'total government is not upon a king'. The religious and constitutional imperatives of covenanting were reaffirmed, the coactive power over monarchy exercised by the political nation was endorsed and the vesting of the right of resistance in those who have power 'as the estates of a land' was reasserted. The ideological fundamentals of covenanting were bluntly justified with respect to Charles I who, 'in a hostile way, set himself to overthrow religion, parliaments, laws and liberties'.[67]

In practice, the proclamation of Charles II had opened up a further British phase of civil war in which the Cromwellian occupation of Scotland was facilitated by the errant capacity of the Covenanters to snatch defeat from the jaws of victory at Dunbar in September 1650; by endemic military and financial exhaustion; and by the erroneous British military strategy of the new king which came to grief at Worcester in September 1651. At the same time, the drive for radical purity in the wake of the Act of Classes had led to the internally damaging split between the Remonstrants (later the Protestors) and the Resolutioners. The Remonstrants, supported by Rutherford and Wariston, were certainly correct in deeming Charles II unreliable and unworthy. Their insistence that their duty to support a covenanted king did not commit them unconditionally to a patently sinful Charles II was constitutionally valid and ideologically consistent with the distinction between the person and the office of monarchy in the covenants. But the Resolutioners, the radical

---

[66] *Acts of the Parliaments of Scotland*, VI (ii), pp. 129 c.13, 133 c.18–19, 143 c.30, 150 c.38, 153 c.47, 172, c.90, 174–81 c.98–102, 195–9 c.112–15, 225 c.171, 436, 446, 486 c.237; Glasgow University Archives, Beith Parish MSS, P/CN vol. II, no. 139.

[67] *The Covenants and the Covenanters*, pp. 348–98.

majority led by Argyll and endorsed by Douglas, claimed with equal validity to adhere to mainstream principles. They countered with the curse of Meroz: that the pursuit of radical purity carried the danger of undefiled inactivity in the face of the external threat from Cromwell. More culpably, the drive for radical purity in the army fatally undermined national independence.[68]

VI

Financial and military exhaustion notwithstanding, the flame of ideological purity was vigorously contested between Protestors and Resolutioners throughout the Cromwellian occupation of the 1650s. Both sides remained impervious to pleas for toleration during Scotland's incorporation in the Commonwealth and the Protectorate. Both these political labels were terms of convenience for the concentration of power that asserted England's intrusive hegemony in the guise of republicanism. The deliberate avoidance of Great Britain for this incorporation denoted not only a chauvinistic disregard for traditional Scottish defences against English overlordship, but also an emphatic rejection of both the Stuart vision of empire and the confederal conception of a kingdom united by covenanting. The appeal for Scots was minimalist, active collaboration being confined to a radical handful. As well as sharing British apocalyptic visions of world reordering, they hoped for Cromwellian support to carry through the social restructuring instigated in the anti-aristocratic parliament of 1649, a programme truncated by the patriotic accommodation.[69]

Presbyterianism in Ulster provided a marked contrast to the Scottish situation. The defensive posture adopted by the Presbytery of Ulster since 1646 was compounded by the withdrawal of covenanting forces in support of the Engagement. Presbyterianism was further compromised in 1649 by association with the Irish version of the patriotic accommodation, which was led by Royalists, not Covenanters, and came to grief at Dundalk. From the draconian onset of the Cromwellian occupation and the expulsion of residual covenanting forces and some ministers to Scotland, Presbyterians were obliged to resort to conventincling in house and field. In the process, they laid claim to be the original, suffering remnant of the godly. However, as the Commonwealth gave way to the

[68] *Ibid.*, pp. 370–2; Balfour, *Historical Works*, IV, pp. 92–109, 141–60, 174–8; *A Source Book of Scottish History*, III, pp. 144–6.

[69] A. H. Williamson, 'Union with England Traditional, Union with England Radical: Sir James Hope and the Mid-Seventeenth Century British State', *EHR*, 110 (1995), pp. 303–22; S. Barber, 'Scotland and Ireland under the Commonwealth: A Question of Loyalty' in S. G. Ellis and S. Barber (eds.), *Conquest and Union: Fashioning a British State, 1485–1725* (London, 1995), pp. 195–221.

Protectorate, the Presbytery of Ulster took advantage of renewed offers of toleration, not by formally engaging with the republican regime but by self-denying ordinances. The acts passed at Bangor in 1654 were designed to neutralise, if not avoid, the spread of the Protestor-Resolutioner controversy as returning exiles and new recruits were attracted from Scotland. So successful were these measures that Presbyterianism on the Scottish model expanded throughout and beyond the confines of Ulster. By 1659, the Presbytery had become the Synod.[70]

Nonetheless, in Ulster as in Scotland, Presbyterian aspirations to reassert respectfully covenanting imperatives at the conclusion of the Cromwellian regime in all three kingdoms were soon dashed. The restoration of Charles II produced a constitutional settlement which revived the Stuarts' *ius imperium* but ruled out the confederal conception of a kingdom united by covenanting. While some influential Resolutioners were won over to erastian Episcopacy, the Protestors provided the mainstay of opposition as covenanting moved from an ideology of power to that of protest. The later covenanting movement in Scotland, which is popularly associated with privation and martyrdom, was contemporaneously identified with militant religious dissent. Pushed to extremes by successive regimes more inclined to repression than conciliation, covenanting ideology was adapted first to covert conventicling and subsequently to vindicate the guerrilla warfare being pursued by the Cameronians during the 1680s.[71]

Covenanting, however, was an ideology of protest not just against an erastian Episcopal establishment, but against the promotion of the military-fiscal state in Scotland, particularly under James Maitland, duke of Lauderdale. However, deprived of the mechanisms of central power and control over constitutional assemblies, covenanting ideologues had no cohesive idea of how their acclaimed coactive power over the monarchy was to be enforced. In like manner, the right of resistance could no longer be vested in a national agency as the movement drew primarily on support from outside the political nation. Pushed to extremes, the pure worship of the godly necessitated secession from a corrupt political establishment in Kirk and state.[72] Thus, the Cameronians disowned Charles II as having forfeited the crown of Scotland by abrogating his religious covenant with God. His usurpation of the crown and royal prerogative was

[70] Adair, *The Presbyterian Church in Ireland*, pp. 135–237; *The Declaration of the British in the North of Ireland*... (London, 1649). Whereas there were no more than twenty-four ministers during the Commonwealth, there were at least eighty during the Protectorate.
[71] J. Buckroyd, *Church and State in Scotland, 1660–1681* (Edinburgh, 1980), pp. 22–67; Cowan, *The Scottish Covenanters 1660–1688*, pp. 103–47.
[72] Cf. J. Stewart, *Ius Populi Vindicatum: The people's right to defend themselves and their covenanted religion vindicated* (n.p., 1669); Reid, *The Party-Coloured Mind*, pp. 111–76.

compounded 'by his tyranny and breach of the very *leges regnandi* in matters civil'. Their ensuing declaration of war, which was reiterated at the accession of James VII in 1685, left unanswered the question of how the imperatives of covenanting were to be enforced.[73]

The Restoration era in Ulster, as elsewhere in the British Isles, was marked by successive outings of nonconformists, by prescription of covenanting and by the public immolation of the Solemn League and Covenant in towns and cities. Despite being tinged through distant association with the Blood Plot of old Cromwellians in and around Dublin during 1663 and despite Ulster featuring occasionally in the preaching circuit of Scottish field conventiclers, Presbyterianism in the province preferred to maintain a passive rather than a militant profile. This profile, characterised by house conventicles and praying societies, enabled Presbyterianism in Ulster to remain a distinctive layer of association within the Church of Ireland. But the association of Presbyterianism and erastian Episcopacy was not necessarily irenecist or indulgent, notwithstanding the resurgence of migration from Scotland and the occasional accommodation offered to Presbyterian ministers removed from the Lowlands. Presbyterian migrants seeking to escape fiscal discrimination in Scotland were not free from civil sanctions in Ulster. The association of covenanting with violence and social disorder provided the excuse for the Society of London to deny Scottish settlers security of tenure in and around Derry in 1670; the irony of this situation was compounded when prominent Ulster Scots actually sounded out Lauderdale on the prospect of military redress for the migrants he had helped hound out.[74]

Throughout the Restoration era in Scotland, recourse to violence by conventiclers and Cameronians as the suffering remnant served as a convenient excuse to impose fines and other fiscal sanctions against the majority of Presbyterians who limited their protests against Episcopacy to non-churchgoing and private prayer meetings. Militant extremists ensured that the religious imperatives of covenanting were set aside at the Revolution when erastian Episcopacy in the Kirk was, much to the chagrin of the Cameronians, replaced by erastian Presbyterianism. Nonetheless, the covenanting legacy of the marquis of Argyll was reasserted constitutionally by his son Archibald, the ninth earl. He justified his refusal to take the Test Act of 1681, which paved the way for the succession of the Catholic James VII and II, by affirming the constitutional

[73] *A Source Book of Scottish History*, III, pp. 174–84; A. Shields, *A Hind Let Loose: An Historical Representation of the Testimonies of the Church of Scotland* (Edinburgh, 1817).
[74] *The Funeral of the Good Old Cause, or A Covenant of Both Houses of parliament against the Solemn League and Covenant* (London, 1661), Adair, *The Presbyterian Church in Ireland*, pp. 238–304; BL, Add. MSS 23,234, f. 23 (Lauderdale Papers).

imperative of limited monarchy.[75] Despite his abortive rising and execution in 1685, the imposition of fiscal sanctions by a state inclined to absolutism ensured that this constitutional imperative was reasserted in the Claim of Right, the foundation of the Revolution Settlement in Scotland.[76]

---

[75] ICA, bundle 56/1. I am grateful to Dr Jane Dawson, Department of Ecclesiastical History, University of Edinburgh for drawing my attention to the ninth earl of Argyll's probable authorship of an undated document in the early 1680s entitled, 'Discussion of nature of monarchy and right to allegiance of the subjects'.

[76] *A Source Book of Scottish History*, III, pp. 200–7.

10   The political economy of Britain and Ireland after the Glorious Revolution

David Armitage

The history of British political thought in the early modern period cannot be written solely within the boundaries of state and nation.[1] However, the Folger Institute's project to construct such a history has been cast largely along national lines, as successive seminars have examined the histories of English, Scottish, Anglo-American and now Irish political thought.[2] During the course of these investigations, it has become clear that the political discourses which are distinctively 'British' have tended to emerge at those points when a nationally bounded conception of the polity becomes inadequate to conceptualise the parameters of politics, and hence when the framework for argument becomes transnational and even international (to appropriate the term coined by Jeremy Bentham amid the reconfigurations of the British Atlantic empire).[3] The most conspicuously 'British' political thinking occurred at moments of union, intersection and competition within and between the Three Kingdoms, in the 1540s or the 1650s or at the time of the regal union of 1603 and the parliamentary union of 1707.[4] Though there were few who identified themselves, and hence their thought, as British in this period, save for Scoto-Britons such as John Mair in the early sixteenth century or Sir William Alexander in the early seventeenth, it was possible to reimagine polities in ways that cut across the rapidly closing boundaries of the

[1] I am especially grateful to the National Humanities Center for its support during the research and writing of this essay, and to Patrick Kelly, Jane Ohlmeyer and John Robertson for their comments on earlier drafts.

[2] J. G. A. Pocock, 'The History of British Political Thought: The Creation of a Center', *Journal of British Studies*, 24 (1985), pp. 283–310; J. G. A. Pocock, Gordon J. Schochet and Lois G. Schwoerer (eds.), *The Varieties of British Political Thought, 1500–1800* (Cambridge, 1993).

[3] Jeremy Bentham, *An Introduction to the Principles of Morals and Legislation* (1780), ed. J. H. Burns and H. L. A. Hart (London, 1970), pp. 6, 296; M. W. Janis, 'Jeremy Bentham and the Fashioning of "International Law"', *American Journal of International Law*, 78 (1984), pp. 408–10.

[4] Roger A. Mason (ed.), *Scots and Britons: Scottish Political Thought and the Union of 1707* (Cambridge, 1994); John Robertson (ed.), *A Union for Empire: Political Thought and the British Union of 1707* (Cambridge, 1995).

British kingdoms. The effort of integrative imagining compelled comparisons as much as it created conjunctions, especially when it was forced to encompass the conceptually ambiguous dependencies of the British monarchies such as Ireland or the colonies and islands of the western Atlantic.

The chronology of the history of British political thought has not always coincided with the parallel chronology established by proponents of the 'New British History'. For these scholars, overwhelmingly drawn from the ranks of mid-seventeenth-century historians, an archipelagic perspective on the high politics of the early modern period has provided a liberation from more circumscribedly nationalist historiographies, especially the Anglocentric narrative that for so long stood proxy for the history of Britain in its widest sense. Their chronology has placed the emphasis on decades such as the 1560s, the 1580s[5] or the 1640s,[6] for example, where conflict rather than convergence dominated Anglo-Scottish and Anglo-Irish relations. However, this approach has tended to overlook other decades in which attention to the British dimension of political thought is equally imperative. The major casualty of this bias towards late Tudor England, late Stewart Scotland and mid-Stuart England has been the twenty-year period after the Glorious Revolution, from the Dutch invasion of England in 1688 through to the Anglo-Scottish union of 1707.[7] This was the era in which a conception of a polity composed of more than the three Anglo-Welsh, Scottish and Irish kingdoms began to emerge under the name of the 'British Empire'. This entity found its fullest expression half a century later in the 1730s and

[5] For example, Stephen Alford, *The Early Elizabethan Polity: William Cecil and the British Succession Crisis 1558–1569* (Cambridge, 1998); Patrick Collinson, 'The Elizabethan Exclusion Crisis and the Elizabethan Polity', *Proceedings of the British Academy*, 84 (1993), pp. 51–92.

[6] For example, Conrad Russell, *The Fall of the British Monarchies 1637–1642* (Oxford, 1991); Michael Perceval-Maxwell, 'Ireland and the Monarchy in the Early Stuart Multiple Kingdom', *The Historical Journal*, 34 (1991), pp. 279–95; John R. Young (ed.), *Celtic Dimensions of the British Civil Wars* (Edinburgh, 1997).

[7] Though for good recent exceptions to this stricture see Toby Barnard, 'Scotland and Ireland in the Later Stewart Monarchy' and David Hayton, 'Constitutional Experiments and Political Expediency, 1689–1725' in Steven G. Ellis and Sarah Barber (eds.), *Conquest and Union: Fashioning a British State 1485–1725* (Harlow, 1995), pp. 250–75, 276–305; Mark Goldie, 'Divergence and Union: Scotland and England, 1660–1707' and Jim Smyth, 'The Communities of Ireland and the British State, 1660–1707' in Brendan Bradshaw and John Morrill (eds.), *The British Problem, c. 1534–1707: State Formation in the Atlantic Archipelago* (Basingstoke, 1996), pp. 220–45, 246–61; Smyth, '"No Remedy More Proper": Anglo-Irish Unionism before 1707' and Colin Kidd, 'Protestantism, Constitutionalism and British Identity under the Later Stuarts' in Brendan Bradshaw and Peter Roberts (eds.), *British Consciousness and Identity: The Making of Britain, 1533–1707* (Cambridge, 1998), pp. 301–20, 321–42.

1740s as the basic conception that would carry the British state up to, and in part beyond, the transatlantic crisis of the third quarter of the eighteenth century.[8]

The British Empire was a polity bounded neither by the state that controlled it nor by the nations which formed part of it. Though historians from J. R. Seeley in the 1880s to John Brewer in the 1980s have conceived of the British Empire as the legal, political and bureaucratic extension of the British state – and hence of the United Kingdom as formally an empire-state – such a perspective has only limited value for the period before the creation of the British (that is, Anglo-Scottish) state itself in 1707.[9] The British Empire was a multinational polity, but it also comprised dependencies which were clearly neither nations nor states, at least until some of them chose to redefine themselves as states in 1776 as they seceded from their allegiance to the Empire.[10] These territories were the colonies or plantations, which lay for the most part in the Caribbean and along the western shores of the Atlantic ocean, though at times they could also be discovered within the Atlantic archipelago itself, where 'Britain' meant solely the Anglo-British state, centred on Westminster and Whitehall, rather than any egalitarian confederation of the Three Kingdoms.

The political thought that defined and shaped the British Empire had its roots within the concerns of British nationality and statehood at least a century before it came to be applied to extra-British territories and peoples.[11] The recurrence of key terms such as 'colony' and 'empire' in the discussion of intra-British relations not only confirms the continuity between the discourses of state and nation and those of empire, but also reveals the ways in which discussions of statehood and nationality were still cast in colonial and imperial language.[12] According to the anonymous author of *The Present State of Ireland* (1673), Ireland was 'one of the chiefest members of the *British* Empire', by which was meant the Anglo-British monarchy based in London that pursued the reduction of Ireland

---

[8] David Armitage, *The Ideological Origins of the British Empire* (Cambridge, 2000), chapter 7.

[9] J. R. Seeley, *The Expansion of England* (London, 1883); John Brewer, *The Sinews of Power: War, Money and the English State, 1688–1783* (London, 1989); Lawrence Stone (ed.), *An Imperial State at War: Britain from 1689 to 1815* (London, 1994).

[10] J. G. A. Pocock, 'States, Republics and Empires: The American Founding in Early-Modern Perspective' in Terence Ball and J. G. A. Pocock (eds.), *Conceptual Change and the Constitution* (Lawrence, Kan., 1988), pp. 55–77.

[11] I argue this at greater length in Armitage, *Ideological Origins of the British Empire*, chapter 2.

[12] On which see also Jacqueline Hill, 'Ireland without Union: Molyneux and his Legacy' in Robertson (ed.), *A Union for Empire*, pp. 271–96.

to civility and order and hence 'like to prove profitable to the Prince, and at all times a good additional strength to the *Brittish Empire*'.[13] From the other side of the confessional divide, the Franciscan Peter Walsh argued in 1674 for a transnational community of British and Irish Catholics, 'those in this famous Empire of *Great Britain*, that continue in Ecclesiastical Communion with the *Catholick* Bishop of old *Rome*'.[14] Walsh denied that there was any necessary collision between allegiance to the Stuart monarchy and communion with Rome, but such an imperial perspective sat more comfortably with the Protestant, Anglo-Irish argument in the 1690s 'that we are of one Religion, that we are a Province of their Empire, and have neither Laws nor Governors but of their sending us'.[15]

Arguments such as these within British and Irish political thought in the late seventeenth century offer the necessary conceptual link between the history of the Three Kingdoms and the history of the British Empire. This has, of course, long been recognised by Irish historians, who have investigated the intellectual, political and commercial links between Ireland and the wider Atlantic world in the eighteenth century.[16] However, the importance of Ireland in such arguments has been less obvious to historians of Britain, whose attempts to bridge the gap between the domestic history of Britain and the transmarine history of 'Greater' Britain have concentrated on the formation of an Anglo-British Empire, within which the Scots were indispensable as soldiers, administrators, merchants, educators and clergy, but to which Ireland, it seems, contributed comparatively little.[17] This is clearly something of an optical illusion, in light of the contributions the Irish made to this larger project in the eighteenth century, but the lacuna remains in the history of the British Empire.[18] The most ambitious attempt to deduce the character of

[13] *The Present State of Ireland: Together with Some Remarques Upon the Antient State Thereof* (London, 1673), sigs. A2v–3r, 79.
[14] Peter Walsh, *A Letter to the Catholicks of England, Ireland, Scotland, and All Other Dominions under His Gracious Majesty Charles II* (London, 1674), p. 1.
[15] [John Hovell,] *A Discourse upon the Woollen Manufactury of Ireland and the Consequences of Prohibiting its Exportation* (London, 1698), p. 8.
[16] For example, Owen Dudley Edwards, 'The American Image of Ireland: A Study of its Early Phases', *Perspectives in American History*, 4 (1970), pp. 199–282; Thomas M. Truxes, *Irish-American Trade, 1660–1783* (Cambridge, 1988).
[17] For example, John M. MacKenzie, 'On Scotland and the Empire', *International History Review*, 15 (1993), pp. 714–39; T. C. Smout, Ned C. Landsman and T. M. Devine, 'Scottish Emigration in the Seventeenth and Eighteenth Centuries' in Nicholas Canny (ed.), *Europeans on the Move: Studies on European Migration, 1500–1800* (Oxford, 1994), pp. 76–112; David Armitage, 'The Scottish Diaspora' in Jenny Wormald (ed.), *The Oxford Illustrated History of Scotland* (Oxford, forthcoming).
[18] Though see Joyce Lorimer (ed.), *English and Irish Settlement on the River Amazon, 1550–1646* (London, 1989); L. M. Cullen, 'The Irish Diaspora of the Seventeenth and Eighteenth Centuries' in Canny (ed.), *Europeans on the Move*, pp. 113–49; Donald

the British Empire from domestic conditions indeed dates the origins of the Empire to the immediately post-Revolutionary decades 'and views [British] imperialism as an attempt to export the Revolution Settlement (and hence to entrench it at home) by creating compliant satellites overseas'.[19] Yet even this account of the Empire as founded on and fuelled by the 'gentlemanly capitalism' of the Financial Revolution finds no place for Ireland in its synthesis, either as a 'compliant satellite' or as a component of the extended metropolitan core.

The anomalous status of Ireland, as both kingdom and colony, generated the most pointed discussions of nation, state and empire in British political thought of the late seventeenth century. This is, again, well known to historians of Ireland,[20] but the history of Irish political thought will only achieve its salutary purpose of dissolving the conventional, national, boundaries of historiography if it can be linked more directly to the wider political arguments within the early modern British Atlantic world. To understand the nature of the arguments regarding Ireland's status as kingdom or colony it is therefore essential to examine parallel arguments about the relationship between the kingdoms of England and Scotland, and about the constitutional and economic status of other colonies, both English and Scottish. The importance of such a comparative approach to Irish political thought – here taken to mean political thought concerning Ireland, as well as the political thought generated within Ireland – is not solely heuristic. It can contribute to the consideration of Ireland in a 'post-nationalist' perspective – a perspective which has already found some measure of fulfilment in the Good Friday Agreement of 1998, with its provisions for shared sovereignty, for a pan-Irish council and for a Council of the Isles – from the standpoint of the debates over sovereignty, political autonomy and economic coordination in the 'pre-nationalist' Ireland of the late seventeenth century.[21] Moreover, for the historian, it has the signal advantage of being idiomatic to the period

Harman Akenson, *If the Irish Ran the World: Montserrat, 1630–1730* (Montreal, 1997); Jane Ohlmeyer, 'Seventeenth-Century Ireland and the New British and Atlantic Histories', *American Historical Review*, 104 (1999), pp. 446–62.
[19] P. J. Cain and A. G. Hopkins, *British Imperialism: Innovation and Expansion 1688–1914* (London, 1993), p. 58.
[20] Karl S. Bottigheimer, 'Kingdom and Colony: Ireland in the Westward Enterprise, 1536–1660' in K. R. Andrews, N. P. Canny and P. E. H. Hair (eds.), *The Westward Enterprise: English Activities in Ireland, the Atlantic, and America, 1480–1650* (Detroit, 1979), pp. 45–65; Nicholas Canny, *Kingdom and Colony: Ireland in the Atlantic World, 1560–1800* (Baltimore, 1988), chapter 4; Patrick Kelly, 'Ireland and the Glorious Revolution: From Kingdom to Colony' in Robert Beddard (ed.), *The Revolutions of 1688: The Andrew Browning Lectures 1988* (Oxford, 1991), pp. 163–90; S. J. Connolly, *Religion, Law, and Power: The Making of Protestant Ireland 1660–1760* (Oxford, 1992), pp. 105–14.
[21] Richard Kearney, *Post-Nationalist Ireland: Politics, Culture, Philosophy* (London, 1997).

itself, in which the concerns of the Three Kingdoms and their dependencies were increasingly linked within the emergent discourse of political economy.[22]

I

Karl Marx attributed the origins of 'classical political economy' to Sir William Petty.[23] He thereby suggested inferentially that Ireland had been present at the birth of the discipline which ran from Locke to Ricardo and which of course culminated with Marx himself. Political economy embraces more than a discipline, and it overflows the boundaries of a canon of classic texts. It is distinct from political theory in defining the polity itself as much in terms of its fiscal, financial and commercial capacities as of its constitutional structure, the civic personality of its citizens or its teleology. Political economy marks a distinctive stage in the history of economic thought, continuous with earlier economic discourse but distinguished from it by the attempt to define the polity itself in economic terms.[24] The emergence of political economy has since Marx been traced back to the methodological innovations in the field of statistics and 'political arithmetic' associated with Petty and his followers.[25] It accords more closely with the perceptions of contemporaries to attribute the novelty of political economy instead to its appreciation that the dynastic states of Europe, even after a century of religious wars, found themselves (often reluctantly, and under mercantile compulsion) adopting commerce as a reason of state in the second half of the seventeenth century. Political economy was the fruit of this quite specific transition from the strenuous paradigm of militarily defined citizenship to the reason-of-state discourse generated by the peculiar strains in the relationship between polities and the wider economy in the late seventeenth century.[26]

The realisation that trade was a determining reason of state was not

[22] For a parallel argument regarding political economy as a transnational political language see John Robertson, 'The Enlightenment above National Context: Political Economy in Eighteenth-Century Scotland and Naples', *The Historical Journal*, 40 (1997), pp. 667–97.
[23] Tony Aspromourgos, 'The Life of William Petty in Relation to his Economics: A Tercentenary Interpretation', *History of Political Economy*, 20 (1988), p. 337. Terence Hutchison, *Before Adam Smith: The Emergence of Political Economy, 1662–1776* (Oxford, 1988), p. 3, is more sceptical of Marx's attribution of paternity to Petty; Neal Wood, *Foundations of Political Economy: Some Early Tudor Views on State and Society* (Berkeley, 1994) proposes instead sixteenth-century, and exclusively English, parentage.
[24] On economic thought before the emergence of political economy see especially Joyce Oldham Appleby, *Economic Thought and Ideology in Seventeenth-Century England* (Princeton, 1978). [25] Hutchison, *Before Adam Smith*, pp. 6–7.
[26] On which see especially Istvan Hont, 'Free Trade and the Economic Limits to Modern Politics: Neo-Machiavellian Political Economy Reconsidered' in John Dunn (ed.), *The Economic Limits to Modern Politics* (Cambridge, 1990), pp. 41–120.

confined to the metropolitan cores of the European state-system. For example, Richard Lawrence, the former Cromwellian colonel and antagonist of Petty on the council of trade, noted in 1682 that for contemporary states it had become 'a principal Piece of State-policy to know how to encrease their own and lessen their neighbours Trade . . . espousing the Interest of Trade as the Darling of State'.[27] Lawrence quoted at length Sir William Temple's *Observations* (1673) to show that Ireland's impoverishment had stemmed from its inadequate ratio of people to land, as well as its population's comparative lack of industriousness.[28] Too few hands being available to cultivate too much soil led inevitably to economic stagnation, while from stagnation could come no improvement in the manufactures essential to compete in international trade; manufactured goods had to be imported into Ireland, worsening its balance of trade and driving it further into poverty. Lawrence noted that Europe's two greatest trading nations, Holland and England, had only a century before been as poor as Ireland was now, and proposed an Irish land-bank on the Dutch model to provide the financial foundation for Irish trade, though he thought Ireland not yet ready for joint-stock trading in the English mode. If population could be increased, and foreign imports restricted, Ireland might yet have the work-force, the manufactures and the institutions necessary for it to compete in a world where commerce was now the leading reason of state. Yet such competition would not be pursued against England, trade would remain in the hands of the Protestant 'English' in Ireland, and the wealth gained by that trade would ultimately be to England's profit.[29]

Lawrence's analysis of the reasons for Ireland's lack of competitiveness was sound enough for the decade before the Williamite wars, especially when the dictates of economic reason of state ensured that the English outside '*West England*'[30] judged Ireland's commercial expansion to be a threat to their own prosperity. Ireland lacked banks and a mint, and hence both cash and credit; the consequently high rates of interest stifled commercial enterprise. The English parliament's Cattle Acts of 1663 and 1667 had restricted one of the most vibrant areas of Ireland's commerce and thereby depleted the supplies of bullion that might have fuelled the economy. Though the Irish economy was expanding in the later

[27] *DNB*, s.v. 'Lawrence, Richard (*fl.* 1643–1682)'; Richard Lawrence, *The Interest of Ireland in Its Trade and Wealth Stated* (Dublin, 1682), part 1, p. 9; compare with Lawrence, *The Interest of England in the Irish Transplantation, Stated* (London, 1655). Also see chapter 3 above.

[28] Sir William Temple, *Observations upon the United Provinces of the Netherlands* (London, 1673), pp. 188–9.

[29] Lawrence, *The Interest of Ireland*, part 2, pp. 1–17 (Temple, *Observations*, quoted, pp. 5–7), 47, 178.   [30] Lawrence, *The Interest of Ireland*, part 2, p. 51.

seventeenth century, these factors nonetheless limited the rate of its growth and the nature of change.[31] Recent scholarship has tended to downplay the impact of English legislation on Irish economic performance, at least in so far as that legislation is seen as the expression of a determined state policy of mercantilist regulation in favour of England.[32] Ireland was subject to discriminatory English legislation throughout the latter half of the seventeenth century, however imperfectly applied. It had been specifically included in the terms of the post-Restoration Navigation Acts, but the inadequate enforcement of the 1663 Staple Act (which required that all enumerated articles be landed in England before re-export to Ireland) led in turn to the 1671 Staple Act, which effectively ended the direct legal flow of sugar and tobacco to Ireland. That act lapsed in 1680 and was not restored until 1685, when English trading interests demanded that Ireland be treated not as a colonial dependency of the English economy but rather as a potential competitor with England, especially in the Atlantic staple trade to the sugar islands of the Caribbean.[33] This shift of emphasis in the legislative regulation of Irish commerce indicated both the increasing viability of the Irish economy in certain areas and English merchants' changing perception of that viability.

Ireland had originally received preferential treatment under the Navigation Acts precisely because it was considered more as a colony than as a kingdom, and hence as a docile dependency of England rather than as a rival to English commerce.[34] By the same logic, Scotland had been excluded from the trading system defined by the Acts, of which England, Ireland and the American and Caribbean colonies were part. The double standard was not lost on contemporaries. '[A]re we not all the Subjects of one King, and Members of the same Commonwealth?' Richard Lawrence asked rhetorically. 'We may be the first', he answered, 'and not the second, though the Scots are Subjects to the same King, yet Members of a distinct Commonwealth, that as *England* makes Laws to secure their Trade from *Scotch* Invasions, so doth *Scotland* for the securing theirs from *English* Retrenchments'.[35] Therein lay the problem, at least for those who did not identify themselves as members of an 'English' interest in Ireland: all might be subjects within the Stuart composite

---

[31] Raymond Gillespie, *The Transformation of the Irish Economy 1550–1700* (Studies in Irish Economic and Social History, 6, Dublin, 1991), pp. 53–7.
[32] Compare Hugh Kearney, 'The Political Background to English Mercantilism, 1695–1700', *Economic History Review*, 11 (1959), pp. 484–96, with Patrick Kelly, 'The Irish Woollen Export Prohibition Act of 1699: Kearney Revisited', *Irish Economic and Social History*, 7 (1980), pp. 22–44.   [33] Truxes, *Irish-American Trade*, pp. 1–16.
[34] [Sir Walter Harris,] *Remarks on the Affairs and Trade of England and Ireland* (London, 1691), pp. 33–9, ventriloquises contemporary Irish complaints.
[35] Lawrence, *The Interest of Ireland*, p. 115.

monarchy, but that would not render them equal citizens of the same commonwealth. The various communities of Britain and Ireland were considered as economically and constitutionally distinct. The main question for English protectionists was whether Ireland or Scotland could command an independent commerce; for their Irish and Scottish counterparts, the question was instead whether such economic independence demanded the sovereignty of an independent legislature as its guarantee and foundation. The decades after the Glorious Revolution brought these two arguments together into the single question of whether it was possible to have economic union without institutional (meaning, above all, parliamentary) union.

The most drastic answer to the dilemma of economic and institutional union came from Sir William Petty in his last major work, 'A Treatise of Ireland' (1687), in which he proposed the transplantation of the majority of the population of Ireland into England.[36] This would have left some 300,000 people in Ireland to administer the country as a cattle-ranching dependency of England. It would also deny Ireland the institutional autonomy it had fitfully claimed through its own parliament: 'Whereas there are Disputes concerning the Superiority of parliament; now there will need no parliament in Ireland to make Laws among the Cow-Herds and Dairy-Women.' Petty's proposal cut across the religious and ethnic divisions of contemporary Ireland by treating its inhabitants solely according to their economic relations, with the crown, their tenants and landlords, whether as employers or employees.[37] His briefer version of the plan, 'A Probleme' (1687), omitted some of the features which made the 'Treatise' a comprehensively British vision of population, power and profit, such as the parallel proposal to depopulate the Scottish Highlands and leave them to the care of 100,000 herdsmen, to the benefit of lowland Scotland and England.[38] Nevertheless, both redactions concluded with similar warnings for the English empire as a whole – that it would not be in England's interests to contemplate any further territorial expansion, and that the substitute for a territorial empire (with all of the military, and hence fiscal, commitments that it raised) should be 'a reall *Mare Clausum*' between and around the islands of Britain and Ireland.[39]

---

[36] On Petty's unionism see James Kelly, 'The Origins of the Act of Union: An Examination of Unionist Opinion in Britain and Ireland, 1650–1800', *IHS*, 25 (1987), pp. 238–40.
[37] Sir William Petty, 'A Treatise of Ireland' (1687), BL, Add. MSS 21128, in *The Economic Writings of Sir William Petty*, ed. Charles Henry Hull (2 vols., Cambridge, 1899), II, pp. 559, 568.
[38] Sir William Petty, 'A Probleme' (1687), BL, Add. MSS 72885, ff. 124r–126r in *The Petty Papers*, ed. Marquis of Lansdowne (2 vols., London, 1927), I, pp. 64–7; Petty, 'A Treatise of Ireland' in *Economic Writings*, p. 572.
[39] Petty, 'A Probleme' in *Petty Papers*, II, p. 67; Petty, 'A Treatise of Ireland' in *Economic Writings*, p. 573.

The 'union' of England and Ireland which forced the latter into agricultural dependency would have been but the first step in Petty's restructuring of the Stuart monarchy as a maritime empire within the late Stuart sovereign's territorial waters. This isolationist and inexpansive empire of the seas would face neither the costs of continental commitments nor the nuisance of internal disputes over sovereignty. As Petty showed in his contemporaneous disquisition on the 'Dominion of the Seas' (1687)[40] the inspiration behind his proposal was the Hobbesian desire for unitary sovereignty as a prophylactic against maritime *'bellum omnium contra Omnes'* in northern Europe; 'Peace & profitt would ensue' only if the sovereigns of Britain, Ireland, Denmark, France, Spain, the United Provinces and the Hanse ceded their claims to dominion over the sea to one of their number, the King of 'Brittayne'.[41] Such unitary sovereignty would only be possible if competing legislatures within Britain and Ireland could be eliminated, and hence the economic interests of the Three Kingdoms simultaneously harmonised into a single polity and economy. Petty's proposals were not therefore solely archipelagic, or even Anglo-Irish, in scope; they encompassed the whole of the Stuart monarchy, and were designed to affect all of the states of Atlantic Europe.[42]

Petty disclaimed any utopianism in his suggestions,[43] and offered a full costing of the transplantation to convince the sceptical of its economic viability and potential profitability. However, his plan was clearly unworkable, not least because it had been addressed in its most elaborate form to James II in the last year of his reign: its fate was to be rendered ridiculous by satiric litotes in Swift's *Modest Proposal* (1729), a satire derived from 'the several *Schemes of other Projectors*', Petty surely among them.[44] As Swift was aware, such reformative utopianism was an unignorable feature of political economy in the half-century on either side of 1700, when it offered some of the most imaginative projections of political thought in post-Restoration Britain in a work such as Andrew Fletcher's *Account of a Conversation Concerning a Right Regulation of Governments for the Common*

---

[40] Petty, 'Dominion of the Seas' (1687), BL, Add. MSS 72865, ff. 119r–138r (another, incomplete, copy is in BL, MS Lansdowne 1228, ff. 58r–74v), in *Petty Papers*, I, pp. 219–41: this must be a draft discussion of 'the Profit and Loss' of a *mare clausum* referred to in 'A Treatise of Ireland' (*Economic Writings*, p. 573); see also Petty, 'Of the *Mare Clausum*' (1687?), BL, Add. MSS 72893, f. 34r, and 'Of a *Mare Clausum*' (1687), BL, Add. MSS 72866, ff. 122r–123v in *Petty Papers*, I, pp. 241–2.

[41] Petty, 'Dominion of the Seas', BL, Add. MSS 72865, f. 128r; *Petty Papers*, I, p. 229.

[42] The designation 'Atlantic Europe' is taken from the work of E. Estyn Evans, *Ireland and the Atlantic Heritage: Selected Writings* (Dublin, 1996).

[43] Petty, 'A Treatise of Ireland' in *Economic Writings*, II, pp. 574–5.

[44] [Jonathan Swift,] *A Modest Proposal for Preventing the Children of Poor People from Being a Burthen to their Parents, or the Country, and for Making them Beneficial to the Publick* (Dublin, 1729), p. 4.

Good of Mankind (1704). That its most conspicuous manifestations should have been reimaginings of the relationship between England, Ireland and Scotland indicates that this critical period in the formation of the British state and Empire led to a fundamental revision of conventional wisdom regarding the relationship between sovereignty and independence, politics and economy. However, the solutions to such problems would ultimately be found in the deliberations of politicians rather than in the visions of theorists. The continuing strain of utopianism in Irish political thought of the eighteenth century – represented in the first half of the century by Samuel Madden, for example[45] – is perhaps also indicative of the continuing failure to reimagine a solid and mutually acceptable basis for Anglo-Irish relations in the aftermath of the Declaratory Act of 1720, after which it could be safely mocked into obsolescence by the illusionless Swift.

II

Petty did not live to see the effects of the Glorious Revolutions on the Three Kingdoms. If he had, the experience might have dampened his enthusiasm for non-sectarian, rationally calculated solutions to the problem of Anglo-Irish political and economic relations. The Three Kingdoms did not benefit equally from the settlements of 1688–9, but the lack of a fully comparative British history of the Glorious Revolutions has obscured the modifications the various arrangements in the Three Kingdoms made upon the conditions of existence of their neighbours. The English elevation of parliamentary sovereignty, for instance, may have been the beginning of a new dispensation of liberty for England, but it could hardly be reconciled with the much more radical reformation of church and state achieved in Scotland, whose political nation took the opportunity to begin and almost complete the modernisation of their country's institutions in the wake of James II's flight. Similarly, the Jacobite War in Ireland made it evident that the Glorious Revolution – perhaps first so-called in Ireland by William Molyneux, in 1698[46] – was far from 'glorious', in the sense that the English understood it: that is, uncontested, non-military and, above all, bloodless. Though it has been argued that the Glorious Revolution represented the victory of law,

---

[45] Samuel Madden, *Memoirs of the Twentieth Century* (London, 1733); Petty's inquisitory and aphoristic style of political projecting also foreshadows the rhetorical method of George Berkeley, *The Querist* (Dublin, 1735–7).

[46] William Molyneux, *The Case of Ireland . . . Stated* (1698), ed. J. G. Simms (Dublin, 1977), p. 113 ('the Glorious Revolution under his Present Majesty'); compare James R. Hertzler, 'Who Dubbed It "The Glorious Revolution"?', *Albion*, 19 (1987), pp. 579–85.

liberty and localism against absolutism, subordination and centralisation, this perspective is only true of England and, possibly, the American mainland colonies, whose own representative institutions took on new powers and confidence in imitation of the metropolitan, English parliament, a development whose profoundest fissile consequences would only be seen in the 1760s and 1770s.[47] As Patrick Kelly has argued, 'Ireland did not experience the Glorious Revolution in the sense in which the term is understood in the history of England and Scotland; even then it should be noted that the term is understood rather differently in the respective histories of England and of Scotland.'[48]

In the short term, Ireland experienced the Glorious Revolution as yet another phase of the Wars of the Three Kingdoms, and hence as a battle for the British monarchy played out on Irish soil which opened up peculiarly Irish divisions. In the medium term, Ireland experienced the Glorious Revolution as the reaffirmation of English claims to parliamentary supremacy, and the reimposition and extension of post-Restoration economic restrictions. As the Anglo-Irish Williamite Richard Cox put it aphoristically in a pamphlet addressed to the Convention Parliament in 1689, 'Ireland is part of the Dominions of *England*, and a Kingdom subordinate to it. . . . Without the Subjection of *Ireland*, *England* cannot flourish, and perhaps subsist.'[49] This may have been partly intended to reassure the Convention that the 'English' in Ireland knew to whom they owed their dutiful obedience at this contested moment, but admissions like this opened the way more broadly for the assertion of English parliamentary supremacy not solely over the settler population in Ireland, but over their own parliament and over their economy too. The Revolution Settlement in Ireland had restored the Irish parliament as a semi-permanent part of government there. This in turn encouraged the potential for collision between the newly self-confident legislatures in England and Ireland,[50] just as the Revolution Settlement in Scotland put the Scottish parliament on the defensive in support of its national interests in the mid-1690s, especially when those interests were construed in the prevailing discourse of national wealth and independence.

---

[47] Jack P. Greene, 'The Glorious Revolution and the British Empire, 1688–1783' in Lois G. Schwoerer (ed.), *The Revolution of 1688–89: Changing Perspectives* (Cambridge, 1992), pp. 260–71. Greene's use of 'Britain' where he in fact means 'England' in this essay obscures the differences between the Revolutions in England, Scotland and Ireland, and makes his Whiggish account of the 'Glorious Revolution' as a single 'British' event untenable, at least for the period 1688–1707.

[48] Patrick Kelly, 'Ireland and the Glorious Revolution' in Beddard (ed.), *The Revolutions of 1688*, p. 163.

[49] [Sir Richard Cox,] *Aphorisms Relating to the Kingdom of Ireland* (London, 1689), pp. 1–2.

[50] Patrick Kelly, 'Ireland and the Glorious Revolution' in Beddard (ed.), *The Revolutions of 1688*, pp. 182–3.

That English Whiggism would bring no immediate advantage to Ireland was evident from the brief burst of unionist sentiment aroused by the uncertainties of the Jacobite War in Ireland.[51] The 'Remarks shewing that it is not in the interest of England that Ireland should remain a separate kingdom' (1690) argued in the language of English whiggery that Ireland was the home of arbitrary government and passive obedience, and that these Jacobite corruptions could easily be reintroduced into England from there. The author was less concerned with the potential benefits of union for Ireland than with the political and moral dangers of maintaining the then current dispensation of domination and dependency between England and Ireland. Even Poynings' Law provided no defence against the influx of arbitrary government from Ireland into the 'English empire', since it placed the ultimate decision-making power in the hands of king and council rather than parliament. The only solution could be complete and incorporating union between England and Ireland on the model of the Anglo-Welsh union of the early sixteenth century which had united the English and the Welsh into one polity, with a single defining 'interest'. Such a union would also allow for the more direct economic exploitation of Ireland than had previously been possible, so that the newly absorbed kingdom 'might be made more profitable to England than all the foreign plantations'. The author presented the Irish economy less as a threat to the English, by virtue of its cheaper costs for labour, production and raw materials, than as the backdoor through which hostile European powers might enter to oppose English economic interests.[52] This analysis was accordingly cast in a comparative geo-political and historical framework, from the Anglo-Welsh union to the contemporary Williamite wars in Europe; by specifically comparing the profits from Ireland with those to be made from the 'foreign plantations' it intimated that the political-economic ambit for considering Ireland was now pan-Atlantic as well as European.

However, the analogy between the economic benefits to be derived from the transatlantic colonies and those from Ireland only encouraged the belief among the English that Ireland should be treated less as a kingdom than as a colony. In the aftermath of the Jacobite War, and the evident pacification of Ireland by force, it also became easier for the English and Anglo-Irish to claim that Ireland had been conquered, and hence that it should be held in subjection by England. The distinction elaborated by Francis Annesley in 1698, between a 'Colony for Trade'

---

[51] James Kelly, 'The Origins of the Act of Union', pp. 240–1; Smyth, '"No Remedy More Proper"' in Bradshaw and Roberts (eds.), *British Consciousness and Identity*, pp. 311–14.
[52] 'Remarks shewing that it is not to the interest of England that Ireland should remain a separate kingdom' (1690), *Cal SP, Domestic: 1690–91* (London, 1898), pp. 201–6.

and a 'Colony for Empire', was a telling one in the case of Ireland. Annesley argued that there were only two ways to keep a conquered country in subjection: by arms or by colonies. The former was always too dangerous and too costly; the latter had the sanction of history, and had been not only the method adopted by Rome, but also what 'our Ancestors did to secure *Ireland*, and is the easiest, least chargeable, and least dangerous Method'.[53] Annesley was clearly drawing upon neoclassical and Machiavellian analyses of territorial expansion, and thereby continued the tradition of Machiavellian theorising on Anglo-Irish relations which had its roots in the works of Sir William Herbert and Richard Beacon in the early 1590s.[54] However, Annesley's deviations from Machiavelli's prescriptions in the *Discorsi* are as significant as his additions to this neoclassical analysis. Though Machiavelli had indeed recommended in both the *Discorsi* and the *Principe* that conquered territories should be held by force of arms, or preferably by colonies, he had also counselled that the best way for a state to expand and maintain its *impero* would be by leagues, whether equal or unequal.[55] In the context of Anglo-Irish relations, this would have implied the necessity of viceregal government or, at best, progress towards ever-closer union.[56] This latter option entailed a recognition that Ireland was a separate but equal kingdom with sovereign institutions capable of making alliances; at least, it demanded the admission that Ireland and England should be partners in a British composite monarchy, joined under the same head, albeit unequal in their relations.

The distinction between 'Colonies for Trade' and 'Colonies for Empire' marked an advance beyond neo-Machiavellian categories into the discourse of political economy.[57] Machiavelli's Livian analysis of the military and diplomatic expedients for expansion had been rendered inadequate, if not anachronistic, by the rise of commerce as a reason of state, as Nicholas Barbon had noted in 1690: 'until *Trade* became necessary to provide Weapons of War, it was always thought Prejudicial to the

---

[53] [Francis Annesley,] *Some Thoughts on the Bill Depending Before the Right Honourable the House of Lords, for Prohibiting the Exportation of the Woollen Manufactures of Ireland to Foreign Parts* (Dublin, 1698), p. 6. Though the pamphlet is usually attributed to Sir Richard Cox, I follow Patrick Kelly, 'The Irish Woollen Export Prohibition Act', p. 35 n.47, in attributing it instead to Annesley.

[54] Sir William Herbert, *Croftus sive de Hibernia Liber* (*c*.1591), ed. Arthur Keaveney and John A. Madden (Dublin, 1992); Richard Beacon, *Solon His Follie* (1594), ed. Clare Carroll and Vincent Carey (Binghamton, NY, 1996).

[55] *Discorsi*, I, vi; II, iv; II, xix; *Principe*, ch. V.

[56] For a Machiavellian analysis of the necessity for viceregal goverment (derived explicitly from *Discorsi*, II, xix), see *The Present State of Ireland*, pp. 165–6.

[57] Hont, 'Free Trade and the Economic Limits to Modern Politics' in Dunn (ed.), *Economic Limits to Modern Politics*, pp. 79–89.

Growth of Empire'.[58] The plantations of the West Indies and the forts and factories of Africa and the East Indies were 'Colonies for Trade' in Annesley's terms, and comprised small groups of metropolitans, either 'sent forth to plant Commodities which your native Country does not produce' or 'to negotiate a Trade with the Natives'. Their trade would therefore be reserved to the metropolis, in return for which the colonists would be defended by the home country and enriched by their risk-taking; such colonists would continue to identify themselves as metropolitans and would thereby present no danger by claiming independence. 'Colonies for Empire', however, were closer to the neoclassical model, and were designed 'to keep great Countries in subjection, and prevent the charge and hazard of constant standing armies'. Their commerce would be unrestrained by the metropolis as the necessary reward for the emigrants' commitment to maintaining the dependency of the conquered territory and its inhabitants.[59] Annesley's two models were each inflected by post-Machiavellian commercial concerns, though only the model of a 'Colonies for Trade' could be usefully applied to Ireland or, more specifically, to the 'English' community in Ireland. 'They are Englishmen sent over to conquer *Ireland*, your Countrymen, your Brothers, your Sons, your Relations, your Acquaintance', he informed the English House of Lords: should they then be subject to economic restrictions that had never even been applied to the 'Irish and Popish' population in Ireland?[60]

Against the English proponents of mercantilist restraint, Annesley argued that the Anglo-Irish had no desire to compete directly with the English in the European race for commercial pre-eminence. 'They are not contending for Power or great Riches; they neither Trade to the *East Indies*, *Turkey*, or *Africa*; they have neither *Hamborough*, *Hudsons-Bay*, *Green-land*, or *Russia* Companies; they have no Fleets or Plantations; they ask only the common Benefits of Earth and Air.'[61] In the context of the late 1690s, this was intended not simply as a reassurance to the English parliament, and to the economic interests represented therein, that Ireland presented no threat to English colonial trade; it was also intended to drive a wedge between the perceived interests of Ireland and those of Scotland within the Williamite composite monarchy. By this time, Scottish political economists had learned their lessons from the English and the Dutch, and realised that the only way to avoid provincial subjection within the Williamite composite monarchy – as Ireland had evidently failed to do – would be for Scotland to pursue an independent colonial

---

[58] Nicholas Barbon, *A Discourse of Trade* (London, 1690), sigs. A3r–v.
[59] [Annesley,] *Some Thoughts on the Bill*, pp. 8–9.   [60] *Ibid.*, pp. 16, 15.   [61] *Ibid.*, p. 8.

trade of its own by instituting a separate system of 'Fleets and Plantations'.[62] The Scottish Privy Council had begun investigating mercantilist means to promote national prosperity after the appointment of James, duke of York, as lord high admiral of Scotland, and to this end they proposed a carrying trade, supported by the protection of domestic shipbuilding and the expansion of the Scottish fleet. This inevitably implied a threat to the Navigation Acts, though that challenge only threatened Anglo-Scottish relations with the resurgence of English parliamentary mercantilism after 1688.[63] The revival in 1693 of plans for an independent Scottish trade to challenge the English acts initially made common cause with English merchants who wished to evade the East India Company's monopoly, so that an Anglo-Scottish trading group proposed setting up a joint-stock company. The East India Company compelled its allies in the English parliament to oppose the move, so that the newly founded Company of Scotland Trading to Africa and the Indies became financed solely by Scottish investment.[64]

The Company of Scotland offered the profits of a 'colony for trade' on the isthmus of Panama as the alternative to dependency within the Williamite composite monarchy, as well as an economic defence against the aspiring universal monarchs of contemporary Europe. The Company's presentation of the potential benefits for Scotland and for the Scots of their plan for an isthmian entrepôt drew support from all but the poorest areas of Scotland.[65] The very willingness of so many Scots to invest in such a speculative venture indicated a major shift in Scottish intellectual life by the 1690s. The economic hardships of that decade, including famine and the effects of the Navigation Acts, had led the Scots into their first encounter with the literature of economic improvement, much of which had indeed been received in Ireland at least a generation earlier from the likes of Samuel Hartlib and William Petty.[66]

[62] The following discussion draws on David Armitage, 'The Scottish Vision of Empire: Intellectual Origins of the Darien Venture' in Robertson (ed.), *A Union for Empire*, pp. 97–118; for the economic background see also Richard Saville, *Bank of Scotland: A History 1695–1995* (Edinburgh, 1996), chapters 1–3.
[63] Eric J. Graham, 'In Defence of the Scottish Maritime Interest, 1681–1713', *SHR*, 71 (1992), pp. 89–90.
[64] G. P. Insh, 'The Founding of the Company of Scotland Trading to Africa and the Indies', *SHR*, 21 (1924), pp. 288–95; Insh, 'The Founders of the Company of Scotland', *SHR*, 25 (1928), pp. 241–54.
[65] *A Perfect List of all the Several Persons Residenters in Scotland, Who Have Subscribed as Adventurers in the Joint-Stock of the Company of Scotland* (Edinburgh, 1696); T. C. Smout, *Scottish Trade on the Eve of Union 1660–1707* (Edinburgh, 1963), pp. 150–1.
[66] Compare T. C. Barnard, 'The Hartlib Circle and the Cult and Culture of Improvement in Ireland' in Mark Greengrass, Michael Leslie and Timothy Raylor (eds.), *Samuel Hartlib and Universal Reformation* (Cambridge, 1994), pp. 281–97, and Ned C. Landsman, *Scotland and Its First American Colony, 1683–1765* (Princeton, 1985), pp. 72–82.

Yet, most importantly, the economic debate surrounding the Company of Scotland marked the beginnings of what would become the Scottish Enlightenment's peculiarly creative engagement with political economy.[67]

III

English political economists saw both Ireland and Scotland as threats to the supremacy of their own economy, but for very different reasons. The possibility that Scotland's potential success in the plantation trade might lead that kingdom to open up Ireland as its primary market made it imperative that Ireland be more closely subjected to English economic regulation. If Scots proposed to use the sovereignty of their parliament and the relative maturity of their financial institutions to promote a colonial empire that might allow it to declare its independence of the English parliament and even the English Protestant succession, then Ireland must more firmly be regulated as a colony and not allowed to pursue its own independent economic destiny as yet another competitive kingdom. This line of argument was pursued by the Bristol merchant John Cary, who perhaps did more than any other English writer of the 1690s to present the political economy of Britain and its dependencies as a single, interdependent system.[68] As Cary put it in his *Essay on the State of England* (1695), 'I take *England* and all its Plantations to be one great Body, those being so many Limbs or Counties belonging to it',[69] though he saw this English colonial empire as being in competition with the Scots to the north and held that Ireland was simply one of those plantations, and should be treated as such. The two major recommendations in the *Essay* struck at Ireland particularly as Cary insisted that the plantation-trade should be made more dependent upon England than hitherto, and that England should become 'a Market for all the Wool of *Christendom*' in order that England should have the economic capacity to continue the Williamite war against France. Ireland should be treated on the same terms as the American plantations by repealing the Cattle Acts, since they had only encouraged the Irish to seek foreign outlets for their products, and hence to become dangerously industrious. It should also have its woollen trade confined to the export of raw material to England; then,

---

[67] John Robertson, 'The Scottish Enlightenment', *Rivista Storica Italiana*, 108 (1996), pp. 808–14.

[68] For a succinct overview of Cary's political economy in its Bristolian context see David Harris Sacks, *The Widening Gate: Bristol and the Atlantic Economy, 1450–1700* (Berkeley, 1991), pp. 339–43.

[69] John Cary, *An Essay on the State of England in Relation to its Trade, its Poor, and its Taxes, For Carrying on the Present War Against France* (Bristol, 1695), pp. 66–7.

like the other colonies, its interests could be entirely subordinated to England's.[70]

Cary became in due course one of the major proponents of the English parliament's bill to restrict the exportation of Irish wool and one of five English authors to offer replies to William Molyneux's *The Case of Ireland . . . Stated* (1698).[71] However, his prominence in these debates has distracted attention from his wider political-economic vision, particularly the connections he made between Ireland, Scotland and the American plantations. The separate publication in 1696 of those sections of his *Essay* that concerned not only Irish but also Scottish trade clarified these connections for his metropolitan English readership.[72] This tract suggested that Cary's target was not solely the Irish woollen manufactory, but also the Scottish parliament with its plans for a joint-stock company. Cary notoriously used the reprint of the *Essay* to reaffirm his argument that the kingdom of Ireland should be reduced to the status of a colony and its products harnessed for the benefit of England. He also drew his English readers' attention to the stirrings of economic innovation in Scotland, where woollen manufactures, a fishery company and plantations were being proposed. Though he discouraged the idea that any nation like Scotland that lacked a vibrant manufacturing base could raise the capital to finance a plantation trade, he nonetheless realised the dangers of a second British kingdom's possession of colonies for trade: 'I cannot see what advantage the *Scotch* can make at this time of day, by setling Plantations; which if they do attempt we must be sure to take care of *Ireland*, and by reducing it to the terms of a Colony, prevent their selling their Product there, which I am apt to think is the main thing they aim at.'[73]

Cary was not alone in perceiving the interconnections between English, Scottish, Irish and colonial commerce. His antagonist Francis

---

[70] Cary, *An Essay on the State of England*, sigs. A4v–[A5]r; 10–11, 97–8; compare [Cary,] *To the Freeholders and Burgesses of the City of Bristol* (n.p., n.d. [Bristol, 1698?]), p. 3. A similar point about the Cattle Acts was made by the Board of Trade, 29 April 1697, PRO, Colonial Office 381/10, f. 44v.

[71] John Cary, *A Vindication of the Parliament of England, In Answer to a Book Written by William Molyneux of Dublin, Esq.* (London, 1698); Patrick Kelly, 'The Irish Woollen Export Prohibition Act', pp. 26–8. Molyneux, *The Case of Ireland . . . Stated*, pp. 143–4, lists the English replies, to which should be added Charles Davenant, *An Essay upon the Probable Means of Making a People Gainers in the Balance of Trade* (1698), in *The Political and Commercial Works of Charles Davenant LL.D.*, ed. Charles Whitworth (5 vols., London, 1771), II, pp. 239–59.

[72] John Cary, *A Discourse Concerning the Trade of Ireland and Scotland* (London, 1696), comprises Cary, *An Essay on the State of England*, pp. 89–113.

[73] Cary, *Discourse*, pp. 12–13 (= Cary, *Essay*, pp. 111–13).

Brewster saw that the success of Scotland's East India trade would only deprive England of such advantages as it had in the Irish market.[74] Cary's ally and interlocutor John Locke, from his vantage-point on the English Board of Trade, had at least as expansive a vision of the British Atlantic world's commerce, even if he did not present a single, comprehensive survey of its interrelations in the way that Cary did. Though Locke's writings on interest and coinage form the most important part of his economic legacy,[75] he also deserves respect for his attention to the workings of the post-Revolutionary Atlantic economy.[76] Locke was the official on the Board of Trade who paid closest heed to the progress of the Company of Scotland's activities in the late 1690s,[77] and it was, of course, Locke who co-ordinated the Board's efforts to promote linen manufacture in Ireland as an alternative to the Irish woollen industry.[78] Locke's interest in the prospects for the English woollen industry had been a central concern of his brief position-paper, 'For a Generall Naturalization' (1693), in which he had also shown himself aware of the dangers that depopulation had posed to the Spanish Monarchy's possessions in the Indies. In line with the prescriptions of other contemporary political economists – including those, like Petty and Sir William Davenant, who counselled the contraction of the English monarchy's territories[79] – Locke argued that wealth no longer lay in land, but rather in trade and hence also in the population necessary for extensive manufactures.[80] In the words of the manuscript addition he made to the *Second Treatise* in the late 1690s, '[t]his shews, how much numbers of men are to be preferd to largenesse of dominions, and that the increase of lands [*Sc.* hands] and

[74] [Sir Francis Brewster,] *A Discourse Concerning Ireland and the Different Interests Thereof, In Answer to the Exon and Barnstaple Petitions* (London, 1698), pp. 52–4.

[75] *Locke on Money*, ed. Patrick Hyde Kelly (2 vols., Oxford, 1991).

[76] On which see especially Louise Fargo Brown, *The First Earl of Shaftesbury* (New York, 1933), chapters 9–10; James Tully, 'Rediscovering America: The *Two Treatises* and Aboriginal Land Rights' in Tully, *An Approach to Political Philosophy: Locke in Contexts* (Cambridge, 1993), pp. 137–76; and Barbara Arneil, *John Locke and America: The Defence of English Colonialism* (Oxford, 1996).

[77] Maurice Cranston, *John Locke: A Biography* (London, 1957), pp. 444–6; Armitage, 'The Scottish Vision of Empire' in Robertson (ed.), *A Union for Empire*, p. 110. For Board of Trade documents relating to the Darien venture see Bodl., MS Locke c. 30, ff. 33r, 49r–52v, 53r, 112r–115v, 116r–118v, 126r, 127r–128v.

[78] See especially [John Locke,] report of the Board of Trade, 31 August 1697 in H. R. Fox Bourne, *The Life of John Locke* (2 vols., London, 1876), II, pp. 363–72, which was the scheme 'pitched upon' by the Board of Trade, PRO, Colonial Office 381/10, f. 107v. For Board of Trade documents relating to the Irish woollen dispute see Bodl., MS Locke c. 30, ff. 65r–66v; 67r–68v, 69r, 70r–77v; 78r–81v; 82r–83v; 84ff.

[79] Charles Davenant, *Discourses on the Public Revenues, and on the Trade of England* (1698) in *Political and Commercial Works*, II, p. 26.

[80] John Locke, 'For a Generall Naturalization' (1693) in *Locke on Money*, II, pp. 487–92.

the right employing of them is the great art of government'.[81] This would be a problem for an extended and composite commonwealth, such as that formed by England and Ireland, as much as for a unitary polity.

IV

Locke's arguments in the 1690s showed his awareness of the larger archipelagic and Atlantic context within which political-economic argument was now necessarily being played out. Yet, as the disputes over the Woollen Bills and the Company of Scotland showed, economic argument in the British Atlantic world after the Glorious Revolution readily became a political and constitutional argument. The existence of three legislatures within the Three Kingdoms, each of which could be used as the instrument for the promotion of competing economic interests, inevitably led to collisions and confrontations, especially when the most powerful of them, the English parliament, had such a freshly renewed sense of its own supremacy. An all-encompassing vision of political economy such as Cary's or Locke's at once allowed all of the British dominions to be seen as part of a single economic system, while the compulsions of contemporary political-economic theory revealed that the parts of that system would necessarily remain in tension with each other so long as they pursued separate economic interests. In order for economic harmony to become possible, it would be necessary to imagine novel constitutional settlements; however, such arrangements would have to be different for kingdoms and colonies. The major difficulty, for Ireland at least, was to decide what dominions should be conceived in which category.

William Molyneux, in *The Case of Ireland . . . Stated,* denied that Ireland should be conceived of in the same terms as the plantations of the Americas: 'Do not the Kings of *England* bear the *Stile of Ireland* amongst the rest of their Kingdoms? Is this Agreeable to the nature of a *Colony?* Do they use the Title of Kings of *Virginia, New-England,* or *Mary-Land?*'[82] On such constitutional grounds, Ireland was not of course a colony in the strict meaning of the term, unlike the plantations on the North American continent. But that did not mean that it was impossible to imagine that the status of Ireland and of the plantations could be considered as equal. Only after the Anglo-Scottish Union of 1707 was it feasible to contemplate that the English would extend to anyone other than themselves their rights of parliamentary representation and free trade within the ambit of

---

[81] John Locke, *Second Treatise,* § 42, ll. 21–3, in *Two Treatises of Government,* ed. Peter Laslett (rev. edn, Cambridge, 1988), pp. 297–8.

[82] Molyneux, *The Case of Ireland . . . Stated,* p. 115. See chapter 4 above.

the Navigation Acts. Even then, the continuing Anglo-Irish disputes over judicial appeals and Wood's Halfpence exacerbated the tensions generated by the failure to extend to Ireland the union that incorporated Scotland with the Anglo-Welsh state in 1707. The Anglo-Scottish Union made it even harder to imagine Ireland as a kingdom, and (in the words of Patrick Kelly) 'the tendency to think of Ireland as merely the first of England's colonies was greatly reinforced'.[83]

As Andrew Fletcher lamented in 1704, 'trade is now become the golden ball, for which all the nations of the world are contending, and the occasion of so great partialities, that not only every nation is endeavouring to possess the trade of the whole world, but every city to draw all to itself'.[84] The logic of political economy compelled every nation to strive for the profits of a colonial empire; equally, that ruthless logic determined that some nations would remain, or at worst become, colonies, in so far as they and their populations were subordinated to the overmastering and unchallengeable economic interests of other nations. Fletcher feared that too ready a capitulation to this political-economic logic by the Scots would lead them to cede their historic status as a separate kingdom, only to be bullied and impoverished into dependency as Ireland had been by England for centuries past. Fletcher's *Account of a Conversation* is remarkable for many reasons, but not the least of those reasons is the impression that Irish political thought after the Glorious Revolution seems to have made upon him. This could perhaps have been expected by any alert contemporary reader, who knew that Sir Edward Seymour – Fletcher's most aggressive English interlocutor in the imaginary dialogue – had been one of the major promoters of the Woollen Bills against Ireland. Yet what is unexpected is the knowledge Fletcher shows of the arguments made by Sir William Petty, William Molyneux and Henry Maxwell in their discussions of the constitutional and economic relations between England and Ireland in the twenty years before Fletcher wrote his dialogue. From Petty, Fletcher appropriated the ironic argument that the population of Ireland should be transplanted to England to prevent any further economic competition. From Molyneux, he drew the arguments that English rule in Ireland was founded on union, not conquest, and that the native Irish were conquered, but the English colony was not, so that Ireland was still a kingdom and not a colony. Finally, from his contemporary, the Irish unionist Henry Maxwell, Fletcher apparently took the Machiavellian

---

[83] Patrick Kelly, 'Ireland and the Glorious Revolution' in Beddard (ed.), *The Revolutions of 1688*, p. 188.
[84] Andrew Fletcher, *An Account of a Conversation Concerning a Right Regulation of Governments for the Common Good of Mankind* (1704) in *Andrew Fletcher: Political Works*, ed. John Robertson (Cambridge, 1997), p. 193.

arguments that the English 'have never shown the least disposition to unite with any other nation, though such as either stood upon equal terms with them, or such as they conquered, or even planted'.[85]

Maxwell's argument concerning the available options for English government of Ireland would, nonetheless, have been chilling for the Scots, and this in itself could explain Fletcher's interest in his prescriptions. Maxwell's Machiavellian analysis led him to conclude that it would be impossible for a free monarchy like England to hold a province like Ireland by force: the only remaining possible strategies were either direct rule (the sixteenth-century pattern); 'to check the growth of that Kingdom in point of Trade and Wealth, so that it may not be able to attempt any thing against the Constitution of *England*', as political economy would dictate (the post-Revolutionary pattern); or incorporating union on the Welsh model (the option Maxwell hoped England would now choose). Maxwell's intended audience was English, not Irish, as the *Essay* presented an Anglo-Irish case for union which would unite the '*British* Inhabitants' in Ireland more closely to the English nation. To prevent union, Maxwell argued, would be to ensure the agricultural impoverishment of Ireland, as the Protestants who led manufacturing would emigrate, leaving Ireland to 'its old Proprietors, who naturally love that lazy Life of Grazing and Droving'. This was Ireland as portrayed by Sir William Temple and envisaged in turn by Petty as an antidote to economic and constitutional competition between the two kingdoms. However, Maxwell concluded, if full political and economic union could be granted to Ireland, as it looked set fair to be offered to Scotland, the expanded Irish trade would flow exclusively to England, and thereby strengthen the metropolis.[86]

The subjection of a subordinate province to the English king-in-parliament was Maxwell's dream but Fletcher's nightmare. Maxwell's stark presentation of the narrow range of options for Ireland clearly

[85] Fletcher, *Account of a Conversation*, in *Political Works*, pp. 194, 199, 196–7: compare Petty, 'A Treatise of Ireland'; Molyneux, *The Case of Ireland . . . Stated*, pp. 30–9; [Henry Maxwell,] *An Essay upon an Union of Ireland with England* (London, 1703), pp. 3–4 (cf. Machiavelli, *Discorsi*, II, iv). The parallels with Petty and Molyneux are noted in Fletcher, *Political Works*, p. 194 n.16, p. 199 n.26. The copy of Maxwell's *Essay* in the Folger Shakespeare Library (shelf-mark DA496 1703 M3 Cage), its cover inscribed 'For Mr Fletcher', is presumably Andrew Fletcher's.
[86] Maxwell, *Essay upon an Union of Ireland with England*, pp. 7, 11–12, 20, 21, 33. My reading of Maxwell is indebted to the only other extensive modern account of the *Essay* in Smyth, '"No Remedy More Proper"' in Bradshaw and Roberts (eds.), *British Consciousness and Identity*, pp. 315–18, though I disagree with Smyth that 'Maxwell differed from Fletcher' in many respects; Maxwell's arguments may have been uncongenial to Fletcher, but their logic confirmed his own arguments against an incorporating union between England and Scotland, and thereby productively accentuated his criticisms of the unionist case.

strengthened Fletcher's conviction that post-Revolutionary Irish political thought was relevant to the equally narrow, but not therefore exactly equivalent, political and economic possibilities open to Scotland. This cross-fertilisation shows that the barriers which might separate Scottish from Irish political thought were, indeed, arbitrary. Fletcher's utopian reimagining, in the *Account of a Conversation*, of the whole of European politics drew upon the historic examples of Ireland and Wales, as well as the contemporary constitutional and economic arguments about the relationships between England, Ireland and the American plantations. In his cosmopolitan comprehensiveness, Fletcher reminds us that, though there were strains of political thought that were distinctive to each of the Three Kingdoms, many others cut across the borders of nation, state and colony, particularly in the pivotal period of European state-formation, unionism and dynastic dispute between 1688 and 1715. Political economy was one; the discourses of union, statehood and empire were others: all intersected during this period. Fletcher's *Account of a Conversation* was so poignant because it tried to imagine a world elsewhere, for western Europe at least, in which the compulsions of political economy and its vehicle, the sovereign nation-state, could be imagined away. But perhaps more poignant still, because more enduring in the political imagination of the eighteenth century, were those strains of Irish political thought that pointed to the economic and constitutional inequalities between England (after 1707, Britain) and Ireland. Utopianism would provide one means of political imagination that could think beyond those inequalities; equally, 'colonial nationalism' in the wake of Molyneux would provide another;[87] but unionism would remain fitfully alive until it won out, in a revived context of European warfare, constitutional contention and economic strife, in 1800.[88] All of these strains of later Irish political thought can be traced back to the decades after the Glorious Revolution. All bore the marks of those earlier attempts to imagine political theories that were adequate for Ireland's equivocal situation. All had drawn upon – just as they also nourished in their turn – contemporary strains of English, Scottish and even 'British' political thought.

---

[87] J. G. Simms, *Colonial Nationalism, 1698–1776: Molyneux's The Case of Ireland . . . Stated* (Cork, 1976); Isolde Victory, 'Colonial Nationalism in Ireland, 1692–1725: From Common Law to Natural Right' (unpublished PhD thesis, Trinity College, Dublin, 1984).

[88] G. C. Bolton, *The Passing of the Irish Act of Union* (Oxford, 1966); W. J. McCormack, *The Pamphlet Debate on the Union between Great Britain and Ireland, 1797–1800* (Blackrock, 1996).

11   From ancient constitution to British empire: William Atwood and the imperial crown of England

Charles C. Ludington

This chapter is not specifically about Irish political thought in the sense that the topic generally has been understood. Rather, it is an examination of the political thought of the English barrister, Whig theorist and chief justice of the royal colony of New York, William Atwood (d. 1712). And yet, this chapter has much to do with Irish political thought, not only because Atwood addressed the question of Irish parliamentary independence in his response to William Molyneux in 1698, but also because the trajectory of Atwood's ideas over the course of his career illustrates the changing British and imperial context in which Irish political thought occurred during the late seventeenth and early eighteenth century, and beyond. That Irish political thought has long been concerned with British and imperial issues is well known. But the popular notion that Ireland's difficulties were uniquely 'Irish' has not entirely dissipated. As David Armitage notes in chapter 10, 'the history of Irish political thought will only achieve its salutary purpose of dissolving the conventional, national, boundaries of historiography, if it can be linked more directly to the wider political arguments within the early modern British Atlantic world'.[1] This chapter is an attempt to make such a link, because Atwood, who spent most of his working career within the confines of central London, imagined one straight, imperial line running from King Arthur to the Stuart monarchs, and from the English parliament to all those places over which the English monarchs reigned. Ireland, in spite of its occasional recalcitrance and divided allegiances, was one such place.

I

William Atwood was a man of many words in his own lifetime, but since his death in 1712 none of his works have been republished, nor has anyone bothered to write much about him. In twentieth-century scholarship, Atwood is sometimes mentioned by historians and political scientists in

---

[1] See p. 252 above.

relation to John Locke, whom he may have known personally and whose works he is certainly known to have admired.[2] J. G. A. Pocock referred to Atwood frequently in his seminal work, *The Ancient Constitution and the Feudal Law*, but he was hardly awed, calling Atwood's mind 'ossified' and his work full of 'misplaced ingenuity'.[3] The Scottish historian William Ferguson dealt more extensively with Atwood in an influential article published in 1974, and was even less impressed than Pocock. 'Indeed', wrote Ferguson, 'his scholarship was weak . . . and his style, if he could be said to have one, was that of a pettifogging attorney'.[4] Even the *Dictionary of National Biography*, not known to be overly critical of patriotic Englishmen, said that, 'As a disputant, he is rather clumsy and ineffective.'[5] It seems odd, then, that William Atwood should be given his own mini-biography in *The Cambridge History of Political Thought 1450–1700* (1991), directly preceding the eminent Francis Bacon.[6] However, when one considers that Atwood was, in the words of Colin Kidd, 'the leading English imperialist theorist',[7] centrally involved in almost every major political debate within England, and between England and her political peripheries, during the period 1680 to 1707 – and that he frequently represented the triumphant Whig point of view – what becomes more surprising is the paucity of writing about him.

The subject of Atwood's works and his prodigious output must be historically understood in the tempestuous and well-known context of nascent party politics.[8] As a major Whig propagandist and ideologue,

---

[2] Richard Ashcraft, *Revolutionary Politics and Locke's Two Treatises of Government* (Princeton, 1986), pp. 585–6. Locke and Atwood had a mutual friend in James Tyrrell and Locke owned copies of Atwood's early works. See John Harrison and Peter Laslett, *The Library of John Locke* (2nd edn, Oxford, 1971), pp. 77, 254.

[3] J. G. A. Pocock, *The Ancient Constitution and the Feudal Law* (Cambridge, 1987 edn), pp. 191 and 193.

[4] William Ferguson, 'Imperial Crowns: A Neglected Facet of the Background to the Treaty of Union of 1707', *SHR*, 53 (1974), p. 29.   [5] *DNB*, I, p. 715.

[6] J. H. Burns (ed.), *The Cambridge History of Political Thought* (Cambridge, 1991), p. 178.

[7] Colin Kidd, 'Religious Realignment between the Restoration and the Union' in John Robertston (ed.), *A Union for Empire: Political Thought and the Union of 1707* (Cambridge, 1995), p. 163.

[8] Atwood appears in some of the following studies that develop this context, but he is only mentioned for his rejection of Locke's *Second Treatise*, or among a list of Whig propagandists. See J. R. Jones, *The First Whigs: The Politics of the Exclusion Crisis, 1678–1683* (London, 1961) and *Court and Country: England 1658–1714* (London, 1978); J. H. Plumb, *The Growth of Political Stability in England* (London, 1967); G. Holmes, *British Politics in the Age of Anne* (London, 1967 edn); J. P. Kenyon, *Revolution Principles: The Politics of Party, 1689–1720* (Cambridge, 1977); G. S. de Krey, *A Fractured Society: The Politics of London in the First Age of Party, 1688–1715* (Oxford, 1985); Clive Jones (ed.), *Britain in the First Age of Party, 1680–1750* (London, 1987); Tim Harris, Paul Seward and Mark Goldie, *The Politics of Religion in Restoration England* (London, 1990); Tim Harris, *Politics under the Later Stuarts: Party Conflict in a Divided Society* (London, 1993); Mark Knights, *Politics and Opinion in Crisis, 1678–81* (Cambridge, 1994).

neither his work nor his career can be separated from the emergent Whig–Tory divide. However, I shall not focus here upon Atwood's writing as a form of Whig propaganda for party debates. Instead, I shall examine how Atwood's domestically shaped Whig ideas were projected on to an English imperial canvas. Bernard Bailyn, and more recently Jack Greene, have described the constitutional and even military conflicts of the Anglo-Atlantic world in the century following the Revolution of 1688–9, as the prolonged struggle between the peripheries and the centre.[9] In Atwood's case, these peripheries were (in the order in which he dealt with them) Ireland, England's North American colonies and Scotland. Atwood believed that England was the centre of a political and legal imperium, as hers was the only imperial crown in the 'British Isles'.[10] The crown, however, had a complex and ultimately subordinate relationship to the English parliament. Thus, the exact locus of power was to be found with the king-*in*-his-English-parliament (not the king-*and*-his-English-parliament) and even more specifically in the English House of Commons, which, according to Atwood and other late seventeenth-century Whig polemicists, had existed from time immemorial. All of these ideas were built upon the ideological foundations of an ancient and immutable constitution, and the concomitant rejection of a Norman Conquest and subsequent 'Norman Yoke'.[11]

According to Pocock, who has done more than anyone to unravel, define and follow the various strands of early modern English and British political thought, Atwood was an 'Old' Whig whose ancient constitutionalism and insistence on the sovereignty of parliament were central to mainstream Whig thought in the late seventeenth and early eighteenth century.[12] What has not been so well studied is the connection between the domestic struggles for power in England, and the development of the English (and later British) Empire.[13] In this context, Atwood provides an excellent barometer for the changing nature of Old Whig thought as it

---

[9] Bernard Bailyn, *The Ideological Origins of the American Revolution* (Cambridge, Mass., 1967) and *The Origins of American Politics* (New York, 1970), and Jack Greene, *Peripheries and Center: Constitutional Development in the Extended Polities of the British Empire and the United States, 1607–1788* (Athens, Georgia, 1986).

[10] I use the controversial term 'British Isles' in a historical sense, as I believe that the growth of and resistance to a pan-British state, which included Ireland, is the key to understanding English (and Welsh), Scottish and Irish relations throughout the early modern period.

[11] For in-depth exploration of these ideas see Pocock, *Ancient Constitution*, and Christopher Hill, 'The Norman Yoke' in *Puritanism and Revolution* (London, 1968), pp. 58–125.

[12] J. G. A. Pocock, 'The Varieties of Whiggism from Exclusion to Reform' in *Virtue, Commerce and History* (Cambridge, 1985), pp. 221–6, 231. Mark Goldie classified Atwood as a 'radical Whig' in 'The Revolution of 1689 and the Structure of Political Argument', *Bulletin of Research in the Humanities*, 73 (1980), p. 508.

[13] This historiographical gap receives full attention in David Armitage, *The Ideological Origins of the British Empire* (Cambridge, 2000).

was transformed from the ancient constitutionalism of Exclusionist Whigs, through the mixed-government ideology and justifications of post-Revolutionary Whigs, to the absolute sovereignty of the-king-in-his-English-parliament Whigs who, by the early eighteenth century, found themselves acting on a British and imperial stage.

The increasingly bold Whig claims of a sovereign English parliament at the centre of the imperium had implications for England's political peripheries, just as the counter-claims of the peripheries brought into question the centrality and power of the English parliament. When the inhabitants of the peripheries did speak out in defiance of their increasingly dependent status, it was often Atwood who responded. And if it was not his exact line of attack or defence that triumphed in each debate, it was frequently the English position he represented that did so. At a time when the constitutional relationships within the British state and between Britain and Ireland are being questioned and scrutinised for a variety of political and economic reasons, the long overlooked treatises of William Atwood remind us of the fundamental connection between the course of internal English debate and the shape of external English expansion.

II

Atwood's early political writings reveal the language and conceptual tools that he was to apply throughout his career.[14] His later efforts, conditioned by changing circumstances, were examples of pouring old wine into new bottles. To his critics, both contemporary and modern, his historically based arguments were a bewildering mix of English common law, suspect evidence and outright myth strung together for the purpose of one essential argument: the supremacy of the English parliament within England, and ultimately, over all the king's dominions. To the degree that these criticisms of Atwood's style are accurate, he does not stand alone among early modern legal antiquarians. And while the quality of his arguments varied, his medium and his message remained remarkably consistent. The question, then, is not whether Atwood was always empirically rigorous, but how he applied his theoretical tools to construct the imperial powers of the English parliament.

As with other early Whig theorists, at the heart of Atwood's work was a belief in the ancient and immemorial English constitution. The maintenance of this idea depended upon denying the Norman Conquest of England, because if William was truly a conqueror who established a

---

[14] Owing to limitations in space, it is not possible to include a full discussion of Atwood's early constitutional arguments written primarily for English debates. The brief account that follows is intended to summarise the development of Atwood's ancient constitutional model that was later projected on to a larger, imperial canvas.

feudal polity with Norman laws, then the rights of the people as represented by parliament were clearly not immemorial. Rather, as products of
a king's will, they were gifts that could be taken away by the king and his
heirs. According to Atwood and other political writers who were concerned with 'preserving' the rights of parliament, William I had merely
taken the crown that was rightfully his, and then confirmed the laws of
Edward the Confessor, laws that were in fact immemorial.[15] Anti-
Normanism was not a Whig invention; it had proliferated throughout the
seventeenth century as a historical justification for limiting the powers of
the monarch.[16] However, it reached its peak during the Exclusion Crisis,
when these first Whigs coalesced in their opposition to Charles II's apparent bid to solidify his political power, and in the Catholic duke of York's
right to succeed. This was construed by both court Whigs and more
radical Commonwealthmen – Atwood seems to have been somewhere in
the middle – as an attempt to gain unprecedented powers over parliament
in order to rule 'absolutely', as did Charles' fellow monarch, mentor and
clandestine paymaster, Louis XIV of France. It was therefore imperative
for Atwood and other opponents of royal power to deny the Norman
Conquest and establish the existence of an immemorial parliament that
was not the product of a king's will. This, thought the anti-Normans,
would prevent the constitution from further encroachment and restore it
to its imagined former state of perfection.[17]

Atwood's earliest known constitutional argument, *Jani Anglorum Facies
Nova* (1680)[18] was written to accompany William Petyt's *The Ancient
Right of the Commons of England Asserted* (1679).[19] Both books followed
the anti-Norman line by rejecting the claims of Sir William Dugdale, Sir
Henry Spelman and Sir Robert Filmer, all of whom had dismissed the
idea of an ancient and thus immemorial English parliament.[20] This
debate, the 'Filmerian Controversy', was ultimately concerned with the

[15] An excellent example of post-Restoration Anglo-Norman studies is the *Argumentum
Anti-Normanicum: Or an Argument Proving, from Ancient Histories and Records, that
William, Duke of Normandy, made no Absolute Conquest of England by the Sword; in the sense
of our Modern Writers* (Derby, 1682). The book was once thought to be by Atwood but is
now generally attributed to Edward Cooke, whom one contemporary called an 'Atwood
in masquerade': David Douglas, *English Scholars, 1660–1730* (London, 1951 edn), pp.
122–3 and 122n. Douglas gave the publishing date as 1680; however, both copies in the
British Library are dated 1682.
[16] Douglas, *English Scholars*, ch. VI, pp. 119–38, and Pocock, *Ancient Constitution*, pp. viii,
125–7, 182–228, 319–21.   [17] Jones, *The First Whigs*, p. 214.
[18] William Atwood, *Jani Anglorum Facies Nova: or Several Monuments of Antiquity touching
the Great Councils of the Kingdom . . .* (London, 1680).
[19] William Petyt was a friend and mentor to Atwood.
[20] Pocock rightly calls *Jani Anglorum* and Petyt's *Ancient Right* 'obscurantist', as both
authors merely insist that parliament and the law are immemorial – 'that is, that at whatever time it is suggested that parliament may have originated, it was already ancient':
Ancient Constitution, p. 191.

issues of co-ordinate sovereignty and the patriarchal theory of kingship. It evolved into the 'Brady Controversy' in 1681 when Dr Robert Brady, a vitriolic Tory, used his rigorous, empirical scholarship to confirm Dugdale's belief that the origins of anything resembling the House of Commons could not have existed before the Act of 49 Henry III (AD 1265).[21] Brady insisted 'that there had been genuine conquest, followed by the introduction of a feudal kingdom that precluded a shared law-making power before time of memory'.[22] In legal terms this meant that the Stuart kings were sovereign on the lines of the Bourbon kings in France and it shattered the myth of the ancient constitution.

To the Whigs, this conclusion could not stand because it denied the truth of the history on which their argument for co-ordinate sovereignty between king, lords and commons was based. Thus, Brady's work elicited a host of responses, among which Atwood's *Jus Anglorum ab Antiquo* (1681)[23] was a notable example. In this work Atwood concluded that the evidence from the Domesday Book, to which Brady had appealed, 'manifestly destroys the Foundations of his Pernicious principles'.[24] Atwood also denied the accusation that he was a 'new Government Maker, in relation to the present Frame,' and turned the argument on his opponent.[25] Atwood's lengthy denial makes it clear that, in searching for political stability, a major Whig dilemma was how to enhance the power of parliament while distancing themselves from the bloody legacy of Interregnum republicanism. Whether this historical severance could be made, and indeed the more radical Whigs did not care to make it, ultimately depended upon the Whig antiquaries' ability to discredit Brady and the Tory feudalists.[26] As it turned out, Atwood's active pen did not overcome

[21] Robert Brady, *A Full and Clear Answer to a Book Written by William Petit, Esq.* (London, 1681), which contained an appendix attacking Atwood's *Jani Anglorum*. Brady revised the book and republished it in 1684 as *Introduction to the Old English History*. See Pocock, *Ancient Constitution*, pp. 182–228, 348.
[22] Corinne Weston, 'England: Ancient Constitution and Common Law' in Burns (ed.), *Political Thought*, p. 407.
[23] William Atwood, *Jus Anglorum ab Antiquo: or, a Confutation of an Impotent Libel Against the Government by King, Lords and Commons. Under pretense of Answering Mr. Petyt, and the Author of Jani Anglorum Facies Nova . . .* (London, 1681).
[24] Atwood, *Jus Anglorum*, p. 26.   [25] *Ibid.*, preface.
[26] Atwood's exact location within the spectrum of Whig political thought during the Exclusion Crisis remains ambiguous. He was among the 'True Whigs' identified by Mark Goldie, and even collaborated with radical republicans; however, his own views made him a moderate during the 1680s and a regime Whig during the next two decades. Mark Goldie, 'The Roots of True Whiggism, 1680–94', *History of Political Thought*, I, 2 (1980), pp. 195–236. Atwood might best be described as a 'domesticated' republican, a type common enough after the Restoration who promoted a doctrine of mixed government. In Petyt's and Atwood's hands, this actually meant the transfer of constitutional sovereignty from king to parliament, but there is no evidence to suggest that Atwood desired to abolish the kingship entirely. J. G. A. Pocock, *The Machiavellian Moment: Florentine Political Thought and the Atlantic Republican Tradition* (Princeton, 1975), pp. 401–22.

Brady's superior scholarship through sheer ambition and insult. It did not have to, as parliamentary power grew in the aftermath of the 'Glorious' Revolution.

Having found himself on the triumphant side of 1688–9, Atwood was free to take part in the necessary historical justification of what had just occurred in a nation where the divine right of kings remained a readily available political discourse, if not still a staunchly held belief.[27] The resultant fashioning of history was a critical component of the Revolution Settlement, and Atwood's contribution, *The Fundamental Constitution of the English Government: Proving King William and Queen Mary our lawful and rightful king and queen* (1690), was an exemplary articulation of Whig constitutional ideology through which the events of the Revolution could be understood. In this work, Atwood went even further than before by asserting that the English kingship had always existed by agreement and consent. Indeed, according to Atwood, it had always been elective. In the course of time the monarchy had become fixed according to hereditary principles, but the king still had to take an oath of coronation and receive indications of consent from parliament.[28] Therefore, the kingship was residually elective, and it was precisely the two Houses' right to choose the king that showed that in fact they were supreme within the constitutional trinity of king, lords and commons.[29]

Atwood's line of argument – which by now fully articulated his idea of parliamentary sovereignty within a mixed government – brought him into conflict with the then anonymous author of the *Two Treatises of Government*, his fellow anti-Filmerian John Locke. The government, according to Atwood, had never visibly ceased and there was no need for a Lockean 'appeal to heaven'. Rather for Atwood (and here he cited Pufendorf), in every agreement of the people to erect a government, there was an implicit proviso intended to avoid dissolution of the government on default of the king.[30] In the case of England in 1688–9 there was no need for the government to revert to the people as such, because the government had not dissolved, but had simply passed into the hands of

[27] Atwood, as we have seen, appealed to that belief as recently as 1681. For more on the post-1689 concept of divine right theory, see Gerard Straka, 'The Final Phase of Divine Right Theory in England, 1688–1702', *EHR*, 77 (1962).
[28] Atwood dated the first historical appearance of the contract in Edward the Confessor's reign, but he went back as far as Egbert of the West Saxons to demonstrate the people's exercise of their rights: *Fundamental Constitution*, pp. 28–84. See also Kenyon, *Revolution Principles*, p. 35.
[29] See Julian Franklin, *John Locke and the Theory of Sovereignty* (Cambridge, 1978), p. 116.
[30] Atwood, *Fundamental Constitution*, p. 100–2; Samuel von Pufendorf, *Law of Nature*, bk VII, ch. VII, 9, p. 1092, cited from Franklin, *John Locke and the Theory of Sovereignty*, p. 106.

parliament alone. As the ultimate source of power, it then became parliament's duty to elect a new king.[31]

Atwood's interpretation of what happened in 1688–9 represented the view of many prominent Whigs. However, it is not clear whether Atwood deputised himself in these debates, was paid by leading Whig parliamentarians to write, or, as a later Scottish critic suggested, was spurred by a business partnership with his publisher.[32] Nor, for that matter, is much known about Atwood's life in London.[33] Obscure to posterity, Atwood's explanation of the Glorious Revolution was central to subsequent 'Whig' versions of English history.[34] Moreover, in 1690 the principles upon which he based his justification of the Revolution and the Revolution Settlement had only begun to run their triumphant course.[35] They were soon called upon when those places that were not so pleased with the newly assertive and centralising role of the English parliament began to speak out.

III

The numerous tracts written in the 1690s and the first years of the eighteenth century concerning the medieval claims of English suzerainty over her neighbours in the British Isles revealed the existence of a deep constitutional crisis – one which concerned not only Ireland and Scotland, but England's Atlantic colonies as well. 'At bottom', wrote William Ferguson, 'these works really illustrate how after the "Glorious Revolution" the old "British problem" was revived in a more extended and subtle form'.[36] It was no longer the king of England who sought to justify his right to exert control over all the British Isles and England's far-flung colonies, it was

---

[31] For a discussion of Atwood's awareness of Locke's radicalism, see Ashcraft, *Revolutionary Politics*, pp. 585–9. Ashcraft says that for Atwood any 'state of nature', should it exist, was tantamount to Hobbes' 'state of war'. Though a Whig, Atwood was not above using this Tory scare tactic to limit the extent of popular sovereignty.

[32] James Anderson, *An Historical Essay Shewing that the Crown and Kingdom of Scotland is Imperial and Independent* (London, 1705), p. 2.

[33] Henry Neville, in his republican tract *Plato Redivivus* (1680), spoke of the 'learned discourse' (*Jani Anglorum Facies Nova*) of 'Mr. Atwood of Grays-Inn', but little other evidence about his life in London remains. Henry Neville, *Plato Redivivus* in Caroline Robbins (ed.), *Two Republican Tracts* (Cambridge, 1969), p. 120. Throughout his career, Atwood's publishers were located adjacent to Gray's Inn, so that much of his working life seems to have revolved in or around his law chambers.

[34] Ashcraft, *Revolutionary Politics*, p. 586.

[35] While I am interested here in why and how constitutional dynamics changed before and after the Revolution, there are two related studies of how the Revolution was seen in retrospect: H. T. Dickinson, 'The Eighteenth Century Debate on the "Glorious Revolution"', *History*, 61 (1976), pp. 28–45; and Kathleen Wilson, 'Inventing Revolution: 1688 and Eighteenth-Century Politics', *Journal of British Studies*, 28 (1989), pp. 349–86.

[36] Ferguson, 'Imperial Crowns', p. 22.

now the English king-in-parliament. This dramatic change raised a host of questions to which the feuding antiquarians addressed themselves. The principal issues of debate concerned the existence and nature of a 'British' crown and the locus of sovereignty within the British Isles. The existence of three kingdoms was not disputed. What was contested was the number of crowns and which ones could claim to be imperial. Most controversial of all (and most diplomatically delicate) was whether the rights of an imperial crown devolved upon the corresponding parliament. These became urgent issues after the Revolution of 1688–9, when English parliamentary power began to threaten the sovereignty of the king's other dominions. The attempts to define, justify and enforce these changing relationships caused vociferous debate. Considering the constitutional issues at hand, it is no surprise that the irascible barrister William Atwood enthusiastically joined the fray.

The growing political powers of Westminster were both a cause and an effect of the fact that England, and London in particular, was rapidly becoming the centre of a commercial and financial empire. This growth spawned new economic attitudes towards the king's poorer dominions – making those same parts increasingly peripheral to the metropolitan centre.[37] English economic growth had very specific consequences for Ireland, one of which was the quashing of the burgeoning Irish woollen industry in 1698–9 by jealous West Country woollen merchants.[38] At the same time, the English House of Lords denied the ultimate appellate jurisdiction of the Irish Lords in a case involving the Bishop of Derry, William King. Into this breach stepped a formerly taciturn member of the Irish parliament, William Molyneux, who responded with what was to become the most famous defence of Irish parliamentary autonomy, *The Case of Ireland's Being Bound by Acts of Parliament in England and elsewhere Stated* (1698).[39]

Molyneux's principal assertion was that Ireland was an independent kingdom and had been so since the time of King John. Historically and constitutionally, it was the king-in-council (not in-his-English-parliament) that had controlled the Irish parliament. It was not clear to him by what right the English parliament had usurped that power since 1689.

---

[37] Istvan Hont, 'Free Trade and the Economic Limits to National Politics: Neo-Machiavellian Political Economy Reconsidered' in John Dunn (ed.), *The Economic Limits to Modern Politics* (Cambridge, 1990), pp. 41–120.

[38] See Hugh Kearney, 'The Political Background to English Mercantilism, 1695–1700', *Economic History Review*, 2nd series, 11 (1959), pp. 484–96, and also Patrick Kelly, 'The Irish Woollen Export Prohibition Act of 1699: Kearney Revisited', *Irish Economic and Social History*, 7 (1980), pp. 22–44.

[39] William Molyneux, *The Case of Ireland's Being Bound by Acts of Parliament in England and elsewhere Stated* (Dublin, 1698). Also see chapter 4 above.

That much of Molyneux's argument was straightforward, but as his case developed he began to hedge his defences. Hoping to gain sympathy from an English Whig audience, Molyneux tried the risky tactic of claiming that 'England may be said much more properly to be conquered by William I than Ireland by Henry II: For we all know with what violence and opposition from Harold, King William obtained the kingdom', whereas 'Henry II received not the least opposition in Ireland'.[40] Molyneux ultimately denied that either kingdom had been conquered, but the tactic backfired, as English Whigs were not amused. The Dubliner's final appeal on the subject of conquest owed much to Locke and through him to Grotius and Sir John Davies.[41] He suggested that even if Ireland had been justly conquered, this would not apply to the descendants of the English in Ireland, for they were among the conquerors.[42]

In order to strengthen his historical and constitutional argument, and no doubt to gain support from England's northern neighbour, Molyneux touched on a subject that was equally troublesome to active political minds in Scotland. He claimed that Ireland and England were distinct kingdoms, 'as are the kingdoms of England and Scotland at this day, without any subordination of the one to the other',[43] and continued with this analogy in a later section, concluding: 'If it be said, that Scotland is an ancient and separate and distinct kingdom from England, I say, so is Ireland.'[44] Changes in his drafts reveal that Molyneux knew that drawing an analogy to Scotland would be to risk the ire rather than the support of the Scots,[45] but his tactic seems to have worked among some, if only posthumously. In 1703, Andrew Fletcher angrily addressed his potential English audience: 'I speak of a nation, who affirm you have no shadow of a right to make law for them; that the power that the King's council has assumed was gotten by surprise; and that their first submission was founded on a treaty of union, which now on account of some rebellions suppressed, is called a conquest. But sure as I said before, you never conquered your own colony, and therefore ought to do them justice.'[46] While Molyneux did not live to hear Fletcher's support, or even much from his colleagues in Ireland, the analogy he drew, although historically and

---

[40] Molyneux, *Case*, p. 9.
[41] Jacqueline Hill, 'Ireland without Union: Molyneux and his Legacy' in Robertson (ed.), *A Union for Empire: Political Thought*, pp. 279–84.   [42] Molyneux, *Case*, pp. 30–34.
[43] *Ibid.*, p. 55.   [44] *Ibid.*, p. 84.
[45] Patrick Kelly, 'The Printer's Copy of the MS of William Molyneux, "The Case of Ireland being bound by Acts of Parliament in England"', *Long Room*, 18–19 (1978–9), pp. 7–13.
[46] Andrew Fletcher, 'Account of a Conversation Concerning a Right Regulation of Governments for the common good of mankind' in John Robertson (ed.), *Andrew Fletcher, Political Works* (Cambridge, 1997), p. 195. Fletcher was referring to Poynings' Law of 1494 ('gotten by surprise') and probably to the rebellions of the 1590s, 1640s and, of course, 1690s. *Political Works*, p. 195n.

legally problematic, forced his Scottish readers to look at their own situation and take note.

The second thrust of Molyneux's defence – and again a form of hedging his bets with the use of Locke – rested on ideas of natural right which he often copied verbatim from the *Second Treatise*. Molyneux argued that the English parliament not only lacked a historical or legal right to subjugate Ireland, but it lacked a moral right as well: ''tis the cause of the whole race of Adam, that I argue: Liberty seems the inherent right of all mankind; and on whatsoever ground any one nation can challenge it to themselves on the same reason may the rest of God's children expect it'.[47] Using a formula that was to become commonplace among British colonists in North America during the late eighteenth century, Molyneux argued that legislation without representation was tantamount to slavery.[48] As William Ferguson stated, 'Molyneux was really condemning the beginnings of the "old colonial system", of which Ireland was the earliest and most severely damaged victim'.[49] While many scholars have pointed out that Molyneux's Irish arguments anticipate the later grievances of British colonists in North America,[50] the propinquity of these instances did not wait until the late eighteenth century to emerge; it became evident long before in the career of William Atwood.

III

It is not clear whether the apparently earnest – and perhaps politically naive[51] – Molyneux actually expected his tract to be calmly received by the English parliament. In any event, it was not. English Whigs, from whom he had gleaned so much about the language of 'rights', were particularly hostile. In June 1698 a Commons committee reported to the House that several passages of *The Case* tended to 'disown and deny' the authority of the English parliament over Ireland. What the committee most objected to was Molyneux's assertion that the English parliament had no right from precedent to legislate for Ireland and that England could more easily be deemed a conquered nation than Ireland. Other paragraphs reproduced for censure were those claiming common law for Ireland as granted by Henry II and his sons, the freedom of the Anglo-Irish (Protestants) by virtue of their English descent, subjection to the king but not to parliament, a forlorn proposal of Irish parliamentary union with

---

[47] Molyneux, *Case*, p. 3. For a longer discussion of Molyneux's use of natural-right arguments, see Robbins, *Commonwealthman*, pp. 134–76.   [48] Molyneux, *Case*, p. 93.
[49] Ferguson, 'Imperial Crowns', p. 25.
[50] J. G. Simms, *William Molyneux of Dublin, 1656–1698* (Dublin, 1982), pp. 116–17; Robbins, *Commonwealthman*, p. 138; C. H. McIlwain, *The American Revolution: A Constitutional Interpretation* (New York, 1923), pp. 35–6, 55–6.   [51] See chapter 4 above.

England, and the comparison with Scotland as an independent nation.[52] Upon hearing the report of the committee, the House of Commons passed a resolution stating that *The Case of Ireland* was dangerous to the crown and people of England because it denied Ireland's subordinate status to the imperial crown of England.

Along with this official reprimand, Molyneux's *Case* prompted three Whig and one Tory responses from England, and a fifth from the Protestant Irish non-juror, Charles Leslie. The Whig responses highlighted what Ferguson called the 'British problem', by presuming the incontrovertible truth of the one, imperial, English crown. Not surprisingly, the lengthiest of these replies was William Atwood's, *The History, and Reasons, of the Dependency of Ireland upon the Imperial Crown of the Kingdom of England* (1698). To Atwood's credit, there were few more practised in the art of ancient constitutional debate than he. As a result, he met Molyneux on his own ground, matching one legal precedent with another and ultimately turning the myth of the ancestral constitution to the disadvantage of Ireland, proving (to his own satisfaction a least) that 'the one imperial crown, upon which Ireland has been, and still is, dependent, is the crown of England'.[53]

In his dedication of *The History and Reasons* to the English House of Commons, Atwood revealed the Hobbesian juncture at which Whig ancient constitutionalism had now arrived. 'Ireland', he wrote, 'as 'tis annexed to the Imperial Crown of this Kingdom; is subjected to that Authority, which is, and must be absolute'.[54] If Ireland was subject to the king but not to the king-in-his-English-parliament, then the king was sovereign after all, and the entire Revolution Settlement could be abrogated. Consequently, *The History and Reasons* was as much a defence of the suzerainty of the English parliament as it was an attack on Molyneux's *Case*.[55] It followed that one of Atwood's primary concerns was to deny Molyneux's claim that William I had conquered England, even though Molyneux had ultimately denied as much. Atwood's reasoning was simple: the English barons had offered William the throne, so he took what was his and then confirmed the ancient laws of Edward the Confessor on his new kingdom.[56] Atwood agreed that Henry II did not really conquer Ireland. Instead, Henry was reasserting the earlier

---

[52] Isolde Victory, 'Colonial Nationalism in Ireland, 1692–1725: From Common Law to Natural Right' (unpublished Ph.D., Trinity College Dublin, 1984), p. 70; William Cobbett *et al.* (eds.), *The Parliamentary History of England* (36 vols., London, Hansard, 1806–20), V, p. 1182.

[53] William Atwood, *The History and Reasons of the Dependency of Ireland upon the Imperial Crown of the Kingdom of England* (London, 1698), p. 72.   [54] *Ibid.*, dedication.

[55] Molyneux hoped for royal support by dedicating *The Case of Ireland* to William III.

[56] Atwood, *History and Reasons*, pp. 133–50.

conquest of King Arthur.[57] This claim gave Henry II and his descendants conqueror's power over Ireland and it took Irish history back to the druidic mists of time immemorial, which was farther than Molyneux had dared to go. Atwood admitted that the Arthurian evidence remained thin, but said that it did not matter as it was clear from the time of King Edgar, that Ireland 'or the greatest part of it', belonged to the crown of England.[58] With nothing in Irish statute books to disprove either the Arthurian or the Anglo-Saxon conquest, Atwood could claim victory in the battle of the ancient constitutions. Moreover, he suggested that Henry II would have had conqueror's rights to Ireland anyway because of the papal licence granted to him in 1154. Pope Adrian IV, the only Englishman ever to sit upon the papal throne, had given Henry II permission to possess Ireland and to reform the wayward church there. A virulent anti-Catholic all his working life, Atwood was willing to give credence to a papal decree when it suited his purpose.[59]

After settling the issue of conquest in his favour, Atwood turned his attention to Molyneux's denial of English parliamentary power. Atwood's own argument was based upon an understanding of the crown to be the 'king-in-parliament' as opposed to the 'king-and-parliament' – even in the twelfth century. Much of Atwood's case rested on this distinction. Thus the Irish submission to Henry II was also a submission to the English parliament, and the granting of common law was the gift of the king-in-parliament, not of the king alone. Molyneux's historically accurate reference to the medieval Irish parliaments as closer in status to councils was used against him by Atwood to show that the Irish parliament was therefore inferior to its English counterpart, which had always been a proper and legitimate parliament, even before it was ever recorded as such.[60] Bringing the argument up to date, Atwood used the Triennial Act of 1689 to demonstrate the superior position of the English parliament, calling it an 'undoubted part of the Fundamental Constitution of the English Monarchy'.[61] Whereas the English parliament now convened regularly according to law, the Irish parliament could still be called and dissolved by the king's will. Atwood also pointed out the contradiction in Molyneux's statement that the king of England was *ipso facto* king of

---

[57] Atwood, *History and Reasons*, pp. 13–14, listed the source of the Arthurian aetiology as 'a very Ancient Manuscript in Latin Verse in the Cotton Library, ascribed to a Gildas who lived in the year 860'.   [58] Atwood, *History and Reasons*, pp. 15–17.
[59] A copy of Atwood's *History and Reasons* (BL, 883 g.15), which belonged to the renowned English legal antiquary and jurist Francis Hargrave (1741–1821), contains the following margin note: 'The ground upon which the author supposes Ireland's dependency on England before the time of Henry 2, seems very slight and fanciful. He even lays some stress on the Pope's bull to Henry. A more injudicious manner of arguing could scarce have struck the imagination of any one.'
[60] Atwood, *History and Reasons*, pp. 93–151. This was the logic that Brady had ridiculed.
[61] *Ibid.*, p. 202.

Ireland but that the Irish parliament nonetheless had to ratify English acts of succession.[62] This was particularly galling to Atwood because he considered it to have been the English parliament's quick action that had repeatedly saved the Irish Protestants from papists and tyrants, and most recently given them an acceptable king in the person of William III. In other words, without English protection, 'those Englishmen who chuse to live in Ireland . . . could not have subsisted in any Age since the Reformation'.[63] Molyneux and his Protestant colleagues in Dublin may have been unchallenged rulers within Ireland since the Treaty of Limerick in 1691, but their status within the English empire was more clearly dependent than ever before.

Atwood dealt only briefly with Molyneux's claim for Irish legislative autonomy as a natural right. He rejected the argument on the same grounds he had rejected Locke's, claiming that Molyneux's appeal tended towards 'a total exemption from all Laws and Government, except such as Adam had a right to in the state of Nature'.[64] In other words, like his friend Locke, Molyneux was accused of condoning anarchy and war. That of course, was not what a representative of the minority Anglo-Irish community desired. In fact, Molyneux had fled Ireland during the fighting there in 1689–90. For obvious reasons, he had never insisted on a people's inherent right to resist. Moreover, his quarrel was with the English parliament, not with a tyrannical monarch; thus there was no apparent need for an 'appeal to heaven'.[65] But Atwood had found the hypocrisy in Molyneux's natural right argument and exploited it wherever it appeared. Thus he rejected Molyneux's suggestion that the 'People of Ireland' (by which Molyneux meant the Anglo-Irish, or members of the Church of Ireland) maintained the same right to representation as native-born Englishmen, saying that all Englishmen were not in parliament and yet they were bound to the laws by the original consent and contract of their forefathers.[66] Finally, he attacked Molyneux on what was his greatest weakness: the use of Lockean conquest theory, which precluded punishing the progeny of the conquered:

and if the Irish natives are not conquered, or if the Right of Conquest over them, ought not to be carryed beyond the reparation of the Damages sustained from them; or if a just Conquest gets no power, but only over those who have actually assisted in that unjust force . . . let the English in Ireland look to it, how to justify those Possessions which they enjoy, by the help of the Crown and Kingdom of England: and if their Consciences are squeamish, let them renounce their Right to the Lands of the Natives; but let them not bring in to question the Right of England to all Foreign Plantations.[67]

[62] *Ibid.*, p. 80.   [63] *Ibid.*, p. 195–6.   [64] *Ibid.*, p. 4.
[65] Hill, 'Ireland without Union', p. 285.   [66] Atwood, *History and Reasons*, p. 196.
[67] *Ibid.*, p. 197–8.

Compared to this one rebuff, which highlighted the contradictions of the post-1691 Irish 'colonial nationalist' position, all of Atwood's prolix recounting of Arthurian legend and medieval legal evidence had been harmless.[68]

Finally, Atwood's argument for one imperial crown in the British Isles could not avoid addressing the status of Scotland, which Molyneux had compared to Ireland as an equal and equally independent kingdom. As he had done in *Jani Anglorum Facies Nova* in 1680, Atwood fired a shot across the Scottish bow, this time claiming that 'when the right of the Crown of *Scotland* came afterwards in James I to be in the same person who had the Crown of *England,* and that without any new acquisition by the Crown or Kingdom of *England,* there was no *merger* of the less Crown: and 'tis certain that in the Judgement of the Law, Palatinates fallen to the Crown continue distinct Royalties'.[69] Atwood acknowledged that there was 'no merger of the less crown', but it was clear which crown that was, and therefore which crown was also the 'palatinate'.

For Atwood and the Whig ideologues, there was but one imperial crown in the British Isles and that belonged to England. Atwood's argument was this: 'The statute, II Jac. I declares him king of England, Scotland, France and Ireland, by God's goodness, and right of descent under one imperial crown.' Having established the one crown, Atwood said, 'the statute, 10 Charles I calls this the imperial crown of England and Ireland'.[70] This second statute suited Atwood perfectly, for it incorporated Ireland into the one crown (and thus in the Whig view under the English parliament), while excluding mention of Scotland altogether. In hindsight, it looks as if Atwood was exploiting the confusion of titles since 1603 in order to reserve the old claim of English suzerainty over Scotland for future use.[71] Indeed, Atwood would deal with Scotland in due time. But first, as a faithful servant of the one imperial crown, he was appointed by the Lords Commissioners of Trade and Plantations to be a judge in the royal colony of New York.

IV

In what little has been written about William Atwood, it is usually mentioned that he served briefly as chief justice in the colony of New York and that he was dismissed on charges of gross corruption and maladministration, which necessitated his escape back to England. Ultimately, Lord

---

[68] For a longer analysis of Molyneux and the 'colonial nationalist' position, see J. G. Simms, *Colonial Nationalism, 1698–1776* (Cork, 1976); and Victory, 'Colonial Nationalism'.
[69] Atwood, *History and Reasons*, p. 56.
[70] Atwood, *History and Reasons*, p. 74, cited these statutes in the margin as 11 Jac. I.C.I. and 10 C. I. Seff. 3.C.3.   [71] Ferguson, 'Imperial Crowns', p. 29.

Cornbury, royal governor of New York, removed Atwood for a host of reasons which imply that the chief justice sought to manipulate the laws to his own political and financial benefit. Cornbury accused Atwood of openly ruling in favour of his own son in cases where the latter was counsel, a practice that not only perverted justice, but brought business to his son and 'large sums of money was by parties given to [Atwood's son] to levy his father's favour'. He also charged Atwood with persecuting the inhabitants of the colony for no apparent reason except to further his own interests, and of rigging justice so as to confiscate estates which were then sold to pay off government debts 'which through their mismanagement were grown to be very considerable'. Furthermore, Cornbury stated that Atwood wrongfully accused officials of treason in order to remove them from office and then practised irregularities in court 'so as to conceal his artifices'.[72]

After his dismissal and escape, Atwood returned to London where he immediately set about trying to right his reputation as an honest man. His version of the story was presented in *The Case of William Atwood, Esq.*, published in 1703. According to Atwood, the principal reason for his dismissal was the treason charges he brought against the colonists Bayard and Hutchins, both Jacobite Tories in that they had supported James II. Atwood defended his actions against them and tried to paint himself as the incorruptible servant of the crown who became a victim of rampant corruption. Specifically, Atwood called the administration of New York before and after the reign of King James II 'Despotick and Arbitrary', a familiar euphemism for the presence of Catholics, Jacobites or Tories in high office.[73] While raising the familiar shibboleths of power hungry Papists and lack of consent of the people – the latter being an idea he had recently rejected for Ireland – Atwood insisted that he was only trying to enforce 'the laws and interest of England'. He concluded by submitting to his readers for consideration 'whether a Dishonest Chief Justice is not the most likely to secure his Status there, or at least to sit easy in it?'[74] Of course, testimony was mixed as to whether Atwood's true interest was enforcing 'the laws and interest of England',[75] or whether he was not himself involved in a 'manner of prohibited trade'. Six years later Atwood was still writing to the Lords of Trade seeking vindication and insisting that his and Governor Bellomont's actions were taken against 'all those who had opposed the revolution' (of 1688–9).[76] Whatever the truth,

---

[72] E. B. O'Callaghan (ed.), *Documents Relative to the Colonial History of the State of New York* (Albany, NY, 1853–87), IV, p. 1010–11. When Cornbury left New York six years later, this was precisely the sort of accusation levelled against him.
[73] Atwood, *The Case*, p. 241.   [74] *Ibid.*, p. 319.   [75] *Ibid.*, p. 282.
[76] O'Callaghan, *Documents*, V, p. 105–8, letter from William Atwood to the Lords of Trade, 26 October 1709. Governor Bellomont, like Atwood, was a liberal Whig; he died suddenly in 1702, and was replaced by the Tory Lord Cornbury.

William Atwood felt the sting of the crown's chief envoy, Lord Cornbury, who used his power to dismiss the judge 'at his pleasure'.

Until very recently, historians of colonial North America had accepted that Cornbury was a despotic Tory governor and a scandalous transvestite. Some of his fiercest opponents at the time claimed that he attempted to represent the office of his cousin Queen Anne by publicly promenading as a woman.[77] Other commentators used more familiar political language to criticise the governor's supposed abuse of power: 'in New Jersey, Edward Hyde, Viscount Cornbury, treated the people not as Free-Men who were to be Governed by Laws, but as Slaves, of whose Persons and Estates he had the sole power of disposing'.[78] It now seems more likely that Cornbury was a victim of political mud-slinging that was as ruthless in the colonies as it was in London.[79] Whatever the truth of the allegations (and there is little substantive evidence for them), when Cornbury was recalled to England in 1708 he left the colonies of New York and New Jersey in massive debt – just as Atwood's friend Governor Bellomont had done before him.

The real problem was that Atwood and Cornbury operated in the twilight of a changing political system.[80] As Jack Greene summarised the situation: 'Long after the crown had given up its rights to veto laws, to prorogue and dissolve legislative bodies and determine the frequency of their meetings, to dismiss judges at pleasure, and to create courts in Britain itself, it continued to claim and actually exert such authority for its governors in the colonies.'[81] Having been sent to a place which made no claims to have its own ancient rights and constitution, but nevertheless whose inhabitants claimed the rights of free-born Englishmen, Cornbury and Atwood were caught in a maelstrom of legal indefinition, what Greene calls 'the single most divisive issue separating metropolis and colonies during the seven decades following the Glorious Revolution'.[82] It was perhaps inevitable that in such an unstable political climate the leading figures were vilified. If the royal governor could be successfully branded a corrupt transvestite, it is little wonder that the chief justice did not remain unscathed.

The legal confusion that Atwood encountered in New York, was, as Molyneux's *Case of Ireland* pointed out, similar to that which existed in the peripheries of the British Isles. The quest of the colonists for specific

---

[77] Patricia Bonomi, *The Lord Cornbury Scandal: The Politics of Reputation in British America* (Chapel Hill, 1998). Bonomi's study is a refutation and explanation of the persistent belief that Cornbury was a transvestite and an inordinately corrupt royal governor.
[78] O'Callaghan (ed.), *Documents*, V, p. 37.   [79] Bonomi, *Lord Cornbury*, chs. 4–7 and 9.
[80] *Ibid.*, p. 78.
[81] Greene, *Peripheries*, p. 20. See also Michael Kammen, *Colonial New York* (Oxford, 1975), ch. 6.   [82] Greene, *Peripheries*, p. 41.

guarantees of their rights to English laws was a recurrent subject of debate
during the century after the Restoration: were all subjects of the English
king or queen entitled to English rights, and if so, which ones?[83] In 1691,
the newly formed Assembly of New York had answered this question by
delineating the 'Rights and Priviledges of their Majesties Subjects'. But
immediately these conflicted with the far less democratic rights of their
Majesties' subjects in England.[84] Unlike the Irish Molyneux, the
American colonists did not dispute that their colonies were initially conquered, or, as with New York, taken from a rival European power. But like
Molyneux, they insisted that the subsequent occupation of those lands by
the natural-born subjects of England and their progeny entitled the
inhabitants to 'the benefit of all the laws of England ... and the rights of
Englishmen'.[85] The issue of which laws applied was further complicated
by the fact that English law was a complex combination of common law
practices as applied by courts and statute law enacted by parliament.[86]
Custom, so important in English law, became equally important wherever English common law was exported, such as to Ireland and the
American colonies. Through an accumulation of cases, each court-
system began to develop its own common law precedents, and in many
cases these superseded the laws of England.

In short, Atwood and Cornbury had unwittingly found themselves in a
world where the vitriol of English party politics met the legal chaos of the
English imperial frontier. The concerns of the inhabitants of New York –
trade, the French, the Indians, religious freedom, citizenship and political
rights – could not fit neatly into the already overlapping Whig and Tory,
court and country divisions of England.[87] The relatively secure world of
ancient constitutional debate was far away. But back in England, with his
own *Case* published in 1703, Atwood felt sufficiently exonerated to make
claims for English parliamentary supremacy.[88] This time the cries of
protest came not from the West or far West, but from the North.

V

In the early 1690s patriotic Scots realised that they had missed a golden
opportunity to negotiate a more equitable union with England immediately after the Revolution.[89] In response to the downtrodden mood

[83] *Ibid.*, p. 23. [84] Kammen, *Colonial New York*, p. 139.
[85] Edward Long, *History of Jamaica* (3 vols., London, 1774), I, p. 160, cited in Greene,
Peripheries, p. 24. [86] Greene, *Peripheries*, p. 25.
[87] Bonomi, *Lord Cornbury*, chs. 8 and 9.
[88] It is not clear whether Atwood returned to Gray's Inn; however, his post-1702 books, as
with the previous ones, were published in the vicinity, suggesting that he resumed many
of his old business connections. [89] Ferguson, 'Imperial Crowns', p. 23.

in Scotland and to increasing English ministerial involvement in Edinburgh's affairs, the Scottish publicist and antiquarian George Ridpath published a manuscript treatise in 1695 on the homage question, written by the early seventeenth-century feudalist Sir Thomas Craig. Craig had denied that the king of Scotland was in any way subordinate to the king of England. In fact, he asserted that the English had given homage to the Romans, Picts, Scots and finally Saxons, who themselves had been forced to pay Danegeld to their Danish conquerors.[90] While its English readers did not appreciate the argument, Craig's claim was hardly new and the English response was muted by the more pressing issues of financing King William's wars against Louis XIV, the existence of a standing army and the constitutional status of Ireland.

But Scotland's English problem did not go away, and tension between the two nations rose again in 1701 when the Act of Settlement was passed in England in order to bar the Catholic Stuarts from returning to the throne. The act devolved the English crown to the Dowager Electress Sophia of Hanover and her issue, but the English parliament did not consult its Scottish counterpart on the measure, thereby implicitly denying the equality of the Scottish crown. The Scots got the message. Andrew Fletcher angrily summarised the snub before a troubled session of the Scottish parliament in 1703:

The English nation did some time past take into consideration the nomination of a successor to that crown; an affair of the highest importance, and one would think of common concernment to both kingdoms. Did they ever require our concurrence? Did they ever desire the late King to cause the parliament of Scotland to meet, in order to take our advice and consent? Was this not to tell us plainly that we ought to be concluded by their determinations and were not worthy to be consulted in the matter?[91]

What really irked the Scots was that the Act of Settlement was reminiscent of the English actions in Ireland, and perceptive Scots drew the analogy.[92] It was in fact a different parallel from the one Molyneux had drawn between Scotland and Ireland as equal, independent kingdoms, but it was inspired by the same source: English political encroachment. An anonymous paper that was circulated at the 1703 Scottish parliamentary session revealed the concern:

My Lord, I shall here beg leave to illustrate the danger of our own constitution as it stands at present by expressing the wretched state of that of our neighbours in

---

[90] Thomas Craig, *Scotland's Sovereignty Asserted being a Dispute concerning Homage against those who maintain that Scotland is a Feu, or Fee Liege of England, and that therefore the King of Scots owes Homage to the King of England* (London, 1695).
[91] Fletcher, *Political Works*, p. 147.
[92] See Hont, 'Free Trade', p. 115; and John Robertson, 'Andrew Fletcher's Vision of Union' in Roger A. Mason (ed.), *Scotland and England, 1286–1815* (Edinburgh, 1987), p. 213.

Ireland, to which ours seems too nearly related . . . I desire to know, then, My Lord, where lies the difference of our case, from that most deplorable state of Irish parliaments, save that in the one case, the legislative is openly determined by command [i.e. Ireland], and in the other by a no less operative influence men. . . .[93]

The question was clear: was Scotland ultimately to be ruled by the parliament of England or was she to rule herself? The answer hinged upon whether the Scottish crown was independent and imperial or whether the Scottish kings once paid homage to the kings of England. The 1703 Scottish parliament emphatically denied the English claim to suzerainty by passing the Act of Security, which asserted the imperial nature of the Scottish crown and therefore Edinburgh's right to nominate its own successor to Queen Anne.

To the English, the Scottish claim of regal equality had been relatively acceptable since 1603. But after 1689, the fear of a Catholic Stuart succession in Scotland, exacerbated by the growing desire for economic dominance by England and its metropolitan centre, made many English minds intolerant. Nor were English claims over Scotland confined to members of the Whig party. A Tory physician, James Drake, launched the first English attack shortly after the stormy 1703 session of the Scottish parliament.[94] The Scots consigned Drake's book to the flames. Undaunted by the fate of Drake's effort, William Atwood responded with the English constitutional case. He was by this time very well practised in the art of lengthy pamphleteering; in this instance he spent 576 pages explaining 'what has occurred to me of that right of the imperial crown of England, which takes from the Scots all occasions, or pretences, for reviving ancient feuds about the right of succession'.[95] Atwood could not immediately invoke the absolute authority of the imperial crown of England as he had done against Molyneux, because Scotland had historical and constitutional leverage that Ireland did not have. Instead, he began his work with a clever, if not impartial declaration of his own Scottish blood, which was 'mingled with an Hereditary Zeal for the Constitution of the British Monarchy'. Thus, he said, 'it may be less strange, that I should be made the first of the Moderns in ascribing to my Countrymen of both Kingdoms, the Honour of being under one Imperial Crown, continued to

---

[93] George Ridpath, *Proceedings of the Scottish Parliament* (Edinburgh, 1704), pp. 304–6. Ferguson stated that he was unable to identify the author of this paper, 'Imperial Crowns', p. 30.

[94] James Drake, *Historia Anglo-Scotica: or an Impartial History of ALL that happen'd between the Kings and Kingdoms of England and Scotland, from the beginning of the Reign of William the Conqueror, to the Reign of Queen Elizabeth* (London, 1703), p. 423.

[95] William Atwood, *The Superiority and Direct Dominion of the Imperial Crown of England, over the Crown and Kingdom of Scotland, and the Divine Right of Succession to both Crowns Inseparable From the Civil* (London, 1704), dedication.

the present Royal Family through a British Channel, not only of consanguinity but of laws'.[96] However, the image of one happy family was a subterfuge:

I cannot but think it my duty to lay before them part of that evidence, which may be thought, rather than the force of arms, to have induced the brave Nation, which now possesses Scotland, as well as their predecessors Picts and Britons, both Princes and People, not only in Words, but notoriety of Facts, to have acknowledged the superiority of England over all parts, which have fallen under the denomination of the kingdom of Scotland; in testimony of which their kings have paid homage both feudal and liege, and the people have sworn allegiance to our king.[97]

Like Englishmen of all political stripes, Atwood was genuinely alarmed by the possibility of the Scots nominating their own successor to Queen Anne. Not only did this pose a frightening military and economic scenario, in which England was faced with a new version of the Auld Alliance, but to Atwood, who had never hidden his views from the Scots, such a move was, or at least should have been, unconstitutional. Scotland's crown, like Ireland's, was subordinate to England's, because the queen herself was subordinate to the English parliament. According to Atwood, since sharing its monarch with England in 1603, Scotland had held the honour of being 'as a Flower in the Imperial Crown of England'.[98] But as England had the only imperial crown in the British Isles, in matters of succession Scotland, like Ireland, had to follow suit. Atwood further contended that the real interest of Scotland would be to acknowledge once and for all the superiority of the English crown as 'it may secure to them a more immediate relation to the head of the British monarchy'.[99] The irony that the reigning monarch's royal house was originally Scottish was apparently lost on Atwood.

Atwood's solution to the British problem was just what the Scots feared, an extension of the powers of the English king-in-parliament to the northernmost end of the British Isles. However, as an ancient constitutionalist, Atwood's claim for English parliamentary suzerainty took the form of a refutation of Sir Thomas Craig's 'Treatises of Homage and Succession'. Along with attacking Craig's works, he intimated that the men who published them were Jacobites. Furthermore, he claimed that Craig himself had acknowledged the legality of a statute of Edward the Confessor which declared the Scots 'to be the subjects of the English monarchy'.[100] If so, one might ask how publishing Craig's works was a sign of Jacobitism, unless Atwood meant to imply that all patriotic Scots

[96] Atwood, *Superiority*, p. 1.   [97] *Ibid.*, pp. 2–3.   [98] *Ibid.*, p. 3.   [99] *Ibid.*, p. 3.
[100] *Ibid.*, pp. 364 and 576.

were inherently Jacobites. But repetition, not consistency, was by now the strength of Atwood's style. Thus he asserted the superiority of the English king-in-parliament by resurrecting the Celtic legend of Arthur and proceeding chronologically from there through the Germanic Saxons, the Francophile and Francophone Plantagenets, the Welsh Tudors right down to the Scottish Stuarts, making them, the English Stuarts, the true, imperial kings of England, unless of course they were Catholic – in which case the issue of a minor German princess would suffice. Once again, Atwood was oblivious to the ironies of his own history. He was not bogged down by the national or cultural origins of so many English monarchs. Instead, he argued for the authority of the English crown against all rivals, a power which was based on the claim that the ancient Britons ruled over the entire island,[101] and that this authority was inherited by the Saxons, who were not conquerors, but rather, like the Normans, happily integrated with their militarily inferior hosts.

Atwood's history was a gallimaufry of fact and fiction; many of his claims were dubious, and others, while documented, were based upon forgeries (some of which he apparently knew about).[102] Nor did concerns of historical accuracy deter him from drawing the formidable conclusion he had only hinted at when rebuking Molyneux for comparing Ireland to Scotland:

Homage for the Kingdom of Scotland, and its dependency upon the superior crown of England continuing, their James VI who had an undoubted right to the crown of England from his father, and to the crown of the dependent kingdom from his mother, being duly recognised king of England, with all its rights, members and appurtenances; no longer can deny that thereby Scotland had granted the investiture to their James I and his heirs, whose sole heir was their James VI our first.[103]

In other words, despite Queen Elizabeth's express renunciation of Scottish suzerainty in January 1568, 'the old English claims . . . over Scotland were never formally abrogated, and were therefore still legally enforceable'.[104]

At the end of his text – and one wonders how many Scottish readers arrived there – Atwood suggested four possible courses for Scotland's future. First, there could be a total separation from England upon a dissolution of government, an idea he ascribed to 'French emissaries' and 'hotheaded republicans'. Second, there could be a joint commonwealth between the two countries, 'which vain chymera could hardly enter into

---

[101] Atwood also argued that the imperial authority of the English crown was matched by a pan-Britannic metropolitan authority in the Archbishopric of Canterbury, *ibid.*, p. 541.
[102] Ferguson, 'Imperial Crowns', p. 36.   [103] Atwood, *Superiority*, p. 553.
[104] Ferguson, 'Imperial Crowns', p. 37.

any sober man's head'. Third, they could have a king which 'can never be limited by the People and consequently . . . must be Absolute'. Fourth, they could have the monarch 'which God Almighty has appointed them, in ratifying the Law of Man, which has settled the Crown of England, with all its Rights, members, and Appurtenances, and among them Scotland'.[105] Knowing Atwood's own preferred choice for the Scots, no one could deny that he was a unionist of sorts. It was just that his vision of union was the complete ingestion of Scotland by England. He wrote in a subsequent work – which was a reply to Ridpath's response to him – 'as queen of England Her Majesty [Queen Anne] cannot make that kingdom (i.e. Scotland) independent, without making it one with England; nor can she give them a free communication of trade, without the consent of the parliament of England'.[106] This type of union, wherein Scotland was clearly the lesser of the two united kingdoms, was precisely what Fletcher and his followers feared most. In fact, it was Atwood's brand of Whig thinking that inspired Fletcher to conceptualise other possibilities for the future of Scotland within a confederated Europe, possibilities that an ancient constitutionalist could not have imagined. In any event, Atwood's protestations that he had Scotland's best interest in mind were not credible in Edinburgh. His work was condemned to be burned by the common hangman.[107]

For Atwood, the task of maintaining parliamentary supremacy over the king within England, necessitated asserting the rights of an imperial English crown over Scotland, to the exclusion of rigorous scholarship.[108] Yet what is revealing here is the similarity of Atwood's claims against Scotland and Ireland, and in both cases his use of the same historical arguments on which he had based his defence of parliamentary sovereignty during the Exclusion Crisis. Taken together, these reveal the concatenation of Whig imperial principles, each of which needed to be maintained lest the logic of the entire chain be broken. The status of the Scottish and Irish crowns and the locus of sovereignty within England had much to do with each other, and everything to do with the English ancient constitution.

---

[105] Atwood, *Superiority*, p. 576.

[106] William Atwood, *The Scotch Patriot Unmask'd* (London, 1705), p. 46.

[107] *Acts of the Parliament of Scotland*, XI, pp. 221–2 and App., p. 81, cited by Ferguson, 'Imperial Crowns', p. 38n.

[108] Aside from using forgeries as Anderson was soon to show, Atwood was incorrect in contending that the term 'imperial crown' was conceived in Scotland only recently in order 'to establish a divine right in a popish successor': Ferguson, 'Imperial Crowns', p. 37. Moreover, the terms 'empire' and 'imperial crown' were in fact used in Scotland as early as 1469 (some sixty years before they were first used in England) and as recently as the reign of Charles II. *Acts of the Parliament of Scotland*, VII, pp. 86–7, and II, p. 95, cited by Ferguson, 'Imperial Crowns', p. 38n.

VI

Atwood's polite attack on the nature of the Scottish crown begot virulent replies, and from Scottish moderates most of all. These were men who were willing to work for a union, but only if Scotland entered as an equal kingdom. The most direct and scathing reply to Atwood was James Anderson's, *An Historical Essay Shewing that the Crown and Kingdom of Scotland is Imperial and Independent* (London, 1705). Anderson's purpose was clearly stated in his title, but his work, like that of many Scottish historians before him, suffered from a dearth of ancient Scottish manuscripts.[109] His rebuttal was therefore based mostly on his ability to show that many of the English charters upon which Atwood made his claims were forgeries. Anderson had a second agenda as well, which was to move this debate and others like it beyond the type of semi-bogus history in which Atwood, Ridpath and many other antiquarians dwelled.[110] In essence, it was a call for a more responsible form of historical investigation.[111] Anderson lived by his own words and one by one dismantled Atwood's 'proofs' of Scottish homage. In the process, he scoffed at the notion of William I not being a conqueror, or of his being the 'King of Britain'.[112] Anderson proclaimed that there is no 'greater Evidence of the Independency and Freedom of a Nation than the Liberties which we find our Ancestors exerted',[113] and marshalled his evidence accordingly. He cited Robert the Bruce and a host of other Scottish kings who clearly did not pay homage to England. However, Anderson was not trying to match Atwood point for point, nor ultimately was he as interested in promoting sound historical method as he was in asserting an equal footing upon which Scotland could enter a union with England.[114] But as he began by scolding Atwood for conspiring against a just and tenable union, so too he finished by accusing Atwood and his ilk of trying to 'Foment and Create Misunderstandings between two Protestant Independent Kingdoms, which I pray God may continue in Peace and Amity, while Sun and Moon endure'.[115]

Atwood and the absolutist Whigs were blind to Anderson's vision of a union of equals, even in its appeal to a common religion. Atwood

---

[109] This problem had plagued George Buchanan and his claims for an ancient Scottish constitution in the sixteenth century. It has been easier for Scottish antiquarians to disprove claims made about Scotland than to assert them. See Hugh Trevor-Roper, 'George Buchanan and the Ancient Scottish Constitution', *EHR*, Supplement 3 (1966).

[110] In 1703, Ridpath published a book of his own, *An Historical Account of the Right and Powers of the parliament of Scotland*, in which he tried to manufacture a Scottish Ancient Constitution grounded in parliamentary tradition.

[111] Anderson, *Historical Essay*, p. 15. [112] *Ibid.*, p. 125. [113] *Ibid.*, p. 257.

[114] *Ibid.*, pp. 279–80. [115] *Ibid.*, p. 280.

responded to the Scots in 1705 with *The Superiority and Direct Dominion of the Imperial Crown of England, over the Crown and Kingdom of Scotland, and the Divine Right of Succession to both Crowns Inseparable From the Civil, Reasserted*, and later in the same year, *The Scotch Patriot Unmask'd*. But Atwood and Anderson were talking past each other despite a shared desire for a limited monarchy.[116] As a result, Anderson and Atwood's competing Whig arguments fell on deaf ears as they crossed the River Tweed. It mattered little. Economic, religious and military concerns out-weighed constitutional matters for both countries, and the ancient constitutionalists remained oblivious to Anglo-Scottish *realpolitik*. In fact, the whole debate over the imperial crown edged towards satire and farce. Ridpath proposed an English army invasion in order to show its dire consequences for both nations,[117] and an anonymous reply to Atwood, entitled *A Pill for Pork Eaters: or a Scots Lancet for an English Swelling*, invoked past Scottish martial success against England. The author also accused Atwood of being a 'hackney-state-scribbler in ordinary to Old England'.[118]

Outside the realm of constitutional debate, Scotland had tried her hand in the late 1690s at gaining an overseas emporium on an isthmus in Panama and had failed. This disappointment led the Scots to 'bemoan the abuse of their imperium at the expense of English trading interests'.[119] It also narrowed the field of Scottish options for emerging from poverty within Europe. Ignoring Andrew Fletcher's pleas to think beyond the either/or options of union or independence,[120] the Scottish parliament, once it had gained satisfactory concessions, chose to take a chance with England. Atwood, meanwhile, had in fact articulated a genuine English concern. Incorporating a relatively poor Scotland was no great gain for England at first; but having a Catholic Stuart and a friend of France on the Scottish throne was potentially disastrous. Thus England was willing to give the Scots their minor concessions. Equal in name, the English were confident that, in economic and political terms, theirs was the superior kingdom. When the Union came about in 1707, it was not with any

---

[116] Colin Kidd, *Subverting Scotland's Past: Scottish Whig Historians and the Creation of an Anglo-British Identity* (Cambridge, 1993), p. 47.

[117] George Ridpath, *The reducing of Scotland by Arms, and Annexing it to England as a Province Considered* (London, 1705?).

[118] *A Pill for Pork Eaters: or a Scots Lancet for an English Swelling* (Edinburgh, 1705), p. 3. Robertson (ed.), *Union for Empire*, p. 211n, says the author was probably William Forbes or Alexander Penacuik.

[119] David Armitage, 'The Scottish Vision of Empire: Intellectual Origins of the Darien Venture, 1695–1707' in Robertson (ed.), *Union for Empire*, p. 117.

[120] See Hont, 'Free Trade' pp. 117–18; John Robertson, 'Andrew Fletcher's Vision of Union' in Mason (ed.), *Scotland and England*, pp. 203–25; and John Robertson, 'Union, State and Empire: The Britain of 1717 in its European Setting' in Lawrence Stone (ed.), *An Imperial State at War: Britain from 1689 to 1815* (London, 1994).

sense of common Britishness or shared Whig values.[121] Rather, it was the power of money, shared Protestantism (although not ecclesiology), the politics of the closet and, for at least a few, a positive vision of an incorporating Union that brought the two uncertain nations together.[122] The duke of Roxburghe was prosaic about the matter: 'Trade with most, Hanover with some, ease and security with others, together with a general aversion to civil disorders', which, he added, meant fear of an English military invasion.[123]

VII

Atwood apparently lived out his final years in tranquillity, or at least his pen was silent.[124] His last works in 1705 were harmless volleys at the Scots. Perhaps he spent the next seven years simply watching what in many ways he had hoped would come to pass. The parliament at Westminster (fully British after the Union with Scotland in 1707) was more powerful than ever before, not because Atwood and other English Whig polemicists had won the constitutional debates in which they had engaged, but because, as Andrew Fletcher foresaw, the metropolitan centre was successfully consolidating its growing political, economic and military might. In spite of this, the debates in which Atwood was involved were not entirely settled. The centre, hungry as it was, could not swallow everything. The kingdom of Ireland was as much a colony for most of the eighteenth century, while the colonies in North America remained largely outside the sphere of metropolitan control. When Westminster tried to rein them in, they successfully rebelled. Inspired by what they saw in America – and France in 1789 – the Irish made a similar attempt in the 1790s. Being closer to the centre and more politically divided, they failed. Only the Scots seem to have been largely satisfied with the status they gained in 1707 as part of the growing 'British' Empire. Much more so than Ireland, Scotland became part of the centre, enjoying her new-found prosperity, politeness, and other effects of commerce and Anglicisation.[125]

---

[121] Kidd, *Subverting Scotland's Past*, p. 49.
[122] Linda Colley, *Britons: Forging the Nation, 1707–1837* (New Haven, 1992), chs. 1 and 2; P. W. J. Riley, *The Union of England and Scotland: A Study in Anglo-Scottish Politics of the Eighteenth Century* (Totowa, NJ, 1978); Brian Levack, *The Formation of the British State: England, Scotland and the Union, 1603–1707* (Oxford, 1987); and John Robertson, 'An Elusive Sovereignty: The Course of the Union Debate in Scotland, 1698–1707' in Robertson (ed.), *Union for Empire*.
[123] P. H. Scott, *1707: The Union of England and Scotland* (Edinburgh, 1979), p. 27.
[124] Many sources including the *DNB* give Atwood's death date as *c.*1705. This is probably based on the fact that he did not publish any works after that year. However, his letter to the Board of Trade in 1709 disproves that date. Burns (ed.), *Cambridge History of Political Thought*, gives his year of death as 1712.
[125] Nicholas Phillipson, 'Politics, Politeness and the Anglicisation of Early Eighteenth-Century Scottish Culture' in Mason (ed.), *Scotland and England*, pp. 226–46.

Throughout his career, Atwood's claims were dubious, his methods were spurious and his style was repetitive. But one can see in his writings, and in the responses to them, the transformation from constitutional debates that were centred around a power struggle in England to those that were inspired by England's struggle for power abroad. In short, his works follow the successful conversion of the English imperial crown into the British Empire. The early stages of this transformation were confusing, and the debates were frequently emotional. Neither Atwood nor anyone else knew what was being created. And yet his involvement in every major centre–periphery debate of the period makes his work and the responses to it uniquely revealing of the changing (and changed) constitutional dynamics within England and the extended dominions of the English empire.

The complexity of the various constitutional and historical debates in the British Isles and the American colonies from the Exclusion Crisis to the Union of 1707, can hardly be exhausted in one chapter. However, Atwood's career illustrates the point that English claims over the peripheries were in fact conditioned by internal English disputes, and that the need to maintain the power of parliament in England had repercussions for those outside.[126] Atwood was, in a sense, getting and keeping England's domestic affairs in order by attempting to consolidate the empire on post-1688 English terms, ones in which confederal relations were not possible because power, supposedly shared between king, lords and commons, was actually understood in absolute terms.[127] The mid-seventeenth-century crisis had shown that there could be but one fount from which all power flowed; ambiguity and divisions of power led to violence and chaos. For Atwood, steeped as he was in the ancient constitution, ultimate power resided with the king-in-his-English-parliament (not a sovereign king *and* his English parliament). That is also why the arguments of fellow Whigs and Commonwealthmen in Ireland, Scotland and America could not be countenanced. If these kingdoms and colonies were subordinate to the one king, they must also be subordinate to that body from which the king received his position and power: the parliament of England. Therefore to claim parliamentary independence for Ireland, as Molyneux had done, was ultimately to deny English parliamentary power *in* England. After all, the centre and peripheries were stitched together by the same imperial thread.

---

[126] John Pocock, 'Conclusion: Contingency, Identity, Sovereignty' in A. Grant and K. Stringer (eds.), *Uniting the Kingdom: The Making of British History* (London, 1995), pp. 292–302.   [127] Kidd, *Subverting Scotland's Past*, pp. 45–9 and 73.

The Third Kingdom in its history: an
afterword

J. G. A. Pocock

The essays in this volume were delivered to a seminar sponsored by the
Folger Institute Centre for the History of British Political Thought, and
to that extent belong in the context currently termed 'the new British
history'.[1] This is a problematic term, since it denotes a problematic
history, and among its problems is the question whether it does so mis-
leadingly. On the one hand, Scottish and Irish historians rightly query
whether the term subjects their national histories to a paradigmatic structure still centred upon England;[2] though it is still unclear whether they
look to the autonomy of those histories or their partial submergence in a
regionalist Europe, which will either generate a history of its own or insist
on the irrelevance of history to its enterprise. Their mistrust of 'British
history' is partly based on an apprehension of the geopolitical term

---

[1] The bibliography of this field of study is growing rapidly. To that contained in Alexander
Grant and Keith J. Stringer (eds), *Uniting the Kingdom? The Making of British History*
(London, 1995) there may now be added Steven G. Ellis and Sarah Barber (eds.), *Conquest
and Union: Fashioning a British State, 1485–1725* (London, 1995), Brendan Bradshaw and
John Morrill (eds.) *The British Problem, c. 1534–1707: State Formation in the Atlantic
Archipelago* (London, 1996), Laurence Brockliss and David Eastwood (eds.), *A Union of
Multiple Identities: The British Isles, c.1750–c.1850* (Manchester, 1997), Brendan Bradshaw
and Peter Roberts (eds.), *British Consciousness and Identity: The Making of Britain,
1533–1707* (Cambridge, 1998), and Alexander Murdoch, *British History, 1660–1832:
National Identity and Local Culture* (London, 1998). This is a selective listing and does not
include the numerous and valuable works which have approached the subject from the
standpoint of literary history. The Folger Institute, having sponsored J. G. A. Pocock
(ed.), *The Varieties of British Political Thought, 1500–1800* (Cambridge, 1994), which is a
mainly English history, went on to sponsor Roger A. Mason (ed.), *Scots and Britons:
Scottish Political Thought and the Union of 1603* (Cambridge, 1994) and John Robertson
(ed.), *A Union for Empire: Political Thought and the Union of 1707* (Cambridge, 1995). Hiram
Morgan (ed.), *Political Ideology in Ireland, 1541–1641* (Dublin, 1999) inaugurates a series on
Irish political thought, of which this is the second volume and Sean Connolly (ed.),
Patriots and Radicals: Political Ideas in Eighteenth-Century Ireland (Dublin, forthcoming)
will be the third. The holdings of the Folger Shakespeare Library delimit the research
seminars that the Centre for the History of British Political Thought sponsors; they do not
therefore extend much beyond the third quarter of the eighteenth century.
[2] See Keith Brown, 'British History: A Sceptical Comment' in Ronald G. Asch (ed.), *Three
Nations – a Common History? England, Scotland, Ireland and British History, c.1600–1900*
(Bochum, 1993); Willy Maley, review article in *History Ireland*, 4 (1996), p.55.

'British Isles', which has been shared by those responsible for mounting the former programme to the point where some have proposed replacing the latter term by 'the Atlantic archipelago'.[3] From another wing of the debate, however, has come a sternly English denunciation of this term of art, as entailing a defeatist willingness to abandon the familiar 'British Isles':[4] a reaction on the whole to be welcomed, as a reminder that 'British history' of England and the English must recognise both their recurrently dominant role and the fact that this role is not the whole of their history.

'British history' is multi-national: a history of nations forming and deforming one another and themselves. It implies the proposition that no nation's history can be understood without that of its interaction with other histories; that national histories have been shaped in the process of shaping other histories and in interaction with the self-shaping of others; and that the identities thus shaped have been so far interactive that there is a high degree of indeterminacy about them and their shaping in a process which never attains finality. We are all left wondering about the identities – in this case national – that have been shaped for us; and this is as it should be. But 'British history' does not lead to the fashionable if under-examined proposition that national history has no meaning and is now to be written out of existence, replaced by a history that recognises only transgressive experiences annihilating the frontiers between identities which they cross. The very concept of transgression implies that there are frontiers to be crossed, and that crossing them both affirms and subjects to scrutiny the identities they demarcate. That every identity is contestable, interactive and negotiable means neither that it does not exist nor that it has not a history. If it is not the whole of the story, it has been part of the shaping of the part of the story that it is.

It follows that any political, national or other community which has generated an image of its own identity as existing over time requires two kinds of history: the one autocentric, a record of how its inhabitants have dealt with one another over time, and the experiences they have undergone in establishing the bases of their existing community; the other heterocentric, a record of how encounters with others, whom they have ruled or been ruled by, have contributed to the shaping and present character of both the 'self' community and the 'others', autonomous or not, now contiguous with it. These two histories can never be separated, but

---

[3] I may have been the first to propose this term in my articles of 1974–5. See also Richard S. Tompson, *The Atlantic Archipelago: A Political History of the British Isles* (Lewiston/Queenston, 1986), p. 1, n1.

[4] See Mark Nicholls, *A History of the Modern British Isles, 1529–1603: The Two Kingdoms* (Oxford, 1999), p.321. Dr Nicholls appears to write on the Eltonian premise that the history of the state is what matters and explains itself; Ireland is therefore a 'shadow kingdom', and its history marginal to that of Scotland and England.

can never be identical; their *dramatis personae* and their plots must overlap, but are organised into distinct narratives. As historians we need the double tongue able to tell both concurrently, but we cannot afford to believe that either annuls the other. In the present case, it is evident that Irish history is not part of British history, because Irish people read it, quite correctly, as resisting inclusion in a British community and ending in an independent association with it; but that it is part of British history for essentially the same reason, namely that neither Irish nor British history – and the same may be said of English and Scottish history – is intelligible without the constant presence of all these peoples to one another.[5] In the same way, though within a different pattern of pressures, the history of England – that is, of how 'England' came to be – is formed both by the dealings those now accounted English have had with one another, and by the interactions they have had with other peoples, some of them included within the narratives constituting 'British history'. This last can be considered, first the history of a series of encounters between janus-headed beings, each regardant of both self and other; second, the history of a problematic, that of whether the encounter between these beings shall assume or retain the form of a lasting association. By calling this a problematic, we provide that any answer to the question may be kept in view, since the end is not yet. 'British history' is neither a concealed imperial enterprise, nor the blueprint of a new confederation, nor the prelude to a 'break-up' or 'unravelling' of Britain;[6] it is the history of how all these possibilities have from time to time come to exist.

In the present volume, the image of an Ireland altogether outside the structures of authority existing in the larger archipelago is present but evanescent, existing in the writings of Conor O'Mahony in Portugal or in the visions of the 'Gaelic Maccabees' in Spanish service. The dominant theme is the obstinate loyalism of the Catholic Old English towards the Stuart, but not the Tudor, occupants of the English throne, and it is here that we are entitled to make, and at the same time to question, the claim that in this part of the story 'Irish history' was part of 'British history' – the term 'British' being at all points contestable and self-contestatory.

---

[5] This is the point at which one is regularly instructed – often in peremptory tones – that English history is to be studied in its 'European' context; that is, in the setting of its relations with its peninsular rather than its insular neighbours. There seems little point in bowing down to this idol. The 'British problem' was archipelagic in character; Spanish, French and Dutch actors intervened in it for good reasons, but it was not produced by their reason of state. The archipelago is neither more nor less 'European' than the subcontinent known by that name.

[6] Tom Nairn, *The Breakup of Britain* (London, 1977); Raphael Samuel, *Island Stories: Unravelling Britain* (London, 1988). These two publicists were not pursuing the same objectives.

The central assertion of the Old English was that Ireland was organically connected with the English crown but that the management of this link lay with Irish counsellors and councils of that crown. The English crown could be thought of as 'British' from the moment of its dynastic but not juridical union with the crown of Scotland, and James VI's Scottishness seems to have made it easier for his Irish subjects to accept him. Nevertheless, the crown of Scotland played no part in the Irish rhetoric reported here, and what they accepted was the crown of England, remaining so even after it had become the crown of 'Great Britain' – an early case of that practice of saying 'Britain' and meaning 'England' with which we are so persistently concerned. Scots settled in Ireland and behaved as Scots after doing so, but brought no flowers of the Scottish crown with them.

How far the older English populations of Ireland referred to themselves as 'British' or 'Britons' is not very clear. This is not surprising, given the rapid changes which 'British' and 'Britain' were undergoing; from being words used by Welsh authors to assert their autonomy within the English kingdom in which they had been incorporated in 1536, these terms were being switched towards denoting the new and limited unity between England and Scotland, forming that *Magna Britannia* to which John Mair had punningly alluded in his *Historia Majoris Britanniae* two generations before.[7] The Irish claim was that their polity constituted a third kingdom, autonomous though subject to the crown of England now linked with that of Scotland, to form the metaphorical rather than juristic entity known by the name of 'Great Britain'. Rather than allow the contestable validity of the term 'British history' to dominate our thinking, it may be better to concede that the Irish claim and the manner of English response to it situate Irish history in the period we have come to term that of the 'Three Kingdoms' – a term as applicable and contestable when applied to Hiram Morgan's volume as to Jane Ohlmeyer's.

The term is contestable, as we learn from the sub-titles of the first two volumes of a new *History of the Modern British Isles*, respectively 'The Two Kingdoms', ending in 1603, and 'The Double Crown', ending in 1707.[8] The language is correct; this was what existed in law, since there was no crown of Ireland. Yet on the presumption that 'British history' is a history of contestation rather than decision, the contention that Ireland was a kingdom was often enough made, recognised and resisted to give heuristic value to the concept of an 'Age of the Three Kingdoms', beginning either in 1541, when the lordship of Ireland was erected into a kingdom,

---

[7] Published 1521; ed. Scottish Historical Society (Edinburgh, 1892).
[8] Nicholls, *A History of the Modern British Isles*, and David L. Smith, *A History of the Modern British Isles, 1603–1707: The Double Crown* (Oxford, 1998).

or in 1603, when the dynastic union faced a single monarch with the problems of exercising kingship in both major islands of the archipelago. This 'Age', including the 'Wars of the Three Kingdoms' from 1637 to 1652 and from 1688 to 1691, may be held to last until 1707, when a 'First Age of Union' begins, followed by a 'Second' lasting from 1801 to 1921. What name to give the succeeding age it would be premature to determine, since once again the end is not yet; but a working periodisation of 'British history' is emerging. To accept 'Three Kingdoms' rather than 'Double Crown' has the advantage of conceding that there is an Irish history made in part by Irish historians, who debate whether Stuart Ireland is to be thought of as a distinct kingdom or an English colony. The answer may be that both readings had validity in the seventeenth century, and therefore for us today; and that there was a complex interplay between them, so that neither excludes the other.

The persistent loyalism of the Old English appears to have two faces and is not merely quixotic (indeed, its windmills were often real giants whose fierceness could not be denied). On its religious face, Irish loyalism was Catholic and made the king an offer he must find it necessary to resist. It invited him to act as the protector of the Catholic majority in his third kingdom, but did so in the knowledge that as king of England he was supreme head and governor of the church in that kingdom, and was committed to the support of a Protestant and Episcopal Church of Ireland of which he was head in the same way. There could be no question, therefore, that James or Charles might become a monster of ecclesiastical triplicity: an Anglican head of state and church in England, a Presbyterian head in Scotland (where he was the only king of a Calvinist kingdom in Europe) and a Catholic king in Ireland. Not even Leviathan might be equal to this triplicity, and the giant of English political philosophy was English enough to pay little attention to the nature of multiple monarchy. Irish loyalism offered allegiance in return for protection; but could the kingdom so defined be more than a protectorate?

Leviathan was a figure born of civil war. Four decades previously, James VI and I might have found his third and Catholic kingdom easier to rule had his ecumenical ambitions for a reconciliation of Christendom borne any fruit at all; we have recently been reminded of what these were and on what presuppositions they must rest.[9] They entailed the vision that every Catholic kingdom might approximate the Gallican position in which the pope received spiritual obedience but exercised no civil authority, and the authority of a general council outweighed his. There is a counter-tridentine vision of the early seventeenth century, helping

[9] W. B. Patterson, *King James VI and I and the Unity of Christendom* (Cambridge, 1997).

account for the reception accorded to Paolo Sarpi; and to understand James' overtures we have to think ourselves back into a world in which lay Catholics and regally minded clergy might be prepared to downplay the papal power in every way possible. Not only, however, was there the claim to a deposing power; there was the resilient ultramontanism whose triumph at Trent Sarpi had recounted; and it is easy for the British historian to tell the story in terms of two immovable objects – papal supremacy and English royal supremacy – brought, however unwillingly, into collision, in such a way that any offer to mitigate the latter produced the paradox of rebellion against it by those so bent on maintaining it that they saw mitigation as a surrender to the former. On another face of the looking-glass world of British politics, the Irish Confederates went into rebellion against the crown because they feared it was about to lose authority, and found their chief enemies to be those determined to restore the crown's authority by parliamentary action independent of it. The logic of rebellion was always more complicated than even Hobbes understood.

Once we introduce the supremacy, however, the story becomes inescapably English-dominated. The War of the Three Kingdoms was long known as 'the English Civil War' for the reason that there was an English civil war, which the English were resolved to settle among themselves, admitting no interference from the associated kingdoms; a war over the location and definition of sovereignty in church and state.[10] They were less intent on maintaining English sovereignty over Scotland or even Ireland than to deny Scots and Irish any role in determining the future of the English kingdom. Allan Macinnes traces the history of the Scottish covenanting attempt to impose a settlement 'British' in the sense of a Presbyterianisation of both church-states in the larger island. Though it failed, it was not unthinkable, since the Church of England could be thought of in Protestant Calvinist terms; and its intellectual symbol was James Ussher, Church of Ireland archbishop of Armagh. The Irish Confederacy, being Catholic, had no 'British' or 'Three Kingdoms' solution open to it. Short of an *ecclesia hibernica* Catholic without being papal, it must aim at either an independent kingdom guaranteed by a foreign prince – it is here that Conor O'Mahony appears the realist who demands the impossible – or a protectorate and subordinate kingdom in which Catholics enjoyed the protection of an Anglican sovereign.

To pursue a redefined subordination by means of armed rebellion appears in hindsight obviously foredoomed, the measure of a colonial status in which even the Catholic Old English found themselves. The

---

[10] Pocock, 'The Atlantic Archipelago and the War of the Three Kingdoms' in Bradshaw and Morrill (eds.), *The British Problem*, pp. 172–91.

formula helps us, however, to pursue the complexities and even confusions of the Confederacy's war as one of the Wars – the plural re-asserts itself – of the Three Kingdoms: a conflict both social, in the sense of one fought among a group of kingdoms in disagreement over the terms of their association, and civil, in the sense of one fought within the Irish kingdom to determine the relations among its inhabitants.[11] The Irish conflict, furthermore, became entangled in both the English and the Scottish wars it had helped precipitate. Alasdair MacColla's campaigns in Argyll and east of the North Channel can be seen in three ways: as part of Montrose's Anglo-Scottish strategy of creating civil war in Scotland; as pursuing in that kingdom the strategic aims (whatever they were) of the Confederacy; and as conducting a strictly ethnic war of Clan Donald against Clan Campbell. MacColla cannot be relegated to a clan world exterior to the state, but there was a clan dimension to what he did.

Within the multiple perspectives of British history, there is an Irish history in which the Confederacy is, or is not, a blind alley, part of the larger failure of the Old English to secure a status for a Catholic Ireland within the multiple monarchy of an otherwise Protestant Stuart dynasty; an enterprise repeatedly wrecked by the English, not only necessitated to maintain control over Ireland but bound to fear any multi-state or multi-church solution as threatening the unity in sovereignty of king and parliament which they had fought civil wars among themselves to maintain. Given Ireland, and given the union of the crowns, the empire of the English over themselves was inseparable from their empire in the archipelago and beyond it in the Atlantic and the American seaboard. The Second War of the Three Kingdoms – which Dr Ohlmeyer prefers to call the War of the Three Kings – was not a general collapse into wars of religion, but the archipelagic face of a European conflict, in which England, Scotland and Ireland became involved in William III's struggle against Louis XIV for supremacy in the Low Counties and lower Germany. At the same time, however, it transformed that conflict, by bringing about the construction of the British fiscal, military and parliamentary state capable of acting as a power in Europe and at the same time exercising empire in Britain, in the archipelago and beyond Europe in America, India and the global oceans.[12] The problems of empire in the Tudor sense

---

[11] For the distinction between 'social' and 'civil' war, *ibid.*

[12] Pocock, 'The Significance of 1688: Some Reflections on Whig History' in Robert Beddard (ed.), *The Revolutions of 1688: The Andrew Browning Lectures, 1988* (Oxford, 1991), pp. 271–92; 'Standing Army and Public Credit: The Institutions of Leviathan' in Dale Hoak and Mordechai Feingold (eds.), *The World of William and Mary: Anglo-Dutch Perspectives on the Revolution of 1688–89* (Stanford, 1996), pp. 87–103.

J. G. A. Pocock

persisted, but their context was enlarged. We enter the First Age of Union, with its climaxes and crises in 1776, 1798 and 1801.

In the cycle of wars from 1688 to 1691 – bloodless in England, civil in Scotland, wars of renewed conquest in Ireland – the distinctively Catholic enterprise of the Old English is held to have ended at Limerick and in its aftermath. It might seem, then, that the history of Catholic loyalism to a Protestant dynasty had met the giant behind the windmill; but Irish history is more complex even than that. In the history of word and discourse, to which volumes originating with a Centre for the History of British Political Thought are necessarily committed, the Old English and the Confederates are seen as leaving something behind them, to be used by others than themselves in history, both Irish, British and American: the claim, originating in the circumstances of the kingdom of Ireland set up in 1534, that this kingdom and its parliament were subject to the crown but not to the parliament of England, so that the crown's authority in Ireland was to be exercised with Irish consent in an Irish parliament. One head and many bodies, or as many heads as there were bodies? Could Leviathan be a hydra, or was this a *monstrum informe, ingens, horridum*? King James had not needed a Hobbes to give him his answer; but the claim was to be pressed again, even while the increasing incorporation of English crown in English parliament – as much a remedy as a cause of civil war – made it seem increasingly monstrous to English understandings. The practical impact of William Molyneux may well have been small, but in retrospect his symbolic importance must appear great; in 1698, a year when Andrew Fletcher was active in Scotland and the English parliament was reacting against the demands of the state being created by King William's wars, he shows us a claim originally Old English passing into the hands and pens of Protestant settlers discontented with the status of a kingdom now their own. In 1707 the Scots were to surrender the opportunity to make such a claim, failing to insist that their union with England should be 'federative' rather than 'incorporating'; and when the issue resurfaced in Ireland about 1780, it was to be in a context where American colonial assemblies had claimed that they too were connected with the crown but not the parliament of England, throwing off the crown only when it would not separate itself from that parliament and inaugurating a third cycle of wars, and this time secessions, within the empire – an empire, be it noted, far more than colonial.[13]

The Irish and American crises are not to be separated in the 'British

---

[13] Pocock, 'Empire, State and Confederation: The War of American Independence as a Crisis in Multiple Monarchy' in John Robertson (ed.), *A Union for Empire: Political Thought and the Union of 1707* (Cambridge, 1995), pp. 318–48.

history' of the late eighteenth century; but that era brings to an end the 'First Age of Union', and it has not been the business of this volume to travel beyond 1707 and the beginnings of that era, which in Irish history is also the Age of the Ascendancy. A further volume is to carry us through that age, towards the maelstrom of 1776–1801; but the purpose of this one has been to effect a transition from the Wars of the Three Kingdoms to the War of the Three Kings and the brink of the age succeeding it. To make it a fully 'British' history, there might perhaps have been a sequel to Allan Macinnes' chapter, exploring in depth the politics of post-covenanting Scotland from the Cromwellian occupation to the Williamite Revolution and the Union which followed; and this might have been in part an Irish history, if the Scots in Ulster were shown responding to what they saw happening in their kingdom of origin. In the next age, again, there can be seen a Dublin Enlightenment visibly English and Whig, an Ulster Enlightenment visibly Scottish, both with their affiliations in America.[14] The focus of this volume, however, has been on Irish history in so far as it was in British history; that is to say, on the history of the Third Kingdom.

Each of the peoples, or nations, of whom 'British history' is made up exists, it is here argued, in two overlapping but distinguishable histories. One is the history of its 'self', as that self has been fashioned in both the relations between those who have come to be its component members and concurrently in relations with 'others' who have not. The other is a history of the relations between selves and others of which its self-fashioning may be seen as a part, but which is not to be written from the standpoint of any 'self' at all, whether individual or comprehensive. In the period with which this volume has been concerned, it might be said that the Third Kingdom – aka 'Ireland' – had not fashioned a coherent self or yet come to exist in a history of its own; both because of the presence of distinct and bitterly contending cultures – this has been a history of Gaelic, Latin and English language, and of Catholic and both forms of British Protestant religion – and because of powerful exterior forces, represented by the English, which was increasingly a British, crown, insisting that the kingdom of Ireland was a dependent, even a conquered, kingdom and to that extent not the author of its own history. From Captain MacMorris to Stephen Dedalus, there are voices in the literature of Ireland expressing the uncertainties of colonial and post-colonial identity. Yet there was a kingdom and the opportunity to fashion it, and this volume contains evidence of vigorous and lasting efforts in that direction.

---

[14] Molyneux and Viscount Molesworth might be held to stand for the former, Francis Hutcheson for the latter.

Leaving aside – perhaps at some risk – the problems of defining a Catholicism which could be neither royal nor fully papal, there has been a history of settler nationalisms able to claim that what indigenous nationalism there was could be comprehended within them. A fully Gaelic nationalism drawing on pre-Norman memories being elusive and little encouraged by the structure of the kingdom of 1541, we have been left with the claim of the Old English to be the true 'Irish nation', founded on the acceptance of the crown by both Norman and Irish consentients as far back as the twelfth century. Whatever the O'Neills, O'Donnells and O'Mahonys may have thought of it, this was a settler nationalism, though the Old English had been in Ireland long enough to be thought, and think themselves, *Hibernicis ipsis Hiberniores*. It issued in the most characteristic of settler nationalist claims, that to the independence of their own parliament in conducting their relations with a multi-national crown of the Three Kingdoms. Here it collided with the central Anglocentricity of British history: the royal supremacy and the civil war producing a compulsive unity and incorporation of English crown with English parliament, meaning that no Irish, Scottish or American legislature could claim a separate relationship with the crown without seeming to threaten the integrity of the English, as well as the United, Kingdom. This is a problem from which in the year 2000 we have by no means escaped, though we are seeking to redraw it.

By the year 1698 the theses of settler nationalism were beginning to pass – not without vigorous counter-moves – into the discourse of a 'Protestant nation' claiming to be at the point of absorbing what remained of its Old Irish and Old English predecessors, so that all Irish could be said to be English. This was no less a nationalism than a colonialism; colonists as well as colonised have their quarrels with the authority that sent them out and seeks to pursue them, and may base claims to autonomy on their wars and treaties with the indigenous peoples preceding them. Thus Peruvian creoles claimed to be the heirs of the Inca, and an Irish Protestant nationalism sought to base itself in a Catholic, Norman and Milesian past. This however, was a phenomenon little seen before 1780 or thereabouts. Molyneux may hint to us how it came to be achieved, but if we take the theme of the present volume to be the assertion and defeat of the Catholic Old English attempt to speak in the name of the kingdom of Ireland, it must be the task of a succeeding volume to pursue Protestant, including Presbyterian, settler nationalisms towards the American and Irish crisis of the last quarter of the eighteenth century. In the second half of the seventeenth century and the First Age of Union, we listen to a diversity of voices fashioning a diversity of selves: a clamour, not a consensus or even a debate.

Index

The following abbreviations are used:
abp   archbishop
bp   bishop
Co.   County
d.   died
LL   lord lieutenant
LD   lord deputy
n   note
OFM   Franciscan
RC   Roman Catholic
SJ   Society of Jesus, Jesuit

Aberdeen, Scotland, 197, 211
Act of Classes (1649), 215, 216
Act of Proscription (1647), 213
Act of Security (1703), 263
Act of Settlement (1701), 262
Acts of Settlement (1652, 1662, 1665), 20, 58, 59, 115, 150
adventurers, 58
Adventurers' Act (1642), 20, 47, 48, 49, 53, 100, 105, 110
Alexander, Sir William, 221
Allestree, Richard, 115
American colonies, 16, 18, 223, 228, 232, 233, 237–8, 240, 246, 251, 254, 258–61, 269–70, 278; *also see* Massachusetts
Anabaptists, 213
Anderson, James, 267, 268
Anglo-Irish, *see* Old English
Anglo-Irish relations, 2, 15, 18–21, chapter 2 *passim*, 83, 85, 86, 87–8, 89, 93, 98, 106, 123, 167, 222, 225, 231–2, 234, 251–3, 254–8; *also see* civilisation; conquest; kingship; parliament; Stuarts
Anglo-Scottish relations, 221–2, 231–2, 235–7, 239, 240–3, 253–4, 261–9; *also see* Covenanters; Union
Annals of the Four Masters, 4
Anne, queen of England, Scotland and Ireland (d. 1714), 260, 263, 264, 266

Anne of Denmark, wife of James I and VI, 167
Annesley, Francis, 100, 103, 233, 235
Annesley Case, 103
Antrim, county, 28, 212
Antrim, earl of, *see* MacDonnell, Randal
Aphorismical Discovery of Treasonable Faction, 19
apocalypticisim, 8, 186, 197n, 198, 212, 217
architecture, 10–11
Argyll, earls of, *see* Campbell, Archibald
Argyllshire, Scotland, 28
armed forces of Dublin government, *see* 'new army'
armed forces of English government, 67, 69, 74, 82
armed forces of Irish, *see* Kilkenny, Confederation of
armed forces of Scots, *see* Covenanters
Arminianism, 193, 195, 197
Atwood, William (d. 1712), 16, 20, 244–7, 248, 250, 251, 252, 254, 256, 257, 258–61, 263, 264, 265, 266, 267, 268, 269, 270
    The History and Reasons, 96, 255
Austria, 210
Austrian Habsburgs, 194, 210

Bacon, Richard, 234
Baltic, 214, 230
Bandon, Co. Cork, 62
Baptists, 56, 66, 69
Barbados, 66, 71
bard, *see* poets/poems
Bardon, Nicholas, 234
Barnewall, family, 59
Barry, family, 62, 63, 64
Bellarmine, Robert, SJ, 22, 160, 162, 163
Bellings, Sir Richard (d. 1677), 7, 26, 120, 172–3
Bellomont, governor of New York, 259, 260
Benburb, battle of (1646), 172, 178, 213

Bermingham, John, 121
Bible, 110, 113, 116, 117, 127
    Old Testament, 60, 159, 163, 172, 176,
        177, 182, 185, 186
Bill of Rights (1689), 102
Binker, John, 124
Birch, John, 89
Bishops' Wars (1639, 1640), 122, 204, 206,
    207
'black oath', 44, 206, 212, 213
Blair, Robert, 196
Blake, Sir Richard, 134
Blood's Plot (1663), 116, 219
Board of Trade, 86, 239
Boate, Gerald, 17
Bohemia, 210
Bolton, Sir Richard, lord chancellor (d.
    1648), 39, 49, 50–1, 92, 96, 100
book trade, 29, 115
books, see print culture
books of survey and distribution, 64
Bordeaux, France, 133
Borlase, Edmund, 17, 29, 127
Bourke, Thomas, 29
Boyle, family, 61
Boyle, Michael, bp of Cork, 31
Boyle, Richard (d. 1643), 1st earl of Cork,
    61, 62
Boyle, Roger (d. 1679), Lord Broghill, earl
    of Orrery, 28, 64, 73, 115, 116, 118,
    119–20
Boyne, battle of (1690), 85
Bradford, William, 80
Brady, Dr Robert, 249, 250
Brewster, Sir Francis, 87, 238–9
Britain, see Anglo-Irish relations; Anglo-
    Scottish relations
British Empire, 221, 222–3, 224, 225, 230,
    231, 246, 269–70, 278
    England's role in, 245–6
    Ireland's role in, 223–4, 257
    Scotland's role in, 224, 235–7, 267–9
Broghill, Lord, see Boyle, Roger
Brouncker, Sir Henry, 148
Bruce, Robert the, 204, 267
Buchanan, George, 201
Burke, family, 188
Burke, Richard (d. 1635), 4th earl of
    Clanricard, 10, 29, 164
Burkhead, Henry, 118
Burnell, Henry, 120–1, 122, 124
Burnet, Gilbert, bp, 31, 102
Butler, James (d. 1688), 12th earl and 1st
    duke of Ormond, LL (1643–9 and
    1662–9), 26, 47, 49–50, 52, 111, 115,
    117, 118, 119–20, 123, 124, 169, 170

Butler, Richard (d. 1686), 1st earl of Arran,
    124

Cahir, Co. Tipperary, 133
Callaghan, John, 25
Calvinism, 193, 194, 197n, 201, 210, 275
Calvin's Case, 95, 96, 99
Cambrensis, Giraldus, 4, 20, 134, 136, 141
Camden, William, 134
Cameronians, 218, 219
Campbell, family (Clan Campbell), 277
Campbell, Archibald (d. 1661), Lord
    Lorne, 8th earl and 1st marquis of
    Argyll, 192–3, 205, 211, 214, 217, 219
Campbell, Archibald (d. 1685), 9th earl of
    Argyll, 219
Campion, Edmund, 67
Canterbury, abp of, see Laud, William
Carew, Sir George, 9
Carribean, 223, 228
cartography, 8
Cary, John, 86, 237, 238, 240
Catholic church/religion, 2, 22–3, 26, 27,
    119, 144, 147, 155, 159, 166, 168, 170,
    174, 194, 224, 276, 280
    bishops, 166, 168
    clergy, 25, 134
    also see Counter-Reformation; Kilkenny,
        Confederation of; Rinuccini
Catholic writers, 4, 16–17, 21–6
Cattle Acts (1665, 1667), 3, 100, 111, 227,
    237
censorship, 29, 115, 163
'cessation of arms' (1643), 109, 119
Chamberlain, Dr Robert, OFM, 180
Charles I, king of England, Scotland and
    Ireland (d. 1649), 2, 15, 24, 44–5, 46,
    47, 51, 121, 147, 156, 167, 169, 183, 192,
    193, 195, 201, 206, 207, 208, 214, 215,
    216, 275
    opponents of, 37–8, 40, 191, 197, 198,
        200, 202, 203, 204, 206
    see also kingship; Stuarts
Charles II, king of England, Scotland and
    Ireland (d. 1685), 25–6, 51, 53, 111, 119,
    125, 147, 149, 150, 154, 193, 216, 218,
    248; also see kingship; Stuarts
Christian IV, king of Denmark-Norway,
    214
Church of England, 193, 210, 276
Church of Ireland, 117, 196, 197n, 219,
    275
civilisation/civility, 4, 8–14, 16, 59–60, 77,
    79–81, 142, 224; also see colonisation
Clan Campbell, see Campbells
Clan Donald, see MacDonalds

Clandeboy, viscount, *see* Hamilton
Clarke, Edward, 87, 104
Clement VIII, pope, 156, 178
Clonmel, Co. Tipperary, 24
Clotworthy, Sir John, 37
Coke, Sir Edward (d. 1634), 40, 95, 96, 99
Colonels' Plot, 182–3
'colonial nationalism', 35, 243, 258
colonies/colonisation, 4–5, 16, 111, 126, 151,
    176, 223, 225, 233, 234, 240
  by English in Ireland, 56, 57, 60, 72–3, 77,
    101, 237, 238
  in America, 77, 79, 237, 251; *also see*
    American colonies
Commission for the Remedy of Defective
    Titles, 36, 145
Committee for Both Kingdoms, 214
Committee of Estates, *see* Tables
Commonwealth and Protectorate, 51, 66,
    119, 217
Company of Scotland, 236, 237, 239, 240
composite monarchy, 35, 37, 150, 151,
    228–9, 234, 235
confederation, 207, 208, 210, 211, 212–13;
    also see Kilkenny, Confederation of
confederalism, *see* Union, confederal
Confederation of Kilkenny, *see* Kilkenny,
    Confederation of
Confession of Faith, 195
Connaught, 188
  proposed plantation in, 36, 37–8, 41
  transplantation to, 58, 59
conquest, nature of, 19–21, 42, 50, 74–5, 94,
    95, 96, 97–8, 101, 102, 135, 145, 148,
    152–3, 159–60, 255-6, 257
  Norman conquest, 246, 247, 248, 255
Conroy, Florence, OFM, 158, 179, 180, 184,
    187
continent, 22, 25, 29, 54
  Irish exiles on, 22-3, 158, 165, 176–9, 187
contractual nature of government/kingship,
    15, 19, 21, 23n, 98, 138, 141, 146–7,
    162–3, 186, 194, 201–2, 250
Convention (1660), 51–2
conventicling movement, 15, 191, 195, 196,
    197, 198, 199, 212, 217, 219
Coote, Sir Charles (d. 1642), 7, 118
Cork, city, 30, 118, 125
Cork, county, 16, 17, 57, 60, 61, 64, 66, 73,
    78
Cork, earl of, *see* Boyle, Roger
Cornbury, lord, 258–9, 260, 261
Counter-Reformation, 194, 200, 212
  ideology, 3, 6, 17, 22–3, 54, 133, 158, 179
court (in London), 123, 126
Court of Chancery, 85, 89

Court of High Commission, 36
Court of King's Bench, 95
Court of Castle Chamber, 36, 38, 44
Covenant, 194, 195
  National, 44, 191, 199, 201, 203, 204,
    206
  Solemn League and, 191, 209, 210, 211,
    212, 213, 214, 219
Covenanters, Scottish, 15, 40, 191, 192, 205,
    209, 214-15, 217; *also see* Tables
  army, 206, 209, 212, 213, 214
  aid to English parliament, 207, 290; *also*
    see London, Treaty of
covenanting ideology, 15, 19, 192, 198, 205,
    209–10, 212-13, 217, 218
Cox, Sir Richard, 7, 232
Craig, Sir Thomas, 262, 264
Cromwell, Henry (d. 1674), LD (1657), LL
    (1658), 66, 69
Cromwell, Oliver (d. 1658), LL (1649–53),
    51, 59, 63, 64, 65, 74, 78, 215, 216, 217
Cromwellian land-settlement, 51, 53, 58–9;
    also see Adventurers' Act;
    transplantation
Cromwellian occupation of Scotland, 191,
    216, 217

Darcy, Patrick (d. 1668), 35, 41–4, 47, 110,
    112, 115, 127, 134; *also see*
    'Declaration'; 'Queries'
  An Argument, 3, 15, 30, 35n, 48, 92, 99,
    106
Davenant, Sir William, 239
Davies, Sir John (d. 1626), 16n, 20, 31, 40,
    43, 67, 75, 146, 147, 253
Dease, Thomas, RC bp of Meath, 166
'Declaration how, and by what means, the
    laws and statutes of England . . .', 48,
    51, 52, 84, 91, 92, 96, 97, 110, 116
Declaratory Act (1689), 55
Declaratory Act (1720), 88, 231
Dempsey, Edward, RC bp of Leighlin,
    172–3
Denmark, 230
depositions ('1641 depositions'), 63, 108–9,
    113
Derry (Londonderry), 114, 122, 212, 219
Desmond, earls of, *see* FitzGerald
Dickson, David, 199
Dieppe, France, 134
diplomacy, 155n
dissemination of political ideas, 27–31,
    111–17, 243; *also see* book trade;
    education; print culture; sermons;
    theatre
Dodwell, Henry, 92

Domville, William, 52, 53, 84, 96
  'A Disquisition touching that Great
    Question . . .', 84, 91, 92, 93, 94, 95, 97
Donegal, county, 212
Dopping, Anthony, bp of Meath, 94
Douai, France, 134
Douglas, Robert, 216, 217
Down, county, 44, 113, 212
Down Survey, 9
Drake, James, 263
Drury, John, 210, 211
Dryden, John, 117
dual monarchy, 102
Dublin, 29, 35, 51, 65, 66, 93, 110, 112, 114,
  115, 117, 119, 122, 123, 126, 219, 257
Dugdale, Sir William, 248
Dunbar, battle of (1650), 216
Dungan's Hill, battle of (1647), 172
Dunkirk, Spanish Netherlands, 78
Dunluce, Co. Antrim, 10
Duns Scotus, John, 22n, 186
Dutch, 211
  revolt, 185
Dutch Republic, 207, 227, 230, 235, 279

East Indies, 235, 236, 239
Edinburgh, 195, 198, 199, 204, 207, 215,
  216, 263, 266
education, 27, 81, 118–19
Edward III, king of England (d. 1377), 94
Eliot, John, 57, 77
Elizabeth I, queen of England and Ireland
  (d. 1603), 158, 167, 265
'engagement' (1648), 191, 215, 217
England, 78, 110, 191, 227, 235
English Civil Wars, see Wars of the Three
  Kingdoms
Enlightenment, 237, 279
Episcopacy, 65, 191, 193, 195, 196, 197n,
  200, 219
Esmond, family, 59
Essex, England, 87, 104
Exclusion Crisis, 248, 270
Exeter, England, 87
exiles, see continent; refugees

Farquhar, George, 28, 122
Fenton, Sir William, 73
Fife, Scotland, 195
Filmer, Sir Robert, 248
FitzGerald family, 188
  earls of Desmond, 46
FitzGerald, Thomas, 157
Fitzmaurice, James, 46, 157, 179
Five Articles (1618–21), 195, 197, 200
Flanders, see Spanish Netherlands

Fleetwood, Charles (d. 1692), LD (1654),
  59, 63, 65, 66, 69
Fletcher, Andrew (d. 1716), 230, 241, 242,
  253, 262, 266, 268-9, 278
Flight of the Earls (1607), 22
France, 100, 132, 134, 211, 230, 237, 261,
  268, 269
Franciscan order, 176, 179, 181, 182, 183,
  186, 187
Frankfurt, Germany, 134
French, Nicholas (d. 1678), RC bp of
  Ferns, 7, 8, 29, 31, 172

Galway, city, 24, 133–4
General Assembly, 195, 204, 211, 212, 216;
  also see Presbyterianism
Germany, 277
Gilbert, Claudius, 70
Glasgow, Scotland, 198
Glenarm, Co. Antrim, 98
Glorious Revolution, 54, 222, 229, 231,
  232, 240, 241, 243, 250, 251, 260
Gookin, Daniel, 16, 57, 61, 77, 78, 79, 81-2
  attitude towards the native Americans,
    79–81
  An historical account . . ., 57, 79
  Historical collections . . ., 57, 79
Gookin, Daniel (senior), 61
Gookin, Robert, 64
Gookin, Vincent, 5, 16, 56, 57, 59, 60, 62,
  63, 64, 65, 66, 69, 70, 74, 75, 76, 78, 79,
  81-2
  attitude towards the Irish, 66–8, 70–2,
    80–1
  The author and case . . ., 66, 76–7
  The great case of transplantation . . ., 56, 66,
    68–72
Gookin, Sir Vincent, 60, 62–3, 78
'Graces' (1628), 36, 37
Graham, James (d. 1650), 5th earl and 1st
  marquis of Montrose, 213, 214, 277
Grotius, Hugo, 146, 147, 253

Hamilton, James (d. 1649), 3rd marquis
  and 1st duke of Hamilton, 209, 215
Hamilton, James, viscount Clandeboy, 44
Harris, Walter, 4, 92, 106
Hartlib, Samuel, 17, 236
Henderson, Alexander, 199, 204
Henrietta Maria, queen of England (d.
  1670), 156, 167
Henry II, king of England (d. 1189), 19, 20,
  52, 90, 94, 95, 96, 99, 101, 137, 141,
  142, 143, 145, 160, 254, 257
Henry VIII, king of England and Ireland
  (d. 1547), 155, 161

Herbert, Sir William, 234
heresy/heretics, 155, 156, 159, 160, 163–4, 167, 168–9, 170
Highlands, Scotland, 193, 229
historiography
    Atlantic, 2, 16, 223–6, 244
    covenanting movement, 191–2
    New British Histories, 2, 14-15, 221–2, 224, 244, 270–80
    political thought, 1, 221, 225, 243, 244
Hobbes, Thomas, 275, 278
Holland, see Dutch Republic
House of Commons (English), 37, 39, 40, 101, 102, 104, 246, 249, 254, 255
House of Commons (Irish), 37, 39, 41, 43, 89
House of Lords (English), 40, 43, 44, 84, 85, 103, 252
House of Lords (Irish), 39, 44, 85, 89, 103, 206, 252
Huguenots, 185, 201
Humanism, 16-17, 67
Hungary, 210
Hyde, Henry, earl of Clarendon, 125

identity formation, 18, 21–6, 38, 57, 60, 66, 72, 97–8, 107, 108, 133, 134-5, 136, 148, 152-4, 159, 164, 179–81, 184, 272, 274–6; also see Old English; native Irish; New English
imperial crown, 246, 252, 255, 258, 263, 264, 266
inauguration, 138, 141
Inchiquin, earl of, see O'Brien, Murrough
Independents, 69, 70
Irish Civil Wars, 107, 108, 109, 113, 127, 135, 147, 148–9, 168, 187
    impact of, 62, 63–4, 131, 132
    also see Wars of the Three Kingdoms; Kilkenny, Confederation of
Irish rebellion (1641), 7n, 8, 23, 27, 47, 53, 62, 70, 76, 108, 126, 165, 183, 209, 212
    origins of, 45–6, 73, 75, 164, 182–3, 208, 276
    also see depositions; 'massacres'
Irish Society of London, 84–5, 101, 103, 218, 219
Israel/Israelites, see Jews

Jacobite War, see 'War of the Three Kings'
Jacobites, 84, 86, 102, 259, 262–3, 264-5
Jamaica, 78
James I and VI (d. 1625), king of Scotland, Ireland and England, 9, 23, 40, 144, 145, 146, 150, 156, 158, 161, 163, 167,

174, 192, 193, 194, 195, 201, 215, 258, 274, 275, 276, 278
James II and VII (d. 1701), king of Scotland, Ireland and England, 2, 21, 26, 54, 114, 124, 125, 219, 230, 231, 236, 248, 259
Jansenism, 17
Jesuit order (Society of Jesus), 27, 118, 161, 165, 167, 175
Jews, 168, 176–7, 179, 184, 186, 187, 198, 201
John, king of England (d. 1216), 39, 96
Johnston, Archibald of Wariston, 199, 216
Jones, Henry, bp of Clogher, 110-11
Jones, Katherine, Lady Ranelagh, 17
Jonson, Ben, 118
judges, Irish, 38, 39, 41, 42, 136; also see Bolton, Richard

Kearney, Michael, 151
Keating, Geoffrey, 19, 131, 133–7, 141, 143, 147, 154
    Foras Feasa ar Éirinn, 6, 29, 131–2, 138–9, 149, 151, 152–3
Kilkenny, city, 27, 30, 71
Kilkenny, Confederation of, 24–5, 29, 30–1, 47, 59, 155, 159, 164, 168, 182–3, 186, 188, 211, 276, 277, 278
    armies of, 166, 213
    factions in, 166, 168, 169, 170
    general assemblies, 172, 184
    negotiations with Charles I, Glamorgan, and Ormond, 27, 49–50, 53, 110, 119, 167, 169, 170, 172
    supreme councils, 24, 142, 167, 173, 184
    also see Oath of Association; Rinuccini
King, Maurice, 28
King, Paul, OFM (d. 1655), 4
King, William, bp of Derry, 84, 88, 95, 100, 103, 252
    Bishop of Derry's case, 84–5, 101, 103
    State of the Protestants, 21, 31, 83
kingship, 15, 18–19, 28, 90, 108, 109, 112, 113, 126, 138, 140, 150, 205, 250, 263
    Irish context, 2, 21–4, 26, 36, 37, 107, 131, 137–41, 143, 146, 151
    prerogative powers, 36, 42, 45, 46, 48, 94, 112, 161–2, 199, 203, 208, 278, 280
    also see contract theory; parliament; Stuarts
Kinsale, Co. Cork, 62, 63
Kirk, 193, 198–9, 203, 218, 219
Knox, John, 201

land settlement, see under Cromwellian land settlement; restoration land settlement

language
  English, 3, 132, 157, 279
  Irish/Gaelic, 3–4, 22, 24, 75, 77, 131–2,
    135, 157, 279
  Latin, 4, 132, 134, 157, 174, 279
Laud, William (d. 1645), apb of
    Canterbury, 195
Laudian rituals, 120-1, 196
Laudabiliter (1155), see papal bulls
law and legal processes, 15, 16, 36-7, 38, 40,
    42, 43, 48, 109, 112, 131, 136, 151, 160,
    161, 177, 261; also see contract theory
Lawrence, Captain Richard, 62, 65, 66, 67,
    69, 73, 74, 75, 227, 228
  The interest of England in Ireland . . ., 56,
    66
Leicester, earl of, see Sidney, Robert
Leslie, Sir Alexander (d. 1661), 1st earl of
    Leven, 207
Leslie, Charles, bp of Down and Connor,
    100-1, 255
A Letter from a Gentleman in the Country, 87,
    88
Leven, earl of, see Leslie, Alexander
library/libraries, 9n, 27n, 28–9, 31, 115, 118
Limerick, city, 109
Limerick, Treaty of (1691), 85, 257, 278
linen manufacture, 86, 239
Lisbon, Portugal, 29
Lisle, Viscount, see Sidney, Philip
literacy, 28, 112-13
Livingstone, John, 196
Locke, John (d. 1704), 15, 84, 86, 88, 91, 93,
    97-8, 101, 103, 104, 106, 239, 240, 245,
    250, 253, 254, 257, 261
Lombard, Peter, RC abp of Armagh (d.
    1625), 23, 29, 157, 162, 163, 167, 168,
    174, 178
London, city, 4, 37, 53, 58, 59, 65, 66, 69,
    103, 115, 122, 126, 223, 251, 259, 260
  financial importance of, 2–3, 225, 252
London, Treaty of (1641), 207, 208, 209
Londonderry, plantation, 84–5, 101
Louis XIV, king of France (d. 1715), 248,
    263, 277
Louvain, Spanish Netherlands, 176, 183,
    185
  St Anthony's College, 2, 22, 179, 180
Low Countries, see Dutch Republic;
    Spanish Netherlands
Lowlands, Scotland, 193, 197, 219
Lucas, Charles, 83, 106
Lutheranism, 210
Lynch, John, RC archdeacon of Tuam (d.
    1673?), 6, 7, 17, 19, 22, 23-4, 25, 131-5,

    136, 154, 157, 158, 160, 161, 168, 169,
      173, 174
  Cambrensis Eversus, 4, 29, 131, 140–53
  Alithinologia, 25, 153
Maccabees, 8, 23, 24, 172, 176, 177–80,
    181–2, 184, 185–8, 273
MacColla, Alasdair, 213, 277
MacDonald/MacDonnell (Clan Donald),
    family, 188, 277
MacDonald, Alasdair (Colketto, Kilketto),
    see MacColla, Alasdair
MacDonnell, Randal, 1st earl of Antrim
    (1620–36), 10, 11
McFarland, Patrick, 28
MacFhirbhisigh, Dubhaltach, 17
Machiavelli, Niccoló, 234, 235, 241-2
MacMahon, family, 188
Madden, Samuel, 231
Magennis, family, 188
Maguire (MacGuire), family, 165, 188
Mair, John, 221, 274
Maitland, James, duke of Lauderdale, 218,
    219
Malone, Thomas, SJ, 169–70
manuscript tradition, 28, 112, 114, 123, 125,
    127, 132, 133
Margretson, James, abp of Armagh, 110-11
Martin, Richard 41
Marvell, Andrew, 74
Marx, Karl, 226
Massachusetts, 16, 77, 78, 79, 81
  Bay Colony, 56, 57, 77, 82
'massacres', 6–7, 24, 60, 70, 148, 163–4,
    165, 170, 171, 209
Maxwell, Henry, 241-2
Maynart, Samuel, 49n, 50, 52, 116
mercantilism, 228, 232, 235, 236; also see
    trade
Mercer, William, 125, 126
Merchants of Waterford Case, 95
Methuen, John, 103, 104
migrant/migration, 196, 197, 208, 212,
    219
millenarianism, 60
Milton, John, 5, 17
Molesworth, Robert, first Viscount, 88, 103
Molina, Luis de, SJ, 160, 162
Molyneux, William (d. 1698), 15, 16, 17, 21,
    28, 31, 91, 95, 98, 104, 105, 106, 107,
    127, 231, 241, 243, 244, 252, 253, 254,
    255-6, 257, 258, 262, 263, 270, 278,
    280
  The Case of Ireland . . . Stated, 20, 83, 84,
    88, 89, 90, 91, 92, 93, 94, 96, 97, 99,
    100-3, 122, 126, 238, 240, 255, 260

legacy of, 82–3, 95, 106, 123, 241, 254
reaction to *The Case*, 82, 87, 103–5
sources for *The Case*, 89–100
Montgomery, Hugh (d. 1663), 3rd Viscount Montgomery of the Ards, 44
Montrose, marquis of, *see* Graham, James
Moravia, 210
Munro, Major General Robert, 110
'multiple kingdoms/monarchies', *see* 'composite monarchy'
Munster, 133, 169
    plantation of, 61

native Americans, 57, 77, 80, 82, 211, 261
native Irish, 18, 22-3, 61, 66, 97, 106, 111, 113, 144, 148, 151, 152, 153, 159, 164, 176, 177–9, 182, 183, 185, 280
natural law, 90–1, 98, 254, 257
Navigation Acts, 3, 100, 111, 228, 236, 241
Negative Confession (1581), 200
'new army', 40, 206
New England, 194, 195, 196, 211
New English, 37, 50, 52, 53, 56, 61, 68, 72, 106, 145; *also see* Old Protestant
New Model Army, 191, 214
New Ross, Co. Wexford, 118
New York, 244, 258, 259, 260, 261
Newfoundland, 196
Nine Years War (1594–1603), 20, 22
Nine Years War (1688–1697), 86, 104, 134, 146, 148
North Channel, 15, 192, 207, 212, 277
    interaction with Ulster, 192, 196, 212; *also see* Ulster
Nugent, family, 59

Oath(s) of Allegiance, 26, 167, 202
Oath(s) of Association, 24, 26, 166–7, 168
O'Brien, earls of Thomond, 161
O'Brien, Murrough (d. 1674), Lord Inchiquin, 63, 109, 169
    'Inchiquin truce' (1648), 25, 30–1, 169
O'Byrne, family, 188
O'Cahan, family, 188
Ó Clérigh, Ludaid, 4, 23
O'Connell, Robert, Capuchin, 25
O'Doherty, family, 188
O'Donnell, family, 280
O'Donnell, Rory, earl of Tyrconnell, 158, 180
O'Ferrall, family, 188
O'Ferrall, Richard, Capuchin, 25, 157, 158–9, 161, 170, 173, 174
O'Flaherty, Roderic, 17
O'Hagan, family, 188

Old English, 18, 21, 23, 36, 37, 41, 45, 46–7, 49, 54, 59, 66, 110, 119, 121, 122, 131, 132–3, 134, 135, 138, 142, 144, 145, 146, 147–9, 150, 151, 152, 153–4, 159, 161, 164, 167, 170, 174, 179, 180, 182–3, 184, 273–4, 275, 276–8, 280
Old Irish, *see* native Irish
Old Protestant, 57, 66, 82, 150, 151; *also see* New English
oligarchy, 192, 208, 212, 214–15
O'Mahony, Conor, SJ, 17, 19, 22n, 27, 157, 160-1, 162, 164, 165, 166, 168, 169, 170, 171, 173, 174, 175, 184–5, 273, 276, 280
    Disputatio apologetica . . ., 17, 24, 159, 167, 172
O'More, family, 188
O'Neill, family, 188, 280
O'Neill, Conn, 27n
O'Neill, Sir Daniel, 44
O'Neill, Hugh (d. 1616), 3rd earl of Tyrone, 46, 135, 146, 157, 158, 161, 164, 179, 180, 181
O'Neill, Owen Roe (d. 1649), 23, 30–1, 44, 164, 165, 169, 176, 178, 180, 181, 182, 183, 185, 187
O'Neill, Sir Phelim of Kinard (d. 1652), 41, 106, 113, 208
O'Reilly, family, 188
Ormond, earl of, *see* Butler, James
Orrery, earl of, *see* Boyle, Roger
O'Sullevane, Thomas, 133
O'Sullivan Beare, Philip, 23, 133, 157, 158, 159, 160
Oxenstierna, Axel, 207, 211
Oxford, England, 214

pageantry, 10, 117, 123–5, 126
Pamphili, cardinal, 155
pamphlets, 86–7
papacy, 4, 54, 156, 157, 169, 181; *also see* Catholic church; Rinuccini
    relations with Irish Catholics, 18, 22, 26, 142
papal authority, 22–3, 26, 141–2, 144, 151, 156, 160, 163, 164, 166, 168, 275, 276, 280
papal bulls
    Laudabiliter (1155), 143, 151
    Regnans in Excelsis (1570), 157-8
Paris, France, 155
parliament (English), 15, 18–20, 26, 35, 37, 46, 48, 49, 50, 51, 83, 89, 93, 102, 103, 106, 149, 191, 206, 207, 209, 212–13, 214, 232, 235, 247, 251, 254, 262, 263;

parliament (English), (cont.)
  also see contract theory; conquest;
  House of Commons; House of Lords
  king-in-parliament, 242, 246, 252, 255,
    256, 264, 270
  perceived rights of, 45–6, 47, 48–9, 50,
    51, 83, 84, 85, 104–5, 232
parliament (Irish), 15, 18–20, 35, 38, 50, 52,
    85, 86, 87, 89, 99, 131, 135, 161, 232,
    252, 257; (1613), 36, 161; (1643–5), 36,
    41; (1640), 36, 122; (1661–6), 150;
    (1689), 86; also see contract theory;
    conquest; House of Commons; House
    of Lords; Kingship Act; Poynings' Act
  early Irish political institutions, 131,
    136–7, 256
  membership and electoral practices, 36,
    41, 66, 149
  opposition in, 36–9, 41, 43, 206
  perceived rights of, 35, 38–40, 41, 43–4,
    48, 50, 52–3, 84, 85, 90–2, 95–6, 99,
    101–3, 110, 136–7, 149–50, 234, 244,
    254, 256, 257
parliament (Scottish Estates), 195, 207,
    209, 215, 232, 237, 238, 261, 262, 263,
    268; also see Tables
Parliamentarians, 148, 209, 214
penal laws, 167, 200
Perrot, John, 71
Petition of Right (1628), 42
Petty, John, 115
Petty, Sir William (d. 1687), 9, 31, 56, 65,
    112, 115, 226, 227, 229–30, 231, 236,
    239, 241, 242; also see Down Survey;
    political economy
Petyt, William, 99, 248
Philip IV, king of Spain (d. 1665), 161
Philips, William, 122
plantations, 60, 73, 223, 235, 238, also see
    Connacht; Londonderry; Munster;
    Ulster plays, see theatre
poets/poems, 124–5, 133, 177, 178
political economy, 9, 16–17, 226, 230, 234,
    235, 237–41; also see Petty, William
Portugal, 17, 161, 184, 273
Portumna, Co. Galway, 10
Poynings' Act (1494), 36, 38, 41, 45, 49, 50,
    55, 86, 102, 106, 111, 233
predestination, 194, 197
Presbyterianism, 15, 23n, 69, 114, 171, 191,
    193, 195, 196, 197, 199, 204, 206, 211,
    212, 215, 217, 218, 219, 275, 276, 280
Preston, battle of (1648), 215
Preston, Jenico, Viscount Gormanston, 23,
    164

print culture, 28–30, 83, 113-14, 123, 125,
    127
privy council
  English, 45
  Irish, 124
  Scottish 236
propaganda, 1, 29–30, 134–5, 157, 159, 164,
    204, 245–6
  history as, 5, 131–2, 152, 265, 267
property, titles to, 36, 37, 44, 45, 135, 144,
    152, 165
'Protestant ascendancy', 72, 280
Protestant Reformation, 157–8, 169, 170,
    171, 194, 201
Protestant writers, 4, 17–18, 20, 21, 31
Protestants, see New English
Protestors, 191, 217, 218
providentialism, 8, 171–2, 173–4
Prynne, William, 99
Puritan, 60, 69, 168, 169, 196, 211
Pym, John (d. 1643), 42

Quakers, 70, 71, 125
'Queries' (1641), 38, 39, 42, 43, 45

radicalism, 192
readership, 3–5, 66, 84–5, 87–8, 122, 131–2,
    134, 142, 157, 159, 163, 166
rebellion of 1641, see Irish rebellion
rebellions, 87, 101, 111, 146, 149, 158, 159,
    165, 276; also see revolution
refugees, Protestant, 17, 100, 257
religious reform, 65, 68, 70, 210
Remonstrance Controversy, 26, 54, 171
Remonstrants, 216
republic/republicanism
  Irish context, 107, 176, 180–1, 183–4, 185
  Scottish context, 192, 203, 217
Resolutioners, 216, 217, 218
Restoration, 66, 91, 132, 219
  in Scotland, 191–2, 218, 219
restoration land-settlement in Ireland, 53,
    54, 100, 105
revolution, 192, 197, 204
Rich, Barnabe, 60
Ridpath, George, 262, 266, 267, 268
Rheims, France, 133
Rinuccini, Giovanni Battista (d. 1653), abp
    of Fermo, 25, 30-1, 142, 144, 155, 158,
    164, 166, 169, 170, 171, 172
  censure of 1648, 25–6, 31, 169
Ripon, Treaty of (1640), 206
Robartes, John, LL (1669–70), 124, 125,
    126
Roche, Patrick, 172

Rome, Italy, 155, 177
  St Isidore's , 186
Rothe, David, bp of Ossory, 17, 142
Rotterdam, Dutch Republic, 29
Rouen, France, 134
royalism, 18n, 25, 106, 109, 205, 209, 216,
  217
Rutherford, Samuel, 197, 204, 216

St John, Oliver, 40, 41
St Patrick, 133, 138, 171
Salamanca, Spain, 186
Scotland, 15, 16, 18, 31, 45, 49, 50, 52, 69,
  121, 171
  links with East Ulster, 15
  National Library of, 28
  also see North Channel
sermons, 27, 110, 127
Service Book, 197, 198, 199
Seymour, Sir Edward, 87, 241
Shirley, James, 120, 122
Sidney, Philip, Viscount Lisle, 5
Sidney, Robert, earl of Leicester, 45
Silesia, 210
Smith, William, 120
social context of political culture, 107–14,
  123, 127
Solemn League and Covenant, see
  Covenant
Somers, lord chancellor, 87, 104
Somerset, England, 87
Sophia of Hanover, 262
Sousa, Antónia de, 161
sovereignty, 135, 136–40, 144–5, 146–7,
  150–1, 154, 160–2; also see kingship;
  Stuarts
Spain, 158, 180, 230
  and Ireland, 46, 158
Spanish Habsburgs, 17, 161, 194, 210
Spanish Netherlands, 180, 185
  Irish regiments in, 179, 180, 188
Speed, John, 9–14
Spelman, Sir Henry, 248
Spenser, Edmund, 4, 60, 67, 73
Stanihurst, Richard, 154, 177
Staple Acts (1663, 1671), 228
Stuart, Elizabeth ('winter queen'), 211
Strafford, earl of, see Wentworth, Thomas
Stuarts, 2, 4, 19, 21, 144, 152, 159, 161–2,
  163, 174, 203, 230, 249, 262, 265, 268,
  277, 278
  allegiance to, 18, 19, 21, 22–4, 26, 46,
  53–5, 147–8, 149–50, 155, 156, 157,
  162–3, 165, 166, 167, 168, 170–1, 183,
  224, 273, 275–6

  also see Charles I; Charles II; Jacobites;
    James I and VI; James II and VII;
    kingship
Suarez, Francisco, SJ, 22n, 160, 162, 163
Supreme Council, see Kilkenny,
  Confederation of
surrender and regrant, 160
Sweden, 206, 208, 211, 214
Swift, Jonathan, 82, 230, 231

Tables, 199, 200, 202, 203, 204, 205,
  206
  Committee of Estates, 205, 206, 208,
    212, 214
  Convention of Estates, 208
  local government, 205, 206
Talbot, Peter, 156
taxation, 51–2, 85, 96
Temple, Sir John, 8, 27, 45, 116, 127
  The Irish Rebellion, 5, 17
Temple, Sir William, 116, 227, 242
Test Act (1681), 219
theatre, 114, 117–23, 125, 126, 127
Thirty Years War (1618–48), 194
Thomond, earls of, see O'Brien
Thurloe, John (d. 1668), 59, 69, 74, 78
Titus; or the Palme of Christian Courage, 27
Tipperary, county, 133
Toland, John, 88
Tone, Wolfe, 106
Tory/Tories, 249, 255, 259, 260, 261, 263
trade, 226, 227, 229, 236, 237, 261, 268
  joint-stock trading, 227, 238
  regulation of Irish trade, 52, 55, 84, 86,
    87, 100, 227-8
  Scottish, 228, 268
Tralee, Co. Kerry, 170
transplantation policies, 56, 57, 58, 59, 60,
  64, 68, 73, 75, 82, 229, 230; also see
  Connacht; Gookin, Vincent;
  Lawrence, Richard
Transylvania, 194
Triennial Act (1689), 256
Trumbull, William, 180
Tyrone, county, 41, 107, 113, 212
Tyrone, earl of, see O'Neill, Hugh

Ulster, 184, 188, 192, 196, 197, 199, 208,
  219, 279; also see conventicling;
  migration; North Channel;
  Presbyterianism
  plantation, 110, 207, 209
  Presbytery of, 212, 213, 217, 218
Ulster rebellion, see Irish rebellion
United Provinces, see Dutch Republic

Union, 229–30, 233, 241
    confederal, 193, 207, 208, 214, 217, 266
    regal (1603), 35, 221, 263, 264, 277
    parliamentary (1707), 221, 222, 223, 229,
      240, 241, 268, 269, 270, 278; (1800),
      83
Ussher, James, abp of Armagh, 8, 17n, 27n,
    174, 276

Verdon, James, 115
Virginia, 57, 77, 61

Wadding, Luke (d. 1657), OFM, 186
Wadding, Luke, RC bp of Ferns, 29
Wales, 18, 50
Walsh, Peter, OFM, 7, 26, 27, 28, 117, 224
War of the League of Augsburg, *see* Nine
    Years War (1688–97)
'War of the Three Kings' (1689–91), 2, 19,
    20, 55, 85, 88, 100, 127, 227, 231, 233,
    247, 252, 277, 278; *also see* Glorious
    Revolution
Ware, Sir James (d. 1666), 4, 17, 67
Ware, Robert, 117
Wars of the Three Kingdoms, 2, 8, 19, 20,
    21, 23, 47, 74, 109, 156, 188, 191, 210,
    232, 270, 275, 276, 277, 279; *also see*
    Irish Civil Wars
Waterford, city, 30

Waterford, county, 133
Wentworth, Thomas (d. 1641), earl of
    Strafford, LD (1633–40), LL (1640), 5,
    35, 41, 120, 122, 123, 206
    impeachment and trial, 37–8, 39, 40, 42,
    207
West Indies, 111, 235
Weston, William, 31
Wetenhall, Edward, bp of Cork, 125
Wexford, county, 73
Whiggamore Raid (1648), 215
Whigs, 102, 104, 233, 244, 245, 246, 247,
    248, 249, 251, 253, 254, 255, 258, 261,
    267, 268, 269
White, Stephen, SJ, 27
William I, king of England (d. 1087), 255
William III, king of England, Scotland and
    Ireland (d. 1702), 21, 54, 55, 85, 93,
    102, 103, 104, 105, 257, 262, 263, 277,
    278
Wilson, John, 124
woollen industry, 84, 85–7, 104, 105, 237,
    238, 239, 240, 241, 252
Worcester, battle of (1651), 216
Worth, Edward, 69, 70
Worth, Susanna, 70

Yonge, Sir Walter, 87, 104
Youghal, Co. Cork, 62, 66

.

For EU product safety concerns, contact us at Calle de José Abascal, 56–1°,
28003 Madrid, Spain or eugpsr@cambridge.org.

www.ingramcontent.com/pod-product-compliance
Ingram Content Group UK Ltd.
Pitfield, Milton Keynes, MK11 3LW, UK
UKHW042154130625
459647UK00011B/1319